The Editor

PATRICIA MEYER SPACKS is Edgar F. Shannon Professor of English at the University of Virginia. She is the author of eleven books including *An Argument of Images: The Poetry of Alexander Pope, The Female Imagination, The Adolescent Idea: Myths of Youth in the Adult Imagination, Desire and Truth: Functions of Plot in Eighteenth-Century English Novels,* and *Boredom: The Literary History of a State of Mind.* Professor Spacks is a contributing editor of *The Norton Anthology of World Masterpieces.*

PERSUASION

AUTHORITATIVE TEXT
BACKGROUNDS AND CONTEXTS
CRITICISM

Jane Austen

PERSUASION

AUTHORITATIVE TEXT
BACKGROUNDS AND CONTEXTS
CRITICISM

Edited by

PATRICIA MEYER SPACKS

UNIVERSITY OF VIRGINIA

W. W. Norton & Company   New York   London

Printed in the United States of America

First Edition

The text of this book is composed in Electra
with the display set in Bernhard Modern
Composition by Vail Composition
Manufacturing by Maple-Vail
Book design by Antonina Krass

Library of Congress Cataloging-in-Publication Data
Austen, Jane, 1775–1817.
Persuasion : an authoritative text, backgrounds, and contexts,
reviews and essays in criticism / Jane Austen ; edited by Patricia
Meyer Spacks.
p.   cm.—(A Norton critical ed.)
Includes bibliographical references.
1. England—Social life and customs—19th century—Fiction.
2. Man-woman relationships—England—Fiction.   3. Austen, Jane,
1775–1817. Persuasion.   I. Spacks, Patricia Ann Meyer.   II. Title.
PR4034.P4   1994
823'.7—dc20   94-4510
ISBN 0-393-96018-8

W. W. Norton & Company, Inc., 500 Fifth Avenue, New York, N.Y. 10110
W. W. Norton & Company Ltd., Castle House, 75/76 Wells Street,
London W1T 3QT

Contents

Preface

Jane Austen wrote *Persuasion*, her last complete novel, while suffering from the illness (Addison's disease) that would kill her. She began work on it in 1815, finishing her alterations of the final chapters on July 18, 1816, precisely a year before she died. Her brother Frank published it, along with *Northanger Abbey* and his own biographical notice of his sister, at the end of 1817.

Certain critics (including some whose work is excerpted in the Backgrounds and Contexts and Criticism sections of this volume) have found in the novel a melancholy strain, attributable, in their view, to the author's illness. Early commentators on *Persuasion*—and some fairly recent ones—glimpsed in the book the sadness of mortality, commenting on its elegiac tone and on a new kind of seriousness in its imagining. Those with a literary-historical bent have noted the incursion of attitudes and assumptions that we associate with romanticism: the novelist who once mocked Marianne's enthusiasm for dead leaves *(Sense and Sensibility)* now allows her heroine, without overt criticism, to take pleasure in evidence of the "declining year." Social critics have found splendid material for investigation in the novel's new emphasis on the life and values of the Royal Navy, discovering that Austen not only drew on knowledge gained from two admiral-brothers but appeared to criticize the aristocracy and welcome the accession to social power of a new class. *Persuasion*, in short, contains something for everybody, a fertile field for varied sorts of critical investigation.

The documents collected in the Backgrounds and Contexts and Criticism sections of this volume suggest a range of possibilities and adumbrate changing attitudes and trends in critical discourse. The excerpt from William Hayley's *Essay on Old Maids* (1785), for instance, implicitly sketches the social context in which Austen chose to investigate the emotional situation of a twenty-seven-year-old unmarried woman. For Austen, at least in her role as fiction maker, as for Hayley, marriage constituted the happy ending of a woman's youth. Within this conceptual framework, however, Austen found it possible to imagine a woman neither preoccupied with marriage nor initially convinced that no female fulfillment can exist outside it. Her letters to Fanny Knight remind us of Jane Austen's comic skepticism about marriage as constituting inevitable female bliss; *Persuasion* helps elucidate that skepticism.

In his memorial notice her brother describes Jane Austen as a woman of notable piety and familial devotion. That woman's last completed novel reminds us how rich an emotional life may underlie exemplary female conduct. One of Austen's communications to Fanny Knight describes Anne Elliot, the heroine of *Persuasion*, as "almost too good for me." Henry Austen's characterization of his sister makes goodness sound like a simple matter. *Persuasion* tells us otherwise. Goodness can include resistance as well as persuadability—and it by no means precludes private judgment.

If such commentators on the social scene as Hayley and such observers of character as Henry Austen call attention to components of conventional female compliance in the late eighteenth and early nineteenth centuries, nineteenth- and early twentieth-century commentary on *Persuasion* tends to stress other stereotypically feminine elements of the novel, notably its alleged emphasis on feeling and its concern for the everyday. Such commentary supports a view of Austen that has long survived; as an unmarried woman living in a village, she knew and cared little about problems and experience beyond her immediate setting. Limited in imaginative range, according to this view, Austen evinced sharp observation, acumen about a fairly restricted realm of emotions, and a gift for sharp, often comic, characterization. Twentieth-century criticism, however, heavily represented in the present volume, considers the Austen of *Persuasion* a serious moralist and a significant commentator on social, even political, issues.

My decision to emphasize recent criticism of *Persuasion* reflects my conviction that the current critical shift has enormous importance for our comprehension of Austen's achievement. New ways of approaching the novels make it possible for the first time to think complexly about Austen in the context of her contemporaries—not only her literary peers, but all the other men and women living through the Napoleonic Wars on the Continent and their political repercussions in England. *Persuasion* speaks of more than life in a village, or even in Bath. It sharply ironizes Austen's well-known profession to her brother about "the little bit (two Inches wide) of Ivory on which I work with so fine a Brush, as produces little effect after much labour." Devoted readers have always denied the claim that Austen works to "little effect"; the notion of her two inches of ivory is equally questionable.

"Pictures of perfection . . . make me sick and wicked," Austen observed, in the letter containing her claim that Anne Elliot was "almost too good" for her. Good though she is, the heroine of *Persuasion* never runs the danger of "perfection." She plays music so that others may dance, cares for a sick child so that her sister and brother-in-law can go out to dinner, changes residence in response to the real or fancied needs of her relatives. Behaving like the very model of a well-bred spinster, she nonetheless vibrates with passion and preserves a will of her own.

The early commentators who praised Austen's characterization and noted the high degree of feeling in *Persuasion* had it right. Thus Julia Kavanagh, in 1862, observes that the portrayal of Anne constitutes "the first genuine picture of that silent torture of an unloved woman." Just so: Austen makes her readers experience vicariously the full intensity of such torture.

But those interested in the social and political implications of Austen's fiction get it right too. The special brilliance of *Persuasion* depends partly on its combined focus on the private experience of a sharply imagined individual and the social actualities that necessarily inform individual experience. As in her other fiction, Austen here provides a penetrating study of self-love in its varied manifestations. The Elliot family supplies numerous examples, from the comic to the simply appalling. Anne's sister Mary, her state of health varying according to the degree of attention others pay her, has found an appropriate mate in Charles, concerned mainly with his hunting, his dogs, and his guns. Elizabeth, the other Elliot sister, resembles her father in vanity and in self-referential snobbery. Sir Walter, for whom his own appearance and rank constitute the primary standard of value against which he judges others (usually to their disadvantage), cares not at all for the welfare of his daughter Anne, whom he considers plain and unlikely to marry well. He and Elizabeth decide, as an economy measure, to bring Anne no gift from their visit to London. The tiny episode epitomizes their utter self-absorption, which signifies a widespread and dangerous social malady.

Less dramatic but more sinister in his self-preoccupation is William Elliot, who calculates his every move in relation to selfish interest. Anne condemns him for lack of "openness" well before she learns of his more openly destructive behavior. He acts like a man of the world—if one defines the world as a place where everyone is out for him- or herself and where success entails winning place, power, and wealth at the expense of others. *Persuasion* raises the question of whether any alternative conception of the world can prove viable.

It does not treat this question as a simple one. As Alexander Pope had recognized ("Self-love, the spring of motion, acts the soul; / Reason's comparing balance rules the whole"), self-interest energizes everyone and provides a fundamental engine of social progress. Anne, to whom her family denies the right of openly expressed self-concern, experiences the omnipresence of individually focused perspectives as she moves from one small social environment to another, to find that the concerns of one household mean nothing at all to residents of another only a few miles away. Driving down a Bath street with Lady Russell, Anne sees only the presence of the man she loves on the sidewalk. What will Lady Russell say about him? she wonders. Lady Russell, of course preoccupied with her own affairs, comments instead on the window curtains she has been contemplating. Anne appropriately recognizes the irony of conflicting personal assignments of significance, but the recognition does not protect her—even her—from seeing in the light of her own feelings, thoughts, and obsessions.

Yet *Persuasion* suggests the possibility of surmounting narrow self-concern, not only through the self-sacrificing "goodness" that Anne at first appears to embody but through a kind of "openness" antithetical to William Elliot's calculation and promising new social horizons. Pope went on from his observation of self-love as energizing principle to the utopian hope that self-love and social might ultimately merge. Austen adumbrates less utopian versions of that merging in the members of the navy she depicts, Admiral and Mrs. Croft, Captain Wentworth, and Anne herself, who becomes Mrs. Wentworth. The Crofts and Captain Wentworth exhibit healthy self-concern. Admiral Croft does not feel shy about drawing his own conclusions as to the character of Sir Walter Elliot; Mrs. Croft speaks her judgments and attitudes forthrightly. Captain Wentworth, in worldly terms successful, has indeed gained his wealth at others' expense, triumphing in naval combat, capturing ships, winning promotion presumably over other people's heads. To some extent, then, the world operates as William Elliot assumes, by clambering competition. Yet these people who have won status and money have not had to sacrifice personal feeling. The Crofts exemplify cooperative and satisfying marriage. Wentworth, despite his hurt feelings over Anne's earlier rejection and his determination to marry anyone but her, finally faces the truth of his emotions and risks rejection once more for the sake of his newly discovered, long-enduring devotion. If we take Anne and her lover as exemplary, it is not quite accurate to generalize, as Anne does, that women love longest when all hope is gone. Men can love just as long—they just have more trouble acknowledging the fact about themselves.

One need not conclude that the navy will replace the aristocracy as center of social power. But the navy epitomizes a better moral as well as social order, specifically in the way its representatives embody a productive union between self-directed and outward-directed interest. Anne, marrying Wentworth, can abandon self-sacrifice for self-fulfillment—which is not to say that she at all abandons her concern for others. The novel's final sentences direct the reader's attention both to the life of personal feeling and to the navy's symbolic connection with private as well as public virtue. "Anne was tenderness itself, and she had the full worth of it in Captain Wentworth's affection. . . . She gloried in being a sailor's wife, but she must pay the tax of quick alarm for belonging to that profession which is, if possible, more distinguished in its domestic virtues than in its national importance." The language of finance ("the full worth of it," "pay the tax") applied to emotions calls attention to the processes of exchange involved in virtually every human transaction.

Ideally one achieves balance between what is given and what received; one does not, like William Elliot, aspire only to take. Being a sailor, or a sailor's wife, allows for intricate balances, between loving and being loved, between pride and fear, but also between personal absorption and public responsibility. The private satisfaction Wentworth receives corresponds to the national service he gives; Anne pays for her pride in his public role by fear for the possibility of her private deprivation. At any moment such precarious balances can tip, but the novel concludes with the imagining of their preservation and of their moral resonance. Such preservation, such resonance signify for national life as well as for a couple's marriage.

The text of *Persuasion* here printed is that of the first edition, dated 1818 but probably issued in late 1817. The printing of the two canceled chapters follows the edition of R. W. Chapman. Ampersands that appeared in the original texts have been spelled out, and superscript letters have been lowered.

The Text of
PERSUASION

Persuasion

Chapter I

Sir Walter Elliot, of Kellynch-hall, in Somersetshire, was a man who, for his own amusement, never took up any book but the Baronet-age;[1] there he found occupation for an idle hour, and consolation in a distressed one; there his faculties were roused into admiration and respect, by contemplating the limited remnant of the earliest patents;[2] there any unwelcome sensations, arising from domestic affairs, changed naturally into pity and contempt. As he turned over the almost endless creations[3] of the last century—and there, if every other leaf were power-less, he could read his own history with an interest which never failed—this was the page at which the favourite volume always opened:

ELLIOT OF KELLYNCH-HALL.

Walter Elliot, born March 1, 1760, married, July 15, 1784, Elizabeth, daughter of James Stevenson, Esq. of South Park, in the county of Gloucester; by which lady (who died 1800) he has issue Elizabeth, born June 1, 1785; Anne, born August 9, 1787; a still-born son, Nov. 5, 1789; Mary, born Nov. 20, 1791.

Precisely such had the paragraph originally stood from the printer's hands; but Sir Walter had improved it by adding, for the information of himself and his family, these words, after the date of Mary's birth—"married, Dec. 16, 1810, Charles, son and heir of Charles Musgrove, Esq. of Uppercross, in the county of Somerset,"—and by inserting most accurately the day of the month on which he had lost his wife.

Then followed the history and rise of the ancient and respectable family, in the usual terms: how it had been first settled in Cheshire; how mentioned in Dugdale—[4] serving the office of High Sheriff, representing a borough in three successive parliaments, exertions of loyalty, and dignity of baronet, in the first year of Charles II., with all the Marys and

---

1. Presumably J. Debrett's *Baronetage of England* (1808).
2. Titles (of nobility).
3. New peerages.
4. Sir William Dugdale, *The Ancient Usage in Bearing of Such Ensigns of Honour as Are Commonly Call'd Arms, with a Catalogue of the Present Nobility of England . . . Scotland . . . and Ireland* (1682).

Elizabeths they had married; forming altogether two handsome duodecimo pages, and concluding with the arms and motto: "Principal seat,
Kellynch hall, in the county of Somerset," and Sir Walter's hand-writ-
ing again in this finale:

"Heir presumptive, William Walter Elliot, Esq., great grandson of
the second Sir Walter."

Vanity was the beginning and the end of Sir Walter Elliot's character;
vanity of person and of situation. He had been remarkably handsome in
his youth; and, at fifty-four, was still a very fine man. Few women could
think more of their personal appearance than he did; nor could the valet
of any new made lord be more delighted with the place he held in
society. He considered the blessing of beauty as inferior only to the blessing of a baronetcy; and the Sir Walter Elliot, who united these gifts, was
the constant object of his warmest respect and devotion.

His good looks and his rank had one fair claim on his attachment;
since to them he must have owed a wife of very superior character to
any thing deserved by his own. Lady Elliot had been an excellent
woman, sensible and amiable; whose judgment and conduct, if they
might be pardoned the youthful infatuation which made her Lady
Elliot, had never required indulgence afterwards.—She had humoured,
or softened, or concealed his failings, and promoted his real respectability for seventeen years; and though not the very happiest being in the
world herself, had found enough in her duties, her friends, and her
children, to attach her to life, and make it no matter of indifference to
her when she was called on to quit them.—Three girls, the two eldest
sixteen and fourteen, was an awful legacy for a mother to bequeath; an
awful charge rather, to confide to the authority and guidance of a conceited, silly father. She had, however, one very intimate friend, a sensible, deserving woman, who had been brought, by strong attachment to
herself, to settle close by her, in the village of Kellynch; and on her
kindness and advice, Lady Elliot mainly relied for the best help and
maintenance of the good principles and instruction which she had been
anxiously giving her daughters.

This friend, and Sir Walter, did *not* marry, whatever might have been
anticipated on that head by their acquaintance.—Thirteen years had
passed away since Lady Elliot's death, and they were still near
neighbours and intimate friends; and one remained a widower, the other
a widow.

That Lady Russell, of steady age and character, and extremely well
provided for, should have no thought of a second marriage, needs no
apology to the public, which is rather apt to be unreasonably discon-
tented when a woman *does* marry again, than when she does *not*; but
Sir Walter's continuing in singleness requires explanation.—Be it
known then, that Sir Walter, like a good father, (having met with one
or two private disappointments in very unreasonable applications) prided

himself on remaining single for his dear daughter's sake. For one daughter, his eldest, he would really have given up any thing, which he had not been very much tempted to do. Elizabeth had succeeded, at sixteen, to all that was possible, of her mother's rights and consequence; and being very handsome, and very like himself, her influence had always been great, and they had gone on together most happily. His two other children were of very inferior value. Mary had acquired a little artificial importance, by becoming Mrs. Charles Musgrove; but Anne, with an elegance of mind and sweetness of character, which must have placed her high with any people of real understanding, was nobody with either father or sister: her word had no weight; her convenience was always to give way;—she was only Anne.

To Lady Russell, indeed, she was a most dear and highly valued goddaughter, favourite and friend. Lady Russell loved them all; but it was only in Anne that she could fancy the mother to revive again.

A few years before, Anne Elliot had been a very pretty girl, but her bloom had vanished early; and as even in its height, her father had found little to admire in her, (so totally different were her delicate features and mild dark eyes from his own); there could be nothing in them now that she was faded and thin, to excite his esteem. He had never indulged much hope, he had now none, of ever reading her name in any other page of his favourite work. All equality of alliance must rest with Elizabeth; for Mary had merely connected herself with an old country family of respectability and large fortune, and had therefore *given* all the honour, and received none: Elizabeth would, one day or other, marry suitably.

It sometimes happens, that a woman is handsomer at twenty-nine than she was ten years before; and, generally speaking, if there has been neither ill health nor anxiety, it is a time of life at which scarcely any charm is lost. It was so with Elizabeth; still the same handsome Miss Elliot that she had begun to be thirteen years ago; and Sir Walter might be excused, therefore, in forgetting her age, or, at least, be deemed only half a fool, for thinking himself and Elizabeth as blooming as ever, amidst the wreck of the good looks of every body else; for he could plainly see how old all the rest of his family and acquaintance were growing. Anne haggard, Mary coarse, every face in the neighbourhood worsting;[5] and the rapid increase of the crow's foot about Lady Russell's temples had long been a distress to him.

Elizabeth did not quite equal her father in personal contentment. Thirteen years had seen her mistress of Kellynch Hall, presiding and directing with a self-possession and decision which could never have given the idea of her being younger than she was. For thirteen years had she been doing the honours, and laying down the domestic law at home,

5. Worsening.

and leading the way to the chaise and four,[6] and walking immediately after Lady Russell out of all the drawing-rooms and dining-rooms in the country. Thirteen winters' revolving frosts had seen her opening every ball of credit which a scanty neighbourhood afforded; and thirteen springs shewn their blossoms, as she travelled up to London with her father, for a few weeks annual enjoyment of the great world. She had the remembrance of all this; she had the consciousness of being nine-and-twenty, to give her some regrets and some apprehensions. She was fully satisfied of being still quite as handsome as ever; but she felt her approach to the years of danger, and would have rejoiced to be certain of being properly solicited by baronet-blood within the next twelve-month or two. Then might she again take up the book of books with as much enjoyment as in her early youth; but now she liked it not. Always to be presented with the date of her own birth, and see no marriage follow but that of a youngest sister, made the book an evil; and more than once, when her father had left it open on the table near her, had she closed it, with averted eyes, and pushed it away.

She had had a disappointment, moreover, which that book, and especially the history of her own family, must ever present the remembrance of. The heir presumptive, the very William Walter Elliot, Esq. whose rights had been so generously supported by her father, had disappointed her.

She had, while a very young girl, as soon as she had known him to be, in the event of her having no brother, the future baronet, meant to marry him; and her father had always meant that she should. He had not been known to them as a boy, but soon after Lady Elliot's death Sir Walter had sought the acquaintance, and though his overtures had not been met with any warmth, he had persevered in seeking it, making allowance for the modest drawing back of youth; and in one of their spring excursions to London, when Elizabeth was in her first bloom, Mr. Elliot had been forced into the introduction.

He was at that time a very young man, just engaged in the study of the law; and Elizabeth found him extremely agreeable, and every plan in his favour was confirmed. He was invited to Kellynch Hall; he was talked of and expected all the rest of the year; but he never came. The following spring he was seen again in town, found equally agreeable, again encouraged, invited and expected, and again he did not come; and the next tidings were that he was married. Instead of pushing his fortune in the line marked out for the heir of the house of Elliot, he had purchased independence by uniting himself to a rich woman of inferior birth.

Sir Walter had resented it. As the head of the house, he felt that he ought to have been consulted, especially after taking the young man so

6. A light, open carriage drawn by four horses.

publicly by the hand: "For they must have been seen together," he observed, "once at Tattersal's,[7] and twice in the lobby of the House of Commons." His disapprobation was expressed, but apparently very little regarded. Mr. Elliot had attempted no apology, and shewn himself as unsolicitous of being longer noticed by the family, as Sir Walter considered him unworthy of it: all acquaintance between them had ceased.

This very awkward history of Mr. Elliot, was still, after an interval of several years, felt with anger by Elizabeth, who had liked the man for himself, and still more for being her father's heir, and whose strong family pride could see only in *him*, a proper match for Sir Walter Elliot's eldest daughter. There was not a baronet from A to Z, whom her feelings could have so willingly acknowledged as an equal. Yet so miserably had he conducted himself, that though she was at this present time, (the summer of 1814,) wearing black ribbons for his wife,[8] she could not admit him to be worth thinking of again. The disgrace of his first marriage might, perhaps, as there was no reason to suppose it perpetuated by offspring, have been got over, had he not done worse; but he had, as by the accustomary intervention of kind friends they had been informed, spoken most disrespectfully of them all, most slightingly and contemptuously of the very blood he belonged to, and the honours which were hereafter to be his own. This could not be pardoned.

Such were Elizabeth Elliot's sentiments and sensations; such the cares to alloy, the agitations to vary, the sameness and the elegance, the prosperity and the nothingness, of her scene of life—such the feelings to give interest to a long, uneventful residence in one country circle, to fill the vacancies which there were no habits of utility abroad, no talents or accomplishments for home, to occupy.

But now, another occupation and solicitude of mind was beginning to be added to these. Her father was growing distressed for money. She knew, that when he now took up the Baronetage, it was to drive the heavy bills of his tradespeople, and the unwelcome hints of Mr. Shepherd, his agent, from his thoughts. The Kellynch property was good, but not equal to Sir Walter's apprehension of the state required in its possessor. While Lady Elliot lived, there had been method, moderation, and economy, which had just kept him within his income; but with her had died all such right-mindedness, and from that period he had been constantly exceeding it. It had not been possible for him to spend less; he had done nothing but what Sir Walter Elliot was imperiously called on to do; but blameless as he was, he was not only growing dreadfully in debt, but was hearing of it so often, that it became vain to attempt concealing it longer, even partially, from his daughter. He had given her some hints of it the last spring in town; he had gone so far even as to say, "Can we retrench? does it occur to you that there is any one

---

7. A center for betting, located in Grosvenor Crescent.
8. Tokens of mourning: his wife had died recently.

article in which we can retrench?"—and Elizabeth, to do her justice, had, in the first ardour of female alarm, set seriously to think what could be done, and had finally proposed these two branches of economy: to cut off some unnecessary charities, and to refrain from new-furnishing the drawing-room; to which expedients she afterwards added the happy thought of their taking no present down to Anne, as had been the usual yearly custom. But these measures, however good in themselves, were insufficient for the real extent of the evil, the whole of which Sir Walter found himself obliged to confess to her soon afterwards. Elizabeth had nothing to propose of deeper efficacy. She felt herself ill-used and unfortunate, as did her father; and they were neither of them able to devise any means of lessening their expenses without compromising their dignity, or relinquishing their comforts in a way not to be borne.

There was only a small part of his estate that Sir Walter could dispose of; but had every acre been alienable,[9] it would have made no difference. He had condescended to mortgage as far as he had the power, but he would never condescend to sell. No; he would never disgrace his name so far. The Kellynch estate should be transmitted whole and entire, as he had received it.

Their two confidential friends, Mr. Shepherd, who lived in the neighbouring market town, and Lady Russell, were called on to advise them; and both father and daughter seemed to expect that something should be struck out by one or the other to remove their embarrassments and reduce their expenditure, without involving the loss of any indulgence of taste or pride.

Chapter II

Mr. Shepherd, a civil, cautious lawyer, who, whatever might be his hold or his views on Sir Walter, would rather have the *disagreeable* prompted by any body else, excused himself from offering the slightest hint, and only begged leave to recommend an implicit deference to the excellent judgment of Lady Russell,—from whose known good sense he fully expected to have just such resolute measures advised, as he meant to see finally adopted.

Lady Russell was most anxiously zealous on the subject, and gave it much serious consideration. She was a woman rather of sound than of quick abilities, whose difficulties in coming to any decision in this instance were great, from the opposition of two leading principles. She was of strict integrity herself, with a delicate sense of honour; but she was as desirous of saving Sir Walter's feelings, as solicitous for the credit of the family, as aristocratic in her ideas of what was due to them, as

---

9. Sellable (i.e., not prevented by legal restriction from being sold).

any body of sense and honesty could well be. She was a benevolent, charitable, good woman, and capable of strong attachments; most correct in her conduct, strict in her notions of decorum, and with manners that were held a standard of good-breeding. She had a cultivated mind, and was, generally speaking, rational and consistent—but she had prejudices on the side of ancestry; she had a value for rank and consequence, which blinded her a little to the faults of those who possessed them. Herself, the widow of only a knight, she gave the dignity of a baronet all its due;[1] and Sir Walter, independent of his claims as an old acquaintance, an attentive neighbour, an obliging landlord, the husband of her very dear friend, the father of Anne and her sisters, was, as being Sir Walter, in her apprehension entitled to a great deal of compassion and consideration under his present difficulties.

They must retrench; that did not admit of a doubt. But she was very anxious to have it done with the least possible pain to him and Elizabeth. She drew up plans of economy, she made exact calculations, and she did, what nobody else thought of doing, she consulted Anne, who never seemed considered by the others as having any interest in the question. She consulted, and in a degree was influenced by her, in marking out the scheme of retrenchment, which was at last submitted to Sir Walter. Every emendation of Anne's had been on the side of honesty against importance. She wanted more vigorous measures, a more complete reformation, a quicker release from debt, a much higher tone of indifference for every thing but justice and equity.

"If we can persuade your father to all this," said Lady Russell, looking over her paper, "much may be done. If he will adopt these regulations, in seven years he will be clear; and I hope we may be able to convince him and Elizabeth, that Kellynch-hall has a respectability in itself, which cannot be affected by these reductions; and that the true dignity of Sir Walter Elliot will be very far from lessened, in the eyes of sensible people, by his acting like a man of principle. What will he be doing, in fact, but what very many of our first families have done,—or ought to do?—There will be nothing singular in his case; and it is singularity which often makes the worst part of our suffering, as it always does of our conduct. I have great hope of our prevailing. We must be serious and decided—for, after all, the person who has contracted debts must pay them; and though a great deal is due to the feelings of the gentleman, and the head of a house, like your father, there is still more due to the character of an honest man."

This was the principle on which Anne wanted her father to be proceeding, his friends to be urging him. She considered it as an act of indispensable duty to clear away the claims of creditors, with all the expedition[2] which the most comprehensive retrenchments could

1. A knight ranked immediately below a baronet in the peerage.
2. Speed.

secure, and saw no dignity in any thing short of it. She wanted it to be prescribed, and felt as a duty. She rated Lady Russell's influence highly, and as to the severe degree of self-denial, which her own conscience prompted, she believed there might be little more difficulty in persuading them to a complete, than to half a reformation. Her knowledge of her father and Elizabeth, inclined her to think that the sacrifice of one pair of horses would be hardly less painful than of both, and so on, through the whole list of Lady Russell's too gentle reductions.

How Anne's more rigid requisitions might have been taken, is of little consequence. Lady Russell's had no success at all—could not be put up with—were not to be borne. "What! Every comfort of life knocked off! Journeys, London, servants, horses, table,—contractions and restrictions every where. To live no longer with the decencies even of a private gentleman! No, he would sooner quit Kellynch-hall at once, than remain in it on such disgraceful terms."

"Quit Kellynch-hall." The hint was immediately taken up by Mr. Shepherd, whose interest was involved in the reality of Sir Walter's retrenching, and who was perfectly persuaded that nothing would be done without a change of abode.—"Since the idea had been started in the very quarter which ought to dictate, he had no scruple," he said, "in confessing his judgment to be entirely on that side. It did not appear to him that Sir Walter could materially alter his style of living in a house which had such a character of hospitality and ancient dignity to support.—In any other place, Sir Walter might judge for himself; and would be looked up to, as regulating the modes of life, in whatever way he might choose to model his household."

Sir Walter would quit Kellynch-hall;—and after a very few days more of doubt and indecision, the great question of whither he should go, was settled, and the first outline of this important change made out.

There had been three alternatives, London, Bath, or another house in the country. All Anne's wishes had been for the latter. A small house in their own neighbourhood, where they might still have Lady Russell's society, still be near Mary, and still have the pleasure of sometimes seeing the lawns and groves of Kellynch, was the object of her ambition. But the usual fate of Anne attended her, in having something very opposite from her inclination fixed on. She disliked Bath, and did not think it agreed with her—and Bath was to be her home.

Sir Walter had at first thought more of London, but Mr. Shepherd felt that he could not be trusted in London, and had been skilful enough to dissuade him from it, and make Bath preferred. It was a much safer place for a gentleman in his predicament:—he might there be important at comparatively little expense.—Two material advantages of Bath over London had of course been given all their weight, its more convenient distance from Kellynch, only fifty miles, and Lady Russell's spending some part of every winter there; and to the very great satisfaction of Lady

Russell, whose first views on the projected change had been for Bath, Sir Walter and Elizabeth were induced to believe that they should lose neither consequence nor enjoyment by settling there.

Lady Russell felt obliged to oppose her dear Anne's known wishes. It would be too much to expect Sir Walter to descend into a small house in his own neighbourhood. Anne herself would have found the mortifications of it more than she foresaw, and to Sir Walter's feelings they must have been dreadful. And with regard to Anne's dislike of Bath, she considered it as a prejudice and mistake, arising first from the circumstance of her having been three years at school there, after her mother's death, and, secondly, from her happening to be not in perfectly good spirits the only winter which she had afterwards spent there with herself.

Lady Russell was fond of Bath in short, and disposed to think it must suit them all; and as to her young friend's health, by passing all the warm months with her at Kellynch-lodge, every danger would be avoided; and it was, in fact, a change which must do both health and spirits good. Anne had been too little from [3] home, too little seen. Her spirits were not high. A larger society would improve them. She wanted her to be more known.

The undesirableness of any other house in the same neighbourhood for Sir Walter, was certainly much strengthened by one part, and a very material part of the scheme, which had been happily engrafted on the beginning. He was not only to quit his home, but to see it in the hands of others; a trial of fortitude, which stronger heads than Sir Walter's have found too much—Kellynch-hall was to be let.[4] This, however, was a profound secret; not to be breathed beyond their own circle.

Sir Walter could not have borne the degradation of being known to design letting his house.—Mr. Shepherd had once mentioned the word, "advertise;"—but never dared approach it again; Sir Walter spurned the idea of its being offered in any manner; forbad the slightest hint being dropped of his having such an intention; and it was only on the supposition of his being spontaneously solicited by some most unexceptionable applicant, on his own terms, and as a great favor, that he would let it at all.

How quick come the reasons for approving what we like!—Lady Russell had another excellent one at hand, for being extremely glad that Sir Walter and his family were to remove from the country. Elizabeth had been lately forming an intimacy, which she wished to see interrupted. It was with a daughter of Mr. Shepherd, who had returned, after an unprosperous marriage, to her father's house, with the additional burthen of two children. She was a clever young woman, who understood the art of pleasing; the art of pleasing, at least, at Kellynch-hall; and who had made herself so acceptable to Miss Elliot, as to have been already

3. Away from.
4. Rented.

staying there more than once, in spite of all that Lady Russell, who thought it a friendship quite out of place, could hint of caution and reserve.

Lady Russell, indeed, had scarcely any influence with Elizabeth, and seemed to love her, rather because she would love her, than because Elizabeth deserved it. She had never received from her more than outward attention, nothing beyond the observances of complaisance; had never succeeded in any point which she wanted to carry, against previous inclination. She had been repeatedly very earnest in trying to get Anne included in the visit to London, sensibly open to all the injustice and all the discredit of the selfish arrangements which shut her out, and on many lesser occasions had endeavoured to give Elizabeth the advantage of her own better judgment and experience—but always in vain; Elizabeth would go her own way—and never had she pursued it in more decided opposition to Lady Russell, than in this selection of Mrs. Clay; turning from the society of so deserving a sister to bestow her affection and confidence on one who ought to have been nothing to her but the object of distant civility.

From situation, Mrs. Clay was, in Lady Russell's estimate, a very unequal, and in her character she believed a very dangerous companion—and a removal that would leave Mrs. Clay behind, and bring a choice of more suitable intimates within Miss Elliot's reach, was therefore an object of first-rate importance.

Chapter III

"I must take leave to observe, Sir Walter," said Mr. Shepherd one morning at Kellynch Hall, as he laid down the newspaper, "that the present juncture is much in our favour. This peace will be turning all our rich Navy Officers ashore.[5] They will be all wanting a home. Could not be a better time, Sir Walter, for having a choice of tenants, very responsible tenants. Many a noble fortune has been made during the war. If a rich Admiral were to come in our way, Sir Walter—"

"He would be a very lucky man, Shepherd," replied Sir Walter, "that's all I have to remark. A prize indeed would Kellynch Hall be to him; rather the greatest prize of all, let him have taken ever so many before—hey, Shepherd?"[6]

Mr. Shepherd laughed, as he knew he must, at this wit, and then added,

"I presume to observe, Sir Walter, that, in the way of business, gentlemen of the navy are well to deal with. I have had a little knowledge of

5. The apparent end of the Napoleonic Wars, signaled by the Treaty of Paris in 1814.
6. Throughout the Napoleonic Wars, the powerful British Navy captured many enemy merchant ships; these "prizes" provided financial rewards for the captain of the conquering vessel.

their methods of doing business, and I am free to confess that they have very liberal notions, and are as likely to make desirable tenants as any set of people one should meet with. Therefore, Sir Walter, what I would take leave to suggest is, that if in consequence of any rumours getting abroad of your intention—which must be contemplated as a possible thing, because we know how difficult it is to keep the actions and designs of one part of the world from the notice and curiosity of the other,—consequence has its tax—I, John Shepherd, might conceal any family-matters that I chose, for nobody would think it worth their while to observe me, but Sir Walter Elliot has eyes upon him which it may be very difficult to elude—and therefore, thus much I venture upon, that it will not greatly surprise me if, with all our caution, some rumour of the truth should get abroad—in the supposition of which, as I was going to observe, since applications will unquestionably follow, I should think any from our wealthy naval commanders particularly worth attending to—and beg leave to add, that two hours will bring me over at any time, to save you the trouble of replying."

Sir Walter only nodded. But soon afterwards, rising and pacing the room, he observed sarcastically,

"There are few among the gentlemen of the navy, I imagine, who would not be surprised to find themselves in a house of this description."

"They would look around them, no doubt, and bless their good fortune," said Mrs. Clay, for Mrs. Clay was present; her father had driven her over, nothing being of so much use to Mrs. Clay's health as a drive to Kellynch: "but I quite agree with my father in thinking a sailor might be a very desirable tenant. I have known a good deal of the profession; and besides their liberality, they are so neat and careful in all their ways! These valuable pictures of yours, Sir Walter, if you chose to leave them, would be perfectly safe. Every thing in and about the house would be taken such excellent care of! the gardens and shrubberies would be kept in almost as high order as they are now. You need not be afraid, Miss Elliot, of your own sweet flower-garden's being neglected."

"As to all that," rejoined Sir Walter coolly, "supposing I were induced to let my house, I have by no means made up my mind as to the privileges to be annexed to it. I am not particularly disposed to favour a tenant. The park would be open to him of course, and few navy officers, or men of any other description, can have had such a range; but what restrictions I might impose on the use of the pleasure-grounds, is another thing. I am not fond of the idea of my shrubberies being always approachable; and I should recommend Miss Elliot to be on her guard with respect to her flower-garden. I am very little disposed to grant a tenant of Kellynch Hall any extraordinary favour, I assure you, be he sailor or soldier."

After a short pause, Mr. Shepherd presumed to say,

"In all these cases, there are established usages which make every thing plain and easy between landlord and tenant. Your interest, Sir Walter, is in pretty safe hands. Depend upon me for taking care that no tenant has more than his just rights. I venture to hint, that Sir Walter Elliot cannot be half so jealous for his own, as John Shepherd will be for him."

Here Anne spoke,—

"The navy, I think, who have done so much for us, have at least an equal claim with any other set of men, for all the comforts and all the privileges which any home can give. Sailors work hard enough for their comforts, we must all allow."

"Very true, very true. What Miss Anne says, is very true," was Mr. Shepherd's rejoinder, and "Oh! certainly," was his daughter's; but Sir Walter's remark was, soon afterwards—

"The profession has its utility, but I should be sorry to see any friend of mine belonging to it."

"Indeed!" was the reply, and with a look of surprise.

"Yes; it is in two points offensive to me; I have two strong grounds of objection to it. First, as being the means of bringing persons of obscure birth into undue distinction, and raising men to honours which their fathers and grandfathers never dreamt of; and secondly, as it cuts up a man's youth and vigour most horribly; a sailor grows old sooner than any other man; I have observed it all my life. A man is in greater danger in the navy of being insulted by the rise of one whose father, his father might have disdained to speak to, and of becoming prematurely an object of disgust himself, than in any other line. One day last spring, in town, I was in company with two men, striking instances of what I am talking of, Lord St. Ives, whose father we all know to have been a country curate, without bread to eat; I was to give place[7] to Lord St. Ives, and a certain Admiral Baldwin, the most deplorable looking personage you can imagine, his face the colour of mahogany, rough and rugged to the last degree, all lines and wrinkles, nine grey hairs of a side, and nothing but a dab of powder at top.—'In the name of heaven, who is that old fellow?' said I, to a friend of mine who was standing near, (Sir Basil Morley.) 'Old fellow!' cried Sir Basil, 'it is Admiral Baldwin. What do you take his age to be?' 'Sixty,' said I, 'or perhaps sixty-two.' 'Forty,' replied Sir Basil, 'forty, and no more.' Picture to yourselves my amazement; I shall not easily forget Admiral Baldwin. I never saw quite so wretched an example of what a sea-faring life can do; but to a degree, I know it is the same with them all: they are all knocked about, and exposed to every climate, and every weather, till they are not fit to be seen. It is a pity they are not knocked on the head at once, before they reach Admiral Baldwin's age."

7. Yield precedence.

"Nay, Sir Walter," cried Mrs. Clay, "this is being severe indeed. Have a little mercy on the poor men. We are not all born to be handsome. The sea is no beautifier, certainly; sailors do grow old betimes; I have often observed it; they soon lose the look of youth. But then, is not it the same with many other professions, perhaps most other? Soldiers, in active service, are not at all better off: and even in the quieter professions, there is a toil and a labour of the mind, if not of the body, which seldom leaves a man's looks to the natural effect of time. The lawyer plods, quite care-worn; the physician is up at all hours, and travelling in all weather; and even the clergyman—" she stopt a moment to consider what might do for the clergyman;—"and even the clergyman, you know, is obliged to go into infected rooms, and expose his health and looks to all the injury of a poisonous atmosphere. In fact, as I have long been convinced, though every profession is necessary and honourable in its turn, it is only the lot of those who are not obliged to follow any, who can live in a regular way, in the country, choosing their own hours, following their own pursuits, and living on their own property, without the torment of trying for more; it is only *their* lot, I say, to hold the blessings of health and a good appearance to the utmost: I know no other set of men but what lose something of their personableness when they cease to be quite young."

It seemed as if Mr. Shepherd, in this anxiety to bespeak Sir Walter's goodwill towards a naval officer as tenant, had been gifted with foresight; for the very first application for the house was from an Admiral Croft, with whom he shortly afterwards fell into company in attending the quarter sessions at Taunton;[8] and indeed, he had received a hint of the admiral from a London correspondent. By the report which he hastened over to Kellynch to make, Admiral Croft was a native of Somersetshire, who having acquired a very handsome fortune, was wishing to settle in his own country, and had come down to Taunton in order to look at some advertised places in that immediate neighbourhood, which, however, had not suited him; that accidentally hearing—(it was just as he had foretold, Mr. Shepherd observed, Sir Walter's concerns could not be kept a secret,)—accidentally hearing of the possibility of Kellynch Hall being to let, and understanding his (Mr. Shepherd's) connection with the owner, he had introduced himself to him in order to make particular inquiries, and had, in the course of a pretty long conference, expressed as strong an inclination for the place as a man who knew it only by description, could feel; and given Mr. Shepherd, in his explicit account of himself, every proof of his being a most responsible, eligible tenant.

"And who is Admiral Croft?" was Sir Walter's cold suspicious inquiry.

8. Court sessions held four times a year by justices of the peace.

Mr. Shepherd answered for his being of a gentleman's family, and mentioned a place; and Anne, after the little pause which followed, added—

"He is rear admiral of the white.[9] He was in the Trafalgar[1] action, and has been in the East Indies since; he has been stationed there, I believe, several years."

"Then I take it for granted," observed Sir Walter, "that his face is about as orange as the cuffs and capes of my livery."

Mr. Shepherd hastened to assure him, that Admiral Croft was a very hale, hearty, well-looking man, a little weather-beaten, to be sure, but not much; and quite the gentleman in all his notions and behaviour;—not likely to make the smallest difficulty about terms;—only wanted a comfortable home, and to get into it as soon as possible;—knew he must pay for his convenience;—knew what rent a ready-furnished house of that consequence might fetch;—should not have been surprised if Sir Walter had asked more;—had inquired about the manor;—would be glad of the deputation,[2] certainly, but made no great point of it;—said he sometimes took out a gun, but never killed;—quite the gentleman.

Mr. Shepherd was eloquent on the subject; pointing out all the circumstances of the admiral's family, which made him peculiarly desirable as a tenant. He was a married man, and without children; the very state to be wished for. A house was never taken good care of, Mr. Shepherd observed, without a lady: he did not know, whether furniture might not be in danger of suffering as much where there was no lady, as where there were many children. A lady, without a family, was the very best preserver of furniture in the world. He had seen Mrs. Croft, too; she was at Taunton with the admiral, and had been present almost all the time they were talking the matter over.

"And a very well-spoken, genteel, shrewd lady, she seemed to be," continued he; "asked more questions about the house, and terms, and taxes, than the admiral himself, and seemed more conversant with business. And moreover, Sir Walter, I found she was not quite unconnected in this country, any more than her husband; that is to say, she is sister to a gentleman who did live amongst us once; she told me so herself: sister to the gentleman who lived a few years back, at Monkford. Bless me! what was his name? At this moment I cannot recollect his name, though I have heard it so lately. Penelope, my dear, can you help me to the name of the gentleman who lived at Monkford—Mrs. Croft's brother?"

But Mrs. Clay was talking so eagerly with Miss Elliot, that she did not hear the appeal.

9. The navy consisted of three squadrons, Red, White, and Blue. Anne's display of knowledge here reveals her special interest in naval affairs, soon to be accounted for.
1. In the Battle of Trafalgar (October 21, 1805), the British Navy triumphed over Napoleon's fleet and definitively established British naval supremacy.
2. The right to shoot game on the property.

"I have no conception whom you can mean, Shepherd; I remember no gentleman resident at Monkford since the time of old Governor Trent."

"Bless me! how very odd! I shall forget my own name soon, I suppose. A name that I am so very well acquainted with; knew the gentleman so well by sight; seen him a hundred times; came to consult me once, I remember, about a trespass of one of his neighbours; farmer's man breaking into his orchard—wall torn down—apples stolen—caught in the fact; and afterwards, contrary to my judgment, submitted to an amicable compromise. Very odd indeed!"

After waiting another moment—

"You mean Mr. Wentworth, I suppose," said Anne.

Mr. Shepherd was all gratitude.

"Wentworth was the very name! Mr. Wentworth was the very man. He had the curacy of Monkford, you know, Sir. Walter, some time back, for two or three years. Came there about the year—5, I take it. You remember him, I am sure."

"Wentworth? Oh! ay,—Mr. Wentworth, the curate of Monkford. You misled me by the term *gentleman*. I thought you were speaking of some man of property: Mr. Wentworth was nobody, I remember; quite unconnected; nothing to do with the Strafford family.[3] One wonders how the names of many of our nobility become so common."

As Mr. Shepherd perceived that this connexion of the Crofts did them no service with Sir Walter, he mentioned it no more; returning, with all his zeal, to dwell on the circumstances more indisputably in their favour; their age, and number, and fortune; the high idea they had formed of Kellynch Hall, and extreme solicitude for the advantage of renting it; making it appear as if they ranked nothing beyond the happiness of being the tenants of Sir Walter Elliot: an extraordinary taste, certainly, could they have been supposed in the secret of Sir Walter's estimate of the dues of a tenant.

It succeeded, however; and though Sir Walter must ever look with an evil eye on any one intending to inhabit that house, and think them infinitely too well off in being permitted to rent it on the highest terms, he was talked into allowing Mr. Shepherd to proceed in the treaty, and authorising him to wait on Admiral Croft, who still remained at Taunton, and fix a day for the house being seen.

Sir Walter was not very wise; but still he had experience enough of the world to feel, that a more unobjectionable tenant, in all essentials, than Admiral Croft bid fair to be, could hardly offer. So far went his understanding; and his vanity supplied a little additional soothing, in the admiral's situation in life, which was just high enough, and not too high. "I have let my house to Admiral Croft," would sound extremely

---

3. "Wentworth" was the family name of the Earls of Strafford.

well; very much better than to any mere *Mr.*——; a *Mr.* (save, perhaps, some half dozen in the nation,) always needs a note of explanation. An admiral speaks his own consequence, and, at the same time, can never make a baronet look small. In all their dealings and intercourse, Sir Walter Elliot must ever have the precedence.

Nothing could be done without a reference to Elizabeth; but her inclination was growing so strong for a removal, that she was happy to have it fixed and expedited by a tenant at hand; and not a word to suspend decision was uttered by her.

Mr. Shepherd was completely empowered to act; and no sooner had such an end been reached, than Anne, who had been a most attentive listener to the whole, left the room, to seek the comfort of cool air for her flushed cheeks; and as she walked along a favourite grove, said, with a gentle sigh, "a few months more, and *he*, perhaps, may be walking here."

Chapter IV

He was not Mr. Wentworth, the former curate of Monkford, however suspicious appearances may be, but a captain Frederick Wentworth, his brother, who being made commander in consequence of the action off St. Domingo,[4] and not immediately employed, had come into Somersetshire, in the summer of 1806; and having no parent living, found a home for half a year, at Monkford. He was, at that time, a remarkably fine young man, with a great deal of intelligence, spirit and brilliancy; and Anne an extremely pretty girl, with gentleness, modesty, taste, and feeling.—Half the sum of attraction, on either side, might have been enough, for he had nothing to do, and she had hardly any body to love; but the encounter of such lavish recommendations could not fail. They were gradually acquainted, and when acquainted, rapidly and deeply in love. It would be difficult to say which had seen highest perfection in the other, or which had been the happiest; she, in receiving his declarations and proposals, or he in having them accepted.

A short period of exquisite felicity followed, and but a short one.— Troubles soon arose. Sir Walter, on being applied to, without actually withholding his consent, or saying it should never be, gave it all the negative of great astonishment, great coldness, great silence, and a professed resolution of doing nothing for his daughter.[5] He thought it a very degrading alliance; and Lady Russell, though with more tempered and pardonable pride, received it as a most unfortunate one.

Anne Elliot, with all her claims of birth, beauty, and mind, to throw

4. A British naval victory in February 1806.
5. Giving her no dowry.

herself away at nineteen; involve herself at nineteen in an engagement with a young man, who had nothing but himself to recommend him, and no hopes of attaining affluence, but in the chances of a most uncertain profession, and no connexions to secure even his farther rise in that profession; would be, indeed, a throwing away, which she grieved to think of! Anne Elliot, so young; known to so few, to be snatched off by a stranger without alliance or fortune; or rather sunk by him into a state of most wearing, anxious, youth-killing dependance! It must not be, if by any fair interference of friendship, any representations from one who had almost a mother's love, and mother's rights, it would be prevented.

Captain Wentworth had no fortune. He had been lucky in his profession, but spending freely, what had come freely, had realized nothing. But, he was confident that he should soon be rich;—full of life and ardour, he knew that he should soon have a ship, and soon be on a station that would lead to every thing he wanted.[6] He had always been lucky; he knew he should be so still.—Such confidence, powerful in its own warmth, and bewitching in the wit which often expressed it, must have been enough for Anne; but Lady Russell saw it very differently.— His sanguine temper, and fearlessness of mind, operated very differently on her. She saw in it but an aggravation of the evil. It only added a dangerous character to himself. He was brilliant, he was headstrong.— Lady Russell had little taste for wit; and of any thing approaching to imprudence a horror. She deprecated the connexion in every light.

Such opposition, as these feelings produced, was more than Anne could combat. Young and gentle as she was, it might yet have been possible to withstand her father's ill-will, though unsoftened by one kind word or look on the part of her sister;—but Lady Russell, whom she had always loved and relied on, could not, with such steadiness of opinion, and such tenderness of manner, be continually advising her in vain. She was persuaded to believe the engagement a wrong thing—indiscreet, improper, hardly capable of success, and not deserving it. But it was not a merely selfish caution, under which she acted, in putting an end to it. Had she not imagined herself consulting his good, even more than her own, she could hardly have given him up.—The belief of being prudent, and self-denying principally for *his* advantage, was her chief consolation, under the misery of a parting—a final parting; and every consolation was required, for she had to encounter all the additional pain of opinions, on his side, totally unconvinced and unbending, and of his feeling himself ill-used by so forced a relinquishment.—He had left the country in consequence.

A few months had seen the beginning and the end of their acquaintance; but, not with a few months ended Anne's share of suffering from it. Her attachment and regrets had, for a long time, clouded every enjoy-

6. He expected to be given command of a ship and assigned to a part of the world that would allow him to capture many enemy vessels.

ment of youth; and an early loss of bloom and spirits had been their lasting effect.

More than seven years were gone since this little history of sorrowful interest had reached its close; and time had softened down much, perhaps nearly all of peculiar attachment to him,—but she had been too dependant on time alone; no aid had been given in change of place, (except in one visit to Bath soon after the rupture,) or in any novelty or enlargement of society.—No one had ever come within the Kellynch circle, who could bear a comparison with Frederick Wentworth, as he stood in her memory. No second attachment, the only thoroughly natural, happy, and sufficient cure, at her time of life, had been possible to the nice[7] tone of her mind, the fastidiousness of her taste, in the small limits of the society around them. She had been solicited, when about two-and-twenty, to change her name, by the young man, who not long afterwards found a more willing mind in her younger sister; and Lady Russell had lamented her refusal; for Charles Musgrove was the eldest son of a man, whose landed property and general importance, were second, in that country, only to Sir Walter's, and of good character and appearance; and however Lady Russell might have asked yet for something more, while Anne was nineteen, she would have rejoiced to see her at twenty-two, so respectably removed from the partialities and injustice of her father's house, and settled so permanently near herself. But in this case, Anne had left nothing for advice to do; and though Lady Russell, as satisfied as ever with her own discretion, never wished the past undone, she began now to have the anxiety which borders on hopelessness for Anne's being tempted, by some man of talents and independence, to enter a state for which she held her to be peculiarly fitted by her warm affections and domestic habits.

They knew not each other's opinion, either its constancy or its change, on the one leading point of Anne's conduct, for the subject was never alluded to,—but Anne, at seven and twenty, thought very differently from what she had been made to think at nineteen.—She did not blame Lady Russell, she did not blame herself for having been guided by her; but she felt that were any young person, in similar circumstances, to apply to her for counsel, they would never receive any of such certain immediate wretchedness, such uncertain future good.—

 She was persuaded that under every disadvantage of disapprobation at home, and every anxiety attending his profession, all their probable fears, delays and disappointments, she should yet have been a happier woman in maintaining the engagement, than she had been in the sacrifice of it; and this, she fully believed, had the usual share, had even more than a usual share of all such solicitudes and suspense been theirs, without reference to the actual results of their case, which, as it happened, would have bestowed earlier prosperity than could be reasonably calculated on. All his sanguine expectations, all his confidence had been justified. His genius and ardour had seemed to foresee and to command his prosperous path. He had, very soon after their engagement ceased, got employ; and all that he had told her would follow, had taken place. He had distinguished himself, and early gained the other step in rank—and must now, by successive captures, have made a handsome fortune. She had only navy lists[8] and newspapers for her authority, but she could not doubt his being rich;—and, in favour of his constancy, she had no reason to believe him married.

How eloquent could Anne Elliot have been,—how eloquent, at least, were her wishes on the side of early warm attachment, and a cheerful confidence in futurity, against that over-anxious caution which seems to insult exertion and distrust Providence!—She had been forced into prudence in her youth, she learned romance as she grew older—the natural sequel of an unnatural beginning.

With all these circumstances, recollections and feelings, she could not hear that Captain Wentworth's sister was likely to live at Kellynch, without a revival of former pain; and many a stroll and many a sigh were necessary to dispel the agitation of the idea. She often told herself it was folly, before she could harden her nerves sufficiently to feel the continual discussion of the Crofts and their business no evil. She was assisted, however, by that perfect indifference and apparent unconsciousness, among the only three of her own friends in the secret of the past, which seemed almost to deny any recollection of it. She could do justice to the superiority of Lady Russell's motives in this, over those of her father and Elizabeth; she could honour all the better feelings of her calmness—but the general air of oblivion among them was highly important, from whatever it sprung; and in the event of Admiral Croft's really taking Kellynch-hall, she rejoiced anew over the conviction which had always been most grateful to her, of the past being known to those three only among her connexions, by whom no syllable, she believed, would ever be whispered, and in the trust that among his, the brother only with whom he had been residing, had received any information of their short-lived engagement.—That brother had been long removed from the country—and being a sensible man, and, moreover, a single man at the time, she had a fond dependance on no human creature's having heard of it from him.

The sister, Mrs. Croft, had then been out of England, accompanying her husband on a foreign station, and her own sister, Mary, had been at school while it all occurred—and never admitted by the pride of some, and the delicacy of others, to the smallest knowledge of it afterwards.

With these supports, she hoped that the acquaintance between herself

8. Official publications of the navy containing lists of officers and other nautical information.

and the Crofts, which, with Lady Russell, still resident in Kellynch, and Mary fixed only three miles off, must be anticipated, need not involve any particular awkwardness.

Chapter V

On the morning appointed for Admiral and Mrs. Croft's seeing Kellynch-hall, Anne found it most natural to take her almost daily walk to Lady Russell's, and keep out of the way till all was over; when she found it most natural to be sorry that she had missed the opportunity of seeing them.

This meeting of the two parties proved highly satisfactory, and decided the whole business at once. Each lady was previously well disposed for an agreement, and saw nothing, therefore, but good manners in the other; and, with regard to the gentlemen, there was such an hearty good humour, such an open, trusting liberality on the Admiral's side, as could not but influence Sir Walter, who had besides been flattered into his very best and most polished behaviour by Mr. Shepherd's assurances of his being known, by report, to the Admiral, as a model of good breeding.

The house and grounds, and furniture, were approved, the Crofts were approved, terms, time, every thing, and every body, was right; and Mr. Shepherd's clerks were set to work, without there having been a single preliminary difference to modify of all that "This indenture sheweth."

Sir Walter, without hesitation, declared the Admiral to be the best-looking sailor he had ever met with, and went so far as to say, that, if his own man might have had the arranging of his hair, he should not be ashamed of being seen with him any where; and the Admiral, with sympathetic cordiality, observed to his wife as they drove back through the Park, "I thought we should soon come to a deal, my dear, in spite of what they told us at Taunton. The baronet will never set the Thames on fire, but there seems no harm in him:"—reciprocal compliments, which would have been esteemed about equal.

The Crofts were to have possession at Michaelmas,[9] and as Sir Walter proposed removing to Bath in the course of the preceding month, there was no time to be lost in making every dependant arrangement.

Lady Russell, convinced that Anne would not be allowed to be of any use, or any importance, in the choice of the house which they were going to secure, was very unwilling to have her hurried away so soon, and wanted to make it possible for her to stay behind, till she might convey her to Bath herself after Christmas; but having engagements of

9. September 29.

her own, which must take her from Kellynch for several weeks, she was unable to give the full invitation she wished; and Anne, though dreading the possible heats of September in all the white glare of Bath, and grieving to forego all the influence so sweet and so sad of the autumnal months in the country, did not think that, every thing considered, she wished to remain. It would be most right, and most wise, and, therefore, must involve least suffering, to go with the others.

Something occurred, however, to give her a different duty. Mary, often a little unwell, and always thinking a great deal of her own complaints, and always in the habit of claiming Anne when any thing was the matter, was indisposed; and foreseeing that she should not have a day's health all the autumn, entreated, or rather required her, for it was hardly entreaty, to come to Uppercross Cottage, and bear her company as long as she should want her, instead of going to Bath.

"I cannot possibly do without Anne," was Mary's reasoning; and Elizabeth's reply was, "Then I am sure Anne had better stay, for nobody will want her in Bath."

To be claimed as a good, though in an improper style, is at least better than being rejected as no good at all; and Anne, glad to be thought of some use, glad to have any thing marked out as a duty, and certainly not sorry to have the scene of it in the country, and her own dear country, readily agreed to stay.

This invitation of Mary's removed all Lady Russell's difficulties, and it was consequently soon settled that Anne should not go to Bath till Lady Russell took her, and that all the intervening time should be divided between Uppercross Cottage and Kellynch-lodge.

So far all was perfectly right; but Lady Russell was almost startled by the wrong of one part of the Kellynch-hall plan, when it burst on her, which was, Mrs. Clay's being engaged to go to Bath with Sir Walter and Elizabeth, as a most important and valuable assistant to the latter in all the business before her. Lady Russell was extremely sorry that such a measure should have been resorted to at all—wondered, grieved, and feared—and the affront it contained to Anne, in Mrs. Clay's being of so much use, while Anne could be of none, was a very sore aggravation.

Anne herself was become hardened to such affronts; but she felt the imprudence of the arrangement quite as keenly as Lady Russell. With a great deal of quiet observation, and a knowledge, which she often wished less, of her father's character, she was sensible that results the most serious to his family from the intimacy, were more than possible. She did not imagine that her father had at present an idea of the kind. Mrs. Clay had freckles, and a projecting tooth, and a clumsy wrist, which he was continually making severe remarks upon, in her absence; but she was young, and certainly altogether well-looking, and possessed, in an acute mind and assiduous pleasing manners, infinitely more dangerous attractions than any merely personal might have been. Anne was so impressed by the degree of their danger, that she could not excuse herself from trying to make it perceptible to her sister. She had little hope of success; but Elizabeth, who in the event of such a reverse would be so much more to be pitied than herself, should never, she thought, have reason to reproach her for giving no warning.

She spoke, and seemed only to offend. Elizabeth could not conceive how such an absurd suspicion should occur to her; and indignantly answered for each party's perfectly knowing their situation.

"Mrs. Clay," said she warmly, "never forgets who she is; and as I am rather better acquainted with her sentiments than you can be, I can assure you, that upon the subject of marriage they are particularly nice; and that she reprobates all inequality of condition and rank more strongly than most people. And as to my father, I really should not have thought that he, who has kept himself single so long for our sakes, need be suspected now. If Mrs. Clay were a very beautiful woman, I grant you, it might be wrong to have her so much with me; not that any thing in the world, I am sure, would induce my father to make a degrading match; but he might be rendered unhappy. But poor Mrs. Clay, who, with all her merits, can never have been reckoned tolerably pretty! I really think poor Mrs. Clay may be staying here in perfect safety. One would imagine you had never heard my father speak of her personal misfortunes, though I know you must fifty times. That tooth of her's! and those freckles! Freckles do not disgust me so very much as they do him: I have known a face not materially disfigured by a few, but he abominates them. You must have heard him notice Mrs. Clay's freckles."

"There is hardly any personal defect," replied Anne, "which an agreeable manner might not gradually reconcile one to."

"I think very differently," answered Elizabeth, shortly; "an agreeable manner may set off handsome features, but can never alter plain ones. However, at any rate, as I have a great deal more at stake on this point than any body else can have, I think it rather unnecessary in you to be advising me."

Anne had done—glad that it was over, and not absolutely hopeless of doing good. Elizabeth, though resenting the suspicion, might yet be made observant by it.

The last office of the four carriage-horses was to draw Sir Walter, Miss Elliot, and Mrs. Clay to Bath. The party drove off in very good spirits; Sir Walter prepared with condescending bows for all the afflicted tenantry and cottagers who might have had a hint to shew themselves: and Anne walked up at the same time, in a sort of desolate tranquillity, to the Lodge, where she was to spend the first week.

Her friend was not in better spirits than herself. Lady Russell felt this break-up of the family exceedingly. Their respectability was as dear to her as her own; and a daily intercourse had become precious by habit.

It was painful to look upon their deserted grounds, and still worse to anticipate the new hands they were to fall into; and to escape the solitariness and the melancholy of so altered a village, and be out of the way when Admiral and Mrs. Croft first arrived, she had determined to make her own absence from home begin when she must give up Anne. Accordingly their removal was made together, and Anne was set down at Uppercross Cottage, in the first stage of Lady Russell's journey.

Uppercross was a moderate-sized village, which a few years back had been completely in the old English style; containing only two houses superior in appearance to those of the yeomen and labourers,—the mansion of the 'squire, with its high walls, great gates, and old trees, substantial and unmodernized—and the compact, tight parsonage, enclosed in its own neat garden, with a vine and a pear-tree trained round its casements; but upon the marriage of the young 'squire, it had received the improvement of a farm-house elevated into a cottage for his residence; and Uppercross Cottage, with its veranda, French windows, and other prettinesses, was quite as likely to catch the traveller's eye, as the more consistent and considerable aspect and premises of the Great House, about a quarter of a mile farther on.

Here Anne had often been staying. She knew the ways of Uppercross as well as those of Kellynch. The two families were so continually meeting, so much in the habit of running in and out of each other's house at all hours, that it was rather a surprise to her to find Mary alone; but being alone, her being unwell and out of spirits, was almost a matter of course. Though better endowed than the elder sister, Mary had not Anne's understanding or temper. While well, and happy, and properly attended to, she had great good humour and excellent spirits; but any indisposition sunk her completely; she had no resources for solitude; and inheriting a considerable share of the Elliot self-importance, was very prone to add to every other distress that of fancying herself neglected and ill-used. In person, she was inferior to both sisters, and had, even in her bloom, only reached the dignity of being "a fine girl." She was now lying on the faded sofa of the pretty little drawing-room, the once elegant furniture of which had been gradually growing shabby, under the influence of four summers and two children; and, on Anne's appearing, greeted her with,

"So, you are come at last! I began to think I should never see you. I am so ill I can hardly speak. I have not seen a creature the whole morning!"

"I am sorry to find you unwell," replied Anne. "You sent me such a good account of yourself on Thursday!"

"Yes, I made the best of it; I always do; but I was very far from well at the time; and I do not think I ever was so ill in my life as I have been all this morning—very unfit to be left alone, I am sure. Suppose I were to be seized of a sudden in some dreadful way, and not able to ring the bell! So, Lady Russell would not get out. I do not think she has been in this house three times this summer."

Anne said what was proper, and enquired after her husband. "Oh! Charles is out shooting. I have not seen him since seven o'clock. He would go, though I told him how ill I was. He said he should not stay out long; but he has never come back, and now it is almost one. I assure you, I have not seen a soul this whole long morning."

"You have had your little boys with you?"

"Yes, as long as I could bear their noise; but they are so unmanageable that they do me more harm than good. Little Charles does not mind a word I say, and Walter is growing quite as bad."

"Well, you will soon be better now," replied Anne, cheerfully. "You know I always cure you when I come. How are your neighbours at the Great House?"

"I can give you no account of them. I have not seen one of them to-day, except Mr. Musgrove, who just stopped and spoke through the window, but without getting off his horse; and though I told him how ill I was, not one of them have been near me. It did not happen to suit the Miss Musgroves, I suppose, and they never put themselves out of their way."

"You will see them yet, perhaps, before the morning is gone. It is early."

"I never want them, I assure you. They talk and laugh a great deal too much for me. Oh! Anne, I am so very unwell! It was quite unkind of you not to come on Thursday."

"My dear Mary, recollect what a comfortable account you sent me of yourself! You wrote in the cheerfullest manner, and said you were perfectly well, and in no hurry for me; and that being the case, you must be aware that my wish would be to remain with Lady Russell to the last: and besides what I felt on her account, I have really been so busy, have had so much to do, that I could not very conveniently have left Kellynch sooner."

"Dear me! what can *you* possibly have to do?"

"A great many things, I assure you. More than I can recollect in a moment: but I can tell you some. I have been making a duplicate of the catalogue of my father's books and pictures. I have been several times in the garden with Mackenzie, trying to understand, and make him understand, which of Elizabeth's plants are for Lady Russell. I have had all my own little concerns to arrange—books and music to divide, and all my trunks to repack, from not having understood in time what was intended as to the waggons. And one thing I have had to do, Mary, of a more trying nature; going to almost every house in the parish, as a sort of take-leave. I was told that they wished it. But all these things took up a great deal of time."

"Oh! well;"—and after a moment's pause, "But you have never asked me one word about our dinner at the Pooles yesterday."

"Did you go then? I have made no enquiries, because I concluded you must have been obliged to give up the party."

"Oh! yes, I went. I was very well yesterday; nothing at all the matter with me till this morning. It would have been strange if I had not gone."

"I am very glad you were well enough, and I hope you had a pleasant party."

"Nothing remarkable. One always knows beforehand what the dinner will be, and who will be there. And it is so very uncomfortable, not having a carriage of one's own. Mr. and Mrs. Musgrove took me, and we were so crowded! They are both so very large, and take up so much room! And Mr. Musgrove always sits forward. So, there was I, crowded into the back seat with Henrietta and Louisa. And I think it very likely that my illness to-day may be owing to it."

A little farther perseverance in patience, and forced cheerfulness on Anne's side, produced nearly a cure on Mary's. She could soon sit upright on the sofa, and began to hope she might be able to leave it by dinner-time. Then, forgetting to think of it, she was at the other end of the room, beautifying a nosegay; then, she ate her cold meat; and then she was well enough to propose a little walk.

"Where shall we go?" said she, when they were ready. "I suppose you will not like to call at the Great House before they have been to see you?"

"I have not the smallest objection on that account," replied Anne. "I should never think of standing on such ceremony with people I know so well as Mrs. and the Miss Musgroves."

"Oh! but they ought to call upon you as soon as possible. They ought to feel what is due to you as *my* sister. However, we may as well go and sit with them a little while, and when we have got that over, we can enjoy our walk."

Anne had always thought such a style of intercourse highly imprudent; but she had ceased to endeavour to check it, from believing that, though there were on each side continual subjects of offence, neither family could now do without it. To the Great House accordingly they went, to sit the full half hour in the old-fashioned square parlour, with a small carpet and shining floor, to which the present daughters of the house were gradually giving the proper air of confusion by a grand piano forte and a harp, flower-stands and little tables placed in every direction. Oh! could the originals of the portraits against the wainscot, could the gentlemen in brown velvet and the ladies in blue satin have seen what was going on, been conscious of such an overthrow of all order and neatness! The portraits themselves seemed to be staring in astonishment.

The Musgroves, like their houses, were in a state of alteration, perhaps of improvement. The father and mother were in the old English style, and the young people in the new. Mr. and Mrs. Musgrove were a very good sort of people; friendly and hospitable, not much educated, and not at all elegant. Their children had more modern minds and manners. There was a numerous family; but the only two grown up, excepting Charles, were Henrietta and Louisa, young ladies of nineteen and twenty, who had brought from a school at Exeter all the usual stock of accomplishments, and were now, like thousands of other young ladies, living to be fashionable, happy, and merry. Their dress had every advantage, their faces were rather pretty, their spirits extremely good, their manners unembarrassed and pleasant; they were of consequence at home, and favourites abroad. Anne always contemplated them as some of the happiest creatures of her acquaintance; but still, saved as we all are by some comfortable feeling of superiority from wishing for the possibility of exchange, she would not have given up her own more elegant and cultivated mind for all their enjoyments; and envied them nothing but that seemingly perfect good understanding and agreement together, that good-humoured mutual affection, of which she had known so little herself with either of her sisters.

They were received with great cordiality. Nothing seemed amiss on the side of the Great House family, which was generally, as Anne very well knew, the least to blame. The half hour was chatted away pleasantly enough; and she was not at all surprised, at the end of it, to have their walking party joined by both the Miss Musgroves, at Mary's particular invitation.

Chapter VI

Anne had not wanted[1] this visit to Uppercross, to learn that a removal from one set of people to another, though at a distance of only three miles, will often include a total change of conversation, opinion, and idea. She had never been staying there before, without being struck by it, or without wishing that other Elliots could have her advantage in seeing how unknown, or unconsidered there, were the affairs which at Kellynch-hall were treated as of such general publicity and pervading interest; yet, with all this experience, she believed she must now submit to feel that another lesson, in the art of knowing our own nothingness beyond our own circle, was become necessary for her;—for certainly, coming as she did, with a heart full of the subject which had been completely occupying both houses in Kellynch for many weeks, she had expected rather more curiosity and sympathy than she found in the separate, but very similar remark of Mr. and Mrs. Musgrove—"So, Miss Anne, Sir Walter and your sister are gone; and what part of Bath do you

1. Needed.

think they will settle in?" and this, without much waiting for an answer;—or in the young ladies' addition of, "I hope *we* shall be in Bath in the winter; but remember, papa, if we do go, we must be in a good situation—none of your Queen-squares for us!" or in the anxious supplement from Mary, of "Upon my word, I shall be pretty well off, when you are all gone away to be happy at Bath!"

She could only resolve to avoid such self-delusion in future, and think with heightened gratitude of the extraordinary blessing of having one such truly sympathising friend as Lady Russell.

The Mr. Musgroves had their own game to guard, and to destroy; their own horses, dogs, and newspapers to engage them; and the females were fully occupied in all the other common subjects of house-keeping, neighbours, dress, dancing, and music. She acknowledged it to be very fitting, that every little social commonwealth should dictate its own matters of discourse; and hoped, ere long, to become a not unworthy member of the one she was now transplanted into.—With the prospect of spending at least two months at Uppercross, it was highly incumbent on her to clothe her imagination, her memory, and all her ideas in as much of Uppercross as possible.

She had no dread of these two months. Mary was not so repulsive[2] and unsisterly as Elizabeth, nor so inaccessible to all influence of hers; neither was there any thing among the other component parts of the cottage inimical to comfort.—She was always on friendly terms with her brother-in-law; and in the children, who loved her nearly as well, and respected her a great deal more than their mother, she had an object of interest, amusement, and wholesome exertion.

Charles Musgrove was civil and agreeable; in sense and temper he was undoubtedly superior to his wife; but not of powers, or conversation, or grace, to make the past, as they were connected together, at all a dangerous contemplation; though, at the same time, Anne could believe, with Lady Russell, that a more equal match might have greatly improved him; and that a woman of real understanding might have given more consequence to his character, and more usefulness, rationality, and elegance to his habits and pursuits. As it was, he did nothing with much zeal, but sport; and his time was otherwise trifled away, without benefit from books, or any thing else. He had very good spirits, which never seemed much affected by his wife's occasional lowness; bore with her unreasonableness sometimes to Anne's admiration; and, upon the whole, though there was very often a little disagreement, (in which she had sometimes more share than she wished, being appealed to by both parties) they might pass for a happy couple. They were always perfectly agreed in the want of more money, and a strong inclination for a handsome present from his father; but here, as on most topics, he had

2. Cold in manner.

the superiority, for while Mary thought it a great shame that such a present was not made, he always contended for his father's having many other uses for his money, and a right to spend it as he liked.

As to the management of their children, his theory was much better than his wife's, and his practice not so bad.—"I could manage them very well, if it were not for Mary's interference,"—was what Anne often heard him say, and had a good deal of faith in; but when listening in turn to Mary's reproach of "Charles spoils the children so that I cannot get them into any order,"—she never had the smallest temptation to say, "Very true."

One of the least agreeable circumstances of her residence there, was her being treated with too much confidence by all parties, and being too much in the secret of the complaints of each house. Known to have some influence with her sister, she was continually requested, or at least receiving hints to exert it, beyond what was practicable. "I wish you could persuade Mary not to be always fancying herself ill," was Charles's language; and, in an unhappy mood, thus spoke Mary;—"I do believe if Charles were to see me dying, he would not think there was any thing the matter with me. I am sure, Anne, if you would, you might persuade him that I really am very ill—a great deal worse than I ever own."

Mary's declaration was, "I hate sending the children to the Great House, though their grandmamma is always wanting to see them, for she humours and indulges them to such a degree, and gives them so much trash and sweet things, that they are sure to come back sick and cross for the rest of the day."—And Mrs. Musgrove took the first opportunity of being alone with Anne, to say, "Oh! Miss Anne, I cannot help wishing Mrs. Charles had a little of your method with those children. They are quite different creatures with you! But to be sure, in general they are so spoilt! It is a pity you cannot put your sister in the way of managing them. They are as fine healthy children as ever were seen, poor little dears, without partiality; but Mrs. Charles knows no more how they should be treated!—Bless me, how troublesome they are sometimes!—I assure you, Miss Anne, it prevents my wishing to see them at our house so often as I otherwise should. I believe Mrs. Charles is not quite pleased with my not inviting them oftener; but you know it is very bad to have children with one, that one is obliged to be checking every moment; 'don't do this, and don't do that;'—or that one can only keep in tolerable order by more cake than is good for them."

She had this communication, moreover, from Mary. "Mrs. Musgrove thinks all her servants so steady, that it would be high treason to call it in question; but I am sure, without exaggeration, that her upper house-maid and laundry-maid, instead of being in their business, are gadding about the village, all day long. I meet them wherever I go; and I declare, I never go twice into my nursery without seeing something of them. If Jemima were not the trustiest, steadiest creature in the world, it would be enough to spoil her; for she tells me, they are always tempting her to take a walk with them." And on Mrs. Musgrove's side, it was,—"I make a rule of never interfering in any of my daughter-in-law's concerns, for I know it would not do; but I shall tell *you*, Miss Anne, because you may be able to set things to rights, that I have no very good opinion of Mrs. Charles's nursery-maid: I hear strange stories of her; she is always upon the gad: and from my own knowledge, I can declare, she is such a fine-dressing lady, that she is enough to ruin any servants she comes near. Mrs. Charles quite swears by her, I know; but I just give you this hint, that you may be upon the watch; because, if you see any thing amiss, you need not be afraid of mentioning it."

Again; it was Mary's complaint that Mrs. Musgrove was very apt not to give her the precedence that was her due, when they dined at the Great House with other families; and she did not see any reason why she was to be considered so much at home as to lose her place. And one day, when Anne was walking with only the Miss Musgroves, one of them, after talking of rank, people of rank, and jealousy of rank, said, "I have no scruple of observing to *you*, how nonsensical some persons are about their place, because, all the world knows how easy and indifferent you are about it: but I wish any body could give Mary a hint that it would be a great deal better if she were not so very tenacious; especially, if she would not be always putting herself forward to take place of mamma. Nobody doubts her right to have precedence of mamma, but it would be more becoming in her not to be always insisting on it. It is not that mamma cares about it the least in the world, but I know it is taken notice of by many persons."

How was Anne to set all these matters to rights? She could do little more than listen patiently, soften every grievance, and excuse each to the other; give them all hints of the forbearance necessary between such near neighbours, and make those hints broadest which were meant for her sister's benefit.

In all other respects, her visit began and proceeded very well. Her own spirits improved by change of place and subject, by being removed three miles from Kellynch: Mary's ailments lessened by having a constant companion; and their daily intercourse with the other family, since there was neither superior affection, confidence, nor employment in the cottage, to be interrupted by it, was rather an advantage. It was certainly carried nearly as far as possible, for they met every morning, and hardly ever spent an evening asunder; but she believed they should not have done so well without the sight of Mr. and Mrs. Musgrove's respectable forms in the usual places, or without the talking, laughing, and singing of their daughters.

She played a great deal better than either of the Miss Musgroves; but having no voice, no knowledge of the harp, and no fond parents to sit by and fancy themselves delighted, her performance was little thought of, only out of civility, or to refresh the others, as she was well aware. She knew that when she played she was giving pleasure only to herself; but this was no new sensation: excepting one short period of her life, she had never, since the age of fourteen, never since the loss of her dear mother, known the happiness of being listened to, or encouraged by any just appreciation or real taste. In music she had been always used to feel alone in the world; and Mr. and Mrs. Musgrove's fond partiality for their own daughters' performance, and total indifference to any other person's, gave her much more pleasure for their sakes, than mortification for her own.

The party at the Great House was sometimes increased by other company. The neighbourhood was not large, but the Musgroves were visited by every body, and had more dinner parties, and more callers, more visitors by invitation and by chance, than any other family. They were more completely popular.

The girls were wild for dancing; and the evenings ended, occasionally, in an unpremeditated little ball. There was a family of cousins within a walk of Uppercross, in less affluent circumstances, who depended on the Musgroves for all their pleasures: they would come at any time, and help play at any thing, or dance any where; and Anne, very much preferring the office of musician to a more active post, played country dances to them by the hour together; a kindness which always recommended her musical powers to the notice of Mr. and Mrs. Musgrove more than any thing else, and often drew this compliment;— "Well done, Miss Anne! very well done indeed! Lord bless me! how those little fingers of yours fly about!"

So passed the first three weeks. Michaelmas came; and now Anne's heart must be in Kellynch again. A beloved home made over to others; all the precious rooms and furniture, groves, and prospects, beginning to own other eyes and other limbs! She could not think of much else on the 29th of September; and she had this sympathetic touch in the evening, from Mary, who, on having occasion to note down the day of the month, exclaimed, "Dear me! is not this the day the Crofts were to come to Kellynch? I am glad I did not think of it before. How low it makes me!"

The Crofts took possession with true naval alertness, and were to be visited. Mary deplored the necessity for herself. "Nobody knew how much she should suffer. She should put it off as long as she could." But was not easy till she had talked Charles into driving her over on an early day; and was in a very animated, comfortable state of imaginary agitation, when she came back. Anne had very sincerely rejoiced in there being no means of her going.[3] She wished, however, to see the Crofts, and was glad to be within when the visit was returned. They came; the

---

3. Because Charles, as we learn later, drives a curricle, which holds only two people.

master of the house was not at home, but the two sisters were together; and as it chanced that Mrs. Croft fell to the share of Anne, while the admiral sat by Mary, and made himself very agreeable by his good-humoured notice of her little boys, she was well able to watch for a likeness, and if it failed her in the features, to catch it in the voice, or the turn of sentiment and expression.

Mrs. Croft, though neither tall nor fat, had a squareness, uprightness, and vigour of form, which gave importance to her person. She had bright dark eyes, good teeth, and altogether an agreeable face; though her reddened and weather-beaten complexion, the consequence of her having been almost as much at sea as her husband, made her seem to have lived some years longer in the world than her real eight and thirty. Her manners were open, easy, and decided, like one who had no distrust of herself, and no doubts of what to do; without any approach to coarseness, however, or any want of good humour. Anne gave her credit, indeed, for feelings of great consideration towards herself, in all that related to Kellynch; and it pleased her: especially, as she had satisfied herself in the very first half minute, in the instant even of introduction, that there was not the smallest symptom of any knowledge or suspicion on Mrs. Croft's side, to give a bias of any sort. She was quite easy on that head, and consequently full of strength and courage, till for a moment electrified by Mrs. Croft's suddenly saying,—

"It was you, and not your sister, I find, that my brother had the pleasure of being acquainted with, when he was in this country."

Anne hoped she had outlived the age of blushing; but the age of emotion she certainly had not.

"Perhaps you may not have heard that he is married," added Mrs. Croft.

She could now answer as she ought; and was happy to feel, when Mrs. Croft's next words explained it to be Mr. Wentworth of whom she spoke, that she had said nothing which might not do for either brother. She immediately felt how reasonable it was, that Mrs. Croft should be thinking and speaking of Edward, and not of Frederick; and with shame at her own forgetfulness, applied herself to the knowledge of their former neighbour's present state, with proper interest.

The rest was all tranquillity; till just as they were moving, she heard the admiral say to Mary,

"We are expecting a brother of Mrs. Croft's here soon; I dare say you know him by name."

He was cut short by the eager attacks of the little boys, clinging to him like an old friend, and declaring he should not go; and being too much engrossed by proposals of carrying them away in his coat pocket, etc. to have another moment for finishing or recollecting what he had begun, Anne was left to persuade herself, as well as she could, that the same brother must still be in question. She could not, however, reach such a degree of certainty, as not to be anxious to hear whether any thing had been said on the subject at the other house, where the Crofts had previously been calling.

The folks of Great House were to spend the evening of this day at the Cottage; and it being now too late in the year for such visits to be made on foot, the coach was beginning to be listened for, when the youngest Miss Musgrove walked in. That she was coming to apologize, and that they should have to spend the evening by themselves, was the first black idea; and Mary was quite ready to be affronted, when Louisa made all right by saying, that she only came on foot, to leave more room for the harp, which was bringing[4] in the carriage.

"And I will tell you our reason," she added, "and all about it. I am come on to give you notice, that papa and mamma are out of spirits this evening, especially mamma; she is thinking so much of poor Richard! And we agreed it would be best to have the harp, for it seems to amuse her more than the piano-forte. I will tell you why she is out of spirits. When the Crofts called this morning, (they called here afterwards, did not they?) they happened to say, that her brother, Captain Wentworth, is just returned to England, or paid off, or something, and is coming to see them almost directly; and most unluckily it came into mamma's head, when they were gone, that Wentworth, or something very like it, was the name of poor Richard's captain, at one time, I do not know when or where, but a great while before he died, poor fellow! And upon looking over his letters and things, she found it was so; and is perfectly sure that this must be the very man, and her head is quite full of it, and of poor Richard! So we must all be as merry as we can, that she may not be dwelling upon such gloomy things."

The real circumstances of this pathetic piece of family history were, that the Musgroves had had the ill fortune of a very troublesome, hopeless son; and the good fortune to lose him before he reached his twentieth year; that he had been sent to sea, because he was stupid and unmanageable on shore; that he had been very little cared for at any time by his family, though quite as much as he deserved; seldom heard of, and scarcely at all regretted, when the intelligence of his death abroad had worked its way to Uppercross, two years before.

He had, in fact, though his sisters were now doing all they could for him, by calling him "poor Richard," been nothing better than a thickheaded, unfeeling, unprofitable Dick Musgrove, who had never done any thing to entitle himself to more than the abbreviation of his name, living or dead.

He had been several years at sea, and had, in the course of those removals to which all midshipmen are liable, and especially such midshipmen as every captain wishes to get rid of, been six months on board

4. Being brought.

Captain Frederick Wentworth's frigate, the Laconia; and from the Laconia he had, under the influence of his captain, written the only two letters which his father and mother had ever received from him during the whole of his absence; that is to say, the only two disinterested letters; all the rest had been mere applications for money.

In each letter he had spoken well of his captain; but yet, so little were they in the habit of attending to such matters, so unobservant and incurious were they as to the names of men or ships, that it had made scarcely any impression at the time; and that Mrs. Musgrove should have been suddenly struck, this very day, with a recollection of the name of Wentworth, as connected with her son, seemed one of those extraordinary bursts of mind which do sometimes occur.

She had gone to her letters, and found it all as she supposed; and the reperusal of these letters, after so long an interval, her poor son gone for ever, and all the strength of his faults forgotten, had affected her spirits exceedingly, and thrown her into greater grief for him than she had known on first hearing of his death. Mr. Musgrove was, in a lesser degree, affected likewise; and when they reached the cottage, they were evidently in want, first, of being listened to anew on this subject, and afterwards, of all the relief which cheerful companions could give.

To hear them talking so much of Captain Wentworth, repeating his name so often, puzzling over past years, and at last ascertaining that it *might*, that it probably *would*, turn out to be the very same Captain Wentworth whom they recollected meeting, once or twice, after their coming back from Clifton;—a very fine young man; but they could not say whether it was seven or eight years ago,—was a new sort of trial to Anne's nerves. She found, however, that it was one to which she must enure herself. Since he actually was expected in the country, she must teach herself to be insensible on such points. And not only did it appear that he was expected, and speedily, but the Musgroves, in their warm gratitude for the kindness he had shewn poor Dick, and very high respect for his character, stamped as it was by poor Dick's having been six months under his care, and mentioning him in strong, though not perfectly well spelt praise, as "a fine dashing felow, only two perticular about the school-master,"[5] were bent on introducing themselves, and seeking his acquaintance, as soon as they could hear of his arrival.

The resolution of doing so helped to form the comfort of their evening.

Chapter VII

A very few days more, and Captain Wentworth was known to be at Kellynch, and Mr. Musgrove had called on him, and come back warm

5. Royal Navy ships all carried schoolmasters.

in his praise, and he was engaged with the Crofts to dine at Uppercross, by the end of another week. It had been a great disappointment to Mr. Musgrove, to find that no earlier day could be fixed, so impatient was he to shew his gratitude, by seeing Captain Wentworth under his own roof, and welcoming him to all that was strongest and best in his cellars.[6] But a week must pass; only a week, in Anne's reckoning, and then, she supposed, they must meet; and soon she began to wish that she could feel secure even for a week.

Captain Wentworth made a very early return to Mr. Musgrove's civility, and she was all but calling there in the same half hour!—She and Mary were actually setting forward for the great house, where, as she afterwards learnt, they must inevitably have found him, when they were stopped by the eldest boy's being at that moment brought home in consequence of a bad fall. The child's situation put the visit entirely aside, but she could not hear of her escape with indifference, even in the midst of the serious anxiety which they afterwards felt on his account.

His collar-bone was found to be dislocated, and such injury received in the back, as roused the most alarming ideas. It was an afternoon of distress, and Anne had every thing to do at once—the apothecary[7] to send for—the father to have pursued and informed—the mother to support and keep from hysterics—the servants to control—the youngest child to banish, and the poor suffering one to attend and soothe;—besides sending, as soon as she recollected it, proper notice to the other house, which brought her an accession rather of frightened, enquiring companions, than of very useful assistants.

Her brother's return was the first comfort; he could take best care of his wife, and the second blessing was the arrival of the apothecary. Till he came and had examined the child, their apprehensions were the worse for being vague;—they suspected great injury, but knew not where; but now the collar-bone was soon replaced, and though Mr. Robinson felt and felt, and rubbed, and looked grave, and spoke low words both to the father and the aunt, still they were all to hope the best, and to be able to part and eat their dinner in tolerable ease of mind; and then it was, just before they parted, that the two young aunts were able so far to digress from their nephew's state, as to give the information of Captain Wentworth's visit;—staying five minutes behind their father and mother, to endeavour to express how perfectly delighted they were with him, how much handsomer, how infinitely more agreeable they thought him than any individual among their male acquaintance, who had been at all a favourite before—how glad they had been to hear papa invite him to stay dinner—how sorry when he said it was quite out of his power—and how glad again, when he had promised in reply to papa and mamma's farther pressing invitations, to come and dine with them

6. Wine cellars.
7. At this time a general medical practitioner.

on the morrow, actually on the morrow!—And he had promised it in so pleasant a manner, as if he felt all the motive of their attention just as he ought!—And, in short, he had looked and said every thing with such exquisite grace, that they could assure them all, their heads were both turned by him!—And off they ran, quite as full of glee as of love, and apparently more full of Captain Wentworth than of little Charles.

The same story and the same raptures were repeated, when the two girls came with their father, through the gloom of the evening, to make enquiries; and Mr. Musgrove, no longer under the first uneasiness about his heir, could add his confirmation and praise, and hope there would be now no occasion for putting Captain Wentworth off, and only be sorry to think that the cottage party, probably, would not like to leave the little boy, to give him the meeting.—"Oh, no! as to leaving the little boy!"—both father and mother were in much too strong and recent alarm to bear the thought; and Anne, in the joy of the escape, could not help adding her warm protestations to theirs.

Charles Musgrove, indeed, afterwards shewed more of inclination; "the child was going on so well—and he wished so much to be introduced to Captain Wentworth, that, perhaps, he might join them in the evening; he would not dine from home, but he might walk in for half an hour." But in this he was eagerly opposed by his wife, with "Oh, no! indeed, Charles, I cannot bear to have you go away. Only think, if any thing should happen!"

The child had a good night, and was going on well the next day. It must be a work of time to ascertain that no injury had been done to the spine, but Mr. Robinson found nothing to increase alarm, and Charles Musgrove began consequently to feel no necessity for longer confinement. The child was to be kept in bed, and amused as quietly as possible; but what was there for a father to do? This was quite a female case, and it would be highly absurd in him, who could be of no use at home, to shut himself up. His father very much wished him to meet Captain Wentworth, and there being no sufficient reason against it, he ought to go; and it ended in his making a bold public declaration, when he came in from shooting, of his meaning to dress directly, and dine at the other house.

"Nothing can be going on better than the child," said he, "so I told my father just now that I would come, and he thought me quite right. Your sister being with you, my love, I have no scruple at all. You would not like to leave him yourself, but you see I can be of no use. Anne will send for me if any thing is the matter."

Husbands and wives generally understand when opposition will be vain. Mary knew, from Charles's manner of speaking, that he was quite determined on going, and that it would be of no use to teaze him. She said nothing, therefore, till he was out of the room, but as soon as there was only Anne to hear,

"So! You and I are to be left to shift by ourselves, with this poor sick child—and not a creature coming near us all the evening! I knew how it would be. This is always my luck! If there is any thing disagreeable going on, men are always sure to get out of it, and Charles is as bad as any of them. Very unfeeling! I must say it is very unfeeling of him, to be running away from his poor little boy; talks of his being going on so well! How does he know that he is going on well, or that there may not be a sudden change half an hour hence? I did not think Charles would have been so unfeeling. So, here he is to go away and enjoy himself, and because I am the poor mother, I am not to be allowed to stir;—and yet, I am sure, I am more unfit than any body else to be about the child. My being the mother is the very reason why my feelings should not be tried. I am not at all equal to it. You saw how hysterical I was yesterday."

"But that was only the effect of the suddenness of your alarm—of the shock. You will not be hysterical again. I dare say we shall have nothing to distress us. I perfectly understand Mr. Robinson's directions, and have no fears; and indeed, Mary, I cannot wonder at your husband. Nursing does not belong to a man, it is not his province. A sick child is always the mother's property, her own feelings generally make it so."

"I hope I am as fond of my child as any mother—but I do not know that I am of any more use in the sick-room than Charles, for I cannot be always scolding and teazing a poor child when it is ill; and you saw, this morning, that if I told him to keep quiet, he was sure to begin kicking about. I have not nerves for the sort of thing."

"But, could you be comfortable yourself, to be spending the whole evening away from the poor boy?"

"Yes; you see his papa can, and why should not I?—Jemima is so careful! And she could send us word every hour how he was. I really think Charles might as well have told his father we would all come. I am not more alarmed about little Charles now than he is. I was dreadfully alarmed yesterday, but the case is very different to-day."

"Well—if you do not think it too late to give notice for yourself, suppose you were to go, as well as your husband. Leave little Charles to my care. Mr. and Mrs. Musgrove cannot think it wrong, while I remain with him."

"Are you serious?" cried Mary, her eyes brightening. "Dear me! that's a very good thought, very good indeed. To be sure I may just as well go as not, for I am of no use at home—am I? and it only harasses me. You, who have not a mother's feelings, are a great deal the properest person. You can make little Charles do any thing; he always minds you at a word. It will be a great deal better than leaving him with only Jemima. Oh! I will certainly go; I am sure I ought if I can, quite as much as Charles, for they want me excessively to be acquainted with Captain Wentworth, and I know you do not mind being left alone. An excellent thought of yours, indeed, Anne! I will go and tell Charles, and get ready directly. You can send for us, you know, at a moment's notice, if any thing is the matter; but I dare say there will be nothing to alarm you. I should not go, you may be sure, if I did not feel quite at ease about my dear child."

The next moment she was tapping at her husband's dressing-room door, and as Anne followed her up stairs, she was in time for the whole conversation, which began with Mary's saying, in a tone of great exultation,

"I mean to go with you, Charles, for I am of no more use at home than you are. If I were to shut myself up for ever with the child, I should not be able to persuade him to do any thing he did not like. Anne will stay; Anne undertakes to stay at home and take care of him. It is Anne's own proposal, and so I shall go with you, which will be a great deal better, for I have not dined at the other house since Tuesday."

"This is very kind of Anne," was her husband's answer, "and I should be very glad to have you go; but it seems rather hard that she should be left at home by herself, to nurse our sick child."

Anne was now at hand to take up her own cause, and the sincerity of her manner being soon sufficient to convince him, where conviction was at least very agreeable, he had no farther scruples as to her being left to dine alone, though he still wanted her to join them in the evening, when the child might be at rest for the night, and kindly urged her to let him come and fetch her; but she was quite unpersuadable; and this being the case, she had ere long the pleasure of seeing them set off together in high spirits. They were gone, she hoped, to be happy, however oddly constructed such happiness might seem; as for herself, she was left with as many sensations of comfort, as were, perhaps, ever likely to be hers. She knew herself to be of the first utility to the child; and what was it to her, if Frederick Wentworth were only half a mile distant, making himself agreeable to others!

She would have liked to know how he felt as to a meeting. Perhaps indifferent, if indifference could exist under such circumstances. He must be either indifferent or unwilling. Had he wished ever to see her again, he need not have waited till this time; he would have done what she could not but believe that in his place she should have done long ago, when events had been early giving him the independence which alone had been wanting.

Her brother and sister came back delighted with their new acquaintance, and their visit in general. There had been music, singing, talking, laughing, all that was most agreeable; charming manners in Captain Wentworth, no shyness or reserve; they seemed all to know each other perfectly, and he was coming the very next morning to shoot with Charles. He was to come to breakfast, but not at the Cottage, though that had been proposed at first; but then he had been pressed to come to the Great House instead, and he seemed afraid of being in Mrs. Charles

Musgrove's way, on account of the child; and therefore, somehow, they hardly knew how, it, ended in Charles's being to meet him to breakfast at his father's.

Anne understood it. He wished to avoid seeing her. He had enquired after her, she found, slightly, as might suit a former slight acquaintance, seeming to acknowledge such as she had acknowledged, actuated, perhaps, by the same view of escaping introduction when they were to meet.

The morning hours of the Cottage were always later than those of the other house; and on the morrow the difference was so great, that Mary and Anne were not more than beginning breakfast when Charles came in to say that they were just setting off, that he was come for his dogs, that his sisters were following with Captain Wentworth, his sisters meaning to visit Mary and the child, and Captain Wentworth proposing also to wait on her for a few minutes, if not inconvenient; and though Charles had answered for the child's being in no such state as could make it inconvenient, Captain Wentworth would not be satisfied without his running on to give notice.

Mary, very much gratified by this attention, was delighted to receive him; while a thousand feelings rushed on Anne, of which this was the most consoling, that it would soon be over. And it was soon over. In two minutes after Charles's preparation, the others appeared; they were in the drawing-room. Her eye half met Captain Wentworth's; a bow, a curtsey passed; she heard his voice—he talked to Mary, said all that was right; said something to the Miss Musgroves, enough to mark an easy footing: the room seemed full—full of persons and voices—but a few minutes ended it. Charles shewed himself at the window, all was ready, their visitor had bowed and was gone; the Miss Musgroves were gone too, suddenly resolving to walk to the end of the village with the sportsmen: the room was cleared, and Anne might finish her breakfast as she could.

"It is over! it is over!" she repeated to herself again, and again, in nervous gratitude. "The worst is over!"

Mary talked, but she could not attend. She had seen him. They had met. They had been once more in the same room!

Soon, however, she began to reason with herself, and try to be feeling less. Eight years, almost eight years had passed, since all had been given up. How absurd to be resuming the agitation which such an interval had banished into distance and indistinctness! What might not eight years do? Events of every description, changes, alienations, removals,—all, all must be comprised in it; and oblivion of the past—how natural, how certain too! It included nearly a third part of her own life.

Alas! with all her reasonings, she found, that to retentive feelings eight years may be little more than nothing.

Now, how were his sentiments to be read? Was this like wishing to

avoid her? And the next moment she was hating herself for the folly
which asked the question.

On one other question, which perhaps her utmost wisdom might not
have prevented, she was soon spared all suspense; for after the Miss
Musgroves had returned and finished their visit at the Cottage, she had
this spontaneous information from Mary:

"Captain Wentworth is not very gallant by you, Anne, though he was
so attentive to me. Henrietta asked him what he thought of you, when
they went away; and he said, 'You were so altered he should not have
known you again.' "

Mary had no feelings to make her respect her sister's in a common
way; but she was perfectly unsuspicious of being inflicting any peculiar
wound.

"Altered beyond his knowledge!" Anne fully submitted, in silent, deep
mortification. Doubtless it was so; and she could take no revenge, for he
was not altered, or not for the worse. She had already acknowledged it
to herself, and she could not think differently, let him think of her as he
would. No; the years which had destroyed her youth and bloom had
only given him a more glowing, manly, open look, in no respect lessening his personal advantages. She had seen the same Frederick Wentworth.

"So altered that he should not have known her again!" These were
words which could not but dwell with her. Yet she soon began to rejoice
that she had heard them. They were of sobering tendency; they allayed
agitation; they composed, and consequently must make her happier.

Frederick Wentworth had used such words, or something like them,
but without an idea that they would be carried round to her. He had
thought her wretchedly altered, and, in the first moment of appeal, had
spoken as he felt. He had not forgiven Anne Elliot. She had used him
ill; deserted and disappointed him; and worse, she had shewn a feebleness of character in doing so, which his own decided, confident temper
could not endure. She had given him up to oblige others. It had been
the effect of <u>over-persuasion</u>. It had been weakness and timidity.

He had been most warmly attached to her, and had never seen a
woman since whom he thought her equal; but, except from some natural sensation of curiosity, he had no desire of meeting her again. Her
power with him was gone for ever.

It was now his object to marry. He was rich, and being turned on
shore, fully intended to settle as soon as he could be properly tempted;
actually looking round, ready to fall in love with all the speed which a
clear head and quick taste could allow. He had a heart for either of the
Miss Musgroves, if they could catch it; a heart, in short, for any pleasing
young woman who came in his way, excepting Anne Elliot. This was
his only secret exception, when he said to his sister, in answer to her
suppositions,

"Yes, here I am, Sophia, quite ready to make a foolish match. Any body between fifteen and thirty may have me for asking. A little beauty, and a few smiles, and a few compliments to the navy, and I am a lost man. Should not this be enough for a sailor, who has had no society among women to make him nice?"

He said it, she knew, to be contradicted. His bright, proud eye spoke the happy conviction that he was nice; and Anne Elliot was not out of his thoughts, when he more seriously described the woman he should wish to meet with. "A strong mind, with sweetness of manner," made the first and the last of the description.

"This is the woman I want," said he. "Something a little inferior I shall of course put up with, but it must not be much. If I am a fool, I shall be a fool indeed, for I have thought on the subject more than most men."

Chapter VIII

From this time Captain Wentworth and Anne Elliot were repeatedly in the same circle. They were soon dining in company together at Mr. Musgrove's, for the little boy's state could no longer supply his aunt with a pretence for absenting herself; and this was but the beginning of other dinings and other meetings.

Whether former feelings were to be renewed, must be brought to the proof; former times must undoubtedly be brought to the recollection of each; *they* could not but be reverted to; the year of their engagement could not but be named by him, in the little narratives or descriptions which conversation called forth. His profession qualified him, his disposition led him, to talk; and "*That* was in the year six;" "*That* happened before I went to sea in the year six," occurred in the course of the first evening they spent together: and though his voice did not falter, and though she had no reason to suppose his eye wandering towards her while he spoke, Anne felt the utter impossibility, from her knowledge of his mind, that he could be unvisited by remembrance any more than herself. There must be the same immediate association of thought, though she was very far from conceiving it to be of equal pain.

They had no conversation together, no intercourse but what the commonest civility required. Once so much to each other! Now nothing! There *had* been a time, when of all the large party now filling the drawing-room at Uppercross, they would have found it most difficult to cease to speak to one another. With the exception, perhaps, of Admiral and Mrs. Croft, who seemed particularly attached and happy, (Anne could allow no other exception even among the married couples) there could have been no two hearts so open, no tastes so similar, no feelings so in unison, no countenances so beloved. Now they were as strangers; nay, worse than strangers, for they could never become acquainted. It was a perpetual estrangement.

When he talked, she heard the same voice, and discerned the same mind. There was a very general ignorance of all naval matters throughout the party; and he was very much questioned, and especially by the two Miss Musgroves, who seemed hardly to have any eyes but for him, as to the manner of living on board, daily regulations, food, hours, etc.; and their surprise at his accounts, at learning the degree of accommodation and arrangement which was practicable, drew from him some pleasant ridicule, which reminded Anne of the early days when she too had been ignorant, and she too had been accused of supposing sailors to be living on board without any thing to eat, or any cook to dress it if there were, or any servant to wait, or any knife and fork to use.

From thus listening and thinking, she was roused by a whisper of Mrs. Musgrove's, who, overcome by fond regrets, could not help saying,

"Ah! Miss Anne, if it had pleased Heaven to spare my poor son, I dare say he would have been just such another by this time."

Anne suppressed a smile, and listened kindly, while Mrs. Musgrove relieved her heart a little more; and for a few minutes, therefore, could not keep pace with the conversation of the others.—When she could let her attention take its natural course again, she found the Miss Musgroves just fetching the navy-list,—(their own navy list, the first that had ever been at Uppercross); and sitting down together to pore over it, with the professed view of finding out the ships which Captain Wentworth had commanded.

"Your first was the Asp, I remember; we will look for the Asp."

"You will not find her there.—Quite worn out and broken up. I was the last man who commanded her.—Hardly fit for service then.—Reported fit for home service for a year or two,—and so I was sent off to the West Indies."

The girls looked all amazement.

"The admiralty," he continued, "entertain themselves now and then, with sending a few hundred men to sea, in a ship not fit to be employed. But they have a great many to provide for; and among the thousands that may just as well go to the bottom as not, it is impossible for them to distinguish the very set who may be least missed."

"Phoo! phoo!" cried the admiral, "what stuff these young fellows talk! Never was a better sloop than the Asp in her day.—For an old built sloop, you would not see her equal. Lucky fellow to get her!—He knows there must have been twenty better men than himself applying for her at the same time. Lucky fellow to get any thing so soon, with no more interest[8] than his."

"I felt my luck, admiral, I assure you;" replied Captain Wentworth,

8. Influence in high places.

seriously.—"I was as well satisfied with my appointment as you can desire. It was a great object with me, at that time, to be at sea,—a very great object. I wanted to be doing something."

"To be sure you did.—What should a young fellow, like you, do ashore, for half a year together?—If a man has not a wife, he soon wants to be afloat again."

"But, Captain Wentworth," cried Louisa, "how vexed you must have been when you came to the Asp, to see what an old thing they had given you."

"I knew pretty well what she was, before that day;" said he, smiling. "I had no more discoveries to make, than you would have as to the fashion and strength of any old pelisse,[9] which you had seen lent about among half your acquaintance, ever since you could remember, and which at last, on some very wet day, is lent to yourself.—Ah! she was a dear old Asp to me. She did all that I wanted. I knew she would.—I knew that we should either go to the bottom together, or that she would be the making of me; and I never had two days of foul weather all the time I was at sea in her; and after taking privateers enough to be very entertaining, I had the good luck, in my passage home the next autumn, to fall in with the very French frigate I wanted.—I brought her into Plymouth; and here was another instance of luck. We had not been six hours in the Sound, when a gale came on, which lasted four days and nights, and which would have done for poor old Asp, in half the time; our touch with the Great Nation[1] not having much improved our condition. Four-and-twenty hours later, and I should only have been a gallant Captain Wentworth, in a small paragraph at one corner of the newspapers; and being lost in only a sloop, nobody would have thought about me."

Anne's shudderings were to herself, alone: but the Miss Musgroves could be as open as they were sincere, in their exclamations of pity and horror.

"And so then, I suppose," said Mrs. Musgrove, in a low voice, as if thinking aloud, "so then he went away to the Laconia, and there he met with our poor boy.—Charles, my dear," (beckoning him to her), "do ask Captain Wentworth where it was he first met with your poor brother. I always forget."

"It was at Gibraltar, mother, I know. Dick had been left ill at Gibraltar, with a recommendation from his former captain to Captain Wentworth."

"Oh!—but, Charles, tell Captain Wentworth, he need not be afraid of mentioning poor Dick before me, for it would be rather a pleasure to hear him talked of, by such a good friend."

9. A long cloak.
1. France, with which Britain had been at war.

Charles, being somewhat more mindful of the probabilities of the case, only nodded in reply, and walked away.

The girls were now hunting for the Laconia; and Captain Wentworth could not deny himself the pleasure of taking the precious volume into his own hands to save them the trouble, and once more read aloud the little statement of her name and rate,[2] and present non-commissioned class, observing over it, that she too had been one of the best friends man ever had.

"Ah! those were pleasant days when I had the Laconia! How fast I made money in her.—A friend of mine, and I, had such a lovely cruise together off the Western Islands.—Poor Harville, sister! You know how much he wanted money—worse than myself. He had a wife.—Excellent fellow! I shall never forget his happiness. He felt it all, so much for her sake.—I wished for him again the next summer, when I had still the same luck in the Mediterranean."

"And I am sure, Sir," said Mrs. Musgrove, "it was a lucky day for *us*, when you were put captain into that ship. *We* shall never forget what you did."

Her feelings made her speak low; and Captain Wentworth, hearing only in part, and probably not having Dick Musgrove at all near his thoughts, looked rather in suspense, and as if waiting for more.

"My brother," whispered one of the girls; "mamma is thinking of poor Richard."

"Poor dear fellow!" continued Mrs. Musgrove; "he was grown so steady, and such an excellent correspondent, while he was under your care! Ah! it would have been a happy thing, if he had never left you. I assure you, Captain Wentworth, we are very sorry he ever left you."

There was a momentary expression in Captain Wentworth's face at this speech, a certain glance of his bright eye, and curl of his handsome mouth, which convinced Anne, that instead of sharing in Mrs. Musgrove's kind wishes, as to her son, he had probably been at some pains to get rid of him; but it was too transient an indulgence of self-amusement to be detected by any who understood him less than herself; in another moment he was perfectly collected and serious; and almost instantly afterwards coming up to the sofa, on which she and Mrs. Musgrove were sitting, took a place by the latter, and entered into conversation with her, in a low voice, about her son, doing it with so much sympathy and natural grace, as shewed the kindest consideration for all that was real and unabsurd in the parent's feelings.

They were actually on the same sofa, for Mrs. Musgrove had most readily made room for him;—they were divided only by Mrs. Musgrove. It was no insignificant barrier indeed. Mrs. Musgrove was of a comfort-

2. Classification of vessels based on their size or strength.

able substantial size, infinitely more fitted by nature to express good
cheer and good humour, than tenderness and sentiment; and while the
agitations of Anne's slender form, and pensive face, may be considered
as very completely screened, Captain Wentworth should be allowed
some credit for the self-command with which he attended to her large
fat sighings over the destiny of a son, whom alive nobody had cared for.

Personal size and mental sorrow have certainly no necessary proportions. A large bulky figure has as good a right to be in deep affliction, as
the most graceful set of limbs in the world. But, fair or not fair, there
are unbecoming conjunctions, which reason will patronize in vain,—
which taste cannot tolerate,—which ridicule will seize.

The admiral, after taking two or three refreshing turns about the room
with his hands behind him, being called to order by his wife, now came
up to Captain Wentworth, and without any observation of what he
might be interrupting, thinking only of his own thoughts, began with,

"If you had been a week later at Lisbon, last spring, Frederick, you
would have been asked to give a passage to Lady Mary Grierson and
her daughters."

"Should I? I am glad I was not a week later then."

The admiral abused him for his want of gallantry. He defended himself; though professing that he would never willingly admit any ladies on
board a ship of his, excepting for a ball, or a visit, which a few hours
might comprehend.

"But, if I know myself," said he, "this is from no want of gallantry
towards them. It is rather from feeling how impossible it is, with all
one's efforts, and all one's sacrifices, to make the accommodations on
board, such as women ought to have. There can be no want of gallantry,
admiral, in rating the claims of women to every personal comfort *high*—
and this is what I do. I hate to hear of women on board, or to see them
on board; and no ship, under my command, shall ever convey a family
of ladies any where, if I can help it."

This brought his sister upon him.

"Oh Frederick!—But I cannot believe it of you.—All idle refinement!—Women may be as comfortable on board, as in the best house
in England. I believe I have lived as much on board as most women,
and I know nothing superior to the accommodations of a man of war. I
declare I have not a comfort or an indulgence about me, even at Kellynch-hall," (with a kind bow to Anne) "beyond what I always had in
most of the ships I have lived in; and they have been five altogether."

"Nothing to the purpose," replied her brother. "You were living with
your husband; and were the only woman on board."

"But you, yourself, brought Mrs. Harville, her sister, her cousin, and
the three children, round from Portsmouth to Plymouth. Where was
this superfine, extraordinary sort of gallantry of yours, then?"

"All merged in my friendship, Sophia. I would assist any brother officer's wife that I could, and I would bring any thing of Harville's from the world's end, if he wanted it. But do not imagine that I did not feel it an evil in itself."

"Depend upon it they were all perfectly comfortable."

"I might not like them the better for that, perhaps. Such a number of women and children have no *right* to be comfortable on board."

"My dear Frederick, you are talking quite idly. Pray, what would become of us poor sailors' wives, who often want to be conveyed to one port or another, after our husbands, if every body had your feelings?"

"My feelings, you see, did not prevent my taking Mrs. Harville, and all her family, to Plymouth."

"But I hate to hear you talking so, like a fine gentleman, and as if women were all fine ladies, instead of rational creatures. We none of us expect to be in smooth water all our days."

"Ah! my dear," said the admiral, "when he has got a wife, he will sing a different tune. When he is married, if we have the good luck to live to another war, we shall see him do as you and I, and a great many others, have done. We shall have him very thankful to any body that will bring him his wife."

"Ay, that we shall."

"Now I have done," cried Captain Wentworth—"When once married people begin to attack me with, 'Oh! you will think very differently, when you are married.' I can only say, 'No, I shall not;' and then they say again, 'Yes, you will,' and there is an end of it."

He got up and moved away.

"What a great traveller you must have been, ma'am!" said Mrs. Musgrove to Mrs. Croft.

"Pretty well, ma'am, in the fifteen years of my marriage; though many women have done more. I have crossed the Atlantic four times, and have been once to the East Indies, and back again; and only once, besides being in different places about home—Cork, and Lisbon, and Gibraltar. But I never went beyond the Streights[3]—and never was in the West Indies. We do not call Bermuda or Bahama, you know, the West Indies."

Mrs. Musgrove had not a word to say in dissent; she could not accuse herself of having ever called them any thing in the whole course of her life.

"And I do assure you, ma'am," pursued Mrs. Croft, "that nothing can exceed the accommodations of a man of war; I speak, you know, of the higher rates. When you come to a frigate, of course, you are more confined—though any reasonable woman may be perfectly happy in one of them; and I can safely say, that the happiest part of my life has been spent on board a ship. While we were together, you know, there

_____

3. The Strait of Gibraltar.

was nothing to be feared. Thank God! I have always been blessed with
excellent health, and no climate disagrees with me. A little disordered
always the first twenty-four hours of going to sea, but never knew what
sickness was afterwards. The only time that I ever really suffered in body
or mind, the only time that I ever fancied myself unwell, or had any
ideas of danger, was the winter that I passed by myself at Deal, when
the Admiral (*Captain* Croft then) was in the North Seas. I lived in
perpetual fright at that time, and had all manner of imaginary complaints from not knowing what to do with myself, or when I should hear
from him next; but as long as we could be together, nothing ever ailed
me, and I never met with the smallest inconvenience."

"Ay, to be sure.—Yes, indeed, oh yes, I am quite of your opinion,
Mrs. Croft," was Mrs. Musgrove's hearty answer. "There is nothing so
bad as a separation. I am quite of your opinion. *I* know what it is, for
Mr. Musgrove always attends the assizes,[4] and I am so glad when they
are over, and he is safe back again."

The evening ended with dancing. On its being proposed, Anne
offered her services, as usual, and though her eyes would sometimes fill
with tears as she sat at the instrument, she was extremely glad to be
employed, and desired nothing in return but to be unobserved.

It was a merry, joyous party, and no one seemed in higher spirits than
Captain Wentworth. She felt that he had every thing to elevate him,
which general attention and deference, and especially the attention of
all the young women could do. The Miss Hayters, the females of the
family of cousins already mentioned, were apparently admitted to the
honour of being in love with him; and as for Henrietta and Louisa, they
both seemed so entirely occupied by him, that nothing but the continued appearance of the most perfect good-will between themselves, could
have made it credible that they were not decided rivals. If he were a little
spoilt by such universal, such eager admiration, who could wonder?

These were some of the thoughts which occupied Anne, while her
fingers were mechanically at work, proceeding for half an hour together,
equally without error, and without consciousness. *Once* she felt that he
was looking at herself—observing her altered features, perhaps, trying to
trace in them the ruins of the face which had once charmed him; and
once she knew that he must have spoken of her;—she was hardly aware
of it, till she heard the answer; but then she was sure of his having asked
his partner whether Miss Elliot never danced? The answer was, "Oh!
no, never; she has quite given up dancing. She had rather play. She is
never tired of playing." Once, too, he spoke to her. She had left the
instrument on the dancing being over, and he had sat down to try to
make out an air which he wished to give the Miss Musgroves an idea of.

4. Periodical sessions of the judges of superior courts, held in every county.

Unintentionally she returned to that part of the room; he saw her, and, instantly rising, said, with studied politeness,

"I beg your pardon, madam, this is your seat;" and though she immediately drew back with a decided negative, he was not to be induced to sit down again.

Anne did not wish for more of such looks and speeches. His cold politeness, his ceremonious grace, were worse than any thing.

Chapter IX

Captain Wentworth was come to Kellynch as to a home, to stay as long as he liked, being as thoroughly the object of the Admiral's fraternal kindness as of his wife's. He had intended, on first arriving, to proceed very soon into Shropshire, and visit the brother settled in that county, but the attractions of Uppercross induced him to put this off. There was so much of friendliness, and of flattery, and of every thing most bewitching in his reception there; the old were so hospitable, the young so agreeable, that he could not but resolve to remain where he was, and take all the charms and perfections of Edward's wife upon credit a little longer.

It was soon Uppercross with him almost every day. The Musgroves could hardly be more ready to invite than he to come, particularly in the morning, when he had no companion at home, for the Admiral and Mrs. Croft were generally out of doors together, interesting themselves in their new possessions, their grass, and their sheep, and dawdling about in a way not endurable to a third person, or driving out in a gig, lately added to their establishment.

Hitherto there had been but one opinion of Captain Wentworth, among the Musgroves and their dependencies. It was unvarying, warm admiration every where. But this intimate footing was not more than established, when a certain Charles Hayter returned among them, to be a good deal disturbed by it, and to think Captain Wentworth very much in the way.

Charles Hayter was the eldest of all the cousins, and a very amiable, pleasing young man, between whom and Henrietta there had been a considerable appearance of attachment previous to Captain Wentworth's introduction. He was in orders,[5] and having a curacy in the neighbourhood where residence was not required, lived at his father's house, only two miles from Uppercross. A short absence from home had left his fair one unguarded by his attentions at this critical period,

5. A clergyman in the Church of England. The curacy he holds makes him assistant or deputy to a rector or vicar.

and when he came back he had the pain of finding very altered manners, and of seeing Captain Wentworth.

Mrs. Musgrove and Mrs. Hayter were sisters. They had each had money, but their marriages had made a material difference in their degree of consequence. Mr. Hayter had some property of his own, but it was insignificant compared with Mr. Musgrove's; and while the Musgroves were in the first class of society in the country,[6] the young Hayters would, from their parents' inferior, retired, and unpolished way of living, and their own defective education, have been hardly in any class at all, but for their connexion with Uppercross; this eldest son of course excepted, who had chosen to be a scholar and a gentleman, and who was very superior in cultivation and manners to all the rest.

The two families had always been on excellent terms, there being no pride on one side, and no envy on the other, and only such a consciousness of superiority in the Miss Musgroves, as made them pleased to improve their cousins.—Charles's attentions to Henrietta had been observed by her father and mother without any disapprobation. "It would not be a great match for her; but if Henrietta liked him,—and Henrietta *did* seem to like him."

Henrietta fully thought so herself, before Captain Wentworth came; but from that time Cousin Charles had been very much forgotten.

Which of the two sisters was preferred by Captain Wentworth was as yet quite doubtful, as far as Anne's observation reached. Henrietta was perhaps the prettiest, Louisa had the higher spirits; and she knew not *now*, whether the more gentle or the more lively character were most likely to attract him.

Mr. and Mrs. Musgrove, either from seeing little, or from an entire confidence in the discretion of both their daughters, and of all the young men who came near them, seemed to leave every thing to take its chance. There was not the smallest appearance of solicitude or remark about them, in the Mansion-house; but it was different at the Cottage: the young couple there were more disposed to speculate and wonder; and Captain Wentworth had not been above four or five times in the Miss Musgroves' company, and Charles Hayter had but just reappeared, when Anne had to listen to the opinions of her brother and sister, as to *which* was the one liked best. Charles gave it for Louisa, Mary for Henrietta, but quite agreeing that to have him marry either would be extremely delightful.

Charles "had never seen a pleasanter man in his life; and from what he had once heard Captain Wentworth himself say, was very sure that he had not made less than twenty thousand pounds by the war. Here was a fortune at once; besides which, there would be the chance of what might be done in any future war; and he was sure Captain Wentworth

6. Neighborhood.

was as likely a man to distinguish himself as any officer in the navy. Oh! it would be a capital match for either of his sisters."

"Upon my word it would," replied Mary. "Dear me! If he should rise to any very great honours! If he should ever be made a Baronet! 'Lady Wentworth' sounds very well. That would be a noble thing, indeed, for Henrietta! She would take place of me then, and Henrietta would not dislike that. Sir Frederick and Lady Wentworth! It would be but a new creation, however, and I never think much of your new creations."

It suited Mary best to think Henrietta the one preferred, on the very account of Charles Hayter, whose pretensions she wished to see put an end to. She looked down very decidedly upon the Hayters, and thought it would be quite a misfortune to have the existing connection between the families renewed—very sad for herself and her children.

"You know," said she, "I cannot think him at all a fit match for Henrietta; and considering the alliances which the Musgroves have made, she has no right to throw herself away. I do not think any young woman has a right to make a choice that may be disagreeable and inconvenient to the *principal* part of her family, and be giving bad connections to those who have not been used to them. And, pray, who is Charles Hayter? Nothing but a country curate. A most improper match for Miss Musgrove, of Uppercross."

Her husband, however, would not agree with her here; for besides having a regard for his cousin, Charles Hayter was an eldest son, and he saw things as an eldest son himself.

"Now you are talking nonsense, Mary," was therefore his answer. "It would not be a *great* match for Henrietta, but Charles has a very fair chance, through the Spicers, of getting something from the Bishop in the course of a year or two; and you will please to remember, that he is the eldest son; whenever my uncle dies, he steps into very pretty property. The estate at Winthrop is not less than two hundred and fifty acres, besides the farm near Taunton, which is some of the best land in the country. I grant you, that any of them but Charles would be a very shocking match for Henrietta, and indeed it could not be; he is the only one that could be possible; but he is a very good-natured, good sort of a fellow; and whenever Winthrop comes into his hands, he will make a different sort of place of it, and live in a very different sort of way; and with that property, he will never be a contemptible man. Good, freehold property.[7] No, no; Henrietta might do worse than marry Charles Hayter; and if she has him, and Louisa can get Captain Wentworth, I shall be very well satisfied."

"Charles may say what he pleases," cried Mary to Anne, as soon as he was out of the room, "but it would be shocking to have Henrietta marry Charles Hayter; a very bad thing for *her*, and still worse for *me*;

7. Property held for life.

and therefore it is very much to be wished that Captain Wentworth may
soon put him quite out of her head, and I have very little doubt that he
has. She took hardly any notice of Charles Hayter yesterday. I wish you
had been there to see her behaviour. And as to Captain Wentworth's
liking Louisa as well as Henrietta, it is nonsense to say so; for he certainly *does* like Henrietta a great deal the best. But Charles is so positive!
I wish you had been with us yesterday, for then you might have decided
between us; and I am sure you would have thought as I did, unless you
had been determined to give it against me."

A dinner at Mr. Musgrove's had been the occasion, when all these
things should have been seen by Anne; but she had staid at home, under
the mixed plea of a head-ache of her own, and some return of indisposition in little Charles. She had thought only of avoiding Captain Wentworth; but an escape from being appealed to as umpire, was now added
to the advantages of a quiet evening.

As to Captain Wentworth's views, she deemed it of more consequence that he should know his own mind, early enough not to be
endangering the happiness of either sister, or impeaching his own honour, than that he should prefer Henrietta to Louisa, or Louisa to Henrietta. Either of them would, in all probability, make him an affectionate,
good-humoured wife. With regard to Charles Hayter, she had delicacy
which must be pained by any lightness of conduct in a well-meaning
young woman, and a heart to sympathize in any of the sufferings it
occasioned; but if Henrietta found herself mistaken in the nature of her
feelings, the alteration could not be understood too soon.

Charles Hayter had met with much to disquiet and mortify him in his
cousin's behaviour. She had too old a regard for him to be so wholly
estranged, as might in two meetings extinguish every past hope, and
leave him nothing to do but to keep away from Uppercross; but there was
such a change as became very alarming, when such a man as Captain
Wentworth was to be regarded as the probable cause. He had been absent
only two Sundays; and when they parted, had left her interested even to
the height of his wishes, in his prospect of soon quitting his present
curacy, and obtaining that of Uppercross instead. It had then seemed the
object nearest her heart, that Dr. Shirley, the rector, who for more than
forty years had been zealously discharging all the duties of his office, but
was now growing too infirm for many of them, should be quite fixed on
engaging a curate; should make his curacy quite as good as he could
afford, and should give Charles Hayter the promise of it. The advantage
of his having to come only to Uppercross, instead of going six miles
another way; of his having, in every respect, a better curacy; of his
belonging to their dear Dr. Shirley, and of dear, good Dr. Shirley's being
relieved from the duty which he could no longer get through without
most injurious fatigue, had been a great deal, even to Louisa, but had
been almost every thing to Henrietta. When he came back, alas! the zeal

of the business was gone by. Louisa could not listen at all to his account of a conversation which he had just held with Dr. Shirley: she was at [the] window, looking out for Captain Wentworth; and even Henrietta had at best only a divided attention to give, and seemed to have forgotten all the former doubt and solicitude of the negociation.

"Well, I am very glad indeed, but I always thought you would have it; I always thought you sure. It did not appear to me that—In short, you know, Dr. Shirley *must* have a curate, and you had secured his promise. Is he coming, Louisa?"

One morning, very soon after the dinner at the Musgroves, at which Anne had not been present, Captain Wentworth walked into the drawing-room at the Cottage, where were only herself and the little invalid Charles, who was lying on the sofa.

The surprise of finding himself almost alone with Anne Elliot, deprived his manners of their usual composure: he started, and could only say, "I thought the Miss Musgroves had been here—Mrs. Musgrove told me I should find them here," before he walked to the window to recollect himself, and feel how he ought to behave.

"They are up stairs with my sister—they will be down in a few moments, I dare say,"—had been Anne's reply, in all the confusion that was natural; and if the child had not called her to come and do something for him, she would have been out of the room the next moment, and released Captain Wentworth as well as herself.

He continued at the window; and after calmly and politely saying, "I hope the little boy is better," was silent.

She was obliged to kneel down by the sofa, and remain there to satisfy her patient; and thus they continued a few minutes, when, to her very great satisfaction, she heard some other person crossing the little vestibule. She hoped, on turning her head, to see the master of the house; but it proved to be one much less calculated for making matters easy— Charles Hayter, probably not at all better pleased by the sight of Captain Wentworth, than Captain Wentworth had been by the sight of Anne.

She only attempted to say, "How do you do? Will not you sit down? The others will be here presently."

Captain Wentworth, however, came from his window, apparently not ill-disposed for conversation; but Charles Hayter soon put an end to his attempts, by seating himself near the table, and taking up the newspaper; and Captain Wentworth returned to his window.

Another minute brought another addition. The younger boy, a remarkable stout, forward child, of two years old, having got the door opened for him by some one without, made his determined appearance among them, and went straight to the sofa to see what was going on, and put in his claim to any thing good that might be giving away.

There being nothing to be eat, he could only have some play; and as his aunt would not let him teaze his sick brother, he began to fasten himself upon her, as she knelt, in such a way that, busy as she was about Charles, she could not shake him off. She spoke to him—ordered, intreated, and insisted in vain. Once she did contrive to push him away, but the boy had the greater pleasure in getting upon her back again directly.

"Walter," said she, "get down this moment. You are extremely troublesome. I am very angry with you."

"Walter," cried Charles Hayter, "why do you not do as you are bid? Do not you hear your aunt speak? Come to me, Walter, come to cousin Charles."

But not a bit did Walter stir.

In another moment, however, she found herself in the state of being released from him; some one was taking him from her, though he had bent down her head so much, that his little sturdy hands were unfastened from around her neck, and he was resolutely borne away, before she knew that Captain Wentworth had done it.

Her sensations on the discovery made her perfectly speechless. She could not even thank him. She could only hang over little Charles, with most disordered feelings. His kindness in stepping forward to her relief—the manner—the silence in which it had passed—the little particulars of the circumstance—with the conviction soon forced on her by the noise he was studiously making with the child, that he meant to avoid hearing her thanks, and rather sought to testify that her conversation was the last of his wants, produced such a confusion of varying, but very painful agitation, as she could not recover from, till enabled by the entrance of Mary and the Miss Musgroves to make over her little patient to their cares, and leave the room. She could not stay. It might have been an opportunity of watching the loves and jealousies of the four; they were now all together, but she could stay for none of it. It was evident that Charles Hayter was not well inclined towards Captain Wentworth. She had a strong impression of his having said, in a vext tone of voice, after Captain Wentworth's interference, "You ought to have minded *me*, Walter; I told you not to teaze your aunt;" and could comprehend his regretting that Captain Wentworth should do what he ought to have done himself. But neither Charles Hayter's feelings, nor any body's feelings, could interest her, till she had a little better arranged her own. She was ashamed of herself, quite ashamed of being so nervous, so overcome by such a trifle; but so it was; and it required a long application of solitude and reflection to recover her.

Chapter X

Other opportunities of making her observations could not fail to occur. Anne had soon been in company with all the four together often enough to have an opinion, though too wise to acknowledge as much at home, where she knew it would have satisfied neither husband nor wife; for while she considered Louisa to be rather the favourite, she could not but think, as far as she might dare to judge from memory and experience, that Captain Wentworth was not in love with either. They were more in love with him; yet there it was not love. It was a little fever of admiration; but it might, probably must, end in love with some. Charles Hayter seemed aware of being slighted, and yet Henrietta had sometimes the air of being divided between them. Anne longed for the power of representing to them all what they were about, and of pointing out some of the evils they were exposing themselves to. She did not attribute guile to any. It was the highest satisfaction to her, to believe Captain Wentworth not in the least aware of the pain he was occasioning. There was no triumph, no pitiful triumph in his manner. He had, probably, never heard, and never thought of any claims of Charles Hayter. He was only wrong in accepting the attentions—(for accepting must be the word) of two young women at once.

After a short struggle, however, Charles Hayter seemed to quit the field. Three days had passed without his coming once to Uppercross; a most decided change. He had even refused one regular invitation to dinner; and having been found on the occasion by Mr. Musgrove with some large books before him, Mr. and Mrs. Musgrove were sure all could not be right, and talked, with grave faces, of his studying himself to death. It was Mary's hope and belief, that he had received a positive dismissal from Henrietta, and her husband lived under the constant dependance of seeing him to-morrow. Anne could only feel that Charles Hayter was wise.

One morning, about this time, Charles Musgrove and Captain Wentworth being gone a shooting together, as the sisters in the cottage were sitting quietly at work, they were visited at the window by the sisters from the mansion-house.

It was a very fine November day, and the Miss Musgroves came through the little grounds, and stopped for no other purpose than to say, that they were going to take a *long* walk, and, therefore, concluded Mary could not like to go with them; and when Mary immediately replied, with some jealousy, at not being supposed a good walker, "Oh, yes, I should like to join you very much, I am very fond of a long walk," Anne felt persuaded, by the looks of the two girls, that it was precisely what they did not wish, and admired [8] again the sort of necessity which the family-habits seemed to produce, of every thing being to be communicated, and every thing being to be done together, however undesired and inconvenient. She tried to dissuade Mary from going, but in vain; and that being the case, thought it best to accept the Miss Musgroves'

much more cordial invitation to herself to go likewise, as she might be useful in turning back with her sister, and lessening the interference in any plan of their own.

"I cannot imagine why they should suppose I should not like a long walk!" said Mary, as she went up stairs. "Every body is always supposing that I am not a good walker! And yet they would not have been pleased, if we had refused to join them. When people come in this manner on purpose to ask us, how can one say no?"

Just as they were setting off, the gentlemen returned. They had taken out a young dog, who had spoilt their sport, and sent them back early. Their time and strength, and spirits, were, therefore, exactly ready for this walk, and they entered into it with pleasure. Could Anne have foreseen such a junction, she would have staid at home; but, from some feelings of interest and curiosity, she fancied now that it was too late to retract, and the whole six set forward together in the direction chosen by the Miss Musgroves, who evidently considered the walk as under their guidance.

Anne's object was, not to be in the way of any body, and where the narrow paths across the fields made many separations necessary, to keep with her brother and sister. Her *pleasure* in the walk must arise from the exercise and the day, from the view of the last smiles of the year upon the tawny leaves and withered hedges, and from repeating to herself some few of the thousand poetical descriptions extant of autumn, that season of peculiar and inexhaustible influence on the mind of taste and tenderness, that season which has drawn from every poet, worthy of being read, some attempt at description, or some lines of feeling. She occupied her mind as much as possible in such like musings and quotations; but it was not possible, that when within reach of Captain Wentworth's conversation with either of the Miss Musgroves, she should not try to hear it; yet she caught little very remarkable. It was mere lively chat,—such as any young persons, on an intimate footing, might fall into. He was more engaged with Louisa than with Henrietta. Louisa certainly put more forward for his notice than her sister. This distinction appeared to increase, and there was one speech of Louisa's which struck her. After one of the many praises of the day, which were continually bursting forth, Captain Wentworth added,

"What glorious weather for the Admiral and my sister! They meant to take a long drive this morning; perhaps we may hail them from some of these hills. They talked of coming into this side of the country. I wonder whereabouts they will upset to-day. Oh! it does happen very often, I assure you—but my sister makes nothing of it—she would as lieve be tossed out as not."

"Ah! You make the most of it, I know," cried Louisa, "but if it were really so, I should do just the same in her place. If I loved a man, as she loves the Admiral, I would be always with him, nothing should ever separate us, and I would rather be overturned by him, than driven safely by anybody else."

It was spoken with enthusiasm.

"Had you?" cried he, catching the same tone; "I honour you!" And there was silence between them for a little while.

Anne could not immediately fall into a quotation again. The sweet scenes of autumn were for a while put by—unless some tender sonnet, fraught with the apt analogy of the declining year, with declining happiness, and the images of youth and hope, and spring, all gone together, blessed her memory. She roused herself to say, as they struck by order into another path, "Is not this one of the ways to Winthrop?" But nobody heard, or, at least, nobody answered her.

Winthrop, however, or its environs—for young men are, sometimes, to be met with, strolling about near home, was their destination; and after another half mile of gradual ascent through large enclosures, where the ploughs at work, and the fresh-made path spoke the farmer, counteracting the sweets of poetical despondence, and meaning to have spring again, they gained the summit of the most considerable hill, which parted Uppercross and Winthrop, and soon commanded a full view of the latter, at the foot of the hill on the other side.

Winthrop, without beauty and without dignity, was stretched before them; an indifferent house, standing low, and hemmed in by the barns and buildings of a farm-yard.

Mary exclaimed, "Bless me! here is Winthrop—I declare I had no idea!—well, now I think we had better turn back; I am excessively tired."

Henrietta, conscious and ashamed, and seeing no cousin Charles walking along any path, or leaning against any gate, was ready to do as Mary wished; but "No," said Charles Musgrove, and "No, no," cried Louisa more eagerly, and taking her sister aside, seemed to be arguing the matter warmly.

Charles, in the meanwhile, was very decidedly declaring his resolution of calling on his aunt, now that he was so near; and very evidently, though more fearfully, trying to induce his wife to go too. But this was one of the points on which the lady shewed her strength, and when he recommended the advantage of resting herself a quarter of an hour at Winthrop, as she felt so tired, she resolutely answered, "Oh! no, indeed!—walking up that hill again would do her more harm than any sitting down could do her good;"—and, in short, her look and manner declared, that go she would not.

After a little succession of these sort of debates and consultations, it was settled between Charles and his two sisters, that he, and Henrietta, should just run down for a few minutes, to see their aunt and cousins, while the rest of the party waited for them at the top of the hill. Louisa seemed the principal arranger of the plan; and, as she went a little way with them, down the hill, still talking to Henrietta, Mary took the opportunity of looking scornfully around her, and saying to Captain Wentworth,

"It is very unpleasant, having such connexions! But I assure you, I have never been in the house above twice in my life."

She received no other answer, than an artificial, assenting smile, followed by a contemptuous glance, as he turned away, which Anne perfectly knew the meaning of.

The brow of the hill, where they remained, was a cheerful spot; Louisa returned, and Mary finding a comfortable seat for herself, on the step of a stile, was very well satisfied so long as the others all stood about her; but when Louisa drew Captain Wentworth away, to try for a gleaning of nuts in an adjoining hedge-row, and they were gone by degrees quite out of sight and sound, Mary was happy no longer; she quarrelled with her own seat,—was sure Louisa had got a much better somewhere,—and nothing could prevent her from going to look for a better also. She turned through the same gate,—but could not see them.—Anne found a nice seat for her, on a dry sunny bank, under the hedge-row, in which she had no doubt of their still being—in some spot or other. Mary sat down for a moment, but it would not do; she was sure Louisa had found a better seat somewhere else, and she would go on, till she overtook her.

Anne, really tired herself, was glad to sit down; and she very soon heard Captain Wentworth and Louisa in the hedge-row, behind her, as if making their way back, along the rough, wild sort of channel, down the centre. They were speaking as they drew near. Louisa's voice was the first distinguished. She seemed to be in the middle of some eager speech. What Anne first heard was,

"And so, I made her go. I could not bear that she should be frightened from the visit by such nonsense. What!—would I be turned back from doing a thing that I had determined to do, and that I knew to be right, by the airs and interference of such a person?—or, of any person I may say. No,—I have no idea of being so easily persuaded. When I have made up my mind, I have made it. And Henrietta seemed entirely to have made up hers to call at Winthrop to-day—and yet, she was as near giving it up, out of nonsensical complaisance!"

"She would have turned back then, but for you?"

"She would indeed. I am almost ashamed to say it."

"Happy for her, to have such a mind as yours at hand!—After the hints you gave just now, which did but confirm my own observations, the last time I was in company with him, I need not affect to have no comprehension of what is going on. I see that more than a mere dutiful morning-visit to your aunt was in question;—and woe betide him, and her too, when it comes to things of consequence, when they are placed in circumstances, requiring fortitude and strength of mind, if she have not resolution enough to resist idle interference in such a trifle as this. Your sister is an amiable creature; but *yours* is the character of decision and firmness, I see. If you value her conduct or happiness, infuse as much of your own spirit into her, as you can. But this, no doubt, you have been always doing. It is the worst evil of too yielding and indecisive a character, that no influence over it can be depended on.—You are never sure of a good impression being durable. Every body may sway it; let those who would be happy be firm.—Here is a nut," said he, catching one down from an upper bough. "To exemplify,—a beautiful glossy nut, which, blessed with original strength, has outlived all the storms of autumn. Not a puncture, not a weak spot any where.—This nut," he continued, with playful solemnity,—"while so many of its brethren have fallen and been trodden under foot, is still in possession of all the happiness that a hazel-nut can be supposed capable of." Then, returning to his former earnest tone: "My first wish for all, whom I am interested in, is that they should be firm. If Louisa Musgrove would be beautiful and happy in her November of life, she will cherish all her present powers of mind."

He had done,—and was unanswered. It would have surprised Anne, if Louisa could have readily answered such a speech—words of such interest, spoken with such serious warmth!—she could imagine what Louisa was feeling. For herself—she feared to move, lest she should be seen. While she remained, a bush of low rambling holly protected her, and they were moving on. Before they were beyond her hearing, however, Louisa spoke again.

"Mary is good-natured enough in many respects," said she; "but she does sometimes provoke me excessively, by her nonsense and her pride; the Elliot pride. She has a great deal too much of the Elliot pride.—We do so wish that Charles had married Anne instead.—I suppose you know he wanted to marry Anne?"

After a moment's pause, Captain Wentworth said,

"Do you mean that she refused him?"

"Oh! yes, certainly."

"When did that happen?"

"I do not exactly know, for Henrietta and I were at school at the time; but I believe about a year before he married Mary. I wish she had accepted him. We should all have liked her a great deal better; and papa and mamma always think it was her great friend Lady Russell's doing, that she did not.—They think Charles might not be learned and bookish enough to please Lady Russell, and that therefore, she persuaded Anne to refuse him."

The sounds were retreating, and Anne distinguished no more. Her own emotions still kept her fixed. She had much to recover from, before she could move. The listener's proverbial fate was not absolutely hers; she had heard no evil of herself,—but she had heard a great deal of very painful import. She saw how her own character was considered by Captain Wentworth; and there had been just that degree of feeling and curiosity about her in his manner, which must give her extreme agitation.

As soon as she could, she went after Mary, and having found, and walked back with her to their former station, by the stile, felt some comfort in their whole party being immediately afterwards collected, and once more in motion together. Her spirits wanted the solitude and silence which only numbers could give.

Charles and Henrietta returned, bringing, as may be conjectured, Charles Hayter with them. The minutiæ of the business Anne could not attempt to understand; even Captain Wentworth did not seem admitted to perfect confidence here; but that there had been a withdrawing on the gentleman's side, and a relenting on the lady's, and that they were now very glad to be together again, did not admit a doubt. Henrietta looked a little ashamed, but very well pleased;—Charles Hayter exceedingly happy, and they were devoted to each other almost from the first instant of their all setting forward for Uppercross.

Every thing now marked out Louisa for Captain Wentworth; nothing could be plainer; and where many divisions were necessary, or even where they were not, they walked side by side, nearly as much as the other two. In a long strip of meadow-land, where there was ample space for all, they were thus divided—forming three distinct parties; and to that party of the three which boasted least animation, and least complaisance, Anne necessarily belonged. She joined Charles and Mary, and was tired enough to be very glad of Charles's other arm;—but Charles, though in very good humour with her, was out of temper with his wife. Mary had shewn herself disobliging to him, and was now to reap the consequence, which consequence was his dropping her arm almost every moment, to cut off the heads of some nettles in the hedge with his switch; and when Mary began to complain of it, and lament her being ill-used, according to custom, in being on the hedge side, while Anne was never incommoded on the other, he dropped the arms of both to hunt after a weasel which he had a momentary glance of; and they could hardly get him along at all.

This long meadow bordered a lane, which their footpath, at the end of it, was to cross; and when the party had all reached the gate of exit, the carriage advancing in the same direction, which had been some time heard, was just coming up, and proved to be Admiral Croft's gig.— He and his wife had taken their intended drive, and were returning home. Upon hearing how long a walk the young people had engaged in, they kindly offered a seat to any lady who might be particularly tired; it would save her full a mile, and they were going through Uppercross. The invitation was general, and generally declined. The Miss Musgroves were not at all tired, and Mary was either offended, by not being asked before any of the others, or what Louisa called the Elliot pride could not endure to make a third in a one horse chaise.

The walking-party had crossed the lane, and were surmounting an opposite stile; and the admiral was putting his horse into motion again, when Captain Wentworth cleared the hedge in a moment to say something to his sister.—The something might be guessed by its effects.

"Miss Elliot, I am sure *you* are tired," cried Mrs. Croft. "Do let us have the pleasure of taking you home. Here is excellent room for three, I assure you. If we were all like you, I believe we might sit four.—You must, indeed, you must."

Anne was still in the lane; and though instinctively beginning to decline, she was not allowed to proceed. The admiral's kind urgency came in support of his wife's; they would not be refused; they compressed themselves into the smallest possible space to leave her a corner, and Captain Wentworth, without saying a word, turned to her, and quietly obliged her to be assisted into the carriage.

Yes,—he had done it. She was in the carriage, and felt that he had placed her there, that his will and his hands had done it, that she owed it to his perception of her fatigue, and his resolution to give her rest. She was very much affected by the view of his disposition towards her which all these things made apparent. This little circumstance seemed the completion of all that had gone before. She understood him. He could not forgive her,—but he could not be unfeeling. Though condemning her for the past, and considering it with high and unjust resentment, though perfectly careless of[9] her, and though becoming attached to another, still he could not see her suffer, without the desire of giving her relief. It was a remainder of former sentiment; it was an impulse of pure, though unacknowledged friendship; it was a proof of his own warm and amiable heart, which she could not contemplate without emotions so compounded of pleasure and pain, that she knew not which prevailed.

Her answers to the kindness and the remarks of her companions were at first unconsciously given. They had travelled half their way along the rough lane, before she was quite awake to what they said. She then found them talking of "Frederick."

"He certainly means to have one or other of those two girls, Sophy," said the admiral;—"but there is no saying which. He has been running after them, too, long enough, one would think, to make up his mind. Ay, this comes of the peace. If it were war, now, he would have settled it long ago.—We sailors, Miss Elliot, cannot afford to make long courtships in time of war. How many days was it, my dear, between the first time of my seeing you, and our sitting down together in our lodgings at North Yarmouth?"

"We had better not talk about it, my dear," replied Mrs. Croft, pleasantly; "for if Miss Elliot were to hear how soon we came to an under-

9. Not caring for.

standing, she would never be persuaded that we could be happy together. I had known you by character, however, long before."

"Well, and I had heard of you as a very pretty girl; and what were we to wait for besides?—I do not like having such things so long in hand. I wish Frederick would spread a little more canvas,[1] and bring us home one of these young ladies to Kellynch. Then, there would always be company for them.—And very nice young ladies they both are; I hardly know one from the other."

"Very good humoured, unaffected girls, indeed," said Mrs. Croft, in a tone of calmer praise, such as made Anne suspect that her keener powers might not consider either of them as quite worthy of her brother; "and a very respectable family. One could not be connected with better people.—My dear admiral, that post!—we shall certainly take that post."

But by coolly giving the reins a better direction herself, they happily passed the danger; and by once afterwards judiciously putting out her hand, they neither fell into a rut, nor ran foul of a dung-cart; and Anne, with some amusement at their style of driving, which she imagined no bad representation of the general guidance of their affairs, found herself safely deposited by them at the cottage.

Chapter XI

The time now approached for Lady Russell's return; the day was even fixed, and Anne, being engaged to join her as soon as she was resettled, was looking forward to an early removal to Kellynch, and beginning to think how her own comfort was likely to be affected by it.

It would place her in the same village with Captain Wentworth, within half a mile of him; they would have to frequent the same church, and there must be intercourse between the two families. This was against her; but, on the other hand, he spent so much of his time at Uppercross, that in removing thence she might be considered rather as leaving him behind, than as going towards him; and, upon the whole, she believed she must, on this interesting question, be the gainer, almost as certainly as in her change of domestic society, in leaving poor Mary for Lady Russell.

She wished it might be possible for her to avoid ever seeing Captain Wentworth at the hall;—those rooms had witnessed former meetings which would be brought too painfully before her; but she was yet more anxious for the possibility of Lady Russell and Captain Wentworth never meeting any where. They did not like each other, and no renewal of acquaintance now could do any good; and were Lady Russell to see

---

1. Put up more or bigger sails, move faster.

them together, she might think that he had too much self-possession, and she too little.

These points formed her chief solicitude in anticipating her removal from Uppercross, where she felt she had been stationed quite long enough. Her usefulness to little Charles would always give some sweetness to the memory of her two months visit there, but he was gaining strength apace, and she had nothing else to stay for.

The conclusion of her visit, however, was diversified in a way which she had not at all imagined. Captain Wentworth, after being unseen and unheard of at Uppercross for two whole days, appeared again among them to justify himself by a relation of what had kept him away.

A letter from his friend, Captain Harville, having found him out at last, had brought intelligence of Captain Harville's being settled with his family at Lyme for the winter; of their being, therefore, quite unknowingly, within twenty miles of each other. Captain Harville had never been in good health since a severe wound which he received two years before, and Captain Wentworth's anxiety to see him had determined him to go immediately to Lyme. He had been there for four-and-twenty hours. His acquittal was complete, his friendship warmly honoured, a lively interest excited for his friend, and his description of the fine country about Lyme so feelingly attended to by the party, that an earnest desire to see Lyme themselves, and a project for going thither was the consequence.

The young people were all wild to see Lyme. Captain Wentworth talked of going there again himself; it was only seventeen miles from Uppercross; though November, the weather was by no means bad; and, in short, Louisa, who was the most eager of the eager, having formed the resolution to go, and besides the pleasure of doing as she liked, being now armed with the idea of merit in maintaining her own way, bore down all the wishes of her father and mother for putting it off till summer; and to Lyme they were to go—Charles, Mary, Anne, Henrietta, Louisa, and Captain Wentworth.

The first heedless scheme had been to go in the morning and return at night, but to this Mr. Musgrove, for the sake of his horses, would not consent; and when it came to be rationally considered, a day in the middle of November would not leave much time for seeing a new place, after deducting seven hours, as the nature of the country required, for going and returning. They were consequently to stay the night there, and not to be expected back till the next day's dinner. This was felt to be a considerable amendment; and though they all met at the Great House at rather an early breakfast hour, and set off very punctually, it was so much past noon before the two carriages, Mr. Musgrove's coach containing the four ladies, and Charles's curricle, in which he drove Captain Wentworth, were descending the long hill into Lyme, and entering upon the still steeper street of the town itself, that it was very evident they would not have more than time for looking about them, before the light and warmth of the day were gone.

After securing accommodations, and ordering a dinner at one of the inns, the next thing to be done was unquestionably to walk directly down to the sea. They were come too late in the year for any amusement or variety which Lyme, as a public place, might offer; the rooms[2] were shut up, the lodgers almost all gone, scarcely any family but of the residents left—and, as there is nothing to admire in the buildings themselves, the remarkable situation of the town, the principal street almost hurrying into the water, the walk to the Cobb,[3] skirting round the pleasant little bay, which in the season is animated with bathing machines and company, the Cobb itself, its old wonders and new improvements, with the very beautiful line of cliffs stretching out to the east of the town, are what the stranger's eye will seek; and a very strange stranger it must be, who does not see charms in the immediate environs of Lyme, to make him wish to know it better. The scenes in its neighbourhood, Charmouth, with its high grounds and extensive sweeps of country, and still more its sweet retired bay, backed by dark cliffs, where fragments of low rock among the sands make it the happiest spot for watching the flow of the tide, for sitting in unwearied contemplation;—the woody varieties of the cheerful village of Up Lyme, and, above all, Pinny, with its green chasms between romantic rocks, where the scattered forest trees and orchards of luxuriant growth declare that many a generation must have passed away since the first partial falling of the cliff prepared the ground for such a state, where a scene so wonderful and so lovely is exhibited, as may more than equal any of the resembling scenes of the far-famed Isle of Wight: these places must be visited, and visited again, to make the worth of Lyme understood.

The party from Uppercross passing down by the now deserted and melancholy looking rooms, and still descending, soon found themselves on the sea shore, and lingering only, as all must linger and gaze on a first return to the sea, who ever deserve to look on it at all, proceeded towards the Cobb, equally their object in itself and on Captain Wentworth's account; for in a small house, near the foot of an old pier of unknown date, were the Harvilles settled. Captain Wentworth turned in to call on his friend; the others walked on, and he was to join them on the Cobb.

They were by no means tired of wondering and admiring; and not even Louisa seemed to feel that they had parted with Captain Wentworth long, when they saw him coming after them, with three companions, all well known already by description to be Captain and Mrs. Harville, and a Captain Benwick, who was staying with them.

Captain Benwick had some time ago been first lieutenant of the Laco-

2. The public assembly rooms.
3. A massive stone breakwater around the harbor.

nia; and the account which Captain Wentworth had given of him, on his return from Lyme before; his warm praise of him as an excellent young man and an officer, whom he had always valued highly, which must have stamped him well in the esteem of every listener, had been followed by a little history of his private life, which rendered him perfectly interesting in the eyes of all the ladies. He had been engaged to Captain Harville's sister, and was now mourning her loss. They had been a year or two waiting for fortune and promotion. Fortune came, his prize-money as lieutenant being great,—promotion, too, came at *last*; but Fanny Harville did not live to know it. She had died the preceding summer, while he was at sea. Captain Wentworth believed it impossible for man to be more attached to woman than poor Benwick had been to Fanny Harville, or to be more deeply afflicted under the dreadful change. He considered his disposition as of the sort which must suffer heavily, uniting very strong feelings with quiet, serious, and retiring manners, and a decided taste for reading, and sedentary pursuits. To finish the interest of the story, the friendship between him and the Harvilles seemed, if possible, augmented by the event which closed all their views of alliance, and Captain Benwick was now living with them entirely. Captain Harville had taken his present house for half a year, his taste, and his health, and his fortune all directing him to a residence unexpensive, and by the sea; and the grandeur of the country, and the retirement of Lyme in the winter, appeared exactly adapted to Captain Benwick's state of mind. The sympathy and good-will excited towards Captain Benwick was very great.

"And yet," said Anne to herself, as they now moved forward to meet the party, "he has not, perhaps, a more sorrowing heart than I have. I cannot believe his prospects so blighted for ever. He is younger than I am; younger in feeling, if not in fact; younger as a man. He will rally again, and be happy with another."

They all met, and were introduced. Captain Harville was a tall, dark man, with a sensible, benevolent countenance; a little lame; and from strong features, and want of health, looking much older than Captain Wentworth. Captain Benwick looked and was the youngest of the three, and, compared with either of them, a little man. He had a pleasing face and a melancholy air, just as he ought to have, and drew back from conversation.

Captain Harville, though not equalling Captain Wentworth in manners, was a perfect gentleman, unaffected, warm, and obliging. Mrs. Harville, a degree less polished than her husband, seemed however to have the same good feelings; and nothing could be more pleasant than their desire of considering the whole party as friends of their own, because the friends of Captain Wentworth, or more kindly hospitable than their entreaties for their all promising to dine with them. The dinner, already ordered at the inn, was at last, though unwillingly, accepted as an excuse; but they seemed almost hurt that Captain Wentworth should have brought any such party to Lyme, without considering it as a thing of course that they should dine with them.

There was so much attachment to Captain Wentworth in all this, and such a bewitching charm in a degree of hospitality so uncommon, so unlike the usual style of give-and-take invitations, and dinners of formality and display, that Anne felt her spirits not likely to be benefited by an increasing acquaintance among his brother-officers. "These would have been all my friends," was her thought; and she had to struggle against a great tendency to lowness.[4]

On quitting the Cobb, they all went indoors with their new friends, and found rooms so small as none but those who invite from the heart could think capable of accommodating so many. Anne had a moment's astonishment on the subject herself; but it was soon lost in the pleasanter feelings which sprang from the sight of all the ingenious contrivances and nice arrangements of Captain Harville, to turn the actual space to the best possible account, to supply the deficiencies of lodging-house furniture, and defend the windows and doors against the winter storms to be expected. The varieties in the fitting-up of the rooms, where the common necessaries provided by the owner, in the common indifferent plight, were contrasted with some few articles of a rare species of wood, excellently worked up, and with something curious and valuable from all the distant countries Captain Harville had visited, were more than amusing to Anne: connected as it all was with his profession, the fruit of its labours, the effect of its influence on his habits, the picture of repose and domestic happiness it presented, made it to her a something more, or less, than gratification.

Captain Harville was no reader; but he had contrived excellent accommodations, and fashioned very pretty shelves, for a tolerable collection of well-bound volumes, the property of Captain Benwick. His lameness prevented him from taking much exercise; but a mind of usefulness and ingenuity seemed to furnish him with constant employment within. He drew, he varnished, he carpentered, he glued; he made toys for the children, he fashioned new netting-needles and pins with improvements; and if every thing else was done, sat down to his large fishing-net at one corner of the room.

Anne thought she left great happiness behind her when they quitted the house; and Louisa, by whom she found herself walking, burst forth into raptures of admiration and delight on the character of the navy— their friendliness, their brotherliness, their openness, their uprightness; protesting that she was convinced of sailors having more worth and warmth than any other set of men in England; that they only knew how to live, and they only deserved to be respected and loved.

4. Depression.

They went back to dress and dine; and so well had the scheme answered[5] already, that nothing was found amiss; though its being "so entirely out of the season," and the "no-thorough-fare of Lyme," and the "no expectation of company," had brought many apologies from the heads of the inn.

Anne found herself by this time growing so much more hardened to being in Captain Wentworth's company than she had at first imagined could ever be, that the sitting down to the same table with him now, and the interchange of the common civilities attending on it—(they never got beyond) was become a mere nothing.

The nights were too dark for the ladies to meet again till the morrow, but Captain Harville had promised them a visit in the evening; and he came, bringing his friend also, which was more than had been expected, it having been agreed that Captain Benwick had all the appearance of being oppressed by the presence of so many strangers. He ventured among them again, however, though his spirits certainly did not seem fit for the mirth of the party in general.

While Captains Wentworth and Harville led the talk on one side of the room, and, by recurring to former days, supplied anecdotes in abundance to occupy and entertain the others, it fell to Anne's lot to be placed rather apart with Captain Benwick; and a very good impulse of her nature obliged her to begin an acquaintance with him. He was shy, and disposed to abstraction; but the engaging mildness of her countenance, and gentleness of her manners, soon had their effect; and Anne was well repaid the first trouble of exertion. He was evidently a young man of considerable taste in reading, though principally in poetry; and besides the persuasion of having given him at least an evening's indulgence in the discussion of subjects, which his usual companions had probably no concern in, she had the hope of being of real use to him in some suggestions as to the duty and benefit of struggling against affliction, which had naturally grown out of their conversation. For, though shy, he did not seem reserved; it had rather the appearance of feelings glad to burst their usual restraints; and having talked of poetry, the richness of the present age, and gone through a brief comparison of opinion as to the first-rate poets, trying to ascertain whether *Marmion* or *The Lady of the Lake* were to be preferred, and how ranked the *Giaour* and *The Bride of Abydos*;[6] and moreover, how the *Giaour* was to be pronounced, he shewed himself so intimately acquainted with all the tenderest songs of the one poet, and all the impassioned descriptions of hopeless agony of the other; he repeated, with such tremulous feeling, the various lines which imaged a broken heart, or a mind destroyed by wretchedness, and looked so entirely as if he meant to be understood,

5. Suited.
6. Titles of romantic poems by Sir Walter Scott (1771–1832) and George Gordon, Lord Byron (1788–1824).

that she ventured to hope he did not always read only poetry; and to say, that she thought it was the misfortune of poetry, to be seldom safely enjoyed by those who enjoyed it completely; and that the strong feelings which alone could estimate it truly, were the very feelings which ought to taste it but sparingly.

His looks shewing him not pained, but pleased with this allusion to his situation, she was emboldened to go on; and feeling in herself the right of seniority of mind, she ventured to recommend a larger allowance of prose in his daily study; and on being requested to particularize, mentioned such works of our best moralists, such collections of the finest letters, such memoirs of characters of worth and suffering, as occurred to her at the moment as calculated to rouse and fortify the mind by the highest precepts, and the strongest examples of moral and religious endurances.

Captain Benwick listened attentively, and seemed grateful for the interest implied; and though with a shake of the head, and sighs which declared his little faith in the efficacy of any books on grief like his, noted down the names of those she recommended, and promised to procure and read them.

When the evening was over, Anne could not but be amused at the idea of her coming to Lyme, to preach patience and resignation to a young man whom she had never seen before; nor could she help fearing, on more serious reflection, that, like many other great moralists and preachers, she had been eloquent on a point in which her own conduct would ill bear examination.

Chapter XII

Anne and Henrietta, finding themselves the earliest of the party the next morning, agreed to stroll down to the sea before breakfast.—They went to the sands, to watch the flowing of the tide, which a fine south-easterly breeze was bringing in with all the grandeur which so flat a shore admitted. They praised the morning; gloried in the sea; sympathized in the delight of the fresh-feeling breeze—and were silent; till Henrietta suddenly began again, with.

"Oh! yes,—I am quite convinced that, with very few exceptions, the sea-air always does good. There can be no doubt of its having been of the greatest service to Dr. Shirley, after his illness, last spring twelve-month.[7] He declares himself, that coming to Lyme for a month, did him more good than all the medicine he took; and, that being by the sea, always makes him feel young again. Now, I cannot help thinking it a pity that he does not live entirely by the sea. I do think he had better

7. A year ago last spring.

leave Uppercross entirely, and fix[8] at Lyme.—Do not you, Anne?—
Do not you agree with me, that it is the best thing he could do, both for
himself and Mrs. Shirley?—She has cousins here, you know, and many
acquaintance, which would make it cheerful for her,—and I am sure
she would be glad to get to a place where she could have medical attendance at hand, in case of his having another seizure. Indeed I think it
quite melancholy to have such excellent people as Dr. and Mrs. Shirley,
who have been doing good all their lives, wearing out their last days in
a place like Uppercross, where, excepting our family, they seem shut
out from all the world. I wish his friends would propose it to him. I
really think they ought. And, as to procuring a dispensation,[9] there
could be no difficulty at his time of life, and with his character. My only
doubt is, whether any thing could persuade him to leave his parish. He
is so very strict and scrupulous in his notions; over-scrupulous, I must
say. Do not you think, Anne, it is being over-scrupulous? Do not you
think it is quite a mistaken point of conscience, when a clergyman sacrifices his health for the sake of duties, which may be just as well per-
formed by another person?—And at Lyme too,—only seventeen miles
off,—he would be near enough to hear, if people thought there was any
thing to complain of."

Anne smiled more than once to herself during this speech, and
entered into the subject, as ready to do good by entering into the feelings
of a young lady as of a young man,—though here it was good of a lower
standard, for what could be offered but general acquiescence?—She said
all that was reasonable and proper on the business; felt the claims of Dr.
Shirley to repose, as she ought; saw how very desirable it was that he
should have some active, respectable young man, as a resident curate,
and was even courteous enough to hint at the advantage of such resident
curate's being married.

"I wish," said Henrietta, very well pleased with her companion, "I
wish Lady Russell lived at Uppercross, and were intimate with Dr. Shirley. I have always heard of Lady Russell, as a woman of the greatest
influence with every body! I always look upon her as able to persuade a
person to any thing! I am afraid of her, as I have told you before, quite
afraid of her, because she is so very clever; but I respect her amazingly,
and wish we had such a neighbour at Uppercross."

Anne was amused by Henrietta's manner of being grateful, and
amused also, that the course of events and the new interests of Henrietta's views should have placed her friend at all in favour with any of the
Musgrove family; she had only time, however, for a general answer, and
a wish that such another woman were at Uppercross, before all subjects
suddenly ceased, on seeing Louisa and Captain Wentworth coming

8. Settle.
9. Dr. Shirley would need special permission from the church to be an absentee vicar—to draw
the income of his post while having Charles Hayter do the actual work.

towards them. They came also for a stroll till breakfast was likely to
be ready; but Louisa recollecting, immediately afterwards, that she had
something to procure at a shop, invited them all to go back with her
into the town. They were all at her disposal.

When they came to the steps, leading upwards from the beach, a
gentleman at the same moment preparing to come down, politely drew
back, and stopped to give them way. They ascended and passed him;
and as they passed, Anne's face caught his eye, and he looked at her
with a degree of earnest admiration, which she could not be insensible
of. She was looking remarkably well; her very regular, very pretty features, having the bloom and freshness of youth restored by the fine wind
which had been blowing on her complexion, and by the animation of
eye which it had also produced. It was evident that the gentleman,
(completely a gentleman in manner) admired her exceedingly. Captain
Wentworth looked round at her instantly in a way which shewed his
noticing of it. He gave her a momentary glance,—a glance of brightness, which seemed to say, "That man is struck with you,—and even I,
at this moment, see something like Anne Elliot again."

After attending Louisa through her business, and loitering about a
little longer, they returned to the inn; and Anne in passing afterwards
quickly from her own chamber to their dining-room, had nearly run
against the very same gentleman, as he came out of an adjoining apartment. She had before conjectured him to be a stranger like themselves,
and determined that a well-looking groom, who was strolling about near
the two inns as they came back, should be his servant. Both master and
man being in mourning, assisted the idea. It was now proved that he
belonged to the same inn as themselves; and this second meeting, short
as it was, also proved again by the gentleman's looks, that he thought
hers very lovely, and by the readiness and propriety of his apologies, that
he was a man of exceedingly good manners. He seemed about thirty,
and, though not handsome, had an agreeable person. Anne felt that she
should like to know who he was.

They had nearly done breakfast, when the sound of a carriage, (almost
the first they had heard since entering Lyme) drew half the party to the
window. "It was a gentleman's carriage—a curricle—but only coming
round from the stable-yard to the front door—Somebody must be going
away.—It was driven by a servant in mourning."

The word curricle made Charles Musgrove jump up, that he might
compare it with his own, the servant in mourning roused Anne's curiosity, and the whole six were collected to look, by the time the owner of
the curricle was to be seen issuing from the door amidst the bows and
civilities of the household, and taking his seat, to drive off.

"Ah!" cried Captain Wentworth, instantly, and with half a glance at
Anne; "it is the very man we passed."

The Miss Musgroves agreed to it; and having all kindly watched him as far up the hill as they could, they returned to the breakfast-table. The waiter came into the room soon afterwards.

"Pray," said Captain Wentworth, immediately, "can you tell us the name of the gentleman who is just gone away?"

"Yes, Sir, a Mr. Elliot; a gentleman of large fortune,—came in last night from Sidmouth,—dare say you heard the carriage, Sir, while you were at dinner; and going on now for Crewkherne, in his way to Bath and London."

"Elliot!"—Many had looked on each other, and many had repeated the name, before all this had been got through, even by the smart rapidity of a waiter.

"Bless me!" cried Mary; "it must be our cousin;—it must be our Mr. Elliot, it must, indeed!—Charles, Anne, must not it? In mourning, you see, just as our Mr. Elliot must be. How very extraordinary! In the very same inn with us! Anne, must not it be our Mr. Elliot; my father's next heir? Pray Sir," (turning to the waiter), "did not you hear—did not his servant say whether he belonged to the Kellynch family?"

"No, ma'am,—he did not mention no particular family; but he said his master was a very rich gentleman, and would be a baronight some day."

"There! you see!" cried Mary, in an ecstacy, "Just as I said! Heir to Sir Walter Elliot!—I was sure that would come out, if it was so. Depend upon it, that is a circumstance which his servants take care to publish wherever he goes. But, Anne, only conceive how extraordinary! I wish I had looked at him more. I wish we had been aware in time, who it was, that he might have been introduced to us. What a pity that we should not have been introduced to each other!—Do you think he had the Elliot countenance? I hardly looked at him, I was looking at the horses; but I think he had something of the Elliot countenance. I wonder the arms [1] did not strike me! Oh!—the great-coat was hanging over the pannel, and hid the arms; so it did, otherwise, I am sure, I should have observed them, and the livery too; if the servant had not been in mourning, one should have known him by the livery."

"Putting all these very extraordinary circumstances together," said Captain Wentworth, "we must consider it to be the arrangement of Providence, that you should not be introduced to your cousin."

When she could command Mary's attention, Anne quietly tried to convince her that their father and Mr. Elliot had not, for many years, been on such terms as to make the power of attempting an introduction at all desirable.

At the same time, however, it was a secret gratification to herself to have seen her cousin, and to know that the future owner of Kellynch was undoubtedly a gentleman, and had an air of good sense. She would

---

1. Coat of arms (which would appear on the side of the carriage).

not, upon any account, mention her having met with him the second time; luckily Mary did not much attend to their having passed close by him in their early walk, but she would have felt quite ill-used by Anne's having actually run against him in the passage, and received his very polite excuses, while she had never been near him at all; no, that cousinly little interview must remain a perfect secret.

"Of course," said Mary, "you will mention our seeing Mr. Elliot, the next time you write to Bath. I think my father certainly ought to hear of it; do mention all about him."

Anne avoided a direct reply, but it was just the circumstance which she considered as not merely unnecessary to be communicated, but as what ought to be suppressed. The offence which had been given her father, many years back, she knew; Elizabeth's particular share in it she suspected; and that Mr. Elliot's idea always produced irritation in both, was beyond a doubt. Mary never wrote to Bath herself; all the toil of keeping up a slow and unsatisfactory correspondence with Elizabeth fell on Anne.

Breakfast had not been long over, when they were joined by Captain and Mrs. Harville, and Captain Benwick, with whom they had appointed to take their last walk about Lyme. They ought to be setting off for Uppercross by one, and in the meanwhile were to be all together, and out of doors as long as they could.

Anne found Captain Benwick getting near her, as soon as they were all fairly in the street. Their conversation, the preceding evening, did not disincline him to seek her again; and they walked together some time, talking as before of Mr. Scott and Lord Byron, and still as unable, as before, and as unable as any other two readers, to think exactly alike of the merits of either, till something occasioned an almost general change amongst their party, and instead of Captain Benwick, she had Captain Harville by her side.

"Miss Elliot," said he, speaking rather low, "you have done a good deed in making that poor fellow talk so much. I wish he could have such company oftener. It is bad for him, I know, to be shut up as he is; but what can we do? we cannot part."

"No," said Anne, "that I can easily believe to be impossible; but in time, perhaps—we know what time does in every case of affliction, and you must remember, Captain Harville, that your friend may yet be called a young mourner—Only last summer, I understand."

"Ay, true enough," (with a deep sigh) "only June."

"And not known to him, perhaps, so soon."

"Not till the first week in August, when he came home from the Cape,—just made into the Grappler.[2] I was at Plymouth, dreading to

2. Promoted into command of a new ship.

hear of him; he sent in letters, but the Grappler was under orders for Portsmouth. There the news must follow him, but who was to tell it? not I. I would as soon have been run up to the yard-arm.[3] Nobody could do it, but that good fellow, (pointing to Captain Wentworth.) The Laconia had come into Plymouth the week before; no danger of her being sent to sea again. He stood his chance for the rest—wrote up for leave of absence, but without waiting the return, travelled night and day till he got to Portsmouth, rowed off to the Grappler that instant, and never left the poor fellow for a week; that's what he did, and nobody else could have saved poor James. You may think, Miss Elliot, whether he is dear to us!"

Anne did think on the question with perfect decision, and said as much in reply as her own feelings could accomplish, or as his seemed able to bear, for he was too much affected to renew the subject—and when he spoke again, it was of something totally different.

Mrs. Harville's giving it as her opinion that her husband would have quite walking enough by the time he reached home, determined the direction of all the party in what was to be their last walk; they would accompany them to their door, and then return and set off themselves. By all their calculations there was just time for this; but as they drew near the Cobb, there was such a general wish to walk along it once more, all were so inclined, and Louisa soon grew so determined, that the difference of a quarter of an hour, it was found, would be no difference at all, so with all the kind leave-taking, and all the kind interchange of invitations and promises which may be imagined, they parted from Captain and Mrs. Harville at their own door, and still accompanied by Captain Benwick, who seemed to cling to them to the last, proceeded to make the proper adieus to the Cobb.

Anne found Captain Benwick again drawing near her. Lord Byron's "dark blue seas"[4] could not fail of being brought forward by their present view, and she gladly gave him all her attention as long as attention was possible. It was soon drawn per force another way.

There was too much wind to make the high part of the new Cobb pleasant for the ladies, and they agreed to get down the steps to the lower, and all were contented to pass quietly and carefully down the steep flight, excepting Louisa; she must be jumped down them by Captain Wentworth. In all their walks, he had had to jump her from the stiles; the sensation was delightful to her. The hardness of the pavement for her feet, made him less willing upon the present occasion; he did it, however; she was safely down, and instantly, to shew her enjoyment, ran up the steps to be jumped down again. He advised her against it, thought the jar too great; but no, he reasoned and talked in vain; she

3. Hanged.
4. Cf. "Roll on, thou deep and dark blue ocean—roll!" (*Childe Harold's Pilgrimage* 4.1603).

smiled and said, "I am determined I will:" he put out his hands; she was too precipitate by half a second, she fell on the pavement on the Lower Cobb, and was taken up lifeless!

There was no wound, no blood, no visible bruise; but her eyes were closed, she breathed not, her face was like death.—The horror of that moment to all who stood around!

Captain Wentworth, who had caught her up, knelt with her in his arms, looking on her with a face as pallid as her own, in an agony of silence. "She is dead! she is dead!" screamed Mary, catching hold of her husband, and contributing with his own horror to make him immoveable; and in another moment, Henrietta, sinking under the conviction, lost her senses too, and would have fallen on the steps, but for Captain Benwick and Anne, who caught and supported her between them.

"Is there no one to help me?" were the first words which burst from Captain Wentworth, in a tone of despair, and as if all his own strength were gone.

"Go to him, go to him," cried Anne, "for heaven's sake go to him. I can support her myself. Leave me, and go to him. Rub her hands, rub her temples; here are salts,[5]—take them, take them."

Captain Benwick obeyed, and Charles at the same moment, disengaging himself from his wife, they were both with him; and Louisa was raised up and supported more firmly between them, and every thing was done that Anne had prompted, but in vain; while Captain Wentworth, staggering against the wall for his support, exclaimed in the bitterest agony,

"Oh God! her father and mother!"

"A surgeon!" said Anne.

He caught the word; it seemed to rouse him at once, and saying only "True, true, a surgeon this instant," was darting away, when Anne eagerly suggested,

"Captain Benwick, would not it be better for Captain Benwick? He knows where a surgeon is to be found."

Every one capable of thinking felt the advantage of the idea, and in a moment (it was all done in rapid moments) Captain Benwick had resigned the poor corpse-like figure entirely to the brother's care, and was off for the town with the utmost rapidity.

As to the wretched party left behind, it could scarcely be said which of the three, who were completely rational, was suffering most, Captain Wentworth, Anne, or Charles, who, really a very affectionate brother, hung over Louisa with sobs of grief, and could only turn his eyes from one sister, to see the other in a state as insensible, or to witness the hysterical agitations of his wife, calling on him for help which he could not give.

5. Smelling salts.

Anne, attending with all the strength and zeal, and thought, which instinct supplied, to Henrietta, still tried, at intervals, to suggest comfort to the others, tried to quiet Mary, to animate Charles, to assuage the feelings of Captain Wentworth. Both seemed to look to her for directions.

"Anne, Anne," cried Charles, "what is to be done next? What, in heaven's name, is to be done next?"

Captain Wentworth's eyes were also turned towards her.

"Had not she better be carried to the inn? Yes, I am sure, carry her gently to the inn."

"Yes, yes, to the inn," repeated Captain Wentworth, comparatively collected, and eager to be doing something. "I will carry her myself. Musgrove, take care of the others."

By this time the report of the accident had spread among the workmen and boatmen about the Cobb, and many were collected near them, to be useful if wanted, at any rate, to enjoy the sight of a dead young lady, nay, two dead young ladies, for it proved twice as fine as the first report. To some of the best-looking of these good people Henrietta was consigned, for, though partially revived, she was quite helpless; and in this manner, Anne walking by her side, and Charles attending to his wife, they set forward, treading back with feelings unutterable, the ground which so lately, so very lately, and so light of heart, they had passed along.

They were not off the Cobb, before the Harvilles met them. Captain Benwick had been seen flying by their house, with a countenance which shewed something to be wrong; and they had set off immediately, informed and directed, as they passed, towards the spot. Shocked as Captain Harville was, he brought senses and nerves that could be instantly useful; and a look between him and his wife decided what was to be done. She must be taken to their house—all must go to their house—and wait the surgeon's arrival there. They would not listen to scruples: he was obeyed; they were all beneath his roof; and while Louisa, under Mrs. Harville's direction, was conveyed up stairs, and given possession of her own bed, assistance, cordials, restoratives were supplied by her husband to all who needed them.

Louisa had once opened her eyes, but soon closed them again, without apparent consciousness. This had been a proof of life, however, of service to her sister; and Henrietta, though perfectly incapable of being in the same room with Louisa, was kept, by the agitation of hope and fear, from a return of her own insensibility. Mary, too, was growing calmer.

The surgeon was with them almost before it had seemed possible. They were sick with horror while he examined; but he was not hopeless. The head had received a severe contusion, but he had seen greater injuries recovered from: he was by no means hopeless; he spoke cheerfully.

That he did not regard it as a desperate case—that he did not say a few hours must end it—was at first felt, beyond the hope of most; and the ecstasy of such a reprieve, the rejoicing, deep and silent, after a few fervent ejaculations of gratitude to Heaven had been offered, may be conceived.

The tone, the look, with which "Thank God!" was uttered by Captain Wentworth, Anne was sure could never be forgotten by her; nor the sight of him afterwards, as he sat near a table, leaning over it with folded arms, and face concealed, as if overpowered by the various feelings of his soul, and trying by prayer and reflection to calm them.

Louisa's limbs had escaped. There was no injury but to the head.

It now became necessary for the party to consider what was best to be done, as to their general situation. They were now able to speak to each other, and consult. That Louisa must remain where she was, however distressing to her friends to be involving the Harvilles in such trouble, did not admit a doubt. Her removal was impossible. The Harvilles silenced all scruples; and, as much as they could, all gratitude. They had looked forward and arranged every thing, before the others began to reflect. Captain Benwick must give up his room to them, and get a bed elsewhere—and the whole was settled. They were only concerned that the house could accommodate no more; and yet perhaps by "putting the children away in the maids' room, or swinging a cot somewhere," they could hardly bear to think of not finding room for two or three besides, supposing they might wish to stay; though, with regard to any attendance on Miss Musgrove, there need not be the least uneasiness in leaving her to Mrs. Harville's care entirely. Mrs. Harville was a very experienced nurse; and her nursery-maid, who had lived with her long and gone about with her every where, was just such another. Between those two, she could want no possible attendance by day or night. And all this was said with a truth and sincerity of feeling irresistible.

Charles, Henrietta, and Captain Wentworth were the three in consultation, and for a little while it was only an interchange of perplexity and terror. "Uppercross,—the necessity of some one's going to Uppercross,—the news to be conveyed—how it could be broken to Mr. and Mrs. Musgrove—the lateness of the morning,—an hour already gone since they ought to have been off,—the impossibility of being in tolerable time. At first, they were capable of nothing more to the purpose than such exclamations; but, after a while, Captain Wentworth, exerting himself, said,

"We must be decided, and without the loss of another minute. Every minute is valuable. Some must resolve on being off for Uppercross instantly. Musgrove, either you or I must go."

Charles agreed; but declared his resolution of not going away. He would be as little incumbrance as possible to Captain and Mrs. Harville; but as to leaving his sister in such a state, he neither ought, nor would.

So far it was decided; and Henrietta at first declared the same. She, however, was soon persuaded to think differently. The usefulness of her staying!—She, who had not been able to remain in Louisa's room, or to look at her, without sufferings which made her worse than helpless! She was forced to acknowledge that she could do no good; yet was still unwilling to be away, till touched by the thought of her father and mother, she gave it up; she consented, she was anxious to be at home.

The plan had reached this point, when Anne, coming quietly down from Louisa's room, could not but hear what followed, for the parlour door was open.

"Then it is settled, Musgrove," cried Captain Wentworth, "that you stay, and that I take care of your sister home. But as to the rest;—as to the others;—If one stays to assist Mrs. Harville, I think it need be only one.—Mrs. Charles Musgrove will, of course, wish to get back to her children; but, if Anne will stay, no one so proper, so capable as Anne!"

She paused a moment to recover from the emotion of hearing herself so spoken of. The other two warmly agreed to what he said, and she then appeared.

"You will stay, I am sure; you will stay and nurse her;" cried he, turning to her and speaking with a glow, and yet a gentleness, which seemed almost restoring the past.—She coloured deeply; and he recollected himself, and moved away.—She expressed herself most willing, ready, happy to remain. "It was what she had been thinking of, and wishing to be allowed to do.—A bed on the floor in Louisa's room would be sufficient for her, if Mrs. Harville would but think so."

One thing more, and all seemed arranged. Though it was rather desirable that Mr. and Mrs. Musgrove should be previously alarmed by some share of delay; yet the time required by the Uppercross horses to take them back, would be a dreadful extension of suspense; and Captain Wentworth proposed, and Charles Musgrove agreed, that it would be much better for him to take a chaise from the inn, and leave Mr. Musgrove's carriage and horses to be sent home the next morning early, when there would be the farther advantage of sending an account of Louisa's night.

Captain Wentworth now hurried off to get every thing ready on his part, and to be soon followed by the two ladies. When the plan was made known to Mary, however, there was an end of all peace in it. She was so wretched, and so vehement, complained so much of injustice in being expected to go away, instead of Anne;—Anne, who was nothing to Louisa, while she was her sister, and had the best right to stay in Henrietta's stead! Why was not she to be as useful as Anne? And to go home without Charles, too—without her husband! No, it was too unkind! And, in short, she said more than her husband could long withstand; and as none of the others could oppose when he gave way, there was no help for it: the change of Mary for Anne was inevitable.

Anne had never submitted more reluctantly to the jealous and ill-judging claims of Mary; but so it must be, and they set off for the town, Charles taking care of his sister, and Captain Benwick attending to her. She gave a moment's recollection, as they hurried along, to the little circumstances which the same spots had witnessed earlier in the morning. There she had listened to Henrietta's schemes for Dr. Shirley's leaving Uppercross; farther on, she had first seen Mr. Elliot; a moment seemed all that could now be given to any one but Louisa, or those who were wrapt up in her welfare.

Captain Benwick was most considerately attentive to her; and, united as they all seemed by the distress of the day, she felt an increasing degree of good-will towards him, and a pleasure even in thinking that it might, perhaps, be the occasion of continuing their acquaintance.

Captain Wentworth was on the watch for them, and a chaise and four in waiting, stationed for their convenience in the lowest part of the street; but his evident surprise and vexation, at the substitution of one sister for the other—the change of his countenance—the astonishment—the expressions begun and suppressed, with which Charles was listened to, made but a mortifying reception of Anne; or must at least convince her that she was valued only as she could be useful to Louisa.

She endeavoured to be composed, and to be just. Without emulating the feelings of an Emma towards her Henry,[6] she would have attended on Louisa with a zeal above the common claims of regard, for his sake; and she hoped he would not long be so unjust as to suppose she would shrink unnecessarily from the office of a friend.

In the meanwhile she was in the carriage. He had handed them both in, and placed himself between them; and in this manner, under these circumstances full of astonishment and emotion to Anne, she quitted Lyme. How the long stage would pass; how it was to affect their manners; what was to be their sort of intercourse, she could not foresee. It was all quite natural, however. He was devoted to Henrietta; always turning towards her; and when he spoke at all, always with the view of supporting her hopes and raising her spirits. In general, his voice and manner were studiously calm. To spare Henrietta from agitation seemed the governing principle. Once only, when she had been grieving over the last ill-judged, ill-fated walk to the Cobb, bitterly lamenting that it ever had been thought of, he burst forth, as if wholly overcome—

"Don't talk of it, don't talk of it," he cried. "Oh God! that I had not given way to her at the fatal moment! Had I done as I ought! But so eager and so resolute! Dear, sweet Louisa!"

Anne wondered whether it ever occurred to him now, to question the justness of his own previous opinion as to the universal felicity and advantage of firmness of character; and whether it might not strike him,

---

6. An allusion to *Henry and Emma, a Poem, upon the Model of the Nut-Brown Maid*, by Matthew Prior (1644–1721), which celebrates at length devoted mutual love.

that, like all other qualities of the mind, it should have its proportions and limits. She thought it could scarcely escape him to feel, that a per-suadable temper might sometimes be as much in favour of happiness, as a very resolute character.

· They got on fast. Anne was astonished to recognise the same hills and the same objects so soon. Their actual speed, heightened by some dread of the conclusion, made the road appear but half as long as on the day before. It was growing quite dusk, however, before they were in the neighbourhood of Uppercross, and there had been total silence among them for some time, Henrietta leaning back in the corner, with a shawl over her face, giving the hope of her having cried herself to sleep; when, as they were going up their last hill, Anne found herself all at once addressed by Captain Wentworth. In a low, cautious voice, he said,

"I have been considering what we had best do. She must not appear at first. She could not stand it. I have been thinking whether you had not better remain in the carriage with her, while I go in and break it to Mr. and Mrs. Musgrove. Do you think this a good plan?"

She did: he was satisfied, and said no more. But the remembrance of the appeal remained a pleasure to her—as a proof of friendship, and of deference for her judgment, a great pleasure; and when it became a sort of parting proof, its value did not lessen.

When the distressing communication at Uppercross was over, and he had seen the father and mother quite as composed as could be hoped, and the daughter all the better for being with them, he announced his intention of returning in the same carriage to Lyme; and when the horses were baited,[7] he was off.

Chapter XIII

The remainder of Anne's time at Uppercross, comprehending only two days, was spent entirely at the mansion-house, and she had the satisfaction of knowing herself extremely useful there, both as an imme-diate companion, and as assisting in all those arrangements for the future, which, in Mr. and Mrs. Musgrove's distressed state of spirits, would have been difficulties.

They had an early account from Lyme the next morning. Louisa was much the same. No symptoms worse than before had appeared. Charles came a few hours afterwards, to bring a later and more particular account. He was tolerably cheerful. A speedy cure must not be hoped, but every thing was going on as well as the nature of the case admitted. In speaking of the Harvilles, he seemed unable to satisfy his own sense of their kindness, especially of Mrs. Harville's exertions as a nurse. "She

7. Fed.

really left nothing for Mary to do. He and Mary had been persuaded to go early to their inn last night. Mary had been hysterical again this morning. When he came away, she was going to walk out with Captain Benwick, which, he hoped, would do her good. He almost wished she had been prevailed on to come home the day before; but the truth was, that Mrs. Harville left nothing for any body to do."

Charles was to return to Lyme the same afternoon, and his father had at first half a mind to go with him, but the ladies could not consent. It would be going only to multiply trouble to the others, and increase his own distress; and a much better scheme followed and was acted upon. A chaise was sent for from Crewkherne, and Charles conveyed back a far more useful person in the old nursery-maid of the family, one who having brought up all the children, and seen the very last, the lingering and long-petted master Harry, sent to school after his brothers, was now living in her deserted nursery to mend stockings, and dress all the blains[8] and bruises she could get near her, and who, consequently, was only too happy in being allowed to go and help nurse dear Miss Louisa. Vague wishes of getting Sarah thither, had occurred before to Mrs. Musgrove and Henrietta; but without Anne, it would hardly have been resolved on, and found practicable so soon.

They were indebted, the next day, to Charles Hayter for all the minute knowledge of Louisa, which it was so essential to obtain every twenty-four hours. He made it his business to go to Lyme, and his account was still encouraging. The intervals of sense and consciousness were believed to be stronger. Every report agreed in Captain Wentworth's appearing fixed in Lyme.

Anne was to leave them on the morrow, an event which they all dreaded. "What should they do without her? They were wretched comforters for one another!" And so much was said in this way, that Anne thought she could not do better than impart among them the general inclination to which she was privy, and persuade them all to go to Lyme at once. She had little difficulty; it was soon determined that they would go, go to-morrow, fix themselves at the inn, or get into lodgings, as it suited, and there remain till dear Louisa could be moved. They must be taking off some trouble from the good people she was with; they might at least relieve Mrs. Harville from the care of her own children; and in short they were so happy in the decision, that Anne was delighted with what she had done, and felt that she could not spend her last morning at Uppercross better than in assisting their preparations, and sending them off at an early hour, though her being left to the solitary range of the house was the consequence.

She was the last, excepting the little boys at the cottage, she was the very last, the only remaining one of all that had filled and animated

---

8. Chilblains (inflammatory swellings produced by cold).

both houses, of all that had given Uppercross its cheerful character. A few days had made a change indeed!

If Louisa recovered, it would all be well again. More than former happiness would be restored. There could not be a doubt, to her mind there was none, of what would follow her recovery. A few months hence, and the room now so deserted, occupied but by her silent, pensive self, might be filled again with all that was happy and gay, all that was glowing and bright in prosperous love, all that was most unlike Anne Elliot!

An hour's complete leisure for such reflections as these, on a dark November day, a small[9] thick rain almost blotting out the very few objects ever to be discerned from the windows, was enough to make the sound of Lady Russell's carriage exceedingly welcome; and yet, though desirous to be gone, she could not quit the mansion-house, or look an adieu to the cottage, with its black, dripping, and comfortless veranda, or even notice through the misty glasses the last humble tenements of the village, without a saddened heart.—Scenes had passed in Uppercross, which made it precious. It stood the record of many sensations of pain, once severe, but now softened; and of some instances of relenting feeling, some breathings of friendship and reconciliation, which could never be looked for again, and which could never cease to be dear. She left it all behind her; all but the recollection that such things had been.

Anne had never entered Kellynch since her quitting Lady Russell's house, in September. It had not been necessary, and the few occasions of its being possible for her to go to the hall she had contrived to evade and escape from. Her first return, was to resume her place in the modern and elegant apartments of the lodge, and to gladden the eyes of its mistress.

There was some anxiety mixed with Lady Russell's joy in meeting her. She knew who had been frequenting Uppercross. But happily, either Anne was improved in plumpness and looks, or Lady Russell fancied her so; and Anne, in receiving her compliments on the occasion, had the amusement of connecting them with the silent admiration of her cousin, and of hoping that she was to be blessed with a second spring of youth and beauty.

When they came to converse, she was soon sensible of some mental change. The subjects of which her heart had been full on leaving Kellynch, and which she had felt slighted, and been compelled to smother among the Musgroves, were now become but of secondary interest. She had lately lost sight even of her father and sister and Bath. Their concerns had been sunk under those of Uppercross, and when Lady Russell reverted to their former hopes and fears, and spoke her satisfaction in

9. Gentle.

the house in Camden-place, which had been taken, and her regret that Mrs. Clay should still be with them, Anne would have been ashamed to have it known, how much more she was thinking of Lyme, and Louisa Musgrove, and all her acquaintance there; how much more interesting to her was the home and the friendship of the Harvilles and Captain Benwick, than her own father's house in Camden-place, or her own sister's intimacy with Mrs. Clay. She was actually forced to exert herself, to meet Lady Russell with any thing like the appearance of equal solicitude, on topics which had by nature the first claim on her.

There was a little awkwardness at first in their discourse on another subject. They must speak of the accident at Lyme. Lady Russell had not been arrived five minutes the day before, when a full account of the whole had burst on her; but still it must be talked of, she must make enquiries, she must regret the imprudence, lament the result, and Captain Wentworth's name must be mentioned by both. Anne was conscious of not doing it so well as Lady Russell. She could not speak the name, and look straight forward to Lady Russell's eye, till she had adopted the expedient of telling her briefly what she thought of the attachment between him and Louisa. When this was told, his name distressed her no longer.

Lady Russell had only to listen composedly, and wish them happy; but internally her heart revelled in angry pleasure, in pleased contempt, that the man who at twenty-three had seemed to understand somewhat of the value of an Anne Elliot, should, eight years afterwards, be charmed by a Louisa Musgrove.

The first three or four days passed most quietly, with no circumstance to mark them excepting the receipt of a note or two from Lyme, which found their way to Anne, she could not tell how, and brought a rather improving account of Louisa. At the end of that period, Lady Russell's politeness could repose no longer, and the fainter self-threatenings of the past, became in a decided tone, "I must call on Mrs. Croft; I really must call upon her soon. Anne, have you courage to go with me, and pay a visit in that house? It will be some trial to us both."

Anne did not shrink from it; on the contrary, she truly felt as she said, in observing,

"I think you are very likely to suffer the most of the two; your feelings are less reconciled to the change than mine. By remaining in the neighbourhood, I am become inured to it."

She could have said more on the subject; for she had in fact so high an opinion of the Crofts, and considered her father so very fortunate in his tenants, felt the parish to be so sure of a good example, and the poor of the best attention and relief, that however sorry and ashamed for the necessity of the removal, she could not but in conscience feel that they were gone who deserved not to stay, and that Kellynch-hall had passed into better hands than its owners'. These convictions must unquestionably have their own pain, and severe was its kind; but they precluded that pain which Lady Russell would suffer in entering the house again, and returning through the well-known apartments.

In such moments Anne had no power of saying to herself, "These rooms ought to belong only to us. Oh, how fallen in their destination! How unworthily occupied! An ancient family to be so driven away! Strangers filling their place!" No, except when she thought of her mother, and remembered where she had been used to sit and preside, she had no sigh of that description to heave.

Mrs. Croft always met her with a kindness which gave her the pleasure of fancying herself a favourite; and on the present occasion, receiving her in that house, there was particular attention.

The sad accident at Lyme was soon the prevailing topic; and on comparing their latest accounts of the invalid, it appeared that each lady dated her intelligence from the same hour of yester morn, that Captain Wentworth had been in Kellynch yesterday—(the first time since the accident) had brought Anne the last note, which she had not been able to trace the exact steps of, had staid a few hours and then returned again to Lyme—and without any present intention of quitting it any more.— He had enquired after her, she found, particularly;—had expressed his hope of Miss Elliot's not being the worse for her exertions, and had spoken of those exertions as great.—This was handsome,—and gave her more pleasure than almost any thing else could have done.

As to the sad catastrophe itself, it could be canvassed only in one style by a couple of steady, sensible women, whose judgments had to work on ascertained events; and it was perfectly decided that it had been the consequence of much thoughtlessness and much imprudence; that its effects were most alarming, and that it was frightful to think, how long Miss Musgrove's recovery might yet be doubtful, and how liable she would still remain to suffer from the concussion hereafter!—The Admiral wound it all up summarily by exclaiming,

"Ay, a very bad business indeed.—A new sort of way this, for a young fellow to be making love, by breaking his mistress's head!—is not it, Miss Elliot?—This is breaking a head and giving a plaister truly!"[1]

Admiral Croft's manners were not quite of the tone to suit Lady Russell, but they delighted Anne. His goodness of heart and simplicity of character were irresistible.

"Now, this must be very bad for you," said he, suddenly rousing from a little reverie, "to be coming and finding us here.—I had not recollected it before, I declare,—but it must be very bad.—But now, do not stand upon ceremony.—Get up and go over all the rooms in the house if you like it."

"Another time, Sir, I thank you, not now."

1. "To break a man's head and give him a plaster" was a proverbial expression, meaning that someone both gives and remedies an injury.

"Well, whenever it suits you.—You can slip in from the shrubbery at any time. And there you will find we keep our umbrellas, hanging up by that door. A good place, is not it? But" (checking himself) "you will not think it a good place, for yours were always kept in the butler's room. Ay, so it always is, I believe. One man's ways may be as good as another's, but we all like our own best. And so you must judge for yourself, whether it would be better for you to go about the house or not."

Anne, finding she might decline it, did so, very gratefully.

"We have made very few changes either!" continued the Admiral, after thinking a moment. "Very few.—We told you about the laundry-door, at Uppercross. That has been a very great improvement. The wonder was, how any family upon earth could bear with the inconvenience of its opening as it did, so long!—You will tell Sir Walter what we have done, and that Mr. Shepherd thinks it the greatest improvement the house ever had. Indeed, I must do ourselves the justice to say, that the few alterations we have made have been all very much for the better. My wife should have the credit of them, however. I have done very little besides sending away some of the large looking-glasses from my dressing-room, which was your father's. A very good man, and very much the gentleman I am sure—but I should think, Miss Elliot" (looking with serious reflection) "I should think he must be rather a dressy man for his time of life.—Such a number of looking-glasses! oh Lord! there was no getting away from oneself. So I got Sophy to lend me a hand, and we soon shifted their quarters; and now I am quite snug, with my little shaving glass in one corner, and another great thing that I never go near."

Anne, amused in spite of herself, was rather distressed for an answer, and the Admiral, fearing he might not have been civil enough, took up the subject again, to say,

"The next time you write to your good father, Miss Elliot, pray give my compliments and Mrs. Croft's, and say that we are settled here quite to our liking, and have no fault at all to find with the place. The break-fast-room chimney smokes a little, I grant you, but it is only when the wind is due north and blows hard, which may not happen three times a winter. And take it altogether, now that we have been into most of the houses hereabouts and can judge, there is not one that we like better than this. Pray say so, with my compliments. He will be glad to hear it."

Lady Russell and Mrs. Croft were very well pleased with each other; but the acquaintance which this visit began, was fated not to proceed far at present; for when it was returned, the Crofts announced themselves to be going away for a few weeks, to visit their connexions[2] in the north

2. Relatives.

of the county, and probably might not be at home again before Lady Russell would be removing to Bath.

So ended all danger to Anne of meeting Captain Wentworth at Kellynch-hall, or of seeing him in company with her friend. Every thing was safe enough, and she smiled over the many anxious feelings she had wasted on the subject.

Chapter XIV

Though Charles and Mary had remained at Lyme much longer after Mr. and Mrs. Musgrove's going, than Anne conceived they could have been at all wanted, they were yet the first of the family to be at home again, and as soon as possible after their return to Uppercross, they drove over to the lodge.—They had left Louisa beginning to sit up; but her head, though clear, was exceedingly weak, and her nerves susceptible to the highest extreme of tenderness; and though she might be pronounced to be altogether doing very well, it was still impossible to say when she might be able to bear the removal home; and her father and mother, who must return in time to receive their younger children for the Christmas holidays, had hardly a hope of being allowed to bring her with them.

They had been all in lodgings together. Mrs. Musgrove had got Mrs. Harville's children away as much as she could, every possible supply from Uppercross had been furnished, to lighten the inconvenience to the Harvilles, while the Harvilles had been wanting them to come to dinner every day; and in short, it seemed to have been only a struggle on each side as to which should be most disinterested and hospitable.

Mary had had her evils; but upon the whole, as was evident by her staying so long, she had found more to enjoy than to suffer.—Charles Hayter had been at Lyme oftener than suited her, and when they dined with the Harvilles there had been only a maid-servant to wait, and at first, Mrs. Harville had always given Mrs. Musgrove precedence; but then, she had received so very handsome an apology from her on finding out whose daughter she was, and there had been so much going on every day, there had been so many walks between their lodgings and the Harvilles, and she had got books from the library and changed them so often, that the balance had certainly been much in favour of Lyme. She had been taken to Charmouth too, and she had bathed,[3] and she had gone to church, and there were a great many more people to look at in the church at Lyme than at Uppercross,—and all this, joined to the sense of being so very useful, had made really an agreeable fortnight.

3. In the public baths of mineral water alleged to have healing properties.

Anne enquired after Captain Benwick. Mary's face was clouded directly. Charles laughed.

"Oh! Captain Benwick is very well, I believe, but he is a very odd young man. I do not know what he would be at. We asked him to come home with us for a day or two; Charles undertook to give him some shooting, and he seemed quite delighted, and for my part, I thought it was all settled; when behold! on Tuesday night, he made a very awkward sort of excuse; "he never shot" and he had "been quite misunderstood,"—and he had promised this and he had promised that, and the end of it was, I found, that he did not mean to come. I suppose he was afraid of finding it dull; but upon my word I should have thought we were lively enough at the Cottage for such a heart-broken man as Captain Benwick."

Charles laughed again and said, "Now Mary, you know very well how it really was.—It was all your doing," (turning to Anne.) "He fancied that if he went with us, he should find you close by; he fancied every body to be living in Uppercross; and when he discovered that Lady Russell lived three miles off, his heart failed him, and he had not courage to come. That is the fact, upon my honour. Mary knows it is."

But Mary did not give into it very graciously; whether from not considering Captain Benwick entitled by birth and situation to be in love with an Elliot, or from not wanting to believe Anne a greater attraction to Uppercross than herself, must be left to be guessed. Anne's goodwill, however, was not to be lessened by what she heard. She boldly acknowledged herself flattered, and continued her enquiries.

"Oh! he talks of you," cried Charles, "in such terms,"—Mary interrupted him. "I declare, Charles, I never heard him mention Anne twice all the time I was there. I declare, Anne, he never talks of you at all."

"No," admitted Charles, "I do not know that he ever does, in a general way—but however, it is a very clear thing that he admires you exceedingly.—His head is full of some books that he is reading upon your recommendation, and he wants to talk to you about them; he has found out something or other in one of them which he thinks—Oh! I cannot pretend to remember it, but it was something very fine—I overheard him telling Henrietta all about it—and then 'Miss Elliot' was spoken of in the highest terms!—Now Mary, I declare it was so, I heard it myself, and you were in the other room.—'Elegance, sweetness, beauty,' Oh! there was no end of Miss Elliot's charms."

"And I am sure," cried Mary warmly, "it was very little to his credit, if he did. Miss Harville only died last June. Such a heart is very little worth having; is it, Lady Russell? I am sure you will agree with me."

"I must see Captain Benwick before I decide," said Lady Russell, smiling.

"And that you are very likely to do very soon, I can tell you, ma'am," said Charles. "Though he had not nerves for coming away with us and setting off again afterwards to pay a formal visit here, he will make his way over to Kellynch one day by himself, you may depend on it. I told him the distance and the road, and I told him of the church's being so very well worth seeing, for as he has a taste for those sort of things, I thought that would be a good excuse, and he listened with all his understanding and soul; and I am sure from his manner that you will have him calling here soon. So, I give you notice, Lady Russell."

"Any acquaintance of Anne's will always be welcome to me," was Lady Russell's kind answer.

"Oh! as to being Anne's acquaintance," said Mary, "I think he is rather my acquaintance, for I have been seeing him every day this last fortnight."

"Well, as your joint acquaintance, then, I shall be very happy to see Captain Benwick."

"You will not find any thing very agreeable in him, I assure you, ma'am. He is one of the dullest young men that ever lived. He has walked with me, sometimes, from one end of the sands to the other, without saying a word. He is not at all a well-bred young man. I am sure you will not like him."

"There we differ, Mary," said Anne. "I think Lady Russell would like him. I think she would be so much pleased with his mind, that she would very soon see no deficiency in his manner."

"So do I, Anne," said Charles. "I am sure Lady Russell would like him. He is just Lady Russell's sort. Give him a book, and he will read all day long."

"Yes, that he will!" exclaimed Mary, tauntingly. "He will sit poring over his book, and not know when a person speaks to him, or when one drops one's scissors, or any thing that happens. Do you think Lady Russell would like that?"

Lady Russell could not help laughing. "Upon my word," said she, "I should not have supposed that my opinion of any one could have admitted of such difference of conjecture, steady and matter of fact as I may call myself. I have really a curiosity to see the person who can give occasion to such directly opposite notions. I wish he may be induced to call here. And when he does, Mary, you may depend upon hearing my opinion; but I am determined not to judge him before-hand."

"You will not like him, I will answer for it."

Lady Russell began talking of something else. Mary spoke with animation of their meeting with, or rather missing, Mr. Elliot so extraordinarily.

"He is a man," said Lady Russell, "whom I have no wish to see. His declining to be on cordial terms with the head of his family, has left a very strong impression in his disfavour with me."

This decision checked Mary's eagerness, and stopped her short in the midst of the Elliot countenance.

With regard to Captain Wentworth, though Anne hazarded no enquiries, there was voluntary communication sufficient. His spirits had been greatly recovering lately, as might be expected. As Louisa improved, he had improved; and he was now quite a different creature from what he had been the first week. He had not seen Louisa; and was so extremely fearful of any ill consequence to her from an interview, that he did not press for it at all; and, on the contrary, seemed to have a plan of going away for a week or ten days, till her head were stronger. He had talked of going down to Plymouth for a week, and wanted to persuade Captain Benwick to go with him; but, as Charles maintained to the last, Captain Benwick seemed much more disposed to ride over to Kellynch.

There can be no doubt that Lady Russell and Anne were both occasionally thinking of Captain Benwick, from this time. Lady Russell could not hear the door-bell without feeling that it might be his herald; nor could Anne return from any stroll of solitary indulgence in her father's grounds, or any visit of charity in the village, without wondering whether she might see him or hear of him. Captain Benwick came not, however. He was either less disposed for it than Charles had imagined, or he was too shy; and after giving him a week's indulgence, Lady Russell determined him to be unworthy of the interest which he had been beginning to excite.

The Musgroves came back to receive their happy boys and girls from school, bringing with them Mrs. Harville's little children, to improve the noise of Uppercross, and lessen that of Lyme. Henrietta remained with Louisa; but all the rest of the family were again in their usual quarters.

Lady Russell and Anne paid their compliments to them once, when Anne could not but feel that Uppercross was already quite alive again. Though neither Henrietta, nor Louisa, nor Charles Hayter, nor Captain Wentworth were there, the room presented as strong a contrast as could be wished, to the last state she had seen it in.

Immediately surrounding Mrs. Musgrove were the little Harvilles, whom she was sedulously guarding from the tyranny of the two children from the Cottage, expressly arrived to amuse them. On one side was a table, occupied by some chattering girls, cutting up silk and gold paper; and on the other were tressels[4] and trays, bending under the weight of brawn and cold pies, where riotous boys were holding high revel; the whole completed by a roaring Christmas fire, which seemed determined to be heard, in spite of all the noise of the others. Charles and Mary also came in, of course, during their visit; and Mrs. Musgrove made a point of paying his respects to Lady Russell, and sat down close to her for ten minutes, talking with a very raised voice, but, from the clamour of the

4. Trestles, supports for the trays that converted them to tables.

children on his knees, generally in vain. It was a fine family-piece.

Anne, judging from her own temperament, would have deemed such a domestic hurricane a bad restorative of the nerves, which Louisa's illness must have so greatly shaken; but Mrs. Musgrove, who got Anne near her on purpose to thank her most cordially, again and again, for all her attentions to them, concluded a short recapitulation of what she had suffered herself, by observing, with a happy glance round the room, that after all she had gone through, nothing was so likely to do her good as a little quiet cheerfulness at home.

Louisa was now recovering apace. Her mother could even think of her being able to join their party at home, before her brothers and sisters went to school again. The Harvilles had promised to come with her and stay at Uppercross, whenever she returned. Captain Wentworth was gone, for the present, to see his brother in Shropshire.

"I hope I shall remember, in future," said Lady Russell, as soon as they were reseated in the carriage, "not to call at Uppercross in the Christmas holidays."

Every body has their taste in noises as well as in other matters; and sounds are quite innoxious, or most distressing, by their sort rather than their quantity. When Lady Russell, not long afterwards, was entering Bath on a wet afternoon, and driving through the long course of streets from the Old Bridge to Camden-place, amidst the dash of other carriages, the heavy rumble of carts and drays, the bawling of newsmen, muffin-men and milk-men, and the ceaseless clink of pattens, she made no complaint. No, these were noises which belonged to the winter pleasures; her spirits rose under their influence; and, like Mrs. Musgrove, she was feeling, though not saying, that, after being long in the country, nothing could be so good for her as a little quiet cheerfulness.

Anne did not share these feelings. She persisted in a very determined, though very silent, disinclination for Bath; caught the first dim view of the extensive buildings, smoking in rain, without any wish of seeing them better; felt their progress through the streets to be, however disagreeable, yet too rapid; for who would be glad to see her when she arrived? And looked back, with fond regret, to the bustles of Uppercross and the seclusion of Kellynch.

Elizabeth's last letter had communicated a piece of news of some interest. Mr. Elliot was in Bath. He had called in Camden-place; had called a second time, a third; had been pointedly attentive: if Elizabeth and her father did not deceive themselves, had been taking as much pains to seek the acquaintance, and proclaim the value of the connection, as he had formerly taken pains to shew neglect. This was very wonderful, if it were true; and Lady Russell was in a state of very agreeable curiosity and perplexity about Mr. Elliot, already recanting the sentiment she had so lately expressed to Mary, of his being "a man whom she had no wish to see." She had a great wish to see him. If he really sought to reconcile himself like a dutiful branch, he must be forgiven for having dismembered himself from the paternal tree.

Anne was not animated to an equal pitch by the circumstance; but she felt that she would rather see Mr. Elliot again than not, which was more than she could say for many other persons in Bath.

She was put down in Camden-place; and Lady Russell then drove to her own lodgings, in Rivers-street.

Chapter XV

Sir Walter had taken a very good house in Camden-place, a lofty, dignified situation, such as becomes a man of consequence; and both he and Elizabeth were settled there, much to their satisfaction.

Anne entered it with a sinking heart, anticipating an imprisonment of many months, and anxiously saying to herself, "Oh! when shall I leave you again?" A degree of unexpected cordiality, however, in the welcome she received, did her good. Her father and sister were glad to see her, for the sake of shewing her the house and furniture, and met her with kindness. Her making a fourth, when they sat down to dinner, was noticed as an advantage.

Mrs. Clay was very pleasant, and very smiling; but her courtesies and smiles were more a matter of course. Anne had always felt that she would pretend what was proper on her arrival; but the complaisance of the others was unlooked for. They were evidently in excellent spirits, and she was soon to listen to the causes. They had no inclination to listen to her. After laying out[5] for some compliments of being deeply regretted in their old neighbourhood, which Anne could not pay, they had only a few faint enquiries to make, before the talk must be all their own. Uppercross excited no interest, Kellynch very little, it was all Bath.

They had the pleasure of assuring her that Bath more than answered their expectations in every respect. Their house was undoubtedly the best in Camden-place; their drawing-rooms had many decided advantages over all the others which they had either seen or heard of; and the superiority was not less in the style of the fitting-up,[6] or the taste of the furniture. Their acquaintance was exceedingly sought after. Every body was wanting to visit them. They had drawn back from many introductions, and still were perpetually having cards left by people of whom they knew nothing.

Here were funds of enjoyment! Could Anne wonder that her father and sister were happy? She might not wonder, but she must sigh that her father should feel no degradation in his change; should see nothing

---

5. Exerting themselves to gain an object.
6. Decorating.

to regret in the duties and dignity of the resident land-holder; should find so much to be vain of in the littlenesses of a town; and she must sigh, and smile, and wonder too, as Elizabeth threw open the folding-doors, and walked with exultation from one drawing-room to the other, boasting of their space, at the possibility of that woman, who had been mistress of Kellynch Hall, finding extent to be proud of between two walls, perhaps thirty feet asunder.

But this was not all which they had to make them happy. They had Mr. Elliot, too. Anne had a great deal to hear of Mr. Elliot. He was not only pardoned, they were delighted with him. He had been in Bath about a fortnight; (he had passed through Bath in November, in his way to London, when the intelligence of Sir Walter's being settled there had of course reached him, though only twenty-four hours in the place, but he had not been able to avail himself of it): but he had now been a fortnight in Bath, and his first object, on arriving, had been to leave his card in Camden-place, following it up by such assiduous endeavours to meet, and, when they did meet, by such great openness of conduct, such readiness to apologize for the past, such solicitude to be received as a relation again, that their former good understanding was completely re-established.

They had not a fault to find in him. He had explained away all the appearance of neglect on his own side. It had originated in misapprehension entirely. He had never had an idea of throwing himself off; he had feared that he was thrown off, but knew not why; and delicacy had kept him silent. Upon the hint of having spoken disrespectfully or carelessly of the family, and the family honours, he was quite indignant. He, who had ever boasted of being an Elliot, and whose feelings, as to connection, were only too strict to suit the unfeudal tone of the present day! He was astonished, indeed! But his character and general conduct must refute it. He could refer Sir Walter to all who knew him; and, certainly, the pains he had been taking on this, the first opportunity of reconciliation, to be restored to the footing of a relation and heir-presumptive, was a strong proof of his opinions on the subject.

The circumstances of his marriage too were found to admit of much extenuation. This was an article not to be entered on by himself; but a very intimate friend of his, a Colonel Wallis, a highly respectable man, perfectly the gentleman, (and not an ill-looking man, Sir Walter added) who was living in very good style in Marlborough Buildings, and had, at his own particular request, been admitted to their acquaintance through Mr. Elliot, had mentioned one or two things relative to the marriage, which made a material difference in the discredit of it.

Colonel Wallis had known Mr. Elliot long, had been well acquainted also with his wife, had perfectly understood the whole story. She was certainly not a woman of family, but well educated, accomplished, rich, and excessively in love with his friend. There had been the charm. She had sought him. Without that attraction, not all her money would have tempted Elliot, and Sir Walter was, moreover, assured of her having been a very fine[7] woman. Here was a great deal to soften the business. A very fine woman, with a large fortune, in love with him! Sir Walter seemed to admit it as complete apology, and though Elizabeth could not see the circumstance in quite so favourable a light, she allowed it be a great extenuation.

Mr. Elliot had called repeatedly, had dined with them once, evidently delighted by the distinction of being asked, for they gave no dinners in general; delighted, in short, by every proof of cousinly notice, and placing his whole happiness in being on intimate terms in Camden-place.

Anne listened, but without quite understanding it. Allowances, large allowances, she knew, must be made for the ideas of those who spoke. She heard it all under embellishment. All that sounded extravagant or irrational in the progress of the reconciliation might have no origin but in the language of the relators. Still, however, she had the sensation of there being something more than immediately appeared, in Mr. Elliot's wishing, after an interval of so many years, to be well received by them. In a worldly view, he had nothing to gain by being on terms with Sir Walter, nothing to risk by a state of variance. In all probability he was already the richer of the two, and the Kellynch estate would as surely be his hereafter as the title. A sensible man! and he had looked like a *very* sensible man, why should it be an object to him? She could only offer one solution; it was, perhaps, for Elizabeth's sake. There might really have been a liking formerly, though convenience and accident had drawn him a different way, and now that he could afford to please himself, he might mean to pay his addresses to her. Elizabeth was certainly very handsome, with well-bred, elegant manners, and her character might never have been penetrated by Mr. Elliot, knowing her but in public, and when very young himself. How her temper and understanding might bear the investigation of his present keener time of life was another concern, and rather a fearful one. Most earnestly did she wish that he might not be too nice, or too observant, if Elizabeth were his object; and that Elizabeth was disposed to believe herself so, and that her friend Mrs. Clay was encouraging the idea, seemed apparent by a glance or two between them, while Mr. Elliot's frequent visits were talked of.

Anne mentioned the glimpses she had had of him at Lyme, but without being much attended to. "Oh! yes, perhaps, it had been Mr. Elliot. They did not know. It might be him, perhaps." They could not listen to her description of him. They were describing him themselves; Sir Walter especially. He did justice to his very gentlemanlike appearance, his

7. Good-looking.

air of elegance and fashion, his good shaped face, his sensible eye, but, at the same time, "must lament his being very much under-hung,[8] a defect which time seemed to have increased; nor could he pretend to say that ten years had not altered almost every feature for the worse. Mr. Elliot appeared to think that he (Sir Walter) was looking exactly as he had done when they last parted;" but Sir Walter had "not been able to return the compliment entirely, which had embarrassed him. He did not mean to complain, however. Mr. Elliot was better to look at than most men, and he had no objection to being seen with him any where."

Mr. Elliot, and his friends in Marlborough Buildings, were talked of the whole evening. "Colonel Wallis had been so impatient to be introduced to them! and Mr. Elliot so anxious that he should!" And there was a Mrs. Wallis, at present only known to them by description, as she was in daily expectation of her confinement;[9] but Mr. Elliot spoke of her as "a most charming woman, quite worthy of being known in Camden-place," and as soon as she recovered, they were to be acquainted. Sir Walter thought much of Mrs. Wallis; she was said to be an excessively pretty woman, beautiful. "He longed to see her. He hoped she might make some amends for the many very plain faces he was continually passing in the streets. The worst of Bath was, the number of its plain women. He did not mean to say that there were no pretty women, but the number of the plain was out of all proportion. He had frequently observed, as he walked, that one handsome face would be followed by thirty, or five and thirty frights; and once, as he had stood in a shop in Bond-street, he had counted eighty-seven women go by, one after another, without there being a tolerable face among them. It had been a frosty morning, to be sure, a sharp frost, which hardly one woman in a thousand could stand the test of. But still, there certainly were a dreadful multitude of ugly women in Bath; and as for the men! they were infinitely worse. Such scare-crows as the streets were full of! It was evident how little the women were used to the sight of any thing tolerable, by the effect which a man of decent appearance produced. He had never walked any where arm in arm with Colonel Wallis, (who was a fine military figure, though sandy-haired) without observing that every woman's eye was upon him; every woman's eye was sure to be upon Colonel Wallis." Modest Sir Walter! He was not allowed to escape, however. His daughter and Mrs. Clay united in hinting that Colonel Wallis's companion might have as good a figure as Colonel Wallis, and certainly was not sandy-haired.

"How is Mary looking?" said Sir Walter, in the height of his good humour. "The last time I saw her, she had a red nose, but I hope that may not happen every day."

"Oh! no, that must have been quite accidental. In general she has

8. Having a projecting lower jaw.
9. Lying-in for childbirth.

been in very good health, and very good looks since Michaelmas."

"If I thought it would not tempt her to go out in sharp winds, and
grow coarse, I would send her a new hat and pelisse."

Anne was considering whether she should venture to suggest that a
gown, or a cap, would not be liable to any such misuse, when a knock
at the door suspended every thing. "A knock at the door! and so late! It
was ten o'clock. Could it be Mr. Elliot? They knew he was to dine in
Lansdown Crescent. It was possible that he might stop in his way home,
to ask them how they did. They could think of no one else. Mrs. Clay
decidedly thought it Mr. Elliot's knock." Mrs. Clay was right. With all
the state which a butler and foot-boy could give, Mr. Elliot was ushered
into the room.

It was the same, the very same man, with no difference but of dress.
Anne drew a little back, while the others received his compliments, and
her sister his apologies for calling at so unusual an hour, but "he could
not be so near without wishing to know that neither she nor her friend
had taken cold the day before, etc. etc." which was all as politely done,
and as politely taken as possible, but her part must follow then. Sir
Walter talked of his youngest daughter; "Mr. Elliot must give him leave
to present him to his youngest daughter"—(there was no occasion for
remembering Mary) and Anne, smiling and blushing, very becomingly
shewed to Mr. Elliot the pretty features which he had by no means
forgotten, and instantly saw, with amusement at his little start of surprise, that he had not been at all aware of who she was. He looked
completely astonished, but not more astonished than pleased; his eyes
brightened, and with the most perfect alacrity he welcomed the relationship, alluded to the past, and entreated to be received as an acquaintance already. He was quite as good-looking as he had appeared at
Lyme, his countenance improved by speaking, and his manners were so
exactly what they ought to be, so polished, so easy, so particularly agreeable, that she could compare them in excellence to only one person's
manners. They were not the same, but they were, perhaps, equally
good.

He sat down with them, and improved their conversation very much.
There could be no doubt of his being a sensible man. Ten minutes were
enough to certify that. His tone, his expressions, his choice of subject,
his knowing where to stop,—it was all the operation of a sensible, discerning mind. As soon as he could, he began to talk to her of Lyme,
wanting to compare opinions respecting the place, but especially wanting to speak of the circumstance of their happening to be guests in the
same inn at the same time, to give his own route, understand something
of hers, and regret that he should have lost such an opportunity of paying his respects to her. She gave him a short account of her party, and
business at Lyme. His regret increased as he listened. He had spent his
whole solitary evening in the room adjoining theirs; had heard voices—

mirth continually; thought they must be a most delightful set of people—longed to be with them; but certainly without the smallest suspicion of his possessing the shadow of a right to introduce himself. If he had but asked who the party were! The name of Musgrove would have told him enough. "Well, it would serve to cure him of an absurd practice of never asking a question at an inn, which he had adopted, when quite a young man, on the principle of its being very ungenteel to be curious.

"The notions of a young man of one or two and twenty," said he, "as to what is necessary in manners to make him quite the thing, are more absurd, I believe, than those of any other set of beings in the world. The folly of the means they often employ is only to be equalled by the folly of what they have in view."

But he must not be addressing his reflections to Anne alone; he knew it; he was soon diffused again among the others, and it was only at intervals that he could return to Lyme.

His enquiries, however, produced at length an account of the scene she had been engaged in there, soon after his leaving the place. Having alluded to "an accident," he must hear the whole. When he questioned, Sir Walter and Elizabeth began to question also; but the difference in their manner of doing it could not be unfelt. She could only compare Mr. Elliot to Lady Russell, in the wish of really comprehending what had passed, and in the degree of concern for what she must have suffered in witnessing it.

He staid an hour with them. The elegant little clock on the mantle-piece had struck "eleven with its silver sounds,"[1] and the watchman was beginning to be heard at a distance telling the same tale, before Mr. Elliot or any of them seemed to feel that he had been there long.

Anne could not have supposed it possible that her first evening in Camden-place could have passed so well!

Chapter XVI

There was one point which Anne, on returning to her family, would have been more thankful to ascertain, even than Mr. Elliot's being in love with Elizabeth, which was, her father's not being in love with Mrs. Clay; and she was very far from easy about it, when she had been at home a few hours. On going down to breakfast the next morning, she found there had just been a decent pretence on the lady's side of meaning to leave them. She could imagine Mrs. Clay to have said, that "now Miss Anne was come, she could not suppose herself at all wanted;" for

1. Perhaps an allusion to Alexander Pope's *The Rape of the Lock* (1714) 1.18: "And the pressed watch returned a silver sound."

Elizabeth was replying, in a sort of whisper, "That must not be any reason, indeed. I assure you I feel it none. She is nothing to me, compared with you;" and she was in full time to hear her father say, "My dear Madam, this must not be. As yet, you have seen nothing of Bath. You have been here only to be useful. You must not run away from us now. You must stay to be acquainted with Mrs. Wallis, the beautiful Mrs. Wallis. To your fine mind, I well know the sight of beauty is a real gratification."

He spoke and looked so much in earnest, that Anne was not surprised to see Mrs. Clay stealing a glance at Elizabeth and herself. Her countenance, perhaps, might express some watchfulness; but the praise of the fine mind did not appear to excite a thought in her sister. The lady could not but yield to such joint entreaties, and promise to stay.

In the course of the same morning, Anne and her father chancing to be alone together, he began to compliment her on her improved looks; he thought her "less thin in her person, in her cheeks; her skin, her complexion, greatly improved—clearer, fresher. Had she been using any thing in particular?" "No, nothing." "Merely Gowland,"[2] he supposed. "No, nothing at all." "Ha! he was surprised at that;" and added, "Certainly you cannot do better than continue as you are; you cannot be better than well; or I should recommend Gowland, the constant use of Gowland, during the spring months. Mrs. Clay has been using it at my recommendation, and you see what it has done for her. You see how it has carried away her freckles."

If Elizabeth could but have heard this! Such personal praise might have struck her, especially as it did not appear to Anne that the freckles were at all lessened. But every thing must take its chance. The evil of the marriage would be much diminished, if Elizabeth were also to marry. As for herself, she might always command a home with Lady Russell.

Lady Russell's composed mind and polite manners were put to some trial on this point, in her intercourse in Camden-place. The sight of Mrs. Clay in such favour, and of Anne so overlooked, was a perpetual provocation to her there; and vexed her as much when she was away, as a person in Bath who drinks the water, gets all the new publications, and has a very large acquaintance, has time to be vexed.

As Mr. Elliot became known to her, she grew more charitable, or more indifferent, towards the others. His manners were an immediate recommendation; and on conversing with him she found the solid so fully supporting the superficial, that she was at first, as she told Anne, almost ready to exclaim, "Can this be Mr. Elliot?" and could not seriously picture to herself a more agreeable or estimable man. Every thing united in him; good understanding, correct opinions, knowledge of the

2. Gowland's lotion, intended for the face, was supposed to remedy ailments of the skin.

world, and a warm heart. He had strong feelings of family-attachment
and family-honour, without pride or weakness; he lived with the liberality of a man of fortune, without display; he judged for himself in every
thing essential, without defying public opinion in any point of worldly
decorum. He was steady, observant, moderate, candid; never run away
with by spirits or by selfishness, which fancied itself strong feeling; and
yet, with a sensibility to what was amiable and lovely, and a value for
all the felicities of domestic life, which characters of fancied enthusiasm
and violent agitation seldom really possess. She was sure that he had not
been happy in marriage. Colonel Wallis said it, and Lady Russell saw
it; but it had been no unhappiness to sour his mind, nor (she began
pretty soon to suspect) to prevent his thinking of a second choice. Her
satisfaction in Mr. Elliot outweighed all the plague of Mrs. Clay.

It was now some years since Anne had begun to learn that she and
her excellent friend could sometimes think differently; and it did not
surprise her, therefore, that Lady Russell should see nothing suspicious
or inconsistent, nothing to require more motives than appeared, in Mr.
Elliot's great desire of a reconciliation. In Lady Russell's view, it was
perfectly natural that Mr. Elliot, at a mature time of life, should feel it a
most desirable object, and what would very generally recommend him,
among all sensible people, to be on good terms with the head of his
family; the simplest process in the world of time upon a head naturally
clear, and only erring in the heyday of youth. Anne presumed, however,
still to smile about it; and at last to mention "Elizabeth." Lady Russell
listened, and looked, and made only this cautious reply: "Elizabeth!
Very well. Time will explain."

It was a reference to the future, which Anne, after a little observation,
felt she must submit to. She could determine nothing at present. In that
house Elizabeth must be first; and she was in the habit of such general
observance as "Miss Elliot," that any particularity of attention seemed
almost impossible. Mr. Elliot, too, it must be remembered, had not
been a widower seven months. A little delay on his side might be very
excusable. In fact, Anne could never see the crape[3] round his hat, without fearing that she was the inexcusable one, in attributing to him such
imaginations; for though his marriage had not been very happy, still it
had existed so many years that she could not comprehend a very rapid
recovery from the awful[4] impression of its being dissolved.

However it might end, he was without any question their pleasantest
acquaintance in Bath; she saw nobody equal to him; and it was a great
indulgence now and then to talk to him about Lyme, which he seemed
to have as lively a wish to see again, and to see more of, as herself. They
went through the particulars of their first meeting a great many times.
He gave her to understand that he had looked at her with some earnest-

3. A sign of mourning.
4. Awe-inspiring.

ness. She knew it well; and she remembered another person's look also.

They did not always think alike. His value for rank and connexion she perceived to be greater than hers. It was not merely complaisance, it must be a liking to the cause, which made him enter warmly into her father and sister's solicitudes on a subject which she thought unworthy to excite them. The Bath paper one morning announced the arrival of the Dowager Viscountess Dalrymple, and her daughter, the Honourable Miss Carteret; and all the comfort of No. —, Camden-place, was swept away for many days; for the Dalrymples (in Anne's opinion, most unfortunately) were cousins of the Elliots; and the agony was, how to introduce themselves properly.

Anne had never seen her father and sister before in contact with nobility, and she must acknowledge herself disappointed. She had hoped better things from their high ideas of their own situation in life, and was reduced to form a wish which she had never foreseen—a wish that they had more pride; for "our cousins Lady Dalrymple and Miss Carteret;" "our cousins, the Dalrymples," sounded in her ears all day long.

Sir Walter had once been in company with the late Viscount, but had never seen any of the rest of the family, and the difficulties of the case arose from there having been a suspension of all intercourse by letters of ceremony, ever since the death of that said late Viscount, when, in consequence of a dangerous illness of Sir Walter's at the same time, there had been an unlucky omission at Kellynch. No letter of condolence had been sent to Ireland. The neglect had been visited on the head of the sinner, for when poor Lady Elliot died herself, no letter of condolence was received at Kellynch, and, consequently, there was but too much reason to apprehend that the Dalrymples considered the relationship as closed. How to have this anxious business set to rights, and be admitted as cousins again, was the question; and it was a question which, in a more rational manner, neither Lady Russell nor Mr. Elliot thought unimportant. "Family connexions were always worth preserving, good company always worth seeking; Lady Dalrymple had taken a house, for three months, in Laura-place, and would be living in style. She had been at Bath the year before, and Lady Russell had heard her spoken of as a charming woman. It was very desirable that the connexion should be renewed, if it could be done, without any compromise of propriety on the side of the Elliots."

Sir Walter, however, would choose his own means, and at last wrote a very fine letter of ample explanation, regret and entreaty, to his right honourable cousin. Neither Lady Russell nor Mr. Elliot could admire the letter; but it did all that was wanted, in bringing three lines of scrawl from the Dowager Viscountess. "She was very much honoured, and should be happy in their acquaintance." The toils of the business were over, the sweets began. They visited in Laura-place, they had the cards of Dowager Viscountess Dalrymple, and the Hon. Miss Carteret, to be arranged wherever they might be most visible; and "Our cousins in Laura-place,"—"Our cousins, Lady Dalrymple and Miss Carteret," were talked of to every body.

Anne was ashamed. Had Lady Dalrymple and her daughter even been very agreeable, she would still have been ashamed of the agitation they created, but they were nothing. There was no superiority of manner, accomplishment, or understanding. Lady Dalrymple had acquired the name of "a charming woman," because she had a smile and a civil answer for every body. Miss Carteret, with still less to say, was so plain and so awkward, that she would never have been tolerated in Camden-place but for her birth.

Lady Russell confessed that she had expected something better; but yet "it was an acquaintance worth having," and when Anne ventured to speak her opinion of them to Mr. Elliot, he agreed to their being nothing in themselves, but still maintained that as a family connexion, as good company, as those who would collect good company around them, they had their value. Anne smiled and said,

"My idea of good company, Mr. Elliot, is the company of clever, well-informed people, who have a great deal of conversation; that is what I call good company."

"You are mistaken," said he gently, "that is not good company, that is the best. Good company requires only birth, education and manners, and with regard to education is not very nice. Birth and good manners are essential; but a little learning is by no means a dangerous thing in good company, on the contrary, it will do very well. My cousin, Anne, shakes her head. She is not satisfied. She is fastidious. My dear cousin, (sitting down by her) you have a better right to be fastidious than almost any other woman I know; but will it answer?[5] Will it make you happy? Will it not be wiser to accept the society of these good ladies in Laura-place, and enjoy all the advantages of the connexion as far as possible? You may depend upon it, that they will move in the first set in Bath this winter, and as rank is rank, your being known to be related to them will have its use in fixing your family (our family let me say) in that degree of consideration which we must all wish for."

"Yes," sighed Anne, "we shall, indeed, be known to be related to them!"—then recollecting herself, and not wishing to be answered, she added, "I certainly do think there has been by far too much trouble taken to procure the acquaintance. I suppose (smiling) I have more pride than any of you; but I confess it does vex me, that we should be so solicitous to have the relationship acknowledged, which we may be very sure is a matter of perfect indifference to them."

"Pardon me, my dear cousin, you are unjust to your own claims. In

5. Suffice, serve the purpose.

London, perhaps, in your present quiet style of living, it might be as you say; but in Bath, Sir Walter Elliot and his family will always be worth knowing, always acceptable as acquaintance."

"Well," said Anne, "I certainly am proud, too proud to enjoy a welcome which depends so entirely upon place."

"I love your indignation," said he; "it is very natural. But here you are in Bath, and the object is to be established here with all the credit and dignity which ought to belong to Sir Walter Elliot. You talk of being proud, I am called proud I know, and I shall not wish to believe myself otherwise, for our pride, if investigated, would have the same object, I have no doubt, though the kind may seem a little different. In one point, I am sure, my dear cousin, (he continued, speaking lower, though there was no one else in the room) in one point, I am sure, we must feel alike. We must feel that every addition to your father's society, among his equals or superiors, may be of use in diverting his thoughts from those who are beneath him."

He looked, as he spoke, to the seat which Mrs. Clay had been lately occupying, a sufficient explanation of what he particularly meant; and though Anne could not believe in their having the same sort of pride, she was pleased with him for not liking Mrs. Clay; and her conscience admitted that his wishing to promote her father's getting great acquaintance, was more than excusable in the view of defeating her.

Chapter XVII

While Sir Walter and Elizabeth were assiduously pushing their good fortune in Laura-place, Anne was renewing an acquaintance of a very different description.

She had called on her former governess, and had heard from her of there being an old school-fellow in Bath, who had the two strong claims on her attention, of past kindness and present suffering. Miss Hamilton, now Mrs. Smith, had shewn her kindness in one of those periods of her life when it had been most valuable. Anne had gone unhappy to school, grieving for the loss of a mother whom she had dearly loved, feeling her separation from home, and suffering as a girl of fourteen, of strong sensibility and not high spirits, must suffer at such a time; and Miss Hamilton, three years older than herself, but still from her want of near relations and a settled home, remaining another year at school, had been useful and good to her in a way which had considerably lessened her misery, and could never be remembered with indifference.

Miss Hamilton had left school, had married not long afterwards, was said to have married a man of fortune, and this was all that Anne had known of her, till now that their governess's account brought her situation forward in a more decided but very different form.

She was a widow, and poor. Her husband had been extravagant; and at his death, about two years before, had left his affairs dreadfully involved. She had had difficulties of every sort to contend with, and in addition to these distresses, had been afflicted with a severe rheumatic fever, which finally settling in her legs, had made her for the present a cripple. She had come to Bath on that account, and was now in lodgings near the hotbaths, living in a very humble way, unable even to afford herself the comfort of a servant, and of course almost excluded from society.

Their mutual friend answered for the satisfaction which a visit from Miss Elliot would give Mrs. Smith, and Anne therefore lost no time in going. She mentioned nothing of what she had heard, or what she intended, at home. It would excite no proper interest there. She only consulted Lady Russell, who entered thoroughly into her sentiments, and was most happy to convey her as near to Mrs. Smith's lodgings in Westgate-buildings, as Anne chose to be taken.

The visit was paid, their acquaintance re-established, their interest in each other more than re-kindled. The first ten minutes had its awkwardness and its emotion. Twelve years were gone since they had parted, and each presented a somewhat different person from what the other had imagined. Twelve years had changed Anne from the blooming, silent, unformed girl of fifteen, to the elegant little woman of seven and twenty, with every beauty excepting bloom, and with manners as consciously right as they were invariably gentle; and twelve years had transformed the fine-looking, well-grown Miss Hamilton, in all the glow of health and confidence of superiority, into a poor, infirm, helpless widow, receiving the visit of her former protegeé as a favour; but all that was uncomfortable in the meeting had soon passed away, and left only the interesting charm of remembering former partialities and talking over old times.

Anne found in Mrs. Smith the good sense and agreeable manners which she had almost ventured to depend on, and a disposition to converse and be cheerful beyond her expectation. Neither the dissipations of the past—and she had lived very much in the world, nor the restrictions of the present; neither sickness nor sorrow seemed to have closed her heart or ruined her spirits.

In the course of a second visit she talked with great openness, and Anne's astonishment increased. She could scarcely imagine a more cheerless situation in itself than Mrs. Smith's. She had been very fond of her husband,—she had buried him. She had been used to affluence,—it was gone. She had no child to connect her with life and happiness again, no relations to assist in the arrangement of perplexed affairs, no health to make all the rest supportable. Her accommodations were limited to a noisy parlour, and a dark bed-room behind, with no possibility of moving from one to the other without assistance, which there was

only one servant in the house to afford, and she never quitted the house
but to be conveyed into the warm bath.[6]—Yet, in spite of all this, Anne
had reason to believe that she had moments only of languor and depression, to hours of occupation and enjoyment. How could it be?—She
watched—observed—reflected—and finally determined that this was
not a case of fortitude or of resignation only.—A submissive spirit might
be patient, a strong understanding would supply resolution, but here
was something more; here was that elasticity of mind, that disposition to
be comforted, that power of turning readily from evil to good, and of
finding employment which carried her out of herself, which was from
Nature alone. It was the choicest gift of Heaven; and Anne viewed her
friend as one of those instances in which, by a merciful appointment, it
seems designed to counterbalance almost every other want.

There had been a time, Mrs. Smith told her, when her spirits had
nearly failed. She could not call herself an invalid now, compared with
her state on first reaching Bath. Then, she had indeed been a pitiable
object—for she had caught cold on the journey, and had hardly taken
possession of her lodgings, before she was again confined to her bed,
and suffering under severe and constant pain; and all this among strangers—with the absolute necessity of having a regular nurse, and finances
at that moment particularly unfit to meet any extraordinary expense.
She had weathered it however, and could truly say that it had done her
good. It had increased her comforts by making her feel herself to be in
good hands. She had seen too much of the world, to expect sudden or
disinterested attachment any where, but her illness had proved to her
that her landlady had a character to preserve, and would not use her ill;
and she had been particularly fortunate in her nurse, as a sister of her
landlady, a nurse by profession, and who had always a home in that
house when unemployed, chanced to be at liberty just in time to attend
her.—"And she," said Mrs. Smith, "besides nursing me most admirably, has really proved an invaluable acquaintance.—As soon as I could
use my hands, she taught me to knit, which has been a great amusement; and she put me in the way of making these little thread-cases,
pin-cushions and card-racks, which you always find me so busy about,
and which supply me with the means of doing a little good to one or
two very poor families in this neighbourhood. She has a large acquaintance, of course professionally, among those who can afford to buy, and
she disposes of my merchandize. She always takes the right time for
applying. Every body's heart is open, you know, when they have
recently escaped from severe pain, or are recovering the blessing of
health, and nurse Rooke thoroughly understands when to speak. She is
a shrewd, intelligent, sensible woman. Hers is a line for seeing human
nature; and she has a fund of good sense and observation which, as a

6. Of the supposedly medicinal waters for which Bath was famous.

companion, make her infinitely superior to thousands of those who having only received "the best education in the world," know nothing worth
attending to. Call it gossip if you will; but when nurse Rooke has half
an hour's leisure to bestow on me, she is sure to have something to relate
that is entertaining and profitable, something that makes one know one's
species better. One likes to hear what is going on, to be *au fait*[7] as to
the newest modes of being trifling and silly. To me, who live so much
alone, her conversation I assure you is a treat."

Anne, far from wishing to cavil at the pleasure, replied, "I can easily
believe it. Women of that class have great opportunities, and if they are
intelligent may be well worth listening to. Such varieties of human
nature as they are in the habit of witnessing! And it is not merely in its
follies, that they are well read; for they see it occasionally under every
circumstance that can be most interesting or affecting. What instances
must pass before them of ardent, disinterested, self-denying attachment,
of heroism, fortitude, patience, resignation—of all the conflicts and all
the sacrifices that ennoble us most. A sick chamber may often furnish
the worth of volumes."

"Yes," said Mrs. Smith more doubtingly, "sometimes it may, though
I fear its lessons are not often in the elevated style you describe. Here
and there, human nature may be great in times of trial, but generally
speaking it is its weakness and not its strength that appears in a sick
chamber; it is selfishness and impatience rather than generosity and fortitude, that one hears of. There is so little real friendship in the world!—
and unfortunately" (speaking low and tremulously) "there are so many
who forget to think seriously till it is almost too late."

Anne saw the misery of such feelings. The husband had not been
what he ought, and the wife had been led among that part of mankind
which made her think worse of the world, than she hoped it deserved.
It was but a passing emotion however with Mrs. Smith, she shook it off,
and soon added in a different tone,

"I do not suppose the situation my friend Mrs. Rooke is in at present,
will furnish much either to interest or edify me.—She is only nursing
Mrs. Wallis of Marlborough-buildings—a mere pretty, silly, expensive,
fashionable woman, I believe—and of course will have nothing to report
but of lace and finery.—I mean to make my profit of Mrs. Wallis, however. She has plenty of money, and I intend she shall buy all the high-
priced things I have in hand now."

Anne had called several times on her friend, before the existence of
such a person was known in Camden-place. At last, it became necessary
to speak of her.—Sir Walter, Elizabeth and Mrs. Clay returned one
morning from Laura-place, with a sudden invitation from Lady Dalrymple for the same evening, and Anne was already engaged, to spend that

7. Aware.

evening in Westgate-buildings. She was not sorry for the excuse. They were only asked, she was sure, because Lady Dalrymple being kept at home by a bad cold, was glad to make use of the relationship which had been so pressed on her,—and she declined on her own account with great alacrity—"She was engaged to spend the evening with an old schoolfellow." They were not much interested in any thing relative to Anne, but still there were questions enough asked, to make it understood what this old schoolfellow was; and Elizabeth was disdainful, and Sir Walter severe.

"Westgate-buildings!" said he; "and who is Miss Anne Elliot to be visiting in Westgate-buildings?—A Mrs. Smith. A widow Mrs. Smith,—and who was her husband? One of the five thousand Mr. Smiths whose names are to be met with every where. And what is her attraction? That she is old and sickly.—Upon my word, Miss Anne Elliot, you have the most extraordinary taste! Every thing that revolts other people, low company, paltry rooms, foul air, disgusting associations are inviting to you. But surely, you may put off this old lady till to-morrow. She is not so near her end, I presume, but that she may hope to see another day. What is her age? Forty?"

"No, Sir, she is not one and thirty; but I do not think I can put off my engagement, because it is the only evening for some time which will at once suit her and myself.—She goes into the warm bath to-morrow, and for the rest of the week you know we are engaged."

"But what does Lady Russell think of this acquaintance?" asked Elizabeth.

"She sees nothing to blame in it," replied Anne; "on the contrary, she approves it; and has generally taken me, when I have called on Mrs. Smith."

"Westgate-buildings must have been rather surprised by the appearance of a carriage drawn up near its pavement!" observed Sir Walter.— "Sir Henry Russell's widow, indeed, has no honours[8] to distinguish her arms; but still, it is a handsome equipage, and no doubt is well known to convey a Miss Elliot.—A widow Mrs. Smith, lodging in Westgate-buildings!—A poor widow, barely able to live, between thirty and forty—a mere Mrs. Smith, an every day Mrs. Smith, of all people and all names in the world, to be the chosen friend of Miss Anne Elliot, and to be preferred by her, to her own family connections among the nobility of England and Ireland! Mrs. Smith, such a name!"

Mrs. Clay, who had been present while all this passed, now thought it advisable to leave the room, and Anne could have said much and did long to say a little, in defence of *her* friend's not very dissimilar claims to theirs, but her sense of personal respect to her father prevented her. She made no reply. She left it to himself to recollect, that Mrs. Smith

---

8. Emblems of special achievement added to a coat of arms.

was not the only widow in Bath between thirty and forty, with little to live on, and no sirname of dignity.

Anne kept her appointment; the others kept theirs, and of course she heard the next morning that they had had a delightful evening.—She had been the only one of the set absent; for Sir Walter and Elizabeth had not only been quite at her ladyship's service themselves, but had actually been happy to be employed by her in collecting others, and had been at the trouble of inviting both Lady Russell and Mr. Elliot; and Mr. Elliot had made a point of leaving Colonel Wallis early, and Lady Russell had fresh arranged all her evening engagements in order to wait on her. Anne had the whole history of all that such an evening could supply, from Lady Russell. To her, its greatest interest must be, in having been very much talked of between her friend and Mr. Elliot, in having been wished for, regretted, and at the same time honoured for staying away in such a cause.—Her kind, compassionate visits to this old schoolfellow, sick and reduced, seemed to have quite delighted Mr. Elliot. He thought her a most extraordinary young woman; in her temper, manners, mind, a model of female excellence. He could meet even Lady Russell in a discussion of her merits; and Anne could not be given to understand so much by her friend, could not know herself to be so highly rated by a sensible man, without many of those agreeable sensations which her friend meant to create.

Lady Russell was now perfectly decided in her opinion of Mr. Elliot. She was as much convinced of his meaning to gain Anne in time, as of his deserving her; and was beginning to calculate the number of weeks which would free him from all the remaining restraints of widowhood, and leave him at liberty to exert his most open powers of pleasing. She would not speak to Anne with half the certainty she felt on the subject, she would venture on little more than hints of what might be hereafter, of a possible attachment on his side, of the desirableness of the alliance, supposing such attachment to be real, and returned. Anne heard her, and made no violent exclamations. She only smiled, blushed, and gently shook her head.

"I am no match-maker, as you well know," said Lady Russell, "being much too well aware of the uncertainty of all human events and calculations. I only mean that if Mr. Elliot should some time hence pay his addresses to you, and if you should be disposed to accept him, I think there would be every possibility of your being happy together. A most suitable connection every body must consider it—but I think it might be a very happy one."

"Mr. Elliot is an exceedingly agreeable man, and in many respects I think highly of him," said Anne; "but we should not suit."

Lady Russell let this pass, and only said in rejoinder, "I own that to be able to regard you as the future mistress of Kellynch, the future Lady Elliot—to look forward and see you occupying your dear mother's place,

succeeding to all her rights, and all her popularity, as well as to all her
virtues, would be the highest possible gratification to me.—You are your
mother's self in countenance and disposition; and if I might be allowed
to fancy you such as she was, in situation, and name, and home, presiding and blessing in the same spot, and only superior to her in being
more highly valued! My dearest Anne, it would give me more delight
than is often felt at my time of life!"

Anne was obliged to turn away, to rise, to walk to a distant table, and,
leaning there in pretended employment, try to subdue the feelings this
picture excited. For a few moments her imagination and her heart were
bewitched. The idea of becoming what her mother had been; of having
the precious name of "Lady Elliot" first revived in herself; of being
restored to Kellynch, calling it her home again, her home for ever, was
a charm which she could not immediately resist. Lady Russell said not
another word, willing to leave the matter to its own operation; and
believing that, could Mr. Elliot at that moment with propriety have
spoken for himself!—She believed, in short, what Anne did not believe.
The same image of Mr. Elliot speaking for himself, brought Anne to
composure again. The charm of Kellynch and of "Lady Elliot" all faded
away. She never could accept him. And it was not only that her feelings
were still adverse to any man save one; her judgment, on a serious consideration of the possibilities of such a case, was against Mr. Elliot.

Though they had now been acquainted a month, she could not be
satisfied that she really knew his character. That he was a sensible man,
an agreeable man,—that he talked well, professed good opinions,
seemed to judge properly and as a man of principle,—this was all clear
enough. He certainly knew what was right, nor could she fix on any one
article of moral duty evidently transgressed; but yet she would have been
afraid to answer for his conduct. She distrusted the past, if not the present. The names which occasionally dropt of former associates, the allu-
sions to former practices and pursuits, suggested suspicions not
favourable of what he had been. She saw that there had been bad habits;
that Sunday-travelling[9] had been a common thing; that there had been
a period of his life (and probably not a short one) when he had been, at
least, careless on all serious matters; and, though he might now think
very differently, who could answer for the true sentiments of a clever,
cautious man, grown old enough to appreciate a fair character?[1] How
could it ever be ascertained that his mind was truly cleansed?

Mr. Elliot was rational, discreet, polished,—but he was not open.
There was never any burst of feeling, any warmth of indignation or
delight, at the evil or good of others. This, to Anne, was a decided
imperfection. Her early impressions were incurable. She prized the
frank, the open-hearted, the eager character beyond all others. Warmth

9. Traveling on Sunday was disapproved of by members of many Protestant denominations.
1. Reputation.

and enthusiasm did captivate her still. She felt that she could so much more depend upon the sincerity of those who sometimes looked or said a careless or a hasty thing, than of those whose presence of mind never varied, whose tongue never slipped.

Mr. Elliot was too generally agreeable. Various as were the tempers in her father's house, he pleased them all. He endured too well,—stood too well with everybody. He had spoken to her with some degree of openness of Mrs. Clay; had appeared completely to see what Mrs. Clay was about, and to hold her in contempt; and yet Mrs. Clay found him as agreeable as anybody.

Lady Russell saw either less or more than her young friend, for she saw nothing to excite distrust. She could not imagine a man more exactly what he ought to be than Mr. Elliot; nor did she ever enjoy a sweeter feeling than the hope of seeing him receive the hand of her beloved Anne in Kellynch church, in the course of the following autumn.

Chapter XVIII

It was the beginning of February; and Anne, having been a month in Bath, was growing very eager for news from Uppercross and Lyme. She wanted to hear much more than Mary communicated. It was three weeks since she had heard at all. She only knew that Henrietta was at home again; and that Louisa, though considered to be recovering fast, was still at Lyme; and she was thinking of them all very intently one evening, when a thicker letter than usual from Mary was delivered to her, and, to quicken the pleasure and surprise, with Admiral and Mrs. Croft's compliments.

The Crofts must be in Bath! A circumstance to interest her. They were people whom her heart turned to very naturally.

"What is this?" cried Sir Walter. "The Crofts arrived in Bath? The Crofts who rent Kellynch? What have they brought you?"

"A letter from Uppercross Cottage, Sir."

"Oh! those letters are convenient passports. They secure an introduction. I should have visited Admiral Croft, however, at any rate. I know what is due to my tenant."

Anne could listen no longer; she could not even have told how the poor Admiral's complexion escaped; her letter engrossed her. It had been begun several days back.

February 1st, ——.

MY DEAR ANNE,

I make no apology for my silence, because I know how little people think of letters in such a place as Bath. You must be a great deal too happy to care for Uppercross, which, as you well know,

affords little to write about. We have had a very dull Christmas;
Mr. and Mrs. Musgrove have not had one dinner-party all the holidays. I do not reckon the Hayters as any body. The holidays, however, are over at last: I believe no children ever had such long ones.
I am sure I had not. The house was cleared yesterday, except of the
little Harvilles; but you will be surprised to hear that they have
never gone home. Mrs. Harville must be an odd mother to part
with them so long. I do not understand it. They are not at all nice
children, in my opinion; but Mrs. Musgrove seems to like them
quite as well, if not better, than her grand-children. What dreadful
weather we have had! It may not be felt in Bath, with your nice
pavements; but in the country it is of some consequence. I have
not had a creature call on me since the second week in January,
except Charles Hayter, who has been calling much oftener than
was welcome. Between ourselves, I think it a great pity Henrietta
did not remain at Lyme as long as Louisa; it would have kept her a
little out of his way. The carriage is gone to-day, to bring Louisa
and the Harvilles to-morrow. We are not asked to dine with them,
however, till the day after, Mrs. Musgrove is so afraid of her being
fatigued by the journey, which is not very likely, considering the
care that will be taken of her; and it would be much more convenient to me to dine there to-morrow. I am glad you find Mr. Elliot
so agreeable, and wish I could be acquainted with him too; but I
have my usual luck, I am always out of the way when any thing
desirable is going on; always the last of my family to be noticed.
What an immense time Mrs. Clay has been staying with Elizabeth!
Does she never mean to go away? But perhaps if she were to leave
the room vacant we might not be invited. Let me know what you
think of this. I do not expect my children to be asked, you know. I
can leave them at the Great House very well, for a month or six
weeks. I have this moment heard that the Crofts are going to Bath
almost immediately; they think the admiral gouty. Charles heard it
quite by chance: they have not had the civility to give me any
notice, or offer to take any thing. I do not think they improve at all
as neighbours. We see nothing of them, and this is really an
instance of gross inattention. Charles joins me in love, and every
thing proper.   Yours affectionately,
                                         MARY M———.

I am sorry to say that I am very far from well; and Jemima has just
told me that the butcher says there is a bad sore-throat very much
about. I dare say I shall catch it; and my sore-throats, you know,
are always worse than anybody's."

So ended the first part, which had been afterwards put into an
envelop, containing nearly as much more.

"I kept my letter open, that I might send you word how Louisa bore her journey, and now I am extremely glad I did, having a great deal to add. In the first place, I had a note from Mrs. Croft yesterday, offering to convey any thing to you; a very kind, friendly note indeed, addressed to me, just as it ought; I shall therefore be able to make my letter as long as I like. The admiral does not seem very ill, and I sincerely hope Bath will do him all the good he wants. I shall be truly glad to have them back again. Our neighbourhood cannot spare such a pleasant family. But now for Louisa. I have something to communicate that will astonish you not a little. She and the Harvilles came on Tuesday very safely, and in the evening we went to ask her how she did, when we were rather surprised not to find Captain Benwick of the party, for he had been invited as well as the Harvilles; and what do you think was the reason? Neither more nor less than his being in love with Louisa, and not choosing to venture to Uppercross till he had had an answer from Mr. Musgrove; for it was all settled between him and her before she came away, and he had written to her father by Captain Harville. True, upon my honour. Are not you astonished? I shall be surprised at least if you ever received a hint of it, for I never did. Mrs. Musgrove protests solemnly that she knew nothing of the matter. We are all very well pleased, however; for though it is not equal to her marrying Captain Wentworth, it is infinitely better than Charles Hayter; and Mr. Musgrove has written his consent, and Captain Benwick is expected to-day. Mrs. Harville says her husband feels a good deal on his poor sister's account; but, however, Louisa is a great favourite with both. Indeed Mrs. Harville and I quite agree that we love her the better for having nursed her. Charles wonders what Captain Wentworth will say; but if you remember, I never thought him attached to Louisa; I never could see any thing of it. And this is the end, you see, of Captain Benwick's being supposed to be an admirer of yours. How Charles could take such a thing into his head was always incomprehensible to me. I hope he will be more agreeable now. Certainly not a great match for Louisa Musgrove; but a million times better than marrying among the Hayters."

Mary need not have feared her sister's being in any degree prepared for the news. She had never in her life been more astonished. Captain Benwick and Louisa Musgrove! It was almost too wonderful for belief; and it was with the greatest effort that she could remain in the room, preserve an air of calmness, and answer the common questions of the moment. Happily for her, they were not many. Sir Walter wanted to know whether the Crofts travelled with four horses, and whether they were likely to be situated in such a part of Bath as it might suit Miss Elliot and himself to visit in; but had little curiosity beyond.

"How is Mary?" said Elizabeth; and without waiting for an answer, "And pray what brings the Crofts to Bath?"

"They come on the Admiral's account. He is thought to be gouty."

"Gout and decrepitude!" said Sir Walter. "Poor old gentleman."

"Have they any acquaintance here?" asked Elizabeth.

"I do not know; but I can hardly suppose that, at Admiral Croft's time of life, and in his profession, he should not have many acquaintance in such a place as this."

"I suspect," said Sir Walter coolly, "that Admiral Croft will be best known in Bath as the renter of Kellynch-hall. Elizabeth, may we venture to present him and his wife in Laura-place?"

"Oh! no, I think not. Situated as we are with Lady Dalrymple, cousins, we ought to be very careful not to embarrass her with acquaintance she might not approve. If we were not related, it would not signify; but as cousins, she would feel scrupulous as to any proposal of ours. We had better leave the Crofts to find their own level. There are several odd-looking men walking about here, who, I am told, are sailors. The Crofts will associate with them!"

This was Sir Walter and Elizabeth's share of interest in the letter; when Mrs. Clay had paid her tribute of more decent attention, in an enquiry after Mrs. Charles Musgrove, and her fine little boys, Anne was at liberty.

In her own room she tried to comprehend it. Well might Charles wonder how Captain Wentworth would feel! Perhaps he had quitted the field, had given Louisa up, had ceased to love, had found he did not love her. She could not endure the idea of treachery or levity, or any thing akin to ill-usage between him and his friend. She could not endure that such a friendship as theirs should be severed unfairly.

Captain Benwick and Louisa Musgrove! The high-spirited, joyous, talking Louisa Musgrove, and the dejected, thinking, feeling, reading Captain Benwick, seemed each of them every thing that would not suit the other. Their minds most dissimilar! Where could have been the attraction? The answer soon presented itself. It had been in situation. They had been thrown together several weeks; they had been living in the same small family party; since Henrietta's coming away, they must have been depending almost entirely on each other, and Louisa, just recovering from illness, had been in an interesting state, and Captain Benwick was not inconsolable. That was a point which Anne had not been able to avoid suspecting before; and instead of drawing the same conclusion as Mary, from the present course of events, they served only to confirm the idea of his having felt some dawning of tenderness toward herself. She did not mean, however, to derive much more from it to gratify her vanity, than Mary might have allowed. She was persuaded that any tolerably pleasing young woman who had listened and seemed to feel for him, would have received the same compliment. He had an affectionate heart. He must love somebody.

She saw no reason against their being happy. Louisa had fine naval fervour to begin with, and they would soon grow more alike. He would gain cheerfulness, and she would learn to be an enthusiast for Scott and Lord Byron; nay, that was probably learnt already; of course they had fallen in love over poetry. The idea of Louisa Musgrove turned into a person of literary taste, and sentimental reflection, was amusing, but she had no doubt of its being so. The day at Lyme, the fall from the Cobb, might influence her health, her nerves, her courage, her character to the end of her life, as thoroughly as it appeared to have influenced her fate.

The conclusion of the whole was, that if the woman who had been sensible of Captain Wentworth's merits could be allowed to prefer another man, there was nothing in the engagement to excite lasting wonder; and if Captain Wentworth lost no friend by it, certainly nothing to be regretted. No, it was not regret which made Anne's heart beat in spite of herself, and brought the colour into her cheeks when she thought of Captain Wentworth unshackled and free. She had some feelings which she was ashamed to investigate. They were too much like joy, senseless joy!

She longed to see the Crofts, but when the meeting took place, it was evident that no rumour of the news had yet reached them. The visit of ceremony was paid and returned, and Louisa Musgrove was mentioned, and Captain Benwick too, without even half a smile.

The Crofts had placed themselves in lodgings in Gay-street, perfectly to Sir Walter's satisfaction. He was not at all ashamed of the acquaintance, and did, in fact, think and talk a great deal more about the Admiral, than the Admiral ever thought or talked about him.

The Crofts knew quite as many people in Bath as they wished for, and considered their intercourse with the Elliots as a mere matter of form, and not in the least likely to afford them any pleasure. They brought with them their country habit of being almost always together. He was ordered to walk, to keep off the gout, and Mrs. Croft seemed to go shares with him in every thing, and to walk for her life, to do him good. Anne saw them wherever she went. Lady Russell took her out in her carriage almost every morning, and she never failed to think of them, and never failed to see them. Knowing their feelings as she did, it was a most attractive picture of happiness to her. She always watched them as long as she could; delighted to fancy she understood what they might be talking of, as they walked along in happy independence, or equally delighted to see the Admiral's hearty shake of the hand when he encountered an old friend, and observe their eagerness of conversation when occasionally forming into a little knot of the navy, Mrs. Croft looking as intelligent and keen as any of the officers around her.

Anne was too much engaged with Lady Russell to be often walking herself, but it so happened that one morning, about a week or ten days after the Crofts' arrival, it suited her best to leave her friend, or her friend's carriage, in the lower part of the town, and return alone to Camden-place; and in walking up Milsom-street, she had the good fortune to meet with the Admiral. He was standing by himself, at a print-shop window, with his hands behind him, in earnest contemplation of some print, and she not only might have passed him unseen, but was obliged to touch as well as address him before she could catch his notice. When he did perceive and acknowledge her, however, it was done with all his usual frankness and good humour. "Ha! is it you? Thank you, thank you. This is treating me like a friend. Here I am, you see, staring at a picture. I can never get by this shop without stopping. But what a thing here is, by way of a boat. Do look at it. Did you ever see the like? What queer fellows your fine painters must be, to think that any body would venture their lives in such a shapeless old cockleshell as that. And yet, here are two gentlemen stuck up in it mightily at their ease, and looking about them at the rocks and mountains, as if they were not to be upset the next moment, which they certainly must be. I wonder where that boat was built!" (laughing heartily) "I would not venture over a horsepond in it. Well," (turning away) "now, where are you bound? Can I go any where for you, or with you? Can I be of any use?"

"None, I thank you, unless you will give me the pleasure of your company the little way our road lies together. I am going home."

"That I will, with all my heart, and farther too. Yes, yes, we will have a snug walk together; and I have something to tell you as we go along. There, take my arm; that's right; I do not feel comfortable if I have not a woman there. Lord! what a boat it is!" taking a last look at the picture, as they began to be in motion.

"Did you say that you had something to tell me, sir?"

"Yes, I have. Presently. But here comes a friend, Captain Brigden; I shall only say, 'How d'ye do,' as we pass, however. I shall not stop. 'How d'ye do.' Brigden stares to see anybody with me but my wife. She, poor soul, is tied by the leg. She has a blister on one of her heels, as large as a three shilling piece. If you look across the street, you will see Admiral Brand coming down and his brother. Shabby fellows, both of them! I am glad they are not on this side of the way. Sophy cannot bear them. They played me a pitiful trick once—got away some of my best men. I will tell you the whole story another time. There comes old Sir Archibald Drew and his grandson. Look, he sees us; he kisses his hand to you; he takes you for my wife. Ah! the peace has come too soon for that younker.[2] Poor old Sir Archibald! How do you like Bath, Miss Elliot? It

---

2. Youngster. The grandson is presumably in the navy.

suits us very well. We are always meeting with some old friend or other; the streets full of them every morning; sure to have plenty of chat; and then we get away from them all, and shut ourselves into our lodgings, and draw in our chairs, and are as snug as if we were at Kellynch, ay, or as we used to be even at North Yarmouth and Deal. We do not like our lodgings here the worse, I can tell you, for putting us in mind of those we first had at North Yarmouth. The wind blows through one of the cupboards just in the same way."

When they were got a little farther, Anne ventured to press again for what he had to communicate. She had hoped, when clear of Milsom-street, to have her curiosity gratified; but she was still obliged to wait, for the Admiral had made up his mind not to begin, till they had gained the greater space and quiet of Belmont, and as she was not really Mrs. Croft, she must let him have his own way. As soon as they were fairly ascending Belmont, he began,

"Well, now you shall hear something that will surprise you. But first of all, you must tell me the name of the young lady I am going to talk about. That young lady, you know, that we have all been so concerned for. The Miss Musgrove, that all this has been happening to. Her christian name—I always forget her christian name."

Anne had been ashamed to appear to comprehend so soon as she really did; but now she could safely suggest the name of "Louisa."

"Ay, ay, Miss Louisa Musgrove, that is the name. I wish young ladies had not such a number of fine christian names. I should never be out, if they were all Sophys, or something of that sort. Well, this Miss Louisa, we all thought, you know, was to marry Frederick. He was courting her week after week. The only wonder was, what they could be waiting for, till the business at Lyme came; then, indeed, it was clear enough that they must wait till her brain was set to right. But even then, there was something odd in their way of going on. Instead of staying at Lyme, he went off to Plymouth, and then he went off to see Edward. When we came back from Minehead, he was gone down to Edward's, and there he has been ever since. We have seen nothing of him since November. Even Sophy could not understand it. But now, the matter has taken the strangest turn of all; for this young lady, this same Miss Musgrove, instead of being to marry Frederick, is to marry James Benwick. You know James Benwick."

"A little. I am a little acquainted with Captain Benwick."

"Well, she is to marry him. Nay, most likely they are married already, for I do not know what they should wait for."

"I thought Captain Benwick a very pleasing young man," said Anne, "and I understand that he bears an excellent character."

"Oh! yes, yes, there is not a word to be said against James Benwick. He is only a commander, it is true, made last summer, and these are bad times for getting on, but he has not another fault that I know of. An

excellent, good-hearted fellow, I assure you, a very active, zealous officer too, which is more than you would think for, perhaps, for that soft
sort of manner does not do him justice."

"Indeed you are mistaken there, sir. I should never augur want of
spirit from Captain Benwick's manners. I thought them particularly
pleasing, and I will answer for it they would generally please."

"Well, well, ladies are the best judges; but James Benwick is rather
too piano[3] for me, and though very likely it is all our partiality, Sophy
and I cannot help thinking Frederick's manners better than his. There
is something about Frederick more to our taste."

Anne was caught. She had only meant to oppose the too-common
idea of spirit and gentleness being incompatible with each other, not at
all to represent Captain Benwick's manners as the very best that could
possibly be, and, after a little hesitation, she was beginning to say, "I was
not entering into any comparison of the two friends," but the Admiral
interrupted her with,

"And the thing is certainly true. It is not a mere bit of gossip. We have
it from Frederick himself. His sister had a letter from him yesterday, in
which he tells us of it, and he had just had it in a letter from Harville,
written upon the spot, from Uppercross. I fancy they are all at
Uppercross."

This was an opportunity which Anne could not resist; she said, therefore, "I hope, Admiral, I hope there is nothing in the style of Captain
Wentworth's letter to make you and Mrs. Croft particularly uneasy. It
did certainly seem, last autumn, as if there were an attachment between
him and Louisa Musgrove; but I hope it may be understood to have
worn out on each side equally, and without violence. I hope his letter
does not breathe the spirit of an ill-used man."

"Not at all, not at all; there is not an oath or a murmur from beginning to end."

Anne looked down to hide her smile.

"No, no; Frederick is not a man to whine and complain; he has too
much spirit for that. If the girl likes another man better, it is very fit she
should have him."

"Certainly. But what I mean is, that I hope there is nothing in Captain Wentworth's manner of writing to make you suppose he thinks himself ill-used by his friend, which might appear, you know, without its
being absolutely said. I should be very sorry that such a friendship as has
subsisted between him and Captain Benwick should be destroyed, or
even wounded, by a circumstance of this sort."

"Yes, yes, I understand you. But there is nothing at all of that nature
in the letter. He does not give the least fling at Benwick; does not so
much as say, 'I wonder at it, I have a reason of my own for wondering

3. Quiet.

at it.' No, you would not guess, from his way of writing, that he had ever thought of this Miss (what's her name?) for himself. He very handsomely hopes they will be happy together, and there is nothing very unforgiving in that, I think."

Anne did not receive the perfect conviction which the Admiral meant to convey, but it would have been useless to press the enquiry farther. She, therefore, satisfied herself with common-place remarks, or quiet attention, and the Admiral had it all his own way.

"Poor Frederick!" said he at last. "Now he must begin all over again with somebody else. I think we must get him to Bath. Sophy must write, and beg him to come to Bath. Here are pretty girls enough, I am sure. It would be of no use to go to Uppercross again, for that other Miss Musgrove, I find, is bespoke by her cousin, the young parson. Do not you think, Miss Elliot, we had better try to get him to Bath?"

Chapter XIX

While Admiral Croft was taking this walk with Anne, and expressing his wish of getting Captain Wentworth to Bath, Captain Wentworth was already on his way thither. Before Mrs. Croft had written, he was arrived; and the very next time Anne walked out, she saw him.

Mr. Elliot was attending his two cousins and Mrs. Clay. They were in Milsom-street. It began to rain, not much, but enough to make shelter desirable for women, and quite enough to make it very desirable for Miss Elliot to have the advantage of being conveyed home in Lady Dalrymple's carriage, which was seen waiting at a little distance; she, Anne, and Mrs. Clay, therefore, turned into Molland's,[4] while Mr. Elliot stepped to Lady Dalrymple, to request her assistance. He soon joined them again, successful, of course; Lady Dalrymple would be most happy to take them home, and would call for them in a few minutes.

Her ladyship's carriage was a barouche,[5] and did not hold more than four with any comfort. Miss Carteret was with her mother; consequently it was not reasonable to expect accommodation for all the three Camden-place ladies. There could be no doubt as to Miss Elliot. Whoever suffered inconvenience, she must suffer none, but it occupied a little time to settle the point of civility between the other two. The rain was a mere trifle, and Anne was most sincere in preferring a walk with Mr. Elliot. But the rain was also a mere trifle to Mrs. Clay; she would hardly allow it even to drop at all, and her boots were so thick! much thicker than Miss Anne's; and, in short, her civility rendered her quite as anxious to be left to walk with Mr. Elliot, as Anne could be, and it was

4. A confectioner's.
5. A carriage with seats for two couples to sit facing each other.

discussed between them with a generosity so polite and so determined, that the others were obliged to settle it for them; Miss Elliot maintaining that Mrs. Clay had a little cold already, and Mr. Elliot deciding on appeal, that his cousin Anne's boots were rather the thickest.

It was fixed accordingly that Mrs. Clay should be of the party in the carriage; and they had just reached this point when Anne, as she sat near the window, descried, most decidedly and distinctly, Captain Wentworth walking down the street.

Her start was perceptible only to herself; but she instantly felt that she was the greatest simpleton in the world, the most unaccountable and absurd! For a few minutes she saw nothing before her. It was all confusion. She was lost; and when she had scolded back her senses, she found the others still waiting for the carriage, and Mr. Elliot (always obliging) just setting off for Union-street on a commission of Mrs. Clay's.

She now felt a great inclination to go to the outer door; she wanted to see if it rained. Why was she to suspect herself of another motive? Captain Wentworth must be out of sight. She left her seat, she would go, one half of her should not be always so much wiser than the other half, or always suspecting the other of being worse than it was. She would see if it rained. She was sent back, however, in a moment by the entrance of Captain Wentworth himself, among a party of gentlemen and ladies, evidently his acquaintance, and whom he must have joined a little below Milsom-street. He was more obviously struck and confused by the sight of her, than she had ever observed before; he looked quite red. For the first time, since their renewed acquaintance, she felt that she was betraying the least sensibility of the two. She had the advantage of him, in the preparation of the last few moments. All the overpowering, blinding, bewildering, first effects of strong surprise were over with her. Still, however, she had enough to feel! It was agitation, pain, pleasure, a something between delight and misery.

He spoke to her, and then turned away. The character of his manner was embarrassment. She could not have called it either cold or friendly, or any thing so certainly as embarrassed.

After a short interval, however, he came towards her and spoke again. Mutual enquiries on common subjects passed; neither of them, probably, much the wiser for what they heard, and Anne continuing fully sensible of his being less at ease than formerly. They had, by dint of being so very much together, got to speak to each other with a considerable portion of apparent indifference and calmness; but he could not do it now. Time had changed him, or Louisa had changed him. There was consciousness of some sort or other. He looked very well, not as if he had been suffering in health or spirits, and he talked of Uppercross, of the Musgroves, nay, even of Louisa, and had even a momentary look of his own arch significance as he named her; but yet it was Captain Wentworth not comfortable, not easy, not able to feign that he was.

It did not surprise, but it grieved Anne to observe that Elizabeth would not know him.[6] She saw that he saw Elizabeth, that Elizabeth saw him, that there was complete internal recognition on each side; she was convinced that he was ready to be acknowledged as an acquaintance, expecting it, and she had the pain of seeing her sister turn away with unalterable coldness.

Lady Dalrymple's carriage, for which Miss Elliot was growing very impatient, now drew up; the servant came in to announce it. It was beginning to rain again, and altogether there was a delay, and a bustle, and a talking, which must make all the little crowd in the shop understand that Lady Dalrymple was calling to convey Miss Elliot. At last Miss Elliot and her friend, unattended but by the servant, (for there was no cousin returned) were walking off; and Captain Wentworth, watching them, turned again to Anne, and by manner, rather than words, was offering his services to her.

"I am much obliged to you," was her answer, "but I am not going with them. The carriage would not accommodate so many. I walk. I prefer walking."

"But it rains."

"Oh! very little. Nothing that I regard."

After a moment's pause he said, "Though I came only yesterday, I have equipped myself properly for Bath already, you see," (pointing to a new umbrella) "I wish you would make use of it, if you are determined to walk; though, I think, it would be more prudent to let me get you a chair."

She was very much obliged to him, but declined it all, repeating her conviction, that the rain would come to nothing at present, and adding, "I am only waiting for Mr. Elliot. He will be here in a moment, I am sure."

She had hardly spoken the words, when Mr. Elliot walked in. Captain Wentworth recollected him perfectly. There was no difference between him and the man who had stood on the steps at Lyme, admiring Anne as she passed, except in the air and look and manner of the privileged relation and friend. He came in with eagerness, appeared to see and think only of her, apologised for his stay, was grieved to have kept her waiting, and anxious to get her away without further loss of time, and before the rain increased; and in another moment they walked off together, her arm under his, a gentle and embarrassed glance, and a "good morning to you," being all that she had time for, as she passed away.

As soon as they were out of sight, the ladies of Captain Wentworth's party began talking of them.

"Mr. Elliot does not dislike his cousin, I fancy?"

6. Would give no sign of recognition.

"Oh! no, that is clear enough. One can guess what will happen there. He is always with them; half lives in the family, I believe. What a very good-looking man!"

"Yes, and Miss Atkinson, who dined with him once at the Wallises, says he is the most agreeable man she ever was in company with."

"She is pretty, I think; Anne Elliot; very pretty, when one comes to look at her. It is not the fashion to say so, but I confess I admire her more than her sister."

"Oh! so do I."

"And so do I. No comparison. But the men are all wild after Miss Elliot. Anne is too delicate for them."

Anne would have been particularly obliged to her cousin, if he would have walked by her side all the way to Camden-place, without saying a word. She had never found it so difficult to listen to him, though nothing could exceed his solicitude and care, and though his subjects were principally such as were wont to be always interesting—praise, warm, just, and discriminating, of Lady Russell, and insinuations highly rational against Mrs. Clay. But just now she could think only of Captain Wentworth. She could not understand his present feelings, whether he were really suffering much from disappointment or not; and till that point were settled, she could not be quite herself.

She hoped to be wise and reasonable in time; but alas! alas! she must confess to herself that she was not wise yet.

Another circumstance very essential for her to know, was how long he meant to be in Bath; he had not mentioned it, or she could not recollect it. He might be only passing through. But it was more probable that he should be come to stay. In that case, so liable as every body was to meet every body in Bath, Lady Russell would in all likelihood see him somewhere.—Would she recollect him? How would it all be?

She had already been obliged to tell Lady Russell that Louisa Musgrove was to marry Captain Benwick. It had cost her something to encounter Lady Russell's surprise; and now, if she were by any chance to be thrown into company with Captain Wentworth, her imperfect knowledge of the matter might add another shade of prejudice against him.

The following morning Anne was out with her friend, and for the first hour, in an incessant and fearful sort of watch for him in vain; but at last, in returning down Pulteney-street, she distinguished him on the right hand pavement at such a distance as to have him in view the greater part of the street. There were many other men about him, many groups walking the same way, but there was no mistaking him. She looked instinctively at Lady Russell; but not from any mad idea of her recognising him so soon as she did herself. No, it was not to be supposed that Lady Russell would perceive him till they were nearly opposite. She looked at her however, from time to time, anxiously; and when the moment approached which must point him out, though not daring to look again (for her own countenance she knew was unfit to be seen), she was yet perfectly conscious of Lady Russell's eyes being turned exactly in the direction for him, of her being in short intently observing him. She could thoroughly comprehend the sort of fascination he must possess over Lady Russell's mind, the difficulty it must be for her to withdraw her eyes, the astonishment she must be feeling that eight or nine years should have passed over him, and in foreign climes and in active service too, without robbing him of one personal grace!

At last, Lady Russell drew back her head.—"Now, how would she speak of him?"

"You will wonder," said she, "what has been fixing my eye so long; but I was looking after some window-curtains, which Lady Alicia and Mrs. Frankland were telling me of last night. They described the drawing-room window-curtains of one of the houses on this side of the way, and this part of the street, as being the handsomest and best hung of any in Bath, but could not recollect the exact number, and I have been trying to find out which it could be; but I confess I can see no curtains hereabouts that answer their description."

Anne sighed and blushed and smiled, in pity and disdain, either at her friend or herself.—The part which provoked her most, was that in all this waste of foresight and caution, she should have lost the right moment for seeing whether he saw them.

A day or two passed without producing any thing.—The theatre or the rooms, where he was most likely to be, were not fashionable enough for the Elliots, whose evening amusements were solely in the elegant stupidity of private parties, in which they were getting more and more engaged; and Anne, wearied of such a state of stagnation, sick of knowing nothing, and fancying herself stronger because her strength was not tried, was quite impatient for the concert evening. It was a concert for the benefit of a person patronised by Lady Dalrymple. Of course they must attend. It was really expected to be a good one, and Captain Wentworth was very fond of music. If she could only have a few minutes conversation with him again, she fancied she should be satisfied; and as to the power of addressing him she felt all over courage if the opportunity occurred. Elizabeth had turned from him, Lady Russell overlooked him; her nerves were strengthened by these circumstances; she felt that she owed him attention.

She had once partly promised Mrs. Smith to spend the evening with her; but in a short hurried call she excused herself and put it off, with the more decided promise of a longer visit on the morrow. Mrs. Smith gave a most good-humoured acquiescence.

"By all means," said she; "only tell me all about it, when you do come. Who is your party?"

Anne named them all. Mrs. Smith made no reply; but when she was

leaving her, said, and with an expression half serious, half arch, "Well,
I heartily wish your concert may answer; and do not fail me to-morrow
if you can come; for I begin to have a foreboding that I may have
many more visits from you."

Anne was startled and confused, but after standing in a moment's
suspense, was obliged, and not sorry to be obliged, to hurry away.

Chapter XX

Sir Walter, his two daughters, and Mrs. Clay, were the earliest of all
their party, at the rooms in the evening; and as Lady Dalrymple must
be waited for, they took their station by one of the fires in the octagon
room. But hardly were they so settled, when the door opened again, and
Captain Wentworth walked in alone. Anne was the nearest to him, and
making yet a little advance, she instantly spoke. He was preparing only
to bow and pass on, but her gentle "How do you do?" brought him out
of the straight line to stand near her, and make enquiries in return, in
spite of the formidable father and sister in the back ground. Their being
in the back ground was a support to Anne; she knew nothing of their
looks, and felt equal to everything which she believed right to be done.

While they were speaking, a whispering between her father and Elizabeth caught her ear. She could not distinguish, but she must guess the
subject; and on Captain Wentworth's making a distant bow, she com-
prehended that her father had judged so well as to give him that simple
acknowledgment of acquaintance, and she was just in time by a side
glance to see a slight curtsey from Elizabeth herself. This, though late
and reluctant and ungracious, was yet better than nothing, and her spirits improved.

After talking however of the weather and Bath and the concert, their
conversation began to flag, and so little was said at last, that she was
expecting him to go every moment; but he did not; he seemed in no
hurry to leave her; and presently with renewed spirit, with a little smile,
a little glow, he said,

"I have hardly seen you since our day at Lyme. I am afraid you must
have suffered from the shock, and the more from its not overpowering
you at the time."

She assured him that she had not.

"It was a frightful hour," said he, "a frightful day!" and he passed his
hand across his eyes, as if the remembrance were still too painful; but in
a moment half smiling again, added, "The day has produced some
effects however—has had some consequences which must be considered
as the very reverse of frightful.—When you had the presence of mind to
suggest that Benwick would be the properest person to fetch a surgeon,

you could have little idea of his being eventually one of those most concerned in her recovery."

"Certainly I could have none. But it appears—I should hope it would be a very happy match. There are on both sides good principles and good temper."

"Yes," said he, looking not exactly forward—"but there I think ends the resemblance. With all my soul I wish them happy, and rejoice over every circumstance in favour of it. They have no difficulties to contend with at home, no opposition, no caprice, no delays.—The Musgroves are behaving like themselves, most honourably and kindly, only anxious with true parental hearts to promote their daughter's comfort. All this is much, very much in favour of their happiness; more than perhaps—"

He stopped. A sudden recollection seemed to occur, and to give him some taste of that emotion which was reddening Anne's cheeks and fixing her eyes on the ground.—After clearing his throat, however, he proceeded thus,

"I confess that I do think there is a disparity, too great a disparity, and in a point no less essential than mind.—I regard Louisa Musgrove as a very amiable, sweet-tempered girl, and not deficient in understanding; but Benwick is something more. He is a clever man, a reading man— and I confess that I do consider his attaching himself to her, with some surprise. Had it been the effect of gratitude, had he learnt to love her, because he believed her to be preferring him, it would have been another thing. But I have no reason to suppose it so. It seems, on the contrary, to have been a perfectly spontaneous, untaught feeling on his side, and this surprises me. A man like him, in his situation! With a heart pierced, wounded, almost broken! Fanny Harville was a very superior creature; and his attachment to her was indeed attachment. A man does not recover from such a devotion of the heart to such a woman!— He ought not—he does not."

Either from the consciousness, however, that his friend had recovered, or from some other consciousness, he went no farther; and Anne, who, in spite of the agitated voice in which the latter part had been uttered, and in spite of all the various noises of the room, the almost ceaseless slam of the door, and ceaseless buzz of persons walking through, had distinguished every word, was struck, gratified, confused, and beginning to breathe very quick, and feel an hundred things in a moment. It was impossible for her to enter on such a subject; and yet, after a pause, feeling the necessity of speaking, and having not the smallest wish for a total change, she only deviated so far as to say,

"You were a good while at Lyme, I think?"

"About a fortnight. I could not leave it till Louisa's doing well was quite ascertained. I had been too deeply concerned in the mischief to be soon at peace. It had been my doing—solely mine. She would not have been obstinate if I had not been weak. The country round Lyme is very fine. I walked and rode a great deal; and the more I saw, the more I found to admire."

"I should very much like to see Lyme again," said Anne.

"Indeed! I should not have supposed that you could have found any thing in Lyme to inspire such a feeling. The horror and distress you were involved in—the stretch of mind, the wear of spirits!—I should have thought your last impressions of Lyme must have been strong disgust."

"The last few hours were certainly very painful," replied Anne: "but when pain is over, the remembrance of it often becomes a pleasure. One does not love a place the less for having suffered in it, unless it has been all suffering, nothing but suffering—which was by no means the case at Lyme. We were only in anxiety and distress during the last two hours; and, previously, there had been a great deal of enjoyment. So much novelty and beauty! I have travelled so little, that every fresh place would be interesting to me—but there is real beauty at Lyme: and in short" (with a faint blush at some recollections) "altogether my impressions of the place are very agreeable."

As she ceased, the entrance door opened again, and the very party appeared for whom they were waiting. "Lady Dalrymple, Lady Dalrymple," was the rejoicing sound; and with all the eagerness compatible with anxious elegance, Sir Walter and his two ladies stepped forward to meet her. Lady Dalrymple and Miss Carteret, escorted by Mr. Elliot and Colonel Wallis, who had happened to arrive nearly at the same instant, advanced into the room. The others joined them, and it was a group in which Anne found herself also necessarily included. She was divided from Captain Wentworth. Their interesting, almost too interesting conversation must be broken up for a time; but slight was the penance compared with the happiness which brought it on! She had learnt, in the last ten minutes, more of his feelings towards Louisa, more of all his feelings, than she dared to think of! and she gave herself up to the demands of the party, to the needful civilities of the moment, with exquisite, though agitated sensations. She was in good humour with all. She had received ideas which disposed her to be courteous and kind to all, and to pity every one, as being less happy than herself.

The delightful emotions were a little subdued, when, on stepping back from the group, to be joined again by Captain Wentworth, she saw that he was gone. She was just in time to see him turn into the concert room. He was gone—he had disappeared: she felt a moment's regret. But "they should meet again. He would look for her—he would find her out long before the evening were over—and at present, perhaps, it was as well to be asunder. She was in need of a little interval for recollection."

Upon Lady Russell's appearance soon afterwards, the whole party was collected, and all that remained, was to marshal themselves, and pro-

ceed into the concert room; and be of all the consequence in their
power, draw as many eyes, excite as many whispers, and disturb as many
people as they could.

Very, very happy were both Elizabeth and Anne Elliot as they walked
in. Elizabeth, arm in arm with Miss Carteret, and looking on the broad
back of the dowager Viscountess Dalrymple before her, had nothing to
wish for which did not seem within her reach; and Anne——but it
would be an insult to the nature of Anne's felicity, to draw any comparison between it and her sister's; the origin of one all selfish vanity, of the
other all generous attachment.

Anne saw nothing, thought nothing of the brilliancy of the room.
Her happiness was from within. Her eyes were bright, and her cheeks
glowed,—but she knew nothing about it. She was thinking only of the
last half hour, and as they passed to their seats, her mind took a hasty
range over it. His choice of subjects, his expressions, and still more his
manner and look, had been such as she could see in only one light.
His opinion of Louisa Musgrove's inferiority, an opinion which he had
seemed solicitous to give, his wonder at Captain Benwick, his feelings
as to a first, strong attachment,—sentences begun which he could not
finish—his half averted eyes, and more than half expressive glance,—
all, all declared that he had a heart returning to her at least; that anger,
resentment, avoidance, were no more; and that they were succeeded,
not merely by friendship and regard, but by the tenderness of the past;
yes, some share of the tenderness of the past. She could not contemplate
the change as implying less.—He must love her.

These were thoughts, with their attendant visions, which occupied
and flurried her too much to leave her any power of observation; and
she passed along the room without having a glimpse of him, without
even trying to discern him. When their places were determined on, and
they were all properly arranged, she looked round to see if he should
happen to be in the same part of the room, but he was not, her eye could
not reach him; and the concert being just opening, she must consent for
a time to be happy in an humbler way.

The party was divided, and disposed of on two contiguous benches:
Anne was among those on the foremost, and Mr. Elliot had manœuvred
so well, with the assistance of his friend Colonel Wallis, as to have a
seat by her. Miss Elliot, surrounded by her cousins, and the principal
object of Colonel Wallis's gallantry, was quite contented.

Anne's mind was in a most favourable state for the entertainment of
the evening: it was just occupation enough: she had feelings for the
tender, spirits for the gay, attention for the scientific, and patience for
the wearisome; and had never liked a concert better, at least during the
first act. Towards the close of it, in the interval[7] succeeding an Italian

7. Intermission.

song, she explained the words of the song to Mr. Elliot.—They had a concert bill[8] between them.

"This," said she, "is nearly the sense, or rather the meaning of the words, for certainly the sense of an Italian love-song must not be talked of,—but it is as nearly the meaning as I can give; for I do not pretend to understand the language. I am a very poor Italian scholar."

"Yes, yes, I see you are. I see you know nothing of the matter. You have only knowledge enough of the language, to translate at sight these inverted, transposed, curtailed Italian lines, into clear, comprehensible, elegant English. You need not say anything more of your ignorance.— Here is complete proof."

"I will not oppose such kind politeness; but I should be sorry to be examined by a real proficient."

"I have not had the pleasure of visiting in Camden-place so long," replied he, "without knowing something of Miss Anne Elliot; and I do regard her as one who is too modest, for the world in general to be aware of half her accomplishments, and too highly accomplished for modesty to be natural in any other woman."

"For shame! for shame!—this is too much of flattery. I forget what we are to have next," turning to the bill.

"Perhaps," said Mr. Elliot, speaking low, "I have had a longer acquaintance with your character than you are aware of."

"Indeed!—How so? You can have been acquainted with it only since I came to Bath, excepting as you might hear me previously spoken of in my own family."

"I knew you by report long before you came to Bath. I had heard you described by those who knew you intimately. I have been acquainted with you by character many years. Your person, your disposition, accomplishments, manner—they were all described, they were all present to me."

Mr. Elliot was not disappointed in the interest he hoped to raise. No one can withstand the charm of such a mystery. To have been described long ago to a recent acquaintance, by nameless people, is irresistible; and Anne was all curiosity. She wondered, and questioned him eagerly—but in vain. He delighted in being asked, but he would not tell.

"No, no—some time or other perhaps, but not now. He would mention no names now; but such, he could assure her, had been the fact. He had many years ago received such a description of Miss Anne Elliot, as had inspired him with the highest idea of her merit, and excited the warmest curiosity to know her."

Anne could think of no one so likely to have spoken with partiality of her many years ago, as the Mr. Wentworth, of Monkford, Captain

8. Program.

Wentworth's brother. He might have been in Mr. Elliot's company, but she had not courage to ask the question.

"The name of Anne Elliot," said he, "has long had an interesting sound to me. Very long has it possessed a charm over my fancy; and, if I dared, I would breathe my wishes that the name might never change."

Such she believed were his words; but scarcely had she received their sound, than her attention was caught by other sounds immediately behind her, which rendered every thing else trivial. Her father and Lady Dalrymple were speaking.

"A well-looking man," said Sir Walter, "a very well-looking man."

"A very fine young man indeed!" said Lady Dalrymple. "More air than one often sees in Bath.—Irish, I dare say."

"No, I just know his name. A bowing acquaintance. Wentworth—Captain Wentworth of the navy. His sister married my tenant in Somersetshire,—the Croft, who rents Kellynch."

Before Sir Walter had reached this point, Anne's eyes had caught the right direction, and distinguished Captain Wentworth, standing among a cluster of men at a little distance. As her eyes fell on him, his seemed to be withdrawn from her. It had that appearance. It seemed as if she had been one moment too late; and as long as she dared observe, he did not look again: but the performance was re-commencing, and she was forced to seem to restore her attention to the orchestra, and look straight forward.

When she could give another glance, he had moved away. He could not have come nearer to her if he would; she was so surrounded and shut in: but she would rather have caught his eye.

Mr. Elliot's speech too distressed her. She had no longer any inclination to talk to him. She wished him not so near her.

The first act was over. Now she hoped for some beneficial change; and, after a period of nothing-saying amongst the party, some of them did decide on going in quest of tea. Anne was one of the few who did not choose to move. She remained in her seat, and so did Lady Russell; but she had the pleasure of getting rid of Mr. Elliot; and she did not mean, whatever she might feel on Lady Russell's account, to shrink from conversation with Captain Wentworth, if he gave her the opportunity. She was persuaded by Lady Russell's countenance that she had seen him.

He did not come however. Anne sometimes fancied she discerned him at a distance, but he never came. The anxious interval wore away unproductively. The others returned, the room filled again, benches were reclaimed and re-possessed, and another hour of pleasure or of penance was to be set out, another hour of music was to give delight or the gapes,[9] as real or affected taste for it prevailed. To Anne, it chiefly

9. Yawns.

wore the prospect of an hour of agitation. She could not quit that room in peace without seeing Captain Wentworth once more, without the interchange of one friendly look.

In re-settling themselves, there were now many changes, the result of which was favourable for her. Colonel Wallis declined sitting down again, and Mr. Elliot was invited by Elizabeth and Miss Carteret, in a manner not to be refused, to sit between them; and by some other removals, and a little scheming of her own, Anne was enabled to place herself much nearer the end of the bench than she had been before, much more within reach of a passer-by. She could not do so, without comparing herself with Miss Larolles, the inimitable Miss Larolles,[1]— but still she did it, and not with much happier effect; though by what seemed prosperity in the shape of an early abdication in her next neighbours, she found herself at the very end of the bench before the concert closed.

Such was her situation, with a vacant space at hand, when Captain Wentworth was again in sight. She saw him not far off. He saw her too; yet he looked grave, and seemed irresolute, and only by very slow degrees came at last near enough to speak to her. She felt that something must be the matter. The change was indubitable. The difference between his present air and what it had been in the octagon room was strikingly great.—Why was it? She thought of her father—of Lady Russell. Could there have been any unpleasant glances? He began by speaking of the concert, gravely; more like the Captain Wentworth of Uppercross; owned himself disappointed, had expected better singing; and, in short, must confess that he should not be sorry when it was over. Anne replied, and spoke in defence of the performance so well, and yet in allowance for his feelings, so pleasantly, that his countenance improved, and he replied again with almost a smile. They talked for a few minutes more; the improvement held; he even looked down towards the bench, as if he saw a place on it well worth occupying; when, at that moment, a touch on her shoulder obliged Anne to turn round.—It came from Mr. Elliot. He begged her pardon, but she must be applied to, to explain Italian again. Miss Carteret was very anxious to have a general idea of what was next to be sung. Anne could not refuse; but never had she sacrificed to politeness with a more suffering spirit.

A few minutes, though as few as possible, were inevitably consumed; and when her own mistress again, when able to turn and look as she had done before, she found herself accosted by Captain Wentworth, in a reserved yet hurried sort of farewell. "He must wish her good night. He was going—he should get home as fast as he could."

"Is not this song worth staying for?" said Anne, suddenly struck by an idea which made her yet more anxious to be encouraging.

1. A minor character in Frances Burney's *Cecilia* (1782) who chooses her seat at public events so as to be in a good position for talking to chosen people.

"No!" he replied impressively, "there is nothing worth my staying for;" and he was gone directly.

Jealousy of Mr. Elliot! It was the only intelligible motive. Captain Wentworth jealous of her affection! Could she have believed it a week ago—three hours ago! For a moment the gratification was exquisite. But alas! there were very different thoughts to succeed. How was such jealousy to be quieted? How was the truth to reach him? How, in all the peculiar disadvantages of their respective situations, would he ever learn her real sentiments? It was misery to think of Mr. Elliot's attentions.— Their evil was incalculable.

Chapter XXI

Anne recollected with pleasure the next morning her promise of going to Mrs. Smith; meaning that it should engage her from home at the time when Mr. Elliot would be most likely to call; for to avoid Mr. Elliot was almost a first object.

She felt a great deal of good will towards him. In spite of the mischief of his attentions, she owed him gratitude and regard, perhaps compassion. She could not help thinking much of the extraordinary circumstances attending their acquaintance; of the right which he seemed to have to interest her, by every thing in situation, by his own sentiments, by his early prepossession. It was altogether very extraordinary.—Flattering, but painful. There was much to regret. How she might have felt, had there been no Captain Wentworth in the case, was not worth enquiry; for there was a Captain Wentworth: and be the conclusion of the present suspense good or bad, her affection would be his for ever. Their union, she believed, could not divide her more from other men, than their final separation.

Prettier musings of high-wrought love and eternal constancy, could never have passed along the streets of Bath, than Anne was sporting with from Camden-place to Westgate-buildings. It was almost enough to spread purification and perfume all the way.

She was sure of a pleasant reception; and her friend seemed this morning particularly obliged to her for coming, seemed hardly to have expected her, though it had been an appointment.

An account of the concert was immediately claimed; and Anne's recollections of the concert were quite happy enough to animate her features, and make her rejoice to talk of it. All that she could tell, she told most gladly; but the all was little for one who had been there, and unsatisfactory for such an enquirer as Mrs. Smith, who had already heard, through the short cut of a laundress and a waiter, rather more of the general success and produce of the evening than Anne could relate; and who now asked in vain for several particulars of the company. Every body of any consequence or notoriety in Bath was well known by name to Mrs. Smith.

"The little Durands were there, I conclude," said she, "with their mouths open to catch the music; like unfledged sparrows ready to be fed. They never miss a concert."

"Yes. I did not see them myself, but I heard Mr. Elliot say they were in the room."

"The Ibbotsons—were they there? and the two new beauties, with the tall Irish officer, who is talked of for one of them."

"I do not know.—I do not think they were."

"Old Lady Mary Maclean? I need not ask after her. She never misses, I know; and you must have seen her. She must have been in your own circle, for as you went with Lady Dalrymple, you were in the seats of grandeur; round the orchestra, of course."

"No, that was what I dreaded. It would have been very unpleasant to me in every respect. But happily Lady Dalrymple always chooses to be farther off; and we were exceedingly well placed—that is for hearing; I must not say for seeing, because I appear to have seen very little."

"Oh! you saw enough for your own amusement.—I can understand. There is a sort of domestic enjoyment to be known even in a crowd, and this you had. You were a large party in yourselves, and you wanted nothing beyond."

"But I ought to have looked about me more," said Anne, conscious while she spoke, that there had in fact been no want of looking about; that the object only had been deficient.

"No, no—you were better employed. You need not tell me that you had a pleasant evening. I see it in your eye. I perfectly see how the hours passed—that you had always something agreeable to listen to. In the intervals of the concert, it was conversation."

Anne half smiled and said, "Do you see that in my eye?"

"Yes, I do. Your countenance perfectly informs me that you were in company last night with the person, whom you think the most agreeable in the world, the person who interests you at this present time, more than all the rest of the world put together."

A blush overspread Anne's cheeks. She could say nothing.

"And such being the case," continued Mrs. Smith, after a short pause, "I hope you believe that I do know how to value your kindness in coming to me this morning. It is really very good of you to come and sit with me, when you must have so many pleasanter demands upon your time."

Anne heard nothing of this. She was still in the astonishment and confusion excited by her friend's penetration, unable to imagine how any report of Captain Wentworth could have reached her. After another short silence—

"Pray," said Mrs. Smith, "is Mr. Elliot aware of your acquaintance with me? Does he know that I am in Bath?"

"Mr. Elliot!" repeated Anne, looking up surprised. A moment's reflection shewed her the mistake she had been under. She caught it instantaneously; and, recovering courage with the feeling of safety, soon added, more composedly, "are you acquainted with Mr. Elliot?"

"I have been a good deal acquainted with him," replied Mrs. Smith, gravely, "but it seems worn out now. It is a great while since we met."

"I was not at all aware of this. You never mentioned it before. Had I known it, I would have had the pleasure of talking to him about you."

"To confess the truth," said Mrs. Smith, assuming her usual air of cheerfulness, "that is exactly the pleasure I want you to have. I want you to talk about me to Mr. Elliot. I want your interest with him. He can be of essential service to me; and if you would have the goodness, my dear Miss Elliot, to make it an object to yourself, of course it is done."

"I should be extremely happy—I hope you cannot doubt my willingness to be of even the slightest use to you," replied Anne; "but I suspect that you are considering me as having a higher claim on Mr. Elliot—a greater right to influence him, than is really the case. I am sure you have, somehow or other, imbibed such a notion. You must consider me only as Mr. Elliot's relation. If in that light, if there is any thing which you suppose his cousin might fairly ask of him, I beg you would not hesitate to employ me."

Mrs. Smith gave her a penetrating glance, and then, smiling, said,

"I have been a little premature, I perceive. I beg your pardon. I ought to have waited for official information. But now, my dear Miss Elliot, as an old friend, do give me a hint as to when I may speak. Next week? To be sure by next week I may be allowed to think it all settled, and build my own selfish schemes on Mr. Elliot's good fortune."

"No," replied Anne, "nor next week, nor next, nor next. I assure you that nothing of the sort you are thinking of will be settled any week. I am not going to marry Mr. Elliot. I should like to know why you imagine I am."

Mrs. Smith looked at her again, looked earnestly, smiled, shook her head, and exclaimed,

"Now, how I do wish I understood you! How I do wish I knew what you were at! I have a great idea that you do not design to be cruel, when the right moment comes. Till it does come, you know, we women never mean to have any body. It is a thing of course among us, that every man is refused—till he offers. But why should you be cruel? Let me plead for my—present friend I cannot call him—but for my former friend. Where can you look for a more suitable match? Where could you expect a more gentlemanlike, agreeable man? Let me recommend Mr. Elliot. I am sure you hear nothing but good of him from Colonel Wallis;

and who can know him better than Colonel Wallis?"

"My dear Mrs. Smith, Mr. Elliot's wife has not been dead much above half a year. He ought not to be supposed to be paying his addresses to any one."

"Oh! if these are your only objections," cried Mrs. Smith, archly, "Mr. Elliot is safe, and I shall give myself no more trouble about him. Do not forget me when you are married, that's all. Let him know me to be a friend of yours, and then he will think little of the trouble required, which it is very natural for him now, with so many affairs and engagements of his own, to avoid and get rid of as he can—very natural, perhaps. Ninety-nine out of a hundred would do the same. Of course, he cannot be aware of the importance to me. Well, my dear Miss Elliot, I hope and trust you will be very happy. Mr. Elliot has sense to understand the value of such a woman. Your peace will not be shipwrecked as mine has been. You are safe in all worldly matters, and safe in his character. He will not be led astray, he will not be misled by others to his ruin."

"No," said Anne, "I can readily believe all that of my cousin. He seems to have a calm, decided temper, not at all open to dangerous impressions. I consider him with great respect. I have no reason, from any thing that has fallen within my observation, to do otherwise. But I have not known him long; and he is not a man, I think, to be known intimately soon. Will not this manner of speaking of him, Mrs. Smith, convince you that he is nothing to me? Surely, this must be calm enough. And, upon my word, he is nothing to me. Should he ever propose to me (which I have very little reason to imagine he has any thought of doing), I shall not accept him. I assure you I shall not. I assure you Mr. Elliot had not the share which you have been supposing, in whatever pleasure the concert of last night might afford:—not Mr. Elliot; it is not Mr. Elliot that—"

She stopped, regretting with a deep blush that she had implied so much; but less would hardly have been sufficient. Mrs. Smith would hardly have believed so soon in Mr. Elliot's failure, but from the perception of there being a somebody else. As it was, she instantly submitted, and with all the semblance of seeing nothing beyond; and Anne, eager to escape farther notice, was impatient to know why Mrs. Smith should have fancied she was to marry Mr. Elliot, where she could have received the idea, or from whom she could have heard it.

"Do tell me how it first came into your head."

"It first came into my head," replied Mrs. Smith, "upon finding how much you were together, and feeling it to be the most probable thing in the world to be wished for by everybody belonging to either of you; and you may depend upon it that all your acquaintance have disposed of you in the same way. But I never heard it spoken of till two days ago."

"And has it indeed been spoken of?"

"Did you observe the woman who opened the door to you, when you called yesterday?"

"No. Was not it Mrs. Speed, as usual, or the maid? I observed no one in particular."

"It was my friend, Mrs. Rooke—Nurse Rooke, who, by the by, had a great curiosity to see you, and was delighted to be in the way to let you in. She came away from Marlborough-buildings only on Sunday; and she it was who told me you were to marry Mr. Elliot. She had had it from Mrs. Wallis herself, which did not seem bad authority. She sat an hour with me on Monday evening, and gave me the whole history."

"The whole history!" repeated Anne, laughing. "She could not make a very long history, I think, of one such little article of unfounded news."

Mrs. Smith said nothing.

"But," continued Anne, presently, "though there is no truth in my having this claim on Mr. Elliot, I should be extremely happy to be of use to you, in any way that I could. Shall I mention to him your being in Bath? Shall I take any message?"

"No, I thank you: no, certainly not. In the warmth of the moment, and under a mistaken impression, I might, perhaps, have endeavoured to interest you in some circumstances. But not now: no, I thank you, I have nothing to trouble you with."

"I think you spoke of having known Mr. Elliot many years?"

"I did."

"Not before he married, I suppose?"

"Yes; he was not married when I knew him first."

"And—were you much acquainted?"

"Intimately."

"Indeed! Then do tell me what he was at that time of life. I have a great curiosity to know what Mr. Elliot was as a very young man. Was he at all such as he appears now?"

"I have not seen Mr. Elliot these three years," was Mrs. Smith's answer, given so gravely that it was impossible to pursue the subject farther; and Anne felt that she had gained nothing but an increase of curiosity. They were both silent—Mrs. Smith very thoughtful. At last,

"I beg your pardon, my dear Miss Elliot," she cried, in her natural tone of cordiality, "I beg your pardon for the short answers I have been giving you, but I have been uncertain what I ought to do. I have been doubting and considering as to what I ought to tell you. There were many things to be taken into the account. One hates to be officious, to be giving bad impressions, making mischief. Even the smooth surface of family-union seems worth preserving, though there may be nothing durable beneath. However, I have determined; I think I am right; I think you ought to be made acquainted with Mr. Elliot's real character. Though I fully believe that, at present, you have not the smallest intention of accepting him, there is no saying what may happen. You might, some time or other, be differently affected towards him. Hear the truth, therefore, now, while you are unprejudiced. Mr. Elliot is a man without heart or conscience; a designing, wary, cold-blooded being, who thinks only of himself; who, for his own interest or ease, would be guilty of any cruelty, or any treachery, that could be perpetrated without risk of his general character. He has no feeling for others. Those whom he has been the chief cause of leading into ruin, he can neglect and desert without the smallest compunction. He is totally beyond the reach of any sentiment of justice or compassion. Oh! he is black at heart, hollow and black!"

Anne's astonished air, and exclamation of wonder, made her pause, and in a calmer manner she added,

"My expressions startle you. You must allow for an injured, angry woman. But I will try to command myself. I will not abuse him. I will only tell you what I have found him. Facts shall speak. He was the intimate friend of my dear husband, who trusted and loved him, and thought him as good as himself. The intimacy had been formed before our marriage. I found them most intimate friends; and I, too, became excessively pleased with Mr. Elliot, and entertained the highest opinion of him. At nineteen, you know, one does not think very seriously, but Mr. Elliot appeared to me quite as good as others, and much more agreeable than most others, and we were almost always together. We were principally in town, living in very good style. He was then the inferior in circumstances, he was then the poor one; he had chambers in the Temple,[2] and it was as much as he could do to support the appearance of a gentleman. He had always a home with us whenever he chose it; he was always welcome; he was like a brother. My poor Charles, who had the finest, most generous spirit in the world, would have divided his last farthing with him; and I know that his purse was open to him; I know that he often assisted him."

"This must have been about that very period of Mr. Elliot's life," said Anne, "which has always excited my particular curiosity. It must have been about the same time that he became known to my father and sister. I never knew him myself, I only heard of him, but there was a something in his conduct then with regard to my father and sister, and afterwards in the circumstances of his marriage, which I never could quite reconcile with present times. It seemed to announce a different sort of man."

"I know it all, I know it all," cried Mrs. Smith. "He had been introduced to Sir Walter and your sister before I was acquainted with him,

---

2. The Inns of Court, in London, where lawyers lived and studied.

but I heard him speak of them for ever. I know he was invited and encouraged, and I know he did not choose to go. I can satisfy you, perhaps, on points which you would little expect; and as to his marriage, I knew all about it at the time. I was privy to all the fors and againsts, I was the friend to whom he confided his hopes and plans, and though I did not know his wife previously, (her inferior situation in society, indeed, rendered that impossible) yet I knew her all her life afterwards, or, at least, till within the last two years of her life, and can answer any question you wish to put."

"Nay," said Anne, "I have no particular enquiry to make about her. I have always understood they were not a happy couple. But I should like to know why, at that time of his life, he should slight my father's acquaintance as he did. My father was certainly disposed to take very kind and proper notice of him. Why did Mr. Elliot draw back?"

"Mr. Elliot," replied Mrs. Smith, "at that period of his life, had one object in view—to make his fortune, and by a rather quicker process than the law. He was determined to make it by marriage. He was determined, at least, not to mar it by an imprudent marriage; and I know it was his belief, (whether justly or not, of course I cannot decide) that your father and sister, in their civilities and invitations, were designing a match between the heir and the young lady; and it was impossible that such a match should have answered his ideas of wealth and independance. That was his motive for drawing back, I can assure you. He told me the whole story. He had no concealments with me. It was curious, that having just left you behind me in Bath, my first and principal acquaintance on marrying, should be your cousin; and that, through him, I should be continually hearing of your father and sister. He described one Miss Elliot, and I thought very affectionately of the other."

"Perhaps," cried Anne, struck by a sudden idea, "you sometimes spoke of me to Mr. Elliot?"

"To be sure I did, very often. I used to boast of my own Anne Elliot, and vouch for your being a very different creature from—"

She checked herself just in time.

"This accounts for something which Mr. Elliot said last night," cried Anne. "This explains it. I found he had been used to hear of me. I could not comprehend how. What wild imaginations one forms, where dear self is concerned! How sure to be mistaken! But I beg your pardon; I have interrupted you. Mr. Elliot married, then, completely for money? The circumstance, probably, which first opened your eyes to his character."

Mrs. Smith hesitated a little here. "Oh! those things are too common. When one lives in the world, a man or woman's marrying for money is too common to strike one as it ought. I was very young, and associated only with the young, and we were a thoughtless, gay set, without any strict rules of conduct. We lived for enjoyment. I think differently now; time and sickness, and sorrow, have given me other notions; but, at that period, I must own I saw nothing reprehensible in what Mr. Elliot was doing. 'To do the best for himself,' passed as a duty."

"But was not she a very low woman?"

"Yes; which I objected to, but he would not regard. Money, money, was all that he wanted. Her father was a grazier,[3] her grandfather had been a butcher, but that was all nothing. She was a fine woman, had had a decent education, was brought forward by some cousins, thrown by chance into Mr. Elliot's company, and fell in love with him; and not a difficulty or a scruple was there on his side, with respect to her birth. All his caution was spent in being secured[4] of the real amount of her fortune, before he committed himself. Depend upon it, whatever esteem Mr. Elliot may have for his own situation in life now, as a young man he had not the smallest value for it. His chance of the Kellynch estate was something, but all the honour of the family he held as cheap as dirt. I have often heard him declare, that if baronetcies were saleable, any body should have his for fifty pounds, arms and motto, name and livery included; but I will not pretend to repeat half that I used to hear him say on that subject. It would not be fair. And yet you ought to have proof; for what is all this but assertion? and you shall have proof."

"Indeed, my dear Mrs. Smith, I want none," cried Anne. "You have asserted nothing contradictory to what Mr. Elliot appeared to be some years ago. This is all in confirmation, rather, of what we used to hear and believe. I am more curious to know why he should be so different now?"

"But for my satisfaction; if you will have the goodness to ring for Mary—stay, I am sure you will have the still greater goodness of going yourself into my bed-room, and bringing me the small inlaid box which you will find on the upper shelf of the closet."

Anne, seeing her friend to be earnestly bent on it, did as she was desired. The box was brought and placed before her, and Mrs. Smith, sighing over it as she unlocked it, said,

"This is full of papers belonging to him, to my husband, a small portion only of what I had to look over when I lost him. The letter I am looking for, was one written by Mr. Elliot to him before our marriage, and happened to be saved; why, one can hardly imagine. But he was careless and immethodical, like other men, about those things; and when I came to examine his papers, I found it with others still more trivial from different people scattered here and there, while many letters and memorandums of real importance had been destroyed. Here it is. I would not burn it, because being even then very little satisfied with Mr. Elliot, I was determined to preserve every document of former intimacy.

3. One who feeds cattle for market: a lower-class occupation.
4. Assured.

I have now another motive for being glad that I can produce it."

This was the letter, directed to "Charles Smith, Esq. Tunbridge Wells," and dated from London, as far back as July, 1803.

> Dear Smith,
>
> I have received yours. Your kindness almost overpowers me. I wish nature had made such hearts as yours more common, but I have lived three and twenty years in the world, and have seen none like it. At present, believe me, I have no need of your services, being in cash again. Give me joy: I have got rid of Sir Walter and Miss. They are gone back to Kellynch, and almost made me swear to visit them this summer, but my first visit to Kellynch will be with a surveyor, to tell me how to bring it with best advantage to the hammer.[5] The baronet, nevertheless, is not unlikely to marry again; he is quite fool enough. If he does, however, they will leave me in peace, which may be a decent equivalent for the reversion.[6] He is worse than last year.
>
> I wish I had any name but Elliot. I am sick of it. The name of Walter I can drop, thank God! and I desire you will never insult me with my second W. again, meaning, for the rest of my life, to be only yours truly,
>
> WM. ELLIOT.

Such a letter could not be read without putting Anne in a glow; and Mrs. Smith, observing the high colour in her face, said,

"The language, I know, is highly disrespectful. Though I have forgot the exact terms, I have a perfect impression of the general meaning. But it shews you the man. Mark his professions to my poor husband. Can any thing be stronger?"

Anne could not immediately get over the shock and mortification of finding such words applied to her father. She was obliged to recollect that her seeing the letter was a violation of the laws of honour, that no one ought to be judged or to be known by such testimonies, that no private correspondence could bear the eye of others, before she could recover calmness enough to return the letter which she had been meditating over, and say,

"Thank you. This is full proof undoubtedly, proof of every thing you were saying. But why be acquainted with us now?"

"I can explain this too," cried Mrs. Smith, smiling.

"Can you really?"

"Yes. I have shewn you Mr. Elliot, as he was a dozen years ago, and I will shew him as he is now. I cannot produce written proof again, but I can give as authentic oral testimony as you can desire, of what he is now wanting, and what he is now doing. He is no hypocrite now. He

---

5. To be auctioned.
6. The passing of the estate to Mr. Elliot if Sir Walter dies without male heirs.

truly wants to marry you. His present attentions to your family are very sincere, quite from the heart. I will give you my authority; his friend Colonel Wallis."

"Colonel Wallis! are you acquainted with him?"

"No. It does not come to me in quite so direct a line as that; it takes a bend or two, but nothing of consequence. The stream is as good as at first; the little rubbish it collects in the turnings, is easily moved away. Mr. Elliot talks unreservedly to Colonel Wallis of his views on you—which said Colonel Wallis I imagine to be in himself a sensible, careful, discerning sort of character; but Colonel Wallis has a very pretty silly wife, to whom he tells things which he had better not, and he repeats it all to her. She, in the overflowing spirits of her recovery, repeats it all to her nurse; and the nurse, knowing my acquaintance with you, very naturally brings it all to me. On Monday evening my good friend Mrs. Rooke let me thus much into the secrets of Marlborough-buildings. When I talked of a whole history therefore, you see, I was not romancing so much as you supposed."

"My dear Mrs. Smith, your authority is deficient. This will not do. Mr. Elliot's having any views on me will not in the least account for the efforts he made towards a reconciliation with my father. That was all prior to my coming to Bath. I found them on the most friendly terms when I arrived."

"I know you did; I know it all perfectly, but"—

"Indeed, Mrs. Smith, we must not expect to get real information in such a line. Facts or opinions which are to pass through the hands of so many, to be misconceived by folly in one, and ignorance in another, can hardly have much truth left."

"Only give me a hearing. You will soon be able to judge of the general credit due, by listening to some particulars which you can yourself immediately contradict or confirm. Nobody supposes that you were his first inducement. He had seen you indeed, before he came to Bath and admired you, but without knowing it to be you. So says my historian at least. Is this true? Did he see you last summer or autumn, 'somewhere down in the west,' to use her own words, without knowing it to be you?"

"He certainly did. So far it is very true. At Lyme; I happened to be at Lyme."

"Well," continued Mrs. Smith triumphantly, "grant my friend the credit due to the establishment of the first point asserted. He saw you then at Lyme, and liked you so well as to be exceedingly pleased to meet with you again in Camden-place, as Miss Anne Elliot, and from that moment, I have no doubt, had a double motive in his visits there. But there was another, and an earlier; which I will now explain. If there is any thing in my story which you know to be either false or improbable, stop me. My account states, that your sister's friend, the lady now stay-ing with you, whom I have heard you mention, came to Bath with Miss

Elliot and Sir Walter as long ago as September, (in short when they first came themselves) and has been staying there ever since; that she is a clever, insinuating, handsome woman, poor and plausible, and altogether such in situation and manner, as to give a general idea among Sir Walter's acquaintance, of her meaning to be Lady Elliot, and as general a surprise that Miss Elliot should be apparently blind to the danger."

Here Mrs. Smith paused a moment; but Anne had not a word to say, and she continued,

"This was the light in which it appeared to those who knew the family, long before your return to it; and Colonel Wallis had his eye upon your father enough to be sensible of it, though he did not then visit in Camden-place; but his regard for Mr. Elliot gave him an interest in watching all that was going on there, and when Mr. Elliot came to Bath for a day or two, as he happened to do a little before Christmas, Colonel Wallis made him acquainted with the appearance of things, and the reports beginning to prevail.—Now you are to understand that time had worked a very material change in Mr. Elliot's opinions as to the value of a baronetcy. Upon all points of blood and connexion, he is a completely altered man. Having long had as much money as he could spend, nothing to wish for on the side of avarice or indulgence, he has been gradually learning to pin his happiness upon the consequence he is heir to. I thought it coming on, before our acquaintance ceased, but it is now a confirmed feeling. He cannot bear the idea of not being Sir William. You may guess therefore that the news he heard from his friend, could not be very agreeable,[7] and you may guess what it produced; the resolution of coming back to Bath as soon as possible, and of fixing himself here for a time, with the view of renewing his former acquaintance and recovering such a footing in the family, as might give him the means of ascertaining the degree of his danger, and of circumventing the lady if he found it material. This was agreed upon between the two friends, as the only thing to be done; and Colonel Wallis was to assist in every way that he could. He was to be introduced, and Mrs. Wallis was to be introduced, and every body was to be introduced. Mr. Elliot came back accordingly; and on application was forgiven, as you know, and re-admitted into the family; and there it was his constant object, and his only object (till your arrival added another motive) to watch Sir Walter and Mrs. Clay. He omitted no opportunity of being with them, threw himself in their way, called at all hours—but I need not be particular on this subject. You can imagine what an artful man would do; and with this guide, perhaps, may recollect what you have seen him do."

"Yes," said Anne, "you tell me nothing which does not accord with

7. Because if Sir Walter marries again, his wife may bear sons.

what I have known, or could imagine. There is always something offensive in the details of cunning. The manœuvres of selfishness and duplicity must ever be revolting, but I have heard nothing which really
surprises me. I know those who would be shocked by such a representation of Mr. Elliot, who would have difficulty in believing it; but I have
never been satisfied. I have always wanted some other motive for his
conduct than appeared.—I should like to know his present opinion, as
to the probability of the event he has been in dread of; whether he considers the danger to be lessening or not."

"Lessening, I understand," replied Mrs. Smith. "He thinks Mrs. Clay
afraid of him, aware that he sees through her, and not daring to proceed
as she might do in his absence. But since he must be absent some time
or other, I do not perceive how he can ever be secure, while she holds
her present influence. Mrs. Wallis has an amusing idea, as nurse tells
me, that it is to be put into the marriage articles when you and Mr.
Elliot marry, that your father is not to marry Mrs. Clay. A scheme,
worthy of Mrs. Wallis's understanding, by all accounts; but my sensible
nurse Rooke sees the absurdity of it.—'Why, to be sure, ma'am,' said
she, 'it would not prevent his marrying any body else.' And indeed, to
own the truth, I do not think nurse in her heart is a very strenuous
opposer of Sir Walter's making a second match. She must be allowed to
be a favourer of matrimony you know, and (since self will intrude) who
can say that she may not have some flying visions of attending the next
Lady Elliot, through Mrs. Wallis's recommendation?"

"I am very glad to know all this," said Anne, after a little thought-
fulness. "It will be more painful to me in some respects to be in company with him, but I shall know better what to do. My line of conduct
will be more direct. Mr. Elliot is evidently a disingenuous, artificial,
worldly man, who has never had any better principle to guide him
than selfishness."

But Mr. Elliot was not yet done with. Mrs. Smith had been carried
away from her first direction, and Anne had forgotten, in the interest of
her own family concerns, how much had been originally implied
against him; but her attention was now called to the explanation of those
first hints, and she listened to a recital which, if it did not perfectly
justify the unqualified bitterness of Mrs. Smith, proved him to have
been very unfeeling in his conduct towards her, very deficient both in
justice and compassion.

She learned that (the intimacy between them continuing unimpaired
by Mr. Elliot's marriage) they had been as before always together, and
Mr. Elliot had led his friend into expenses much beyond his fortune.
Mrs. Smith did not want to take blame to herself, and was most tender
of throwing any on her husband; but Anne could collect that their
income had never been equal to their style of living, and that from the
first, there had been a great deal of general and joint extravagance. From

his wife's account of him, she could discern Mr. Smith to have been a man of warm feelings, easy temper, careless habits, and not strong understanding, much more amiable than his friend, and very unlike him—led by him, and probably despised by him. Mr. Elliot, raised by his marriage to great affluence, and disposed to every gratification of pleasure and vanity which could be commanded without involving himself, (for with all his self-indulgence he had become a prudent man) and beginning to be rich, just as his friend ought to have found himself to be poor, seemed to have had no concern at all for that friend's probable finances, but, on the contrary, had been prompting and encouraging expenses, which could end only in ruin. And the Smiths accordingly had been ruined.

The husband had died just in time to be spared the full knowledge of it. They had previously known embarrassments enough to try the friendship of their friends, and to prove that Mr. Elliot's had better not be tried; but it was not till his death that the wretched state of his affairs was fully known. With a confidence in Mr. Elliot's regard, more creditable to his feelings than his judgment, Mr. Smith had appointed him the executor of his will; but Mr. Elliot would not act, and the difficulties and distresses which this refusal had heaped on her, in addition to the inevitable sufferings of her situation, had been such as could not be related without anguish of spirit, or listened to without corresponding indignation.

Anne was shewn some letters of his on the occasion, answers to urgent applications from Mrs. Smith, which all breathed the same stern resolution of not engaging in a fruitless trouble, and, under a cold civility, the same hard-hearted indifference to any of the evils it might bring on her. It was a dreadful picture of ingratitude and inhumanity; and Anne felt at some moments, that no flagrant open crime could have been worse. She had a great deal to listen to; all the particulars of past sad scenes, all the minutiæ of distress upon distress, which in former conversations had been merely hinted at, were dwelt on now with a natural indulgence. Anne could perfectly comprehend the exquisite relief, and was only the more inclined to wonder at the composure of her friend's usual state of mind.

There was one circumstance in the history of her grievances of particular irritation. She had good reason to believe that some property of her husband in the West Indies, which had been for many years under a sort of sequestration for the payment of its own incumbrances,[8] might be recoverable by proper measures; and this property, though not large, would be enough to make her comparatively rich. But there was nobody to stir in it. Mr. Elliot would do nothing, and she could do nothing herself, equally disabled from personal exertion by her state of bodily

8. The income of the estate has been assigned, presumably by legal action, to pay legal claims against the owner.

weakness, and from employing others by her want of money. She had no natural connexions to assist her even with their counsel, and she could not afford to purchase the assistance of the law. This was a cruel aggravation of actually streightened[9] means. To feel that she ought to be in better circumstances, that a little trouble in the right place might do it, and to fear that delay might be even weakening her claims, was hard to bear!

It was on this point that she had hoped to engage Anne's good offices with Mr. Elliot. She had previously, in the anticipation of their marriage, been very apprehensive of losing her friend by it; but on being assured that he could have made no attempt of that nature, since he did not even know her to be in Bath, it immediately occurred, that something might be done in her favour by the influence of the woman he loved, and she had been hastily preparing to interest Anne's feelings, as far as the observances due to Mr. Elliot's character would allow, when Anne's refutation of the supposed engagement changed the face of every thing, and while it took from her the new-formed hope of succeeding in the object of her first anxiety, left her at least the comfort of telling the whole story her own way.

After listening to this full description of Mr. Elliot, Anne could not but express some surprise at Mrs. Smith's having spoken of him so favourably in the beginning of their conversation. "She had seemed to recommend and praise him!"

"My dear," was Mrs. Smith's reply, "there was nothing else to be done. I considered your marrying him as certain, though he might not yet have made the offer, and I could no more speak the truth of him, than if he had been your husband. My heart bled for you, as I talked of happiness. And yet, he is sensible, he is agreeable, and with such a woman as you, it was not absolutely hopeless. He was very unkind to his first wife. They were wretched together. But she was too ignorant and giddy for respect, and he had never loved her. I was willing to hope that you must fare better."

Anne could just acknowledge within herself such a possibility of having been induced to marry him, as made her shudder at the idea of the misery which must have followed. It was just possible that she might have been persuaded by Lady Russell! And under such a supposition, which would have been most miserable, when time had disclosed all, too late?

It was very desirable that Lady Russell should be no longer deceived; and one of the concluding arrangements of this important conference, which carried them through the greater part of the morning, was, that Anne had full liberty to communicate to her friend every thing relative to Mrs. Smith, in which his conduct was involved.

9. Straitened, reduced.

Chapter XXII

Anne went home to think over all that she had heard. In one point, her feelings were relieved by this knowledge of Mr. Elliot. There was no longer any thing of tenderness due to him. He stood, as opposed to Captain Wentworth, in all his own unwelcome obtrusiveness; and the evil of his attentions last night, the irremediable mischief he might have done, was considered with sensations unqualified, unperplexed.—Pity for him was all over. But this was the only point of relief. In every other respect, in looking around her, or penetrating forward, she saw more to distrust and to apprehend. She was concerned for the disappointment and pain Lady Russell would be feeling, for the mortifications which must be hanging over her father and sister, and had all the distress of foreseeing many evils, without knowing how to avert any one of them.—She was most thankful for her own knowledge of him. She had never considered herself as entitled to reward for not slighting an old friend like Mrs. Smith, but here was a reward indeed springing from it!—Mrs. Smith had been able to tell her what no one else could have done. Could the knowledge have been extended through her family!— But this was a vain idea. She must talk to Lady Russell, tell her, consult with her, and having done her best, wait the event[1] with as much composure as possible; and after all, her greatest want of composure would be in that quarter of the mind which could not be opened to Lady Russell, in that flow of anxieties and fears which must be all to herself.

She found, on reaching home, that she had, as she intended, escaped seeing Mr. Elliot; that he had called and paid them a long morning visit; but hardly had she congratulated herself, and felt safe till to-morrow, when she heard that he was coming again in the evening.

"I had not the smallest intention of asking him," said Elizabeth, with affected carelessness, "but he gave so many hints; so Mrs. Clay says, at least."

"Indeed I do say it. I never saw any body in my life spell[2] harder for an invitation. Poor man! I was really in pain for him; for your hard-hearted sister, Miss Anne, seems bent on cruelty."

"Oh!" cried Elizabeth, "I have been rather too much used to the game to be soon overcome by a gentleman's hints. However, when I found how excessively he was regretting that he should miss my father this morning, I gave way immediately, for I would never really omit an opportunity of bringing him and Sir Walter together. They appear to so much advantage in company with each other! Each behaving so pleasantly! Mr. Elliot looking up with so much respect!"

"Quite delightful!" cried Mrs. Clay, not daring, however, to turn her

1. Outcome.
2. Suggest a desire.

eyes towards Anne. "Exactly like father and son! Dear Miss Elliot, may I not say father and son?"

"Oh! I lay no embargo on any body's words. If you will have such ideas! But, upon my word, I am scarcely sensible of his attentions being beyond those of other men."

"My dear Miss Elliot!" exclaimed Mrs. Clay, lifting up her hands and eyes, and sinking all the rest of her astonishment in a convenient silence.

"Well, my dear Penelope, you need not be so˙alarmed about him. I did invite him, you know. I sent him away with smiles. When I found he was really going to his friends at Thornberry-park for the whole day tomorrow, I had compassion on him."

Anne admired the good acting of the friend, in being able to shew such pleasure as she did, in the expectation, and in the actual arrival of the very person whose presence must really be interfering with her prime object. It was impossible but that Mrs. Clay must hate the sight of Mr. Elliot; and yet she could assume a most obliging, placid look, and appear quite satisfied with the curtailed license of devoting herself only half as much to Sir Walter as she would have done otherwise.

To Anne herself it was most distressing to see Mr. Elliot enter the room; and quite painful to have him approach and speak to her. She had been used before to feel that he could not be always quite sincere, but now she saw insincerity in every thing. His attentive deference to her father, contrasted with his former language, was odious; and when she thought of his cruel conduct towards Mrs. Smith, she could hardly bear the sight of his present smiles and mildness, or the sound of his artificial good sentiments. She meant to avoid any such alteration of manners as might provoke a remonstrance on his side. It was a great object with her to escape all enquiry or eclat;[3] but it was her intention to be as decidedly cool to him as might be compatible with their relationship, and to retrace, as quietly as she could, the few steps of unnecessary intimacy she had been gradually led along. She was accordingly more guarded, and more cool, than she had been the night before.

He wanted to animate her curiosity again as to how and where he could have heard her formerly praised; wanted very much to be gratified by more solicitation; but the charm was broken: he found that the heat and animation of a public room were necessary to kindle his modest cousin's vanity; he found, at least, that it was not to be done now, by any of those attempts which he could hazard among the too-commanding claims of the others. He little surmised that it was a subject acting now exactly against his interest, bringing immediately into her thoughts all those parts of his conduct which were least excusable.

She had some satisfaction in finding that he was really going out of

3. Notoriety, conspicuousness.

Bath the next morning, going early, and that he would be gone the greater part of two days. He was invited again to Camden-place the very evening of his return; but from Thursday to Saturday evening his absence was certain. It was bad enough that a Mrs. Clay should be always before her; but that a deeper hypocrite should be added to their party, seemed the destruction of every thing like peace and comfort. It was so humiliating to reflect on the constant deception practised on her father and Elizabeth; to consider the various sources of mortification preparing for them! Mrs. Clay's selfishness was not so complicate nor so revolting as his; and Anne would have compounded for the marriage at once, with all its evils, to be clear of Mr. Elliot's subtleties, in endeavouring to prevent it.

On Friday morning she meant to go very early to Lady Russell, and accomplish the necessary communication; and she would have gone directly after breakfast but that Mrs. Clay was also going out on some obliging purpose of saving her sister trouble, which determined her to wait till she might be safe from such a companion. She saw Mrs. Clay fairly off, therefore, before she began to talk of spending the morning in Rivers-street.

"Very well," said Elizabeth, "I have nothing to send but my love. Oh! you may as well take back that tiresome book she would lend me, and pretend I have read it through. I really cannot be plaguing myself for ever with all the new poems and states of the nation that come out. Lady Russell quite bores one with her new publications. You need not tell her so, but I thought her dress hideous the other night. I used to think she had some taste in dress, but I was ashamed of her at the concert. Something so formal and *arrangé*[4] in her air! and she sits so upright! My best love, of course."

"And mine," added Sir Walter. "Kindest regards. And you may say, that I mean to call upon her soon. Make a civil message. But I shall only leave my card.[5] Morning visits are never fair by women at her time of life, who make themselves up so little. If she would only wear rouge, she would not be afraid of being seen; but last time I called, I observed the blinds were let down immediately."

While her father spoke, there was a knock at the door. Who could it be? Anne, remembering the preconcerted visits, at all hours, of Mr. Elliot, would have expected him, but for his known engagement seven miles off. After the usual period of suspense, the usual sounds of approach were heard, and "Mr. and Mrs. Charles Musgrove" were ushered into the room.

Surprise was the strongest emotion raised by their appearance; but Anne was really glad to see them; and the others were not so sorry but

4. Artificial.
5. Calling card: Sir Walter will leave his card, in token of having called, but will not ask to see Lady Russell.

that they could put on a decent air of welcome; and as soon as it became clear that these, their nearest relations, were not arrived with any views of accommodation in that house, Sir Walter and Elizabeth were able to rise in cordiality, and do the honours of it very well. They were come to Bath for a few days with Mrs. Musgrove, and were at the White Hart. So much was pretty soon understood; but till Sir Walter and Elizabeth were walking Mary into the other drawing-room, and regaling themselves with her admiration, Anne could not draw upon Charles's brain for a regular history of their coming, or an explanation of some smiling hints of particular business, which had been ostentatiously dropped by Mary, as well as of some apparent confusion as to whom their party consisted of.

She then found that it consisted of Mrs. Musgrove, Henrietta, and Captain Harville, beside their two selves. He gave her a very plain, intelligible account of the whole; a narration in which she saw a great deal of most characteristic proceeding. The scheme had received its first impulse by Captain Harville's wanting to come to Bath on business. He had begun to talk of it a week ago; and by way of doing something, as shooting was over, Charles had proposed coming with him, and Mrs. Harville had seemed to like the idea of it very much, as an advantage to her husband; but Mary could not bear to be left, and had made herself so unhappy about it that, for a day or two, every thing seemed to be in suspense, or at an end. But then, it had been taken up by his father and mother. His mother had some old friends in Bath, whom she wanted to see; it was thought a good opportunity for Henrietta to come and buy wedding-clothes for herself and her sister; and, in short, it ended in being his mother's party, that every thing might be comfortable and easy to Captain Harville; and he and Mary were included in it, by way of general convenience. They had arrived late the night before. Mrs. Harville, her children, and Captain Benwick, remained with Mr. Musgrove and Louisa at Uppercross.

Anne's only surprise was, that affairs should be in forwardness enough for Henrietta's wedding-clothes to be talked of: she had imagined such difficulties of fortune to exist there as must prevent the marriage from being near at hand; but she learned from Charles that, very recently, (since Mary's last letter to herself) Charles Hayter had been applied to by a friend to hold a living for a youth who could not possibly claim it under many years;[6] and that, on the strength of this present income, with almost a certainty of something more permanent long before the term in question, the two families had consented to the young people's wishes, and that their marriage was likely to take place in a few months, quite as soon as Louisa's. "And a very good living it was," Charles added,

6. Charles, as a young clergyman, has been asked to serve as temporary pastor for a congregation that has been promised to someone still too young to be ordained. Many pastoral positions in England at this time were assigned by large landowners as a matter of patronage.

"only five-and-twenty miles from Uppercross, and in a very fine country—fine part of Dorsetshire. In the centre of some of the best preserves[7]
in the kingdom, surrounded by three great proprietors, each more careful and jealous than the other; and to two of the three, at least, Charles
Hayter might get a special recommendation. Not that he will value it as
he ought," he observed, "Charles is too cool about sporting. That's the
worst of him."

"I am extremely glad, indeed," cried Anne, "particularly glad that this
should happen: and that of two sisters, who both deserve equally well,
and who have always been such good friends, the pleasant prospects of
one should not be dimming those of the other—that they should be so
equal in their prosperity and comfort. I hope your father and mother are
quite happy with regard to both."

"Oh! yes. My father would be as well pleased if the gentlemen were
richer, but he has no other fault to find. Money, you know, coming
down with money[8]—two daughters at once—it cannot be a very agreeable operation, and it streightens him as to many things. However, I do
not mean to say they have not a right to it. It is very fit they should have
daughters' shares; and I am sure he has always been a very kind, liberal
father to me. Mary does not above half like Henrietta's match. She
never did, you know. But she does not do him justice, nor think enough
about Winthrop. I cannot make her attend to the value of the property.
It is a very fair match, as times go; and I have liked Charles Hayter all
my life, and I shall not leave off now."

"Such excellent parents as Mr. and Mrs. Musgrove," exclaimed
Anne, "should be happy in their children's marriages. They do every
thing to confer happiness, I am sure. What a blessing to young people
to be in such hands! Your father and mother seem so totally free from
all those ambitious feelings which have led to so much misconduct and
misery, both in young and old! I hope you think Louisa perfectly recovered now?"

He answered rather hesitatingly, "Yes, I believe I do—very much
recovered; but she is altered: there is no running or jumping about, no
laughing or dancing; it is quite different. If one happens only to shut the
door a little hard, she starts and wriggles like a young dab chick in the
water; and Benwick sits at her elbow, reading verses, or whispering to
her, all day long."

Anne could not help laughing. "That cannot be much to your taste,
I know," said she; "but I do believe him to be an excellent young man."

"To be sure he is. Nobody doubts it; and I hope you do not think I
am so illiberal as to want every man to have the same objects and pleasures as myself. I have a great value for Benwick; and when one can but
get him to talk, he has plenty to say. His reading has done him no

---

7. Game preserves, where animals were nurtured for the purpose of hunting them.
8. For dowries.

harm, for he has fought as well as read. He is a brave fellow. I got more acquainted with him last Monday than ever I did before. We had a famous set-to at rat-hunting all the morning, in my father's great barns; and he played his part so well, that I have liked him the better ever since."

Here they were interrupted by the absolute necessity of Charles's following the others to admire mirrors and china; but Anne had heard enough to understand the present state of Uppercross, and rejoice in its happiness; and though she sighed as she rejoiced, her sigh had none of the ill-will of envy in it. She would certainly have risen to their blessings if she could, but she did not want to lessen theirs.

The visit passed off altogether in high good humour. Mary was in excellent spirits, enjoying the gaiety and the change; and so well satisfied with the journey in her mother-in-law's carriage with four horses, and with her own complete independence of Camden-place, that she was exactly in a temper to admire every thing as she ought, and enter most readily into all the superiorities of the house, as they were detailed to her. She had no demands on her father or sister, and her consequence was just enough increased by their handsome drawing-rooms.

Elizabeth was, for a short time, suffering a good deal. She felt that Mrs. Musgrove and all her party ought to be asked to dine with them, but she could not bear to have the difference of style, the reduction of servants, which a dinner must betray, witnessed by those who had been always so inferior to the Elliots of Kellynch. It was a struggle between propriety and vanity; but vanity got the better, and then Elizabeth was happy again. These were her internal persuasions.—"Old fashioned notions—country hospitality—we do not profess to give dinners—few people in Bath do—Lady Alicia never does; did not even ask her own sister's family, though they were here a month: and I dare say it would be very inconvenient to Mrs. Musgrove—put her quite out of her way. I am sure she would rather not come—she cannot feel easy with us. I will ask them all for an evening; that will be much better—that will be a novelty and a treat. They have not seen two such drawing rooms before. They will be delighted to come to-morrow evening. It shall be a regular party—small, but most elegant." And this satisfied Elizabeth: and when the invitation was given to the two present, and promised for the absent, Mary was as completely satisfied. She was particularly asked to meet Mr. Elliot, and be introduced to Lady Dalrymple and Miss Carteret, who were fortunately already engaged to come; and she could not have received a more gratifying attention. Miss Elliot was to have the honour of calling on Mrs. Musgrove in the course of the morning, and Anne walked off with Charles and Mary, to go and see her and Henrietta directly.

Her plan of sitting with Lady Russell must give way for the present. They all three called in Rivers-street for a couple of minutes; but Anne convinced herself that a day's delay of the intended communication could be of no consequence, and hastened forward to the White Hart, to see again the friends and companions of the last autumn, with an eagerness of good will which many associations contributed to form.

They found Mrs. Musgrove and her daughter within, and by themselves, and Anne had the kindest welcome from each. Henrietta was exactly in that state of recently-improved views, of fresh-formed happiness, which made her full of regard and interest for every body she had ever liked before at all; and Mrs. Musgrove's real affection had been won by her usefulness when they were in distress. It was a heartiness, and a warmth, and a sincerity which Anne delighted in the more, from the sad want of such blessings at home. She was intreated to give them as much of her time as possible, invited for every day and all day long, or rather claimed as a part of the family; and in return, she naturally fell into all her wonted ways of attention and assistance, and on Charles's leaving them together, was listening to Mrs. Musgrove's history of Louisa, and to Henrietta's of herself, giving opinions on business, and recommendations to shops; with intervals of every help which Mary required, from altering her ribbon to settling her accounts, from finding her keys, and assorting her trinkets, to trying to convince her that she was not ill used by any body; which Mary, well amused as she generally was in her station at a window overlooking the entrance to the pump-room,[9] could not but have her moments of imagining.

A morning of thorough confusion was to be expected. A large party in an hotel ensured a quick-changing, unsettled scene. One five minutes brought a note, the next a parcel, and Anne had not been there half an hour, when their dining-room, spacious as it was, seemed more than half filled: a party of steady old friends were seated round Mrs. Musgrove, and Charles came back with Captains Harville and Wentworth. The appearance of the latter could not be more than the surprise of the moment. It was impossible for her to have forgotten to feel, that this arrival of their common friends must be soon bringing them together again. Their last meeting had been most important in opening his feelings; she had derived from it a delightful conviction; but she feared from his looks, that the same unfortunate persuasion, which had hastened him away from the concert room, still governed. He did not seem to want to be near enough for conversation.

She tried to be calm, and leave things to take their course; and tried to dwell much on this argument of rational dependance—"Surely, if there be constant attachment on each side, our hearts must understand each other ere long. We are not boy and girl, to be captiously irritable, misled by every moment's inadvertence, and wantonly playing with our own happiness." And yet, a few minutes afterwards, she felt as if their

9. A central room in the public baths, where people assembled for social as well as medical reasons.

being in company with each other, under their present circumstances, could only be exposing them to inadvertencies and misconstructions of the most mischievous kind.

"Anne," cried Mary, still at her window, "there is Mrs. Clay, I am sure, standing under the colonnade, and a gentleman with her. I saw them turn the corner from Bath-street just now. They seem deep in talk. Who is it?—Come, and tell me. Good heavens! I recollect.—It is Mr. Elliot himself."

"No," cried Anne quickly, "it cannot be Mr. Elliot, I assure you. He was to leave Bath at nine this morning, and does not come back till to-morrow."

As she spoke, she felt that Captain Wentworth was looking at her; the consciousness of which vexed and embarrassed her, and made her regret that she had said so much, simple as it was.

Mary, resenting that she should be supposed not to know her own cousin, began talking very warmly about the family features, and protesting still more positively that it was Mr. Elliot, calling again upon Anne to come and look herself; but Anne did not mean to stir, and tried to be cool and unconcerned. Her distress returned, however, on perceiving smiles and intelligent glances pass between two or three of the lady visitors, as if they believed themselves quite in the secret. It was evident that the report concerning her had spread; and a short pause succeeded, which seemed to ensure that it would now spread farther.

"Do come, Anne," cried Mary, "come and look yourself. You will be too late, if you do not make haste. They are parting, they are shaking hands. He is turning away. Not know Mr. Elliot, indeed!—You seem to have forgot all about Lyme."

To pacify Mary, and perhaps screen her own embarrassment, Anne did move quietly to the window. She was just in time to ascertain that it really was Mr. Elliot (which she had never believed), before he disappeared on one side, as Mrs. Clay walked quickly off on the other; and checking the surprise which she could not but feel at such an appearance of friendly conference between two persons of totally opposite interests, she calmly said, "Yes, it is Mr. Elliot certainly. He has changed his hour of going, I suppose, that is all—or I may be mistaken; I might not attend;" and walked back to her chair, recomposed, and with the comfortable hope of having acquitted herself well.

The visitors took their leave; and Charles, having civilly seen them off, and then made a face at them, and abused them for coming, began with—

"Well, mother, I have done something for you that you will like. I have been to the theatre, and secured a box for to-morrow night. A'n't I a good boy? I know you love a play; and there is room for us all. It holds nine. I have engaged Captain Wentworth. Anne will not be sorry to join us, I am sure. We all like a play. Have not I done well, mother?"

Mrs. Musgrove was good humouredly beginning to express her perfect readiness for the play, if Henrietta and all the others liked it, when Mary eagerly interrupted her by exclaiming,

"Good heavens, Charles! how can you think of such a thing? Take a box for to-morrow night! Have you forgot that we are engaged to Camden-place to-morrow night? and that we were most particularly asked on purpose to meet Lady Dalrymple and her daughter, and Mr. Elliot—all the principal family connexions—on purpose to be introduced to them? How can you be so forgetful?"

"Phoo! phoo!" replied Charles, "what's an evening party? Never worth remembering. Your father might have asked us to dinner, I think, if he had wanted to see us. You may do as you like, but I shall go to the play."

"Oh! Charles, I declare it will be too abominable if you do! when you promised to go."

"No, I did not promise. I only smirked and bowed, and said the word 'happy.' There was no promise."

"But you must go, Charles. It would be unpardonable to fail. We were asked on purpose to be introduced. There was always such a great connexion between the Dalrymples and ourselves. Nothing ever happened on either side that was not announced immediately. We are quite near relations, you know: and Mr. Elliot too, whom you ought so particularly to be acquainted with! Every attention is due to Mr. Elliot. Consider, my father's heir—the future representative of the family."

"Don't talk to me about heirs and representatives," cried Charles. "I am not one of those who neglect the reigning power to bow to the rising sun. If I would not go for the sake of your father, I should think it scandalous to go for the sake of his heir. What is Mr. Elliot to me?"

The careless expression was life to Anne, who saw that Captain Wentworth was all attention, looking and listening with his whole soul; and that the last words brought his enquiring eyes from Charles to herself.

Charles and Mary still talked on in the same style; he, half serious and half jesting, maintaining the scheme for the play; and she, invariably serious, most warmly opposing it, and not omitting to make it known, that however determined to go to Camden-place herself, she should not think herself very well used, if they went to the play without her. Mrs. Musgrove interposed.

"We had better put it off. Charles, you had much better go back, and change the box for Tuesday. It would be a pity to be divided, and we should be losing Miss Anne too, if there is a party at her father's; and I am sure neither Henrietta nor I should care at all for the play, if Miss Anne could not be with us."

Anne felt truly obliged to her for such kindness; and quite as much so, moreover, for the opportunity it gave her of decidedly saying—

"If it depended only on my inclination, ma'am, the party at home (excepting on Mary's account) would not be the smallest impediment. I have no pleasure in the sort of meeting, and should be too happy to change it for a play, and with you. But, it had better not be attempted, perhaps."

She had spoken it; but she trembled when it was done, conscious that her words were listened to, and daring not even to try to observe their effect.

It was soon generally agreed that Tuesday should be the day, Charles only reserving the advantage of still teasing his wife, by persisting that he would go to the play to-morrow, if nobody else would.

Captain Wentworth left his seat, and walked to the fire-place; probably for the sake of walking away from it soon afterwards, and taking a station, with less barefaced design, by Anne.

"You have not been long enough in Bath," said he, "to enjoy the evening parties of the place."

"Oh! no. The usual character of them has nothing for me. I am no card-player."

"You were not formerly, I know. You did not use to like cards; but time makes many changes."

"I am not yet so much changed," cried Anne, and stopped, fearing she hardly knew what misconstruction. After waiting a few moments he said—and as if it were the result of immediate feeling—"It is a period, indeed! Eight years and a half is a period!"

Whether he would have proceeded farther was left to Anne's imagination to ponder over in a calmer hour; for while still hearing the sounds he had uttered, she was startled to other subjects by Henrietta, eager to make use of the present leisure for getting out, and calling on her companions to lose no time, lest somebody else should come in.

They were obliged to move. Anne talked of being perfectly ready, and tried to look it; but she felt that could Henrietta have known the regret and reluctance of her heart in quitting that chair, in preparing to quit the room, she would have found, in all her own sensations for her cousin, in the very security of his affection, wherewith to pity her.

Their preparations, however, were stopped short. Alarming sounds were heard; other visitors approached, and the door was thrown open for Sir Walter and Miss Elliot, whose entrance seemed to give a general chill. Anne felt an instant oppression, and, wherever she looked, saw symptoms of the same. The comfort, the freedom, the gaiety of the room was over, hushed into cold composure, determined silence, or insipid talk, to meet the heartless elegance of her father and sister. How mortifying to feel that it was so!

Her jealous eye was satisfied in one particular. Captain Wentworth was acknowledged again by each, by Elizabeth more graciously than before. She even addressed him once, and looked at him more than once. Elizabeth was, in fact, revolving a great measure. The sequel explained it. After the waste of a few minutes in saying the proper nothings, she began to give the invitation which was to comprise all the remaining dues of the Musgroves. "To-morrow evening, to meet a few friends, no formal party." It was all said very gracefully, and the cards with which she had provided herself, the "Miss Elliot at home," were laid on the table, with a courteous, comprehensive smile to all; and one smile and one card more decidedly for Captain Wentworth. The truth was, that Elizabeth had been long enough in Bath, to understand the importance of a man of such an air and appearance as his. The past was nothing. The present was that Captain Wentworth would move about well in her drawing-room. The card was pointedly given, and Sir Walter and Elizabeth arose and disappeared.

The interruption had been short, though severe; and ease and animation returned to most of those they left, as the door shut them out, but not to Anne. She could think only of the invitation she had with such astonishment witnessed; and of the manner in which it had been received, a manner of doubtful meaning, of surprise rather than gratification, of polite acknowledgment rather than acceptance. She knew him; she saw disdain in his eye, and could not venture to believe that he had determined to accept such an offering, as atonement for all the insolence of the past. Her spirits sank. He held the card in his hand after they were gone, as if deeply considering it.

"Only think of Elizabeth's including every body!" whispered Mary very audibly. "I do not wonder Captain Wentworth is delighted! You see he cannot put the card out of his hand."

Anne caught his eye, saw his cheeks glow, and his mouth form itself into a momentary expression of contempt, and turned away, that she might neither see nor hear more to vex her.

The party separated. The gentlemen had their own pursuits, the ladies proceeded on their own business, and they met no more while Anne belonged to them. She was earnestly begged to return and dine, and give them all the rest of the day; but her spirits had been so long exerted, that at present she felt unequal to more, and fit only for home, where she might be sure of being as silent as she chose.

Promising to be with them the whole of the following morning, therefore, she closed the fatigues of the present, by a toilsome walk to Camden-place, there to spend the evening chiefly in listening to the busy arrangements of Elizabeth and Mrs. Clay for the morrow's party, the frequent enumeration of the persons invited, and the continually improving detail of all the embellishments which were to make it the most completely elegant of its kind in Bath, while harassing herself in secret with the never-ending question, of whether Captain Wentworth would come or not? They were reckoning him as certain, but, with her, it was a gnawing solicitude never appeased for five minutes together. She generally thought he would come, because she generally thought he ought; but it was a case which she could not so shape into any positive act of duty or discretion, as inevitably to defy the suggestions of very opposite feelings.

She only roused herself from the broodings of this restless agitation, to let Mrs. Clay know that she had been seen with Mr. Elliot three hours after his being supposed to be out of Bath; for having watched in vain for some intimation of the interview from the lady herself, she determined to mention it; and it seemed to her that there was guilt in Mrs. Clay's face as she listened. It was transient, cleared away in an instant, but Anne could imagine she read there the consciousness of having, by some complication of mutual trick, or some overbearing authority of his, been obliged to attend (perhaps for half an hour) to his lectures and restrictions on her designs on Sir Walter. She exclaimed, however, with a very tolerable imitation of nature,

"Oh dear! very true. Only think, Miss Elliot, to my great surprise I met with Mr. Elliot in Bath-street! I was never more astonished. He turned back and walked with me to the Pump-yard. He had been prevented setting off for Thornberry, but I really forget by what—for I was in a hurry, and could not much attend, and I can only answer for his being determined not to be delayed in his return. He wanted to know how early he might be admitted to-morrow. He was full of 'to-morrow;' and it is very evident that I have been full of it too ever since I entered the house, and learnt the extension of your plan, and all that had happened, or my seeing him could never have gone so entirely out of my head."

Chapter XXIII

One day only had passed since Anne's conversation with Mrs. Smith; but a keener interest had succeeded, and she was now so little touched by Mr. Elliot's conduct, except by its effects in one quarter, that it became a matter of course the next morning, still to defer her explanatory visit in Rivers-street. She had promised to be with the Musgroves from breakfast to dinner. Her faith was plighted, and Mr. Elliot's character, like the Sultaness Scheherazade's head,[1] must live another day.

She could not keep her appointment punctually, however; the weather was unfavourable, and she had grieved over the rain on her friends' account, and felt it very much on her own, before she was able to attempt the walk. When she reached the White Hart, and made her way to the proper apartment, she found herself neither arriving quite in time, nor the first to arrive. The party before her were Mrs. Musgrove, talking to Mrs. Croft, and Captain Harville to Captain Wentworth, and

1. Scheherazade, in the *Arabian Nights' Entertainment*, saved herself from beheading, night after night, by the enthralling stories that she told the sultan.

she immediately heard that Mary and Henrietta, too impatient to wait, had gone out the moment it had cleared, but would be back again soon, and that the strictest injunctions had been left with Mrs. Musgrove, to keep her there till they returned. She had only to submit, sit down, be outwardly composed, and feel herself plunged at once in all the agitations which she had merely laid her account of[2] tasting a little before the morning closed. There was no delay, no waste of time. She was deep in the happiness of such misery, or the misery of such happiness, instantly. Two minutes after her entering the room, Captain Wentworth said,

"We will write the letter we were talking of, Harville, now, if you will give me materials."

Materials were all at hand, on a separate table; he went to it, and nearly turning his back on them all, was engrossed by writing.

Mrs. Musgrove was giving Mrs. Croft the history of her eldest daughter's engagement, and just in that inconvenient tone of voice which was perfectly audible while it pretended to be a whisper. Anne felt that she did not belong to the conversation, and yet, as Captain Harville seemed thoughtful and not disposed to talk, she could not avoid hearing many undesirable particulars, such as "how Mr. Musgrove and my brother Hayter had met again and again to talk it over; what my brother Hayter had said one day, and what Mr. Musgrove had proposed the next, and what had occurred to my sister Hayter, and what the young people had wished, and what I said at first I never could consent to, but was afterwards persuaded to think might do very well," and a great deal in the same style of open-hearted communication—Minutiæ which, even with every advantage of taste and delicacy which good Mrs. Musgrove could not give, could be properly interesting only to the principals. Mrs. Croft was attending with great good humour, and whenever she spoke at all, it was very sensibly. Anne hoped the gentlemen might each be too much self-occupied to hear.

"And so, ma'am, all these things considered," said Mrs. Musgrove in her powerful whisper, "though we could have wished it different, yet altogether we did not think it fair to stand out any longer; for Charles Hayter was quite wild about it, and Henrietta was pretty near as bad; and so we thought they had better marry at once, and make the best of it, as many others have done before them. At any rate, said I, it will be better than a long engagement."

"That is precisely what I was going to observe," cried Mrs. Croft. "I would rather have young people settle on a small income at once, and have to struggle with a few difficulties together, than be involved in a long engagement. I always think that no mutual—"

"Oh! dear Mrs. Croft," cried Mrs. Musgrove, unable to let her finish

2. Reckoned on, anticipated.

her speech, "there is nothing I so abominate for young people as a long engagement. It is what I always protested against for my children. It is all very well, I used to say, for young people to be engaged, if there is a certainty of their being able to marry in six months, or even in twelve, but a long engagement!"

"Yes, dear ma'am," said Mrs. Croft, "or an uncertain engagement; an engagement which may be long. To begin without knowing that at such a time there will be the means of marrying, I hold to be very unsafe and unwise, and what, I think, all parents should prevent as far as they can."

Anne found an unexpected interest here. She felt its application to herself, felt it in a nervous thrill all over her, and at the same moment that her eyes instinctively glanced towards the distant table, Captain Wentworth's pen ceased to move, his head was raised, pausing, listening, and he turned round the next instant to give a look—one quick, conscious look at her.

The two ladies continued to talk, to re-urge the same admitted truths, and enforce them with such examples of the ill effect of a contrary practice, as had fallen within their observation, but Anne heard nothing distinctly; it was only a buzz of words in her ear, her mind was in confusion.

Captain Harville, who had in truth been hearing none of it, now left his seat, and moved to a window; and Anne seeming to watch him, though it was from thorough absence of mind, became gradually sensible that he was inviting her to join him where he stood. He looked at her with a smile, and a little motion of the head, which expressed, "Come to me, I have something to say;" and the unaffected, easy kindness of manner which denoted the feelings of an older acquaintance than he really was, strongly enforced the invitation. She roused herself and went to him. The window at which he stood, was at the other end of the room from where the two ladies were sitting, and though nearer to Captain Wentworth's table, not very near. As she joined him, Captain Harville's countenance reassumed the serious, thoughtful expression which seemed its natural character.

"Look here," said he, unfolding a parcel in his hand, and displaying a small miniature painting, "do you know who that is?"

"Certainly, Captain Benwick."

"Yes, and you may guess who it is for. But (in a deep tone) it was not done for her. Miss Elliot, do you remember our walking together at Lyme, and grieving for him? I little thought then—but no matter. This was drawn at the Cape. He met with a clever young German artist at the Cape, and in compliance with a promise to my poor sister, sat to him, and was bringing it home for her. And I have now the charge of getting it properly set for another! It was a commission to me! But who else was there to employ? I hope I can allow for him. I am not sorry, indeed, to make it over to another. He undertakes it—(looking towards

Captain Wentworth) he is writing about it now." And with a quivering lip he wound up the whole by adding, "Poor Fanny! she would not have forgotten him so soon!"

"No," replied Anne, in a low feeling voice. "That, I can easily believe."

"It was not in her nature. She doated on him."

"It would not be the nature of any woman who truly loved."

Captain Harville smiled, as much as to say, "Do you claim that for your sex?" and she answered the question, smiling also, "Yes. We certainly do not forget you, so soon as you forget us. It is, perhaps, our fate rather than our merit. We cannot help ourselves. We live at home, quiet, confined, and our feelings prey upon us. You are forced on exertion. You have always a profession, pursuits, business of some sort or other, to take you back into the world immediately, and continual occupation and change soon weaken impressions."

"Granting your assertion that the world does all this so soon for men, (which, however, I do not think I shall grant) it does not apply to Benwick. He has not been forced upon any exertion. The peace turned him on shore at the very moment, and he has been living with us, in our little family-circle, ever since."

"True," said Anne, "very true; I did not recollect; but what shall we say now, Captain Harville? If the change be not from outward circumstances, it must be from within; it must be nature, man's nature, which has done the business for Captain Benwick."

"No, no, it is not man's nature. I will not allow it to be more man's nature than woman's to be inconstant and forget those they do love, or have loved. I believe the reverse. I believe in a true analogy between our bodily frames and our mental; and that as our bodies are the strongest, so are our feelings; capable of bearing most rough usage, and riding out the heaviest weather."

"Your feelings may be the strongest," replied Anne, "but the same spirit of analogy will authorise me to assert that ours are the most tender. Man is more robust than woman, but he is not longer-lived; which exactly explains my view of the nature of their attachments. Nay, it would be too hard upon you, if it were otherwise. You have difficulties, and privations, and dangers enough to struggle with. You are always labouring and toiling, exposed to every risk and hardship. Your home, country, friends, all quitted. Neither time, nor health, nor life, to be called your own. It would be too hard indeed" (with a faltering voice) "if woman's feelings were to be added to all this."

"We shall never agree upon this question"—Captain Harville was beginning to say, when a slight noise called their attention to Captain Wentworth's hitherto perfectly quiet division of the room. It was nothing more than that his pen had fallen down, but Anne was startled at finding him nearer than she had supposed, and half inclined to suspect that the pen had only fallen, because he had been occupied by them, striving to catch sounds, which yet she did not think he could have caught.

"Have you finished your letter?" said Captain Harville.

"Not quite, a few lines more. I shall have done in five minutes."

"There is no hurry on my side. I am only ready whenever you are.— I am in very good anchorage here," (smiling at Anne) "well supplied, and want for nothing.—No hurry for a signal at all.—Well, Miss Elliot," (lowering his voice) "as I was saying, we shall never agree I suppose upon this point. No man and woman would, probably. But let me observe that all histories are against you, all stories, prose and verse. If I had such a memory as Benwick, I could bring you fifty quotations in a moment on my side the argument, and I do not think I ever opened a book in my life which had not something to say upon woman's inconstancy. Songs and proverbs, all talk of woman's fickleness. But perhaps you will say, these were all written by men."

"Perhaps I shall.—Yes, yes, if you please, no reference to examples in books. Men have had every advantage of us in telling their own story. Education has been theirs in so much higher a degree; the pen has been in their hands. I will not allow books to prove any thing."

"But how shall we prove any thing?"

"We never shall. We never can expect to prove any thing upon such a point. It is a difference of opinion which does not admit of proof. We each begin probably with a little bias towards our own sex, and upon that bias build every circumstance in favour of it which has occurred within our own circle; many of which circumstances (perhaps those very cases which strike us the most) may be precisely such as cannot be brought forward without betraying a confidence, or in some respect saying what should not be said."

"Ah!" cried Captain Harville, in a tone of strong feeling, "if I could but make you comprehend what a man suffers when he takes a last look at his wife and children, and watches the boat that he has sent them off in, as long as it is in sight, and then turns away and says, 'God knows whether we ever meet again!' And then, if I could convey to you the glow of his soul when he does see them again; when, coming back after a twelvemonth's absence perhaps, and obliged to put into another port, he calculates how soon it be possible to get them there, pretending to deceive himself, and saying, 'They cannot be here till such a day,' but all the while hoping for them twelve hours sooner, and seeing them arrive at last, as if Heaven had given them wings, by many hours sooner still! If I could explain to you all this, and all that a man can bear and do, and glories to do for the sake of these treasures of his existence! I speak, you know, only of such men as have hearts!" pressing his own with emotion.

"Oh!" cried Anne eagerly, "I hope I do justice to all that is felt by you, and by those who resemble you. God forbid that I should undervalue the warm and faithful feelings of any of my fellow-creatures. I should deserve utter contempt if I dared to suppose that true attachment and constancy were known only by woman. No, I believe you capable of every thing great and good in your married lives. I believe you equal to every important exertion, and to every domestic forbearance, so long as—if I may be allowed the expression, so long as you have an object. I mean, while the woman you love lives, and lives for you. All the privilege I claim for my own sex (it is not a very enviable one, you need not covet it) is that of loving longest, when existence or when hope is gone."

She could not immediately have uttered another sentence; her heart was too full, her breath too much oppressed.

"You are a good soul," cried Captain Harville, putting his hand on her arm quite affectionately. "There is no quarrelling with you.—And when I think of Benwick, my tongue is tied."

Their attention was called towards the others.—Mrs. Croft was taking leave.

"Here, Frederick, you and I part company, I believe," said she. "I am going home, and you have an engagement with your friend.—To-night we may have the pleasure of all meeting again, at your party," (turning to Anne.) "We had your sister's card yesterday, and I understood Frederick had a card too, though I did not see it—and you are disengaged, Frederick, are you not, as well as ourselves?"

Captain Wentworth was folding up a letter in great haste, and either could not or would not answer fully.

"Yes," said he, "very true; here we separate, but Harville and I shall soon be after you, that is, Harville, if you are ready, I am in half a minute. I know you will not be sorry to be off. I shall be at your service in half a minute."

Mrs. Croft left them, and Captain Wentworth, having sealed his letter with great rapidity, was indeed ready, and had even a hurried, agitated air, which shewed impatience to be gone. Anne knew not how to understand it. She had the kindest "Good morning, God bless you," from Captain Harville, but from him not a word, nor a look. He had passed out of the room without a look!

She had only time, however, to move closer to the table where he had been writing, when footsteps were heard returning; the door opened; it was himself. He begged their pardon, but he had forgotten his gloves, and instantly crossing the room to the writing table, and standing with his back towards Mrs. Musgrove, he drew out a letter from under the scattered paper, placed it before Anne with eyes of glowing entreaty fixed on her for a moment, and hastily collecting his gloves, was again out of the room, almost before Mrs. Musgrove was aware of his being in it—the work of an instant!

The revolution which one instant had made in Anne, was almost beyond expression. The letter, with a direction hardly legible, to "Miss A. E.—." was evidently the one which he had been folding so hastily. While supposed to be writing only to Captain Benwick, he had been also addressing her! On the contents of that letter depended all which this world could do for her! Any thing was possible, any thing might be defied rather than suspense. Mrs. Musgrove had little arrangements of her own at her own table; to their protection she must trust, and sinking into the chair which he had occupied, succeeding to the very spot where he had leaned and written, her eyes devoured the following words:

> I can listen no longer in silence. I must speak to you by such means as are within my reach. You pierce my soul. I am half agony, half hope. Tell me not that I am too late, that such precious feelings are gone for ever. I offer myself to you again with a heart even more your own, than when you almost broke it eight years and a half ago. Dare not say that man forgets sooner than woman, that his love has an earlier death. I have loved none but you. Unjust I may have been, weak and resentful I have been, but never inconstant. You alone have brought me to Bath. For you alone I think and plan.—Have you not seen this? Can you fail to have understood my wishes?—I had not waited even these ten days, could I have read your feelings, as I think you must have penetrated mine. I can hardly write. I am every instant hearing something which overpowers me. You sink your voice, but I can distinguish the tones of that voice, when they would be lost on others.—Too good, too excellent creature! You do us justice indeed. You do believe that there is true attachment and constancy among men. Believe it to be most fervent, most undeviating in
>
> F. W.
>
> I must go, uncertain of my fate; but I shall return hither, or follow your party, as soon as possible. A word, a look will be enough to decide whether I enter your father's house this evening, or never.

Such a letter was not to be soon recovered from. Half an hour's solitude and reflection might have tranquillized her; but the ten minutes only, which now passed before she was interrupted, with all the restraints of her situation, could do nothing towards tranquillity. Every moment rather brought fresh agitation. It was an overpowering happiness. And before she was beyond the first stage of full sensation, Charles, Mary, and Henrietta all came in.

The absolute necessity of seeming like herself produced then an immediate struggle; but after a while she could do no more. She began not to understand a word they said, and was obliged to plead indisposition and excuse herself. They could then see that she looked very ill— were shocked and concerned—and would not stir without her for the world. This was dreadful! Would they only have gone away, and left her in the quiet possession of that room, it would have been her cure; but to have them all standing or waiting around her was distracting, and, in desperation, she said she would go home.

"By all means, my dear," cried Mrs. Musgrove, "go home directly and take care of yourself, that you may be fit for the evening. I wish Sarah was here to doctor you, but I am no doctor myself. Charles, ring and order a chair. She must not walk."

But the chair would never do. Worse than all! To lose the possibility of speaking two words to Captain Wentworth in the course of her quiet, solitary progress up the town (and she felt almost certain of meeting him) could not be borne. The chair was earnestly protested against; and Mrs. Musgrove, who thought only of one sort of illness, having assured herself, with some anxiety, that there had been no fall in the case; that Anne had not, at any time lately, slipped down, and got a blow on her head; that she was perfectly convinced of having had no fall, could part with her cheerfully, and depend on finding her better at night.

Anxious to omit no possible precaution, Anne struggled, and said,

"I am afraid, ma'am, that it is not perfectly understood. Pray be so good as to mention to the other gentlemen that we hope to see your whole party this evening. I am afraid there has been some mistake; and I wish you particularly to assure Captain Harville, and Captain Wentworth, that we hope to see them both."

"Oh! my dear, it is quite understood, I give you my word. Captain Harville has no thought but of going."

"Do you think so? But I am afraid; and I should be so very sorry! Will you promise me to mention it, when you see them again? You will see them both again this morning, I dare say. Do promise me."

"To be sure I will, if you wish it. Charles, if you see Captain Harville any where, remember to give Miss Anne's message. But indeed, my dear, you need not be uneasy. Captain Harville holds himself quite engaged, I'll answer for it; and Captain Wentworth the same, I dare say."

Anne could do no more; but her heart prophesied some mischance, to damp the perfection of her felicity. It could not be very lasting, however. Even if he did not come to Camden-place himself, it would be in her power to send an intelligible sentence by Captain Harville.

Another momentary vexation occurred. Charles, in his real concern and good-nature, would go home with her; there was no preventing him. This was almost cruel! But she could not be long ungrateful; he was sacrificing an engagement at a gunsmith's to be of use to her; and she set off with him, with no feeling but gratitude apparent.

They were in Union-street, when a quicker step behind, a something of familiar sound, gave her two moments preparation for the sight of Captain Wentworth. He joined them; but, as if irresolute whether to join or to pass on, said nothing—only looked. Anne could command herself enough to receive that look, and not repulsively. The cheeks which had been pale now glowed, and the movements which had hesitated were decided. He walked by her side. Presently, struck by a sudden thought, Charles said,

"Captain Wentworth, which way are you going? only to Gay-street, or farther up the town?"

"I hardly know," replied Captain Wentworth, surprised.

"Are you going as high as Belmont? Are you going near Camden-place? Because if you are, I shall have no scruple in asking you to take my place, and give Anne your arm to her father's door. She is rather done for this morning, and must not go so far without help. And I ought to be at that fellow's in the market-place. He promised me the sight of a capital gun he is just going to send off; said he would keep it unpacked to the last possible moment, that I might see it; and if I do not turn back now, I have no chance. By his description, a good deal like the second-sized double-barrel of mine, which you shot with one day, round Winthrop."

There could not be an objection. There could be only a most proper alacrity, a most obliging compliance for public view; and smiles reined in and spirits dancing in private rapture. In half a minute, Charles was at the bottom of Union-street again, and the other two proceeding together; and soon words enough had passed between them to decide their direction towards the comparatively quiet and retired gravel-walk, where the power of conversation would make the present hour a blessing indeed; and prepare for it all the immortality which the happiest recollections of their own future lives could bestow. There they exchanged again those feelings and those promises which had once before seemed to secure every thing, but which had been followed by so many, many years of division and estrangement. There they returned again into the past, more exquisitely happy, perhaps, in their re-union, than when it had been first projected; more tender, more tried, more fixed in a knowledge of each other's character, truth, and attachment; more equal to act, more justified in acting. And there, as they slowly paced the gradual ascent, heedless of every group around them, seeing neither sauntering politicians, bustling house-keepers, flirting girls, nor nursery-maids and children, they could indulge in those retrospections and acknowledgments, and especially in those explanations of what had directly preceded the present moment, which were so poignant and so ceaseless in interest. All the little variations of the last week were gone through; and of yesterday and to-day there could scarcely be an end.

She had not mistaken him. Jealousy of Mr. Elliot had been the retarding weight, the doubt, the torment. That had begun to operate in the very hour of first meeting her in Bath; that had returned, after a short suspension, to ruin the concert; and that had influenced him in every thing he had said and done, or omitted to say and do, in the last four-and-twenty hours. It had been gradually yielding to the better hopes which her looks, or words, or actions occasionally encouraged; it had been vanquished at last by those sentiments and those tones which had reached him while she talked with Captain Harville; and under the irresistible governance of which he had seized a sheet of paper, and poured out his feelings.

Of what he had then written, nothing was to be retracted or qualified. He persisted in having loved none but her. She had never been supplanted. He never even believed himself to see her equal. Thus much indeed he was obliged to acknowledge—that he had been constant unconsciously, nay unintentionally; that he had meant to forget her, and believed it to be done. He had imagined himself indifferent, when he had only been angry; and he had been unjust to her merits, because he had been a sufferer from them. Her character was now fixed on his mind as perfection itself, maintaining the loveliest medium of fortitude and gentleness; but he was obliged to acknowledge that only at Uppercross had he learnt to do her justice, and only at Lyme had he begun to understand himself.

At Lyme, he had received lessons of more than one sort. The passing admiration of Mr. Elliot had at least roused him, and the scenes on the Cobb, and at Captain Harville's, had fixed her superiority.

In his preceding attempts to attach himself to Louisa Musgrove (the attempts of angry pride), he protested that he had for ever felt it to be impossible; that he had not cared, could not care for Louisa; though, till that day, till the leisure for reflection which followed it, he had not understood the perfect excellence of the mind with which Louisa's could so ill bear a comparison; or the perfect, unrivalled hold it possessed over his own. There, he had learnt to distinguish between the steadiness of principle and the obstinacy of self-will, between the darings of heedlessness and the resolution of a collected mind. There, he had seen every thing to exalt in his estimation the woman he had lost, and there begun to deplore the pride, the folly, the madness of resentment, which had kept him from trying to regain her when thrown in his way.

From that period his penance had become severe. He had no sooner been free from the horror and remorse attending the first few days of Louisa's accident, no sooner begun to feel himself alive again, than he had begun to feel himself, though alive, not at liberty.

"I found," said he, "that I was considered by Harville an engaged man! That neither Harville nor his wife entertained a doubt of our mutual attachment. I was startled and shocked. To a degree, I could contradict this instantly; but, when I began to reflect that others might have felt the same—her own family, nay, perhaps herself, I was no longer at my own disposal. I was hers in honour if she wished it. I had been unguarded. I had not thought seriously on this subject before. I had not considered that my excessive intimacy must have its danger of ill consequence in many ways: and that I had no right to be trying whether I could attach myself to either of the girls, at the risk of raising even an unpleasant report, were there no other ill effects. I had been grossly wrong, and must abide the consequences."

He found too late, in short, that he had entangled himself; and that precisely as he became fully satisfied of his not caring for Louisa at all, he must regard himself as bound to her, if her sentiments for him were what the Harvilles supposed. It determined him to leave Lyme, and await her complete recovery elsewhere. He would gladly weaken, by any fair means, whatever feelings or speculations concerning him might exist; and he went, therefore, to his brother's, meaning after a while to return to Kellynch, and act as circumstances might require.

"I was six weeks with Edward," said he, "and saw him happy. I could have no other pleasure. I deserved none. He enquired after you very particularly; asked even if you were personally altered, little suspecting that to my eye you could never alter."

Anne smiled, and let it pass. It was too pleasing a blunder for a reproach. It is something for a woman to be assured, in her eight-and-twentieth year, that she has not lost one charm of earlier youth: but the value of such homage was inexpressibly increased to Anne, by comparing it with former words, and feeling it to be the result, not the cause of a revival of his warm attachment.

He had remained in Shropshire, lamenting the blindness of his own pride, and the blunders of his own calculations, till at once released from Louisa by the astonishing and felicitous intelligence of her engagement with Benwick.

"Here," said he, "ended the worst of my state; for now I could at least put myself in the way of happiness, I could exert myself, I could do something. But to be waiting so long in inaction, and waiting only for evil, had been dreadful. Within the first five minutes I said, 'I will be at Bath on Wednesday,' and I was. Was it unpardonable to think it worth my while to come? and to arrive with some degree of hope? You were single. It was possible that you might retain the feelings of the past, as I did; and one encouragement happened to be mine. I could never doubt that you would be loved and sought by others, but I knew to a certainty that you had refused one man at least, of better pretensions than myself: and I could not help often saying, Was this for me?"

Their first meeting in Milsom-street afforded much to be said, but the concert still more. That evening seemed to be made up of exquisite moments. The moment of her stepping forward in the octagon-room to speak to him, the moment of Mr. Elliot's appearing and tearing her away, and one or two subsequent moments, marked by returning hope or increasing despondence, were dwelt on with energy.

"To see you," cried he, "in the midst of those who could not be my well-wishers, to see your cousin close by you, conversing and smiling, and feel all the horrible eligibilities and proprieties of the match! To consider it as the certain wish of every being who could hope to influence you! Even, if your own feelings were reluctant or indifferent, to consider what powerful supports would be his! Was it not enough to make the fool of me which I appeared? How could I look on without agony? Was not the very sight of the friend who sat behind you, was not the recollection of what had been, the knowledge of her influence, the indelible, immoveable impression of what persuasion had once done— was it not all against me?"

"You should have distinguished," replied Anne. "You should not have suspected me now; the case so different, and my age so different. If I was wrong in yielding to persuasion once, remember that it was to persuasion exerted on the side of safety, not of risk. When I yielded, I thought it was to duty; but no duty could be called in aid here. In marrying a man indifferent to me, all risk would have been incurred, and all duty violated."

"Perhaps I ought to have reasoned thus," he replied. "but I could not. I could not derive benefit from the late knowledge I had acquired of your character. I could not bring it into play: it was overwhelmed, buried, lost in those earlier feelings which I had been smarting under year after year. I could think of you only as one who had yielded, who had given me up, who had been influenced by any one rather than by me. I saw you with the very person who had guided you in that year of misery. I had no reason to believe her of less authority now.—The force of habit was to be added."

"I should have thought," said Anne, "that my manner to yourself might have spared you much or all of this."

"No, no! your manner might be only the ease which your engagement to another man would give. I left you in this belief; and yet—I was determined to see you again. My spirits rallied with the morning, and I felt that I had still a motive for remaining here."

At last Anne was at home again, and happier than any one in that house could have conceived. All the surprise and suspense, and every other painful part of the morning dissipated by this conversation, she re-entered the house so happy as to be obliged to find an alloy in some momentary apprehensions of its being impossible to last. An interval of meditation, serious and grateful, was the best corrective of every thing dangerous in such high-wrought felicity; and she went to her room, and grew steadfast and fearless in the thankfulness of her enjoyment.

The evening came, the drawing-rooms were lighted up, the company assembled. It was but a card-party, it was but a mixture of those who had never met before, and those who met too often—a common-place business, too numerous for intimacy, too small for variety; but Anne had never found an evening shorter. Glowing and lovely in sensibility and happiness, and more generally admired than she thought about or cared for, she had cheerful or forbearing feelings for every creature around her. Mr. Elliot was there; she avoided, but she could pity him. The Wallises; she had amusement in understanding them. Lady Dalrymple and Miss Carteret; they would soon be innoxious cousins to her. She cared not for Mrs. Clay, and had nothing to blush for in the public manners of her father and sister. With the Musgroves, there was the happy chat of perfect ease; with Captain Harville, the kind-hearted intercourse of brother and sister; with Lady Russell, attempts at conversation, which a delicious consciousness cut short; with Admiral and Mrs. Croft, every thing of peculiar cordiality and fervent interest, which the same consciousness sought to conceal;—and with Captain Wentworth, some moments of communication continually occurring, and always the hope of more, and always the knowledge of his being there!

It was in one of these short meetings, each apparently occupied in admiring a fine display of green-house plants, that she said—

"I have been thinking over the past, and trying impartially to judge of the right and wrong, I mean with regard to myself; and I must believe that I was right, much as I suffered from it, that I was perfectly right in being guided by the friend whom you will love better than you do now. To me, she was in the place of a parent. Do not mistake me, however. I am not saying that she did not err in her advice. It was, perhaps, one of those cases in which advice is good or bad only as the event decides; and for myself, I certainly never should, in any circumstance of tolerable similarity, give such advice. But I mean, that I was right in submitting to her, and that if I had done otherwise, I should have suffered more in continuing the engagement than I did even in giving it up, because I should have suffered in my conscience. I have now, as far as such a sentiment is allowable in human nature, nothing to reproach myself with; and if I mistake not, a strong sense of duty is no bad part of a woman's portion."

He looked at her, looked at Lady Russell, and looking again at her, replied, as if in cool deliberation,

"Not yet. But there are hopes of her being forgiven in time. I trust to being in charity with her soon. But I too have been thinking over the past, and a question has suggested itself, whether there may not have been one person more my enemy even than that lady? My own self. Tell me if, when I returned to England in the year eight, with a few thousand pounds, and was posted into the Laconia, if I had then written to you, would you have answered my letter? would you, in short, have renewed the engagement then?"

"Would I!" was all her answer; but the accent was decisive enough.

"Good God!" he cried, "you would! It is not that I did not think of it, or desire it, as what could alone crown all my other success. But I was proud, too proud to ask again. I did not understand you. I shut my eyes, and would not understand you, or do you justice. This is a recollection which ought to make me forgive every one sooner than myself. Six years of separation and suffering might have been spared. It is a sort of pain, too, which is new to me. I have been used to the gratification of believing myself to earn every blessing that I enjoyed. I have valued myself on honourable toils and just rewards. Like other great men under reverses," he added with a smile, "I must endeavour to subdue my mind to my fortune. I must learn to brook being happier than I deserve."

Chapter XXIV

Who can be in doubt of what followed? When any two young people take it into their heads to marry, they are pretty sure by perseverance to carry their point, be they ever so poor, or ever so imprudent, or ever so little likely to be necessary to each other's ultimate comfort. This may be bad morality to conclude with, but I believe it to be truth; and if such parties succeed, how should a Captain Wentworth and an Anne Elliot, with the advantage of maturity of mind, consciousness of right, and one independent fortune between them, fail of bearing down every opposition? They might in fact have borne down a great deal more than they met with, for there was little to distress them beyond the want of graciousness and warmth.—Sir Walter made no objection, and Elizabeth did nothing worse than look cold and unconcerned. Captain Wentworth, with five-and-twenty thousand pounds, and as high in his profession as merit and activity could place him, was no longer nobody. He was now esteemed quite worthy to address the daughter of a foolish, spendthrift baronet, who had not had principle or sense enough to maintain himself in the situation in which Providence had placed him, and who could give his daughter at present but a small part of the share of ten thousand pounds which must be hers hereafter.

Sir Walter indeed, though he had no affection for Anne, and no vanity flattered, to make him really happy on the occasion, was very far from thinking it a bad match for her. On the contrary, when he saw more of Captain Wentworth, saw him repeatedly by daylight and eyed him well, he was very much struck by his personal claims, and felt that his superiority of appearance might be not unfairly balanced against her superiority of rank; and all this, assisted by his well-sounding name, enabled Sir Walter at last to prepare his pen with a very good grace for the insertion of the marriage in the volume of honour.

The only one among them, whose opposition of feeling could excite any serious anxiety, was Lady Russell. Anne knew that Lady Russell must be suffering some pain in understanding and relinquishing Mr. Elliot, and be making some struggles to become truly acquainted with, and do justice to Captain Wentworth. This however was what Lady Russell had now to do. She must learn to feel that she had been mistaken with regard to both; that she had been unfairly influenced by appearances in each; that because Captain Wentworth's manners had not suited her own ideas, she had been too quick in suspecting them to indicate a character of dangerous impetuosity; and that because Mr. Elliot's manners had precisely pleased her in their propriety and correctness, their general politeness and suavity, she had been too quick in receiving them as the certain result of the most correct opinions and well regulated mind. There was nothing less for Lady Russell to do, than to admit that she had been pretty completely wrong, and to take up a new set of opinions and of hopes.

There is a quickness of perception in some, a nicety in the discernment of character, a natural penetration, in short, which no experience in others can equal, and Lady Russell had been less gifted in this part of understanding than her young friend. But she was a very good woman, and if her second object was to be sensible and well-judging, her first was to see Anne happy. She loved Anne better than she loved her own abilities; and when the awkwardness of the beginning was over, found little hardship in attaching herself as a mother to the man who was securing the happiness of her other child.

Of all the family, Mary was probably the one most immediately gratified by the circumstance. It was creditable to have a sister married, and she might flatter herself with having been greatly instrumental to the connexion, by keeping Anne with her in the autumn; and as her own sister must be better than her husband's sisters, it was very agreeable that Captain Wentworth should be a richer man than either Captain Benwick or Charles Hayter.—She had something to suffer perhaps when they came into contact again, in seeing Anne restored to the rights of seniority, and the mistress of a very pretty landaulette;[3] but she had a future to look forward to, of powerful consolation. Anne had no Uppercross-hall before her, no landed estate, no headship of a family; and if they could but keep Captain Wentworth from being made a baronet, she would not change situations with Anne.

It would be well for the eldest sister if she were equally satisfied with her situation, for a change is not very probable there. She had soon the mortification of seeing Mr. Elliot withdraw; and no one of proper condition has since presented himself to raise even the unfounded hopes which sunk with him.

The news of his cousin Anne's engagement burst on Mr. Elliot most unexpectedly. It deranged his best plan of domestic happiness, his best hope of keeping Sir Walter single by the watchfulness which a son-in-law's rights would have given. But, though discomfited and disappointed, he could still do something for his own interest and his own enjoyment. He soon quitted Bath; and on Mrs. Clay's quitting it likewise soon afterwards, and being next heard of as established under his protec-

3. A small carriage.

tion in London, it was evident how double a game he had been playing, and how determined he was to save himself from being cut out by one artful woman, at least.

Mrs. Clay's affections had overpowered her interest, and she had sacrificed, for the young man's sake, the possibility of scheming longer for Sir Walter. She has abilities, however, as well as affections; and it is now a doubtful point whether his cunning, or hers, may finally carry the day; whether, after preventing her from being the wife of Sir Walter, he may not be wheedled and caressed at last into making her the wife of Sir William.

It cannot be doubted that Sir Walter and Elizabeth were shocked and mortified by the loss of their companion, and the discovery of their deception in her. They had their great cousins, to be sure, to resort to for comfort; but they must long feel that to flatter and follow others, without being flattered and followed in turn, is but a state of half enjoyment.

Anne, satisfied at a very early period of Lady Russell's meaning to love Captain Wentworth as she ought, had no other alloy to the happiness of her prospects than what arose from the consciousness of having no relations to bestow on him which a man of sense could value. There she felt her own inferiority keenly. The disproportion in their fortune was nothing; it did not give her a moment's regret; but to have no family to receive and estimate him properly; nothing of respectability, of harmony, of good-will to offer in return for all the worth and all the prompt welcome which met her in his brothers and sisters, was a source of as lively pain as her mind could well be sensible of, under circumstances of otherwise strong felicity. She had but two friends in the world to add to his list, Lady Russell and Mrs. Smith. To those, however, he was very well disposed to attach himself. Lady Russell, in spite of all her former transgressions, he could now value from his heart. While he was not obliged to say that he believed her to have been right in originally dividing them, he was ready to say almost every thing else in her favour; and as for Mrs. Smith, she had claims of various kinds to recommend her quickly and permanently.

Her recent good offices by Anne had been enough in themselves; and their marriage, instead of depriving her of one friend, secured her two. She was their earliest visitor in their settled life; and Captain Wentworth, by putting her in the way of recovering her husband's property in the West Indies; by writing for her, acting for her, and seeing her through all the petty difficulties of the case, with the activity and exertion of a fearless man and a determined friend, fully requited the services which she had rendered, or ever meant to render, to his wife.

Mrs. Smith's enjoyments were not spoiled by this improvement of income, with some improvement of health, and the acquisition of such friends to be often with, for her cheerfulness and mental alacrity did not fail her; and while these prime supplies of good remained, she might have bid defiance even to greater accessions of worldly prosperity. She might have been absolutely rich and perfectly healthy, and yet be happy. Her spring of felicity was in the glow of her spirits, as her friend Anne's was in the warmth of her heart. Anne was tenderness itself, and she had the full worth of it in Captain Wentworth's affection. His profession was all that could ever make her friends wish that tenderness less; the dread of a future war all that could dim her sunshine. She gloried in being a sailor's wife, but she must pay the tax of quick alarm for belonging to that profession which is, if possible, more distinguished in its domestic virtues than in its national importance.

THE END

[The Original Ending of *Persuasion*] †

[The two chapters here printed comprise Austen's original ending to *Persuasion*. They were replaced by the final two chapters of the present text.]

CHAPTER 10

July 8.

    With all this knowledge of Mr E—and this authority to impart it, Anne left Westgate Buildgs—her mind deeply busy in revolving what she had heard, feeling, thinking, recalling and forseeing everything; shocked at Mr Elliot—sighing over future Kellynch, and pained for Lady Russell, whose confidence in him had been entire.—The Embarrassment which must be felt from this hour in his presence!—How to behave to him?—how to get rid of him?—what to do by any of the Party at home?—where to be blind? where to be active?—It was altogether a confusion of Images and Doubts—a perplexity, an agitation which she could not see the end of—and she was in Gay St and still so much engrossed, that she started on being addressed by Adml Croft, as if he were a person unlikely to be met there. It was within a few steps of his own door.—"You are going to call upon my wife, said he, she will be very glad to see you."—Anne denied it "No—she really had not time, she was in her way home"—but while she spoke, the Adml had stepped back and knocked at the door, calling out, "Yes, yes, do go in; she is all alone. go in and rest yourself."—Anne felt so little disposed at this time to be in company of any sort, that it vexed her to be thus constrained—but she was obliged to stop. "Since you are so very kind, said she, I will just ask Mrs Croft how she does, but I really cannot stay 5 minutes.—You are sure she is quite alone."—The possibility of Capt. W. had

† Reprinted from *Jane Austen's Autograph*, edited by R. W. Chapman (Oxford: Clarendon Press, 1926) by permission of Oxford University Press.

occurred—and most fearfully anxious was she to be assured—either that he was within or that he was not; *which*, might have been a question.— "Oh! yes, quite alone—Nobody but her Mantuamaker with her, and they have been shut up together this half hour, so it must be over soon."—"Her Mantua maker!—then I am sure my calling now, would be most inconvenient.—Indeed you must allow me to leave my Card and be so good as to explain it afterwards to Mrs C." "No, no, not at all, not at all. She will be very happy to see you. Mind—I will not swear that she has not something particular to say to you—but *that* will all come out in the right place. I give no hints.—Why, Miss Elliot, we begin to hear strange things of you—(smiling in her face)—But you have not much the Look of it—as Grave as a little Judge." —Anne blushed.—"Aye, aye, that will do. Now, it is right. I *thought* we were not mistaken." She was left to guess at the direction of his Suspicions;— the first wild idea had been of some disclosure from his Br in law—but she was ashamed the next moment—and felt how far more probable that he should be meaning Mr E.—The door was opened—and the Man evidently beginning to *deny* his Mistress, when the sight of his Master stopped him. The Adml enjoyed the joke exceedingly. Anne thought his triumph over Stephen rather too long. At last however, he was able to invite her upstairs, and stepping before her said—"I will just go up with you myself and shew you in—. I cannot stay, because I must go to the P. Office, but if you will only sit down for 5 minutes I am sure Sophy will come—and you will find nobody to disturb you—there is nobody but Frederick here—" opening the door as he spoke.—Such a person to be passed over as a Nobody to *her*!—After being allowed to feel quite secure—indifferent—at her ease, to have it burst on her that she was to be the next moment in the same room with him!—No time for recollection!—for planning behaviour, or regulating manners!— There was time only to turn pale, before she had passed through the door, and met the astonished eyes of Capt. W——. who was sitting by the fire pretending to read and prepared for no greater surprise than the Admiral's hasty return.—Equally unexpected was the meeting, on each side. There was nothing to be done however, but to stifle feelings and be quietly polite;—and the Admiral was too much on the alert, to leave any troublesome pause.—He repeated again what he had said before about his wife and everybody—insisted on Anne's sitting down and being perfectly comfortable, was sorry he must leave her himself, but was sure Mrs Croft would be down very soon, and would go upstairs and give her notice directly.—Anne *was* sitting down, but now she arose again—to entreat him not to interrupt Mrs C—and re-urge the wish of going away and calling another time.—But the Adml would not hear of it;—and if she did not return to the charge with unconquerable Perseverance, or did not with a more passive Determination walk quietly out of the room—(as certainly she might have done) may she not be pardoned?—If she *had* no horror of a few minutes Tête-à-Tête with Capt. W—, may she not be pardoned for not wishing to give him the idea that she *had?*—She reseated herself, and the Adml took leave; but on reaching the door, said, "Frederick, a word with *you*, if you please."—Capt. W— went to him; and instantly, before they were well out of the room, the Adml continued—"As I am going to leave you together, it is but fair I should give you something to talk of—and so, if you please—" Here the door was very firmly closed; she could guess by which of the two; and she lost entirely what immediately followed; but it was impossible for her not to distinguish parts of the rest, for the Adml on the strength of the Door's being shut was speaking without any management of voice, tho' she could hear his companion trying to check him.—She could not doubt their being speaking of her. She heard her own name and *Kellynch* repeatedly—she was very much distressed. She knew not what to do, or what to expect—and among other agonies felt the possibility of Capt. W—'s not returning into the room at all, which after *her* consenting to stay would have been—too bad for Language.—They seemed to be talking of the Admls Lease of Kellynch. She heard him say something of "the Lease being signed or not signed"—*that* was not likely to be a very agitating subject—but then followed "I hate to be at an uncertainty—I must know at once—Sophy thinks the same." Then, in a lower tone, Capt. W— seemed remonstrating—wanting to be excused—wanting to put something off. "Phoo, Phoo—answered the Admiral now is the Time. If *you* will not speak, I will stop and speak myself."—"Very well Sir, very well Sir, followed with some impatience from his companion, opening the door as he spoke.—"You will then— you promise you will?" replied the Admiral, in all the power of his natural voice, unbroken even by one thin door.—"Yes—Sir—Yes." And the Adml was hastily left, the door was closed, and the moment arrived in which Anne was alone with Capt. W—. She could not attempt to see how he looked; but he walked immediately to a window, as if irresolute and embarrassed;—and for about the space of 5 seconds, she repented what she had done—censured it as unwise, blushed over it as indelicate.—She longed to be able to speak of the weather or the Concert—but could only compass the releif of taking a Newspaper in her hand.—The distressing pause was soon over however; he turned round in half a minute, and coming towards the Table where she sat, said, in a voice of effort and constraint— "You must have heard too much already Madam to be in any doubt of my having promised Adml Croft to speak to you on some particular subject—and this conviction determines me to do it—however repugnant to my—to all my sense of propriety, to be taking so great a liberty.—You will acquit me of Impertinence I trust, by considering me as speaking only for another, and speaking by Necessity;—and the Adml is a Man who can never be thought Impertinent by one who knows him as you do—. His Intentions are always the kindest and the Best;—and you will perceive that he is actuated by none other, in the application which I am now with—with very peculiar feelings—obliged to make."—He stopped—but merely to recover breath;—not seeming to expect any answer.—Anne listened, as if her Life depended on the issue of his Speech.—He proceeded, with a forced alacrity.—"The Adml, Madam, was this morning confidently informed that you were—upon my word I am quite at a loss, ashamed—(breathing and speaking quick)—the awkwardness of *giving* Information of this sort to one of the Parties—You can be at no loss to understand me—It was very confidently said that Mr Elliot—that everything was settled in the family for an Union between Mr Elliot—and yourself. It was added that you were to live at Kellynch—that Kellynch was to be given up. This, the Admiral knew could not be correct—But it occurred to him that it might be the *wish* of the Parties—And my commission from him Madam, is to say, that if the Family wish is such, his Lease of Kellynch shall be cancel'd, and he and my sister will provide themselves with another home, without imagining themselves to be doing anything which under similar circumstances wd not be done for *them*.—This is all Madam.—A very few words in reply from you will be sufficient.—That *I* should be the person commissioned on this subject is extraordinary!—and beleive me Madam, it is no less painful.—A very few words however will put an end to the awkwardness and distress we may *both* be feeling." Anne spoke a word or two, but they were unintelligible—And before she could command herself, he added,—"If you only tell me that the Adml may address a Line to Sir Walter, it will be enough. Pronounce only the words, *he may*.—I shall immediately follow him with your message.—" This was spoken, as with a fortitude which seemed to meet the message.—"No Sir—said Anne—There is no message.—You are misin—the Adml is misinformed.—I do justice to the kindness of his Intentions, but he is quite mistaken. There is no Truth in any such report."—He was a moment silent.—She turned her eyes towards him for the first time since his re-entering the room. His colour was varying—and he was looking at her with all the Power and Keenness, which she believed no other eyes than his, possessed. "No Truth in any such report!—he repeated.—No Truth in any *part* of it?"—"None."—He had been standing by a chair—enjoying the releif of leaning on it—or of playing with it;—he now sat down—drew it a little nearer to her—and looked, with an expression which had something more than penetration in it, something softer;—Her Countenance did not discourage.—It was a silent, but a very powerful Dialogue;—on his side, Supplication, on her's acceptance.—Still, a little nearer—and a hand taken and pressed—and "Anne, my own dear Anne!"—bursting forth in the fullness of exquisite feeling—and all Suspense and Indecision were over.—They were re-united. They were restored to all that had been lost. They were carried back to the past, with only an increase of attachment and confidence, and only such a flutter of present Delight as made them little fit for the interruption of Mrs Croft, when she joined them not long afterwards.—*She* probably, in the observations of the next ten minutes, saw something to suspect—and tho' it was hardly possible for a woman of her description to wish the Mantuamaker had imprisoned her longer, she might be very likely wishing for some excuse to run about the house, some storm to break the windows above, or a summons to the Admiral's Shoemaker below.—Fortune favoured them all however in another way—in a gentle, steady rain—just happily set in as the Admiral returned and Anne rose to go.—She was earnestly invited to stay dinner;—a note was dispatched to Camden Place—and she staid;—staid till 10 at night. And during that time, the Husband and wife, either by the wife's contrivance, or by simply going on in their usual way, were frequently out of the room together—gone up stairs to hear a noise, or down stairs to settle their accounts, or upon the Landing place to trim the Lamp.—And these precious moments were turned to so good an account that all the most anxious feelings of the past were gone through.—Before they parted at night, Anne had the felicity of being assured in the first place that—(so far from being altered for the worse!)—she had *gained* inexpressibly in personal Loveliness; and that as to Character—her's was now fixed on his Mind as Perfection itself—maintaining the just Medium of Fortitude and Gentleness;—that he had never ceased to love and prefer her, though it had been only at Uppercross that he had learn't to do her Justice—and only at Lyme that he had begun to understand his own sensations;—that at Lyme he had received Lessons of more than one kind;—the passing admiration of Mr Elliot had at least *roused* him, and the scenes on the Cobb and at Capt. Harville's had fixed her superiority.—In his preceding *attempts* to attach himself to Louisa Musgrove, (the attempts of Anger and Pique)—he protested that he had continually felt the impossibility of really caring for Louisa, though till *that day*, till the leisure for reflection which followed it, he had not understood the perfect excellence of the Mind, with which Louisa's could so ill bear a comparison, or the perfect, the unrivalled hold it possessed over his own.—There he had learnt to distinguish between the steadiness of Principle and the Obstinacy of Self-will, between the Darings of Heedlessness, and the Resolution of a collected Mind—there he had seen everything to exalt in his estimation the Woman he had lost, and there begun to deplore the pride, the folly, the madness of resentment which had kept him from trying to regain her, when thrown in his way. From that period to the present had his penance been the most severe.—He had no sooner been free from the horror and remorse attending the first few days of Louisa's accident, no sooner begun to feel himself alive again, than he had begun to feel himself though alive, not at liberty.—He found that he was considered by his friend Harville, as an engaged Man. The Harvilles entertained not a doubt of a mutual attachment between him and Louisa—and though this to a *degree*, was contradicted instantly—it yet made him feel that perhaps by *her* family, by everybody, by *herself* even, the same idea might be held—and that he was not *free* in honour—though, if such were to be the conclusion, too free alas! in Heart.—He had never thought justly on this subject before—he had not sufficiently considered that his excessive Intimacy at Uppercross must have it's danger of ill consequence in many ways, and that while trying whether he *could* attach himself to either of the Girls, he might be exciting unpleasant reports, if not, raising unrequited regard!—He found, too late, that he had entangled himself—and that precisely as he became thoroughly satisfied of his not *caring* for Louisa at all, he must regard himself as bound to her, if her feelings for him, were what the Harvilles supposed.—It determined him to leave Lyme—and await her perfect recovery elsewhere. He would gladly weaken, by any *fair* means, whatever sentiments or speculations concerning him might exist; and he went therefore into Shropshire meaning after a while, to return to the Crofts at Kellynch, and act as he found requisite.—He had remained in Shropshire, lamenting the Blindness of his own Pride, and the Blunders of his own Calculations, till at once released from Louisa by the astonishing felicity of her engagement with Benwicke. Bath, Bath—had instantly followed, in *Thought*; and not long after, in *fact*. To Bath, to arrive with Hope, to be torn by Jealousy at the first sight of Mr E—, to experience all the changes of each at the Concert, to be miserable by this morning's circumstantial report, to be now, more happy than Language could express, or any heart but his own be capable of.

He was very eager and very delightful in the description of what he had felt at the Concert.—The Eveng seemed to have been made up of exquisite moments;—the moment of her stepping forward in the Octagon Room to speak to him—the moment of Mr E's appearing and tearing her away, and one or two subsequent moments, marked by returning hope, or increasing Despondence, were all dwelt on with energy. "To see you, cried he, in the midst of those who could not be *my* well-wishers, to see your Cousin close by you—conversing and smiling—and feel all the horrible Eligibilities and Proprieties of the Match!—to consider it as the certain wish of every being who could hope to influence you—even, if your own feelings were reluctant, or indifferent—to consider what powerful supports would be his!—Was not it enough to make the fool of me, which my behaviour expressed?—How could I look on without agony?—Was not the very sight of the *Friend* who sat behind you?—was not the recollection of what *had* been—the knowledge of her Influence—the indelible, immoveable Impression of what *Persuasion* had *once* done, was not it all against me?"—

"You should have distinguished—replied Anne—You should not have suspected me *now*;—The case so different, and my age so different!—If I *was* wrong, in yeilding to Persuasion once, remember that it was to Persuasion exerted on the side of Safety, not of Risk. When I yeilded, I thought it was to *Duty*.—But no *Duty* could be called in aid here.—In marrying a Man indifferent to me, all Risk would have been incurred, and all Duty violated."—"Perhaps I ought to have reasoned thus, he replied, but I could not.—I could not derive benefit from the later knowledge of your Character which I had acquired, I could not bring it into play, it was overwhelmed, buried, lost in those earlier feelings, which I had been smarting under Year after Year.—I could think of you only as one who *had* yeilded, who *had* given me up, who *had* been influenced by any one rather than by *me*—I saw you with the very Person who had guided you in that year of Misery—I had no reason to think her of less authority now;—the force of Habit was to be added."—"I should have thought, said Anne, that my Manner to yourself, might have spared you much, or all of this."—"No—No—Your manner might be only the ease, which your engagement to another Man would give.—I left you with this beleif.—And yet—I was determined to see you again.—My spirits rallied with the morning, and I felt that I had still a motive for remaining here.—The Admirals news indeed, was a revulsion. Since that moment, I have been decided what to do—and had it been confirmed, this would have been my *last day* in Bath."

There was time for all this to pass—with such Interruptions only as enhanced the charm of the communication—and Bath could scarcely contain any other two Beings at once so rationally and so rapturously happy as during that eveng occupied the Sopha of Mrs Croft's Drawing room in Gay St.

Capt. W.— had taken care to meet the Adml as he returned into the house, to satisfy him as to Mr E— and Kellynch;—and the delicacy of the Admiral's good nature kept him from saying another word on the subject to Anne.—He was quite concerned lest he might have been giving her pain by touching a tender part. Who could say?—She might be liking her Cousin, better than he liked her.—And indeed, upon recollection, if they had been to marry at all why should they have waited so long?—

When the Eveng closed, it is probable that the Adml received some new Ideas from his Wife;—whose particularly friendly manner in parting with her, gave Anne the gratifying persuasion of her seeing and approving.

It had been such a day to Anne!—the hours which had passed since her leaving Camden Place, had done so much!—She was almost bewildered, almost too happy in looking back.—It was necessary to sit up half the Night and lie awake the remainder to comprehend with composure her present state, and pay for the overplus of Bliss, by Headake and Fatigue.—

CHAPTER 11

Who can be in doubt of what followed?—When any two Young People take it into their heads to marry, they are pretty sure by perseverance
to carry their point—be they ever so poor, or ever so imprudent, or ever
so little likely to be necessary to each other's ultimate comfort. This may
be bad Morality to conclude with, but I beleive it to be Truth—and if
such parties succeed, how should a Capt. W— and an Anne E—, with
the advantage of maturity of Mind, consciousness of Right, and one
Independant Fortune between them, fail of bearing down every opposition? They might in fact, have born down a great deal more than they
met with, for there was little to distress them beyond the want of Graciousness and Warmth. Sir W. made no objection, and Elizth did nothing worse than look cold and unconcerned.—Capt. W— with
£25,000—and as high in his Profession as Merit & Activity could place
him, was no longer nobody. He was now esteemed quite worthy to
address the Daughter of a foolish spendthrift Baronet, who had not had
Principle or sense enough to maintain himself in the Situation in which
Providence had placed him, and who could give his Daughter but a
small part of the share of ten Thousand pounds which must be her's
hereafter.—Sir Walter indeed tho' he had no affection for his Daughter
and no vanity flattered to make him really happy on the occasion, was
very far from thinking it a bad match for her.—On the contrary when
he saw more of Capt. W.— and eyed him well, he was very much struck
by his personal claims and felt that *his* superiority of appearance might
be not unfairly balanced against *her* superiority of Rank;—and all this,
together with his well-sounding name, enabled Sir W. at last to prepare
his pen with a very good grace for the insertion of the Marriage in the
volume of Honour.—The only person among them whose opposition
of feelings could excite any serious anxiety, was Lady Russel.—Anne
knew that Lady R— must be suffering some pain in understanding and
relinquishing Mr E— and be making some struggles to become truly
acquainted with and do justice to Capt. W.—This however, was what
Lady R— had now to do. She must learn to feel that she had been
mistaken with regard to both—that she had been unfairly influenced by
appearances in each—that, because Capt. W.'s manners had not suited
her own ideas, she had been too quick in suspecting them to indicate a
Character of dangerous Impetuosity, and that because Mr Elliot's manners had precisely pleased her in their propriety and correctness, their
general politeness and suavity, she had been too quick in receiving them
as the certain result of the most correct opinions and well regulated
Mind.—There was nothing less for Lady R. to do than to admit that she
had been pretty completely wrong, and to take up a new set of opinions
and hopes.—There *is* a quickness of perception in some, a nicety in the
discernment of character—a natural Penetration in short which no

Experience in others can equal—and Lady R. had been less gifted in this part of Understanding than her young friend;—but she was a very good Woman; and if her second object was to be sensible and well judging, her first was to see Anne happy. She loved Anne better than she loved her own abilities—and when the awkwardness of the Beginning was over, found little hardship in attaching herself as a Mother to the Man who was securing the happiness of her Child. Of all the family, Mary was probably the one most immediately gratified by the circumstance. It was creditable to have a Sister married, and she might flatter herself that she had been greatly instrumental to the connection, by having Anne staying with her in the Autumn; and as her own Sister must be better than her Husbands Sisters, it was very agreable that Captn W— should be a richer Man than either Capt. B. or Charles Hayter.— She had something to suffer perhaps when they came into contact again, in seeing Anne restored to the rights of Seniority and the Mistress of a very pretty Landaulet—but *she* had a *future* to look forward to, of powerful consolation—Anne had no Uppercross Hall before her, no Landed Estate, no Headship of a family, and if they could but keep Capt. W— from being made a Baronet, she would not change situations with Anne.—It would be well for the *Eldest* Sister if she were equally satisfied with *her* situation, for a change is not very probable there.—She had soon the mortification of seeing Mr E. withdraw, and no one of proper condition has since presented himself to raise even the unfounded hopes which sunk with *him*. The news of his Cousin Anne's engagement burst on Mr Elliot most unexpectedly. It deranged his best plan of domestic Happiness, his best hopes of keeping Sir Walter single by the watchfulness which a son in law's rights would have given—But tho' discomfited and disappointed, he could still do something for his own interest and his own enjoyment. He soon quitted Bath and on Mrs Clay's quitting it likewise soon afterwards and being next heard of, as established under his Protection in London, it was evident how double a Game he had been playing, and how determined he was to save himself from being cut out by *one* artful woman at least.—Mrs Clay's affections had overpowered her Interest, and she had sacrificed for the Young Man's sake, the possibility of scheming longer for Sir Walter;—she has Abilities however as well as Affections, and it is now a doubtful point whether his cunning or hers may finally carry the day, whether, after preventing her from being the wife of Sir Walter, he may not be wheedled and caressed at last into making her the wife of Sir William.—

It cannot be doubted that Sir Walter and Eliz: were shocked and mortified by the loss of their companion and the discovery of their deception in her. They had their great cousins to be sure, to resort to for comfort— but they must long feel that to flatter and follow others, without being flattered and followed themselves is but a state of half enjoyment.

Anne, satisfied at a very early period, of Lady Russel's *meaning* to love Capt. W— as she ought, had no other alloy to the happiness of her prospects, than what arose from the consciousness of having no relations to bestow on him which a Man of Sense could value.—There, she felt her own Inferiority keenly.—The disproportion in their fortunes was nothing;—it did not give her a moment's regret;—but to have no Family to receive and estimate him properly, nothing of respectability, of Harmony, of Goodwill to offer in return for all the Worth and all the prompt welcome which met her in his Brothers and Sisters, was a source of as lively pain, as her Mind could well be sensible of, under circumstances of otherwise strong felicity.—She had but two friends in the World, to add to his List, Lady R. and Mrs Smith.—To those however, he was very well-disposed to attach himself. Lady R— inspite of all her former transgressions, he could now value from his heart;—while he was not obliged to say that he beleived her to have been right in originally dividing them, he was ready to say almost anything else in her favour;—and as for Mrs Smith, she had claims of various kinds to recommend her quickly and permanently.—Her recent good offices by Anne had been enough in themselves—and their marriage, instead of depriving her of one friend secured her two. She was one of their first visitors in their settled Life—and Capt. Wentworth, by putting her in the way of recovering her Husband's property in the W. Indies, by writing for her, and acting for her, and seeing her through all the petty Difficulties of the case, with the activity and exertion of a fearless Man, and a determined friend, fully requited the services she had rendered, or had ever meant to render, to his Wife. Mrs Smith's enjoyments were not *spoiled* by this improvement of Income, with some improvement of health, and the acquisition of such friends to be often with, for her chearfulness and mental Activity did not fail her, and while those prime supplies of Good remained, she might have bid defiance even to greater accessions of worldly Prosperity. She might have been absolutely rich and perfectly healthy, and yet be happy.—*Her* spring of Felicity was in the glow of her Spirits—as her friend Anne's was in the warmth of her Heart.—Anne was Tenderness itself;—and she had the full worth of it in Captn Wentworth's affection. His Profession was all that could ever make her friends wish *that* Tenderness less; the dread of a future War, all that could dim her Sunshine.—She gloried in being a Sailor's wife, but she must pay the tax of quick alarm, for belonging to that Profession which is—if possible—more distinguished in it's Domestic Virtues, than in it's National Importance.—

FINIS

July 18.—1816.

BACKGROUNDS AND CONTEXTS

[WILLIAM HAYLEY]

[On Old Maids] †

[This passage from the third volume of William Hayley's anonymously published treatise on old maids belongs to an extended fantasy: the narrator's
dream-vision. It consists mainly of an oration delivered by a speaker at an
imagined banquet. The previous speaker (referred to in the *his* of the first
sentence) has presented the claims of widows.]

* * * When his peroration was ended, which, being tender and pathetic,
formed a pleasing contrast to the humorous arguments of his predecessor, a
gentleman arose, who possessed, with a very graceful person, an uncommon
archness of countenance; and in a voice peculiarly melodious, he delivered
the following oration:

Mr. President,
  Though I was aware that a very formidable majority of speakers would
appear against me, it is yet with confidence that I engage on the unpopu-
lar side of the present question; a question upon which the prejudices,
the passions, and the practice of mankind, are in direct opposition to
the clearest dictates of reason and of justice! Yes! Sir, I will be so bold
as to affirm, that if the conduct and the opinions of men were under the
steady guidance of equity, this question could not remain doubtful for a
single minute, in the mind of any man; it must be decided, without a
moment's hesitation, in favour of that injured, that derided being, the
involuntary Old Maid, whose advocate I profess myself: nor would such
a decision depend on any prior sentiments, which the arbiter might
form, to the discredit, or to the glory, of wedlock; for, whether we consider marriage as a burthen or as an enjoyment, it is equally unjust that
any female should twice suffer that burthen, or be twice indulged in that
enjoyment, while another, at the same period of life, is kept an utter
stranger to the cares or to the delights of an important office, which she
is equally ready to assume, and equally able to support. This position is,
I trust, so evident, that, if I could convert this assembly into the supreme
court of judicature, and bring to its bar both the Widow and the Old
Maid, as rival claimants of the nuptial coronet, on the mere principles
of right, I am persuaded the integrity of this audience would soon terminate the contest, and ratify the title of my client by an unanimous
decree. But alas! in this point there is no tribunal on earth, to which the
disconsolate Old Maiden can successfully apply for substantial justice.

† From [William Hayley], A *Philosophical, Historical, and Moral Essay on Old Maids*, 3 vols.
  (London, 1785), 3: 176–196. All notes are by the editor of this Norton Critical Edition.

The clamour of prejudice is against her, and her pretensions are derided; while custom and commodity,

> *That smooth-fac'd gentleman, tickling commodity,*

are such active and prosperous agents for her antagonist, the Widow, that she, this insidious antagonist! is admitted, perhaps, three, four, or even five times to the recent altar of Hymen,[1] while my unfortunate client, the neglected Old Maid, however wishfully she may look towards the portal, is not allowed to find even a temporary shelter within a portico of the temple.—Can this, Sir, be called equity? Is it not injustice? Is it not barbarity?—But I may be told, that in the common occurrences of life, in a transaction such as marriage, peculiarly subject to fancy and caprice, we must not expect, we must not require men to observe the nicer dictates of strict equity, and a speculative rule of right.—Be it so!— I will not, therefore, on this important question, appeal solely to the consciences of men; I will appeal to their interests. I will prove to them, that he who marries an Old Maid, has a much greater chance of being invariably beloved by his wife, or, in other words, of being happy in wedlock, than he has, who rashly throws himself into the open arms of a Widow.—Sir, I flatter myself, it will require no long chain of arguments to establish and fortify, on the most solid ground, this momentous position. I trust, that I shall be able to accomplish it, merely by reminding this audience of a propensity in the human mind, which cannot be called in question; I mean the propensity to exalt in our estimation those possessions of which we are deprived, and to sink the value of what is actually in our hands.—Sir, the first part of this propensity is so general, and it operates with such amazing force on the character to whom I wish to apply it, that I remember the admirable Fielding,[2] with a most happy coincidence of humour and of truth, calls the death of an husband 'an infallible recipe to recover the lost affections of a wife.'

Let me, Sir, entreat this assembly to retain in their thoughts the propensity I have mentioned, and then to contemplate with me the feelings of the late Widow towards her second or third husband, and the feelings of the quondam Old Maid, now joyfully united to her first and only love.—Sir, the affection of the re-married Widow is a pocket telescope; she directs the magnifying end of it towards her good man in the grave, and it enlarges to a marvellous degree all the mental and all the personal endowments of the dear departed. She then turns the inverted glass to his diminishing successor, and, whatever his proportion of excellence may be, the poor luckless living mortal soon dwindles in her sight to a comparative pigmy. But, Sir, this is not the case with our quondam Old Maid. No! Sir—her affection is a portable microscope, which magnifies

---

1. God of marriage.
2. Henry Fielding (1707–1754), author of *Tom Jones*. The quoted phrase occurs in a chapter title (bk. 2, chap. 8).

in a stupendous manner all the attractive merits and powers of pleasing, however inconsiderable they may be, in the favourite creature upon whom she gazes. Like an inexperienced but a passionate naturalist, she continues to survey the new and sole object of her contemplation, not only with unremitted assiduity, but with increasing amazement and delight. He fills her eye; he occupies her mind; he engrosses her heart.

But it may be said in reply, If the man who marries an Old Maid has this superior chance of being uniformly beloved by his wife, since it is certainly the wish of every man who marries to be so, how happens it that men decide so preposterously against themselves, and perpetually prefer the Widow to the Old Maid? Is not this constant preference a very strong argument in favour of the character so preferred? Does it not prove, that the Widow has acquired the art, or the power, of conferring more happiness on her second husband than the Old Maid is able to bestow upon her first? for can we suppose that men, instructed by the experience of ages, would continue to act in constant opposition to their own domestic happiness, in the most important article of human life?

Alas! Sir, I fear there are more articles than one, in which we inconsiderate mortals may be frequently observed to act against experience, against our reason, and against our felicity. That the Widow is constantly preferred to the Old Maid, I most readily admit; nay, I complain of it as an inveterate grievance; but I trust, Sir, that I can account for this unreasonable preference, without adding a single grain to the weight, or rather to the empty scale, of the Widow.

I believe, Sir, a very simple metaphor will illustrate the whole affair on both sides.

The Widow is an experienced and a skilful angler, who has acquired patience to wait for the favourable minute, and rapidity to strike in the very instant when the fish has fairly risen to the hook. By this double excellence her success is ensured. But alas! Sir, the Old Maid is an angler, whom fruitless expectation has rendered both impatient and unskilful; she is thrown into trepidation by the first appearance of *a nibble*, and by making a too hasty movement at that critical juncture, she too often renders her bait, however sweet it may be, an object of terror, instead of allurement, to what she wishes to catch. Though my allusion may sound a little coarsely, let me entreat you, Sir, not to imagine that I mean to express any degree of disrespect to my honest and worthy client, the unprosperous Old Maid. Allow me, Sir, to remind you, that ingenuous and unhacknied spirits, though actively inclined, are often reduced to do nothing, by their too eager desire to do well; and this is frequently the case of the good and delicate Old Maid, in her laudable project of securing a husband: so that even when she is herself the cause of her own failure in this worthy purpose; she deserves not our censure but our compassion. Yes! Sir, the partizans of the Widow may smile, if they please, at my assertion; but I scruple not to affirm, that the solitary, neglected Old Maid is more truly entitled to pity, that soft harbinger of love, than the weeping Widow herself. Much has been said, and, I confess, with great eloquence, on the Widow's attractive sorrow. It is, indeed, *attractive*; and so attractive, that it has frequently recalled to my imagination the moan of the hyæna, that artful, destructive, and insatiable creature, who is said by the ancient naturalists to lure into her den, by a treacherous cry of distress, the unwary traveller whom she intends to devour. This insidious behaviour of the hyæna is a questionable fact, that no one, perhaps, can fully prove or refute; but all persons of any experience in the world have seen instances of men, who have been allured into the snare of the Widow, and have lamented, when it was too late to retreat, that they fell the victims of their own generous, but misplaced compassion.

The habit of changing is very apt to produce a passion for novelty; and the wife, who has buried one or two husbands, on a slight disagreement with her second or third, will soon wish him to sleep in peace with his departed predecessor, from her hope of being more lucky in her next adventure. You may remember, Sir, that our old poet Chaucer, that admirable and exact painter of life and manners! has very happily marked this prevalent disposition of the re-married Widow, in the long prologue which he assigns to his Wife of Bath. That good lady glories in having already buried four husbands, and expresses a perfect readiness, whenever Heaven may give her the opportunity, to engage with a sixth. Let it not be said, that this character is a mere phantom, created by the lively imagination of a satirical and facetious poet! No! Sir, this venerable, though sportive old bard, copied nature most faithfully: and, as a proof that he did so in the present case, I will mention a more marvellous example of this passion in the re-marrying Widow for an unlimited succession of novelties. Sir, the example I mean, is recorded in an ecclesiastical writer of great authority, whose name I cannot in this moment recollect; but I remember he mentions it as a fact, which happened at Rome, and to which he was himself an eye-witness. This fact, Sir, was the marriage of a widow to her *twenty-second husband*. The man also had buried *twenty wives*; and all the eyes of Rome were fixed on this singular pair, as on a couple of gladiators, anxious to see which would conduct the other to the grave. If I remember right, the woman, after all her funeral triumphs, was the victim in this wonderful conflict: but the story, however it might terminate, sufficiently proves the passion for novelty, which I have ascribed to the Widow. Now, Sir, if the second or third husband of a Widow may have frequent cause to imagine, that his lady's transferrable affections are veering toward his probable successor, he cannot surely be so happy, or secure, as the man who has more wisely united himself to a worthy Old Maid. She, good soul! remembering how long she waited for her first husband, instead of hastily looking forward to a second, will direct all her attention to cherish and preserve the dear creature, whom she at last acquired after tedious expectation. Her good man has no rival to fear, either among the living or the dead, and may securely enjoy the delightful prerogative of believing himself the absolute master of his wife's affections. I entreat you, Sir, to observe how very different the case is with the inconsiderate man, who rashly married a Widow! He has not only to apprehend, that the changeable tenderness of his lady may take a sudden turn towards his probable successor, but, if her thoughts are too faithful, and too virtuous, to wander towards the living, even then, Sir, after all his endeavours to take full possession of her heart, though he may delude himself with the vain idea of being its sole proprietor, he will frequently find, that he has only entered into partnership with a ghost. Yes! Sir, though my opponents may treat the expression as ludicrous, I will maintain that it is literally just. I repeat, he has entered into partnership with a ghost, and I will add, Sir, the very probable consequence of such a partnership; he will soon find, that by the subtle illusions of his invisible partner, he has lost even his poor moiety in that precarious possession, the heart of a remarried Widow! and will find himself, at the same time, a real bankrupt in happiness. Since my antagonists have been pleased to smile at my expression, as the language rather of fancy than of truth, suffer me, Mr. President, to quote a case, in which this dead, this derided partner made his actual appearance, and was bold enough to urge an exclusive claim. Sir, I trust the case I allude to is a case directly in point; it is quoted, indeed, on a different occasion, by the admirable Addison,[3] from the seventeenth book of the Jewish historian, Josephus. I mean the case of the Widow Glaphyra, who, having been twice a Widow, took for her third husband Archelaus. You may remember, Sir, that the thoughts of this lady, after her third adventure, ran so much on her first lord, that she saw the good man in a vision—'Glaphyra,' said the phantom, 'thou hast made good the old saying, that women are not to be trusted. Was not I the husband of thy virginity? Have I not children by thee? How couldst thou forget our loves so far, as to enter into a second marriage, and after that into a third?—But for our passed loves I will free thee from thy present reproach, and make thee mine for ever.'—Glaphyra related her dream, and died soon after. This, Sir, is a serious and tragical proof, how dangerous it is to marry a Widow. Surely no considerate man would chuse to incur the hazard of having his bride thus torn from his embraces by so arrogant a phantom.—Allow me, Sir, to relate a story of a comic cast, which will equally prove the secret perils of such a marriage. I received it from a very worthy old gentleman, not unknown to this assembly. He was acquainted, in his youth, with a famous mimic of the last century, who was the principal actor in this comic or rather farcical scene, and related it circumstantially to my friend. This mimic,

3. Joseph Addison (1672–1719), essayist, founder (with Richard Steele) of *The Spectator*, a popular weekly periodical.

Sir, a man of pleasantry and adventure, courted, in the early part of his life, a very handsome and opulent Widow; she gave him the highest encouragement; but, as avarice was her foible, she at last jilted him for a wealthy suitor, who, though of a very timid constitution, was rash enough to marry this very tempting Widow. The discarded mimic was inflamed with a variety of passions, and determined to take some very signal revenge. An opportunity of vengeance occurred to him, which, as he knew the extreme timidity of his fortunate rival, he seized without the pause of apprehension. His valet had intrigued with the favourite abigail[4] of the Widow, and by her assistance the mimic commanded[5] the nuptial chamber of the bride. He had known the person of her first husband, and, having concealed himself under a toilet,[6] till the hour of consummation, he then made his appearance, assuming the most exact similitude, both in figure and voice, to the dear departed. He had hardly undrawn the curtain, when the affrighted bride fell into a fit. The bridegroom, who had also known his deceased predecessor, was seized with a panic still worse, and his trembling body soon diffused so powerful an effluvia, that although it contributed nothing to his own relief, it recovered the lady from her swoon. She revived in perfect possession of her senses, and, finding the dead husband vanished, and the living one unfit for a companion, she hastily arose. As she loved money, she had taken the prudent precaution of securing to herself the enjoyment of her own fortune, and, having some suspicion of the trick which had been played against her, she resolved to make a wise use of it, and declared, that she would never proceed to consummate her marriage with a man, who had not resolution enough to protect her from a ghost. She persisted in this conduct, and the luckless derided bridegroom remained, through life, a melancholy example to confirm the wisdom of that adage, which says, that he should, indeed, be a bold man, who enters into the service of a Widow.

Sir, I should entreat your pardon for having trespassed on the patience of this assembly by the recital of so long a story, did I not flatter myself that it will have a happy tendency to guard the single gentlemen, who hear me, from the iniquitous temerity of preferring a Widow to an Old Maid.

I might alledge, Sir, many arguments which I have not hitherto touched upon, in favour of my client. I might shew of what infinite importance it is to matrimonial felicity, that the husband should receive into his arms a partner for life, whose disposition and habits, instead of being fixed already by a former lord, are yet to be moulded according to the will and abilities of her first and only director. Sir, in this point, the Widow is a piece of warped wood, which the most skilful workman may

4. Maidservant.
5. Took possession of.
6. Dressing table.

find himself unable to shape as he wishes; but the Old Maid, Sir, is the pliant virgin wax, which follows, with the most happy ductility, every serious design, every ingenious device, every sportive whim, of the modeller.

But I will relinquish the innumerable arguments that I might yet adduce in support of the Old Maid; I will rest her cause on that solid rock, which I have endeavoured, Sir, to exhibit in different points of view, I mean the superior security with which her husband may depend on the stability of her affection. I will conclude by conjuring every gentleman, who may happen to hesitate between a Widow and an Old Maid, to remember, that reason and experience, that equity and the general interest of mankind, all loudly plead for his preferring the latter: I will conjure him to recollect, that the man who marries a Widow has great cause to apprehend unreasonable expectations, unpleasant comparisons, and variable affection; while he, who marries an Old Maid, may with confidence prepare to meet unexacting tenderness, increasing gratitude, and perpetual endearments.

JANE AUSTEN

Letters about *Persuasion* †

To Fanny Knight

Chawton, Thursday March 13. [1817]

As to making any adequate return for such a Letter as yours my dearest Fanny, it is absolutely impossible; if I were to labour at it all the rest of my Life and live to the age of Methuselah, I could never accomplish anything so long and so perfect; but I cannot let William go without a few Lines of acknowledgement and reply. I have pretty well done with Mr. Wildman. By your description he can*not* be in love with you, however he may try at it, and I could not wish the match unless there were a great deal of Love on his side. I do not know what to do about Jemima Branfill. What does her dancing away with so much spirit, mean? that she does not care for him, or only wishes to *appear* not to care for him?—Who can understand a young Lady?—Poor Mrs. C. Milles, that she should die on a wrong day at last, after being about it so long!—It was unlucky that the Goodnestone Party could not meet you, and I hope her friendly, obliging, social Spirit, which delighted in drawing People together, was not conscious of the division and disappoint-

† From *Jane Austen's Letters*, edited by R. W. Chapman, 2nd ed. (London: Oxford UP, 1959), letters 141 and 142. Reprinted by permission of Oxford University Press. All notes are by the editor of this Norton Critical Edition.

ment she was occasioning. I am sorry and surprised that you speak of
her as having little to leave, and must feel for Miss Milles, though she
is Molly, if a material loss of Income is to attend her other loss.—Single
Women have a dreadful propensity for being poor—which is one very
strong argument in favour of Matrimony, but I need not dwell on such
arguments with *you*, pretty Dear, you do not want inclination.—Well,
I shall say, as I have often said before, Do not be in a hurry; depend
upon it, the right Man will come at last; you will in the course of the
next two or three years, meet with somebody more generally unexceptionable than anyone you have yet known, who will love you as warmly
as ever *He* did, and who will so completely attach you, that you will feel
you never really loved before.—And then, by not beginning the business
of Mothering quite so early in life, you will be young in Constitution,
spirits, figure and countenance, while Mrs Wm Hammond is growing
old by confinements and nursing. Do none of the Plumtres ever come
to Balls now?—You have never mentioned them as being at any?—And
what do you hear of the Gipps or of Fanny and her Husband?—Mrs F.
A.[1] is to be confined the middle of April, and is by no means remarkably
Large for *her*.—Aunt Cassandra walked to Wyards yesterday with Mrs.
Digweed. Anna has had a bad cold, looks pale, and we fear something
else. She has just weaned Julia.—How soon, the difference of temper
in Children appears!—Jemima has a very irritable bad Temper (her
Mother says so)—and Julia a very sweet one, always pleased and
happy.—I hope as Anna is so early sensible of it's defects, that she will
give Jemima's disposition the early and steady attention it must
require.—*I* have also heard lately from your Aunt Harriot, and cannot
understand their plans in parting with Miss S—whom she seems very
much to value, now that Harriot and Eleanor are both of an age for a
Governess to be so useful to;—especially as when Caroline was sent to
School some years, *Miss Bell* was still retained, though the others were
then mere Nursery Children.—They have some good reason I dare say,
though I cannot penetrate it, and till I know what it is I shall invent a
bad one, and amuse myself with accounting for the difference of measures by supposing Miss S. to be a superior sort of Woman, who has
never stooped to recommend herself to the Master of the family by Flattery, as Miss Bell did.—I *will* answer your kind questions more than you
expect. Miss Catherine[2] is put upon the Shelve for the present, and I
do not know that she will ever come out;—but I have a something ready
for Publication, which may perhaps appear about a twelvemonth hence.
It is short, about the length of Catherine.—This is for yourself alone.
Neither Mr. Salusbury nor Mr. Wildman are to know of it.

   I am got tolerably well again, quite equal to walking about and
enjoying the Air; and by sitting down and resting a good while between

1. Mrs. Frederick Austen, her sister-in-law. "Confined" means confined for childbirth.
2. Presumably *Northanger Abbey*, whose heroine is Catherine Morland.

my Walks, I get exercise enough. I have a scheme however for accomplishing more, as the weather grows springlike. I mean to take to riding the Donkey. It will be more independant & less troublesome than the use of the carriage, & I shall be able to go about with At Cassandra in her walks to Alton and Wyards.—I hope you will think Wm. looking well. He was bilious the other day, and Aunt Cass: supplied him with a Dose at his own request, which seemed to have good effect.—I was sure *you* would have approved it. Wm. and I are the best of friends. I love him very much. Everything is so *natural* about him, his affections, his Manners and his Drollery. He entertains and interests us extremely.— Max: Hammond and A. M. Shaw are people whom I cannot care for, in themselves, but I enter into their situation and am glad they are so happy.—If I were the Duchess of Richmond, I should be very miserable about my son's choice. What can be expected from a Paget, born and brought up in the centre of conjugal Infidelity & Divorces?—I will *not* be interested about Lady Caroline. I abhor all the race of Pagets.—Our fears increase for poor little Harriet; the latest account is that Sir Ev: Home is confirmed in his opinion of there being water on the brain.— I hope Heaven in its mercy will take her soon. Her poor Father will be quite worn out by his feelings for her.—He cannot spare Cassy at present, she is an occupation and a comfort to him.

Adieu my dearest Fanny. Nothing could be more delicious than your Letter; and the assurance of your feeling releived by writing it, made the pleasure perfect.—But how could it possibly be any new idea to you that you have a great deal of Imagination?—You are all over Imagination.— The most astonishing part of your Character is, that with so much Imagination, so much flight of Mind, such unbounded Fancies, you should have such excellent Judgement in what you do!—Religious Principle I fancy must explain it.—Well, good bye and God bless you.

Yrs very affecly
J. Austen

To Fanny Knight

Chawton, Sunday March 23. [1817]

I am very much obliged to you my dearest Fanny for sending me Mr. Wildman's conversation, I had great amusement in reading it, and I *hope* I am not affronted and do not think the worse of him for having a Brain so very different from mine, but my strongest sensation of all is *astonishment* at your being able to press him on the subject so perseveringly—and I agree with your Papa, that it was not fair. When he knows the truth he will be uncomfortable.—You are the oddest Creature!— Nervous enough in some respects, but in others perfectly without nerves!—Quite unrepulsible, hardened and impudent. Do not oblige him to read any more.—Have mercy on him, tell him the truth and make him an apology. He and I should not in the least agree of course, in our ideas of Novels and Heroines;—pictures of perfection as you know make me sick and wicked—but there is some very good sense in what he says, and I particularly respect him for wishing to think well of all young Ladies; it shews an amiable and a delicate Mind.—And he deserves better treatment than to be obliged to read any more of my Works.—Do not be surprised at finding Uncle Henry acquainted with my having another ready for publication. I could not say No when he asked me, but he knows nothing more of it.—You will not like it, so you need not be impatient. You may *perhaps* like the Heroine, as she is almost too good for me.—Many thanks for your kind care for my health; I certainly have not been well for many weeks, and about a week ago I was very poorly, I have had a good deal of fever at times and indifferent nights, but am considerably better now, and recovering my Looks a little, which have been bad enough, black and white and every wrong colour. I must not depend upon being ever very blooming again. Sickness is a dangerous Indulgence at my time of Life. Thank you for everything you tell me;—I do not feel worthy of it by anything I can say in return, but I assure you my pleasure in your Letters is quite as great as ever, and I am interested and amused just as you could wish me. If there is a *Miss* Marsden, I perceive whom she will marry.

Eveng.—I was languid and dull and very bad company when I wrote the above; I am better now—to my own feelings at least—and wish I may be more agreable. We are going to have Rain, and after that, very pleasant genial weather, which will exactly do for me, as my Saddle will then be completed—and air and exercise is what I want. Indeed I shall be very glad when the event at Scarlets[3] is over, the expectation of it keeps us in a worry, your Grandmama especially; she sits brooding over Evils which cannot be remedied and Conduct impossible to be understood.—Now, the reports from Keppel St. are rather better, little Harriet's headaches are abated, and Sir Evd: is satisfied with the effect of the Mercury, and does not despair of a Cure. The Complaint I find is not considered Incurable nowadays, provided the Patient be young enough not to have the Head hardened. The Water in that case may be drawn off by Mercury. But though this is a new idea to us, perhaps it may have been long familiar to you, through your friend Mr. Scud:—I hope his high renown is maintained by driving away William's cough. Tell William that Triggs is as beautiful and condescending as ever, and was so good as to dine with us today, and tell him that I often play at *Nines* and think of him.—Anna has not a chance of escape; her husband called here the other day, and said she was *pretty* well but not *equal* to so long a walk; she *must come in* her *Donkey Carriage.*—Poor Animal, she will be worn out before she is thirty.—I am very sorry for her.—Mrs Clem-

3. Home of Mr. and Mrs. James Leigh Perrot, Austen's uncle and aunt.

ent too is in that way again. I am quite tired of so many Children.—
Mrs Benn has a 13th.—The Papillons came back on friday night, but I
have not seen them yet, as I do not venture to Church. I cannot hear
however, but that they are the same Mr. P. and his sister they used to
be. She has engaged a new Maidservant in Mrs. Calker's room, whom
she means to make also Housekeeper under herself.—Old Philmore was
buried yesterday, and I, by way of saying something to Triggs, observed
that it had been a very handsome Funeral, but his manner of reply made
me suppose that it was not generally esteemed so. I can only be sure of
one part being very handsome, Triggs himself, walking behind in his
Green Coat.—Mrs. Philmore attended as chief Mourner, in Bombasin,
made very short, and flounced with Crape.

Tuesday.—I have had various plans as to this Letter, but at last I have
determined that Un: Henry shall forward it from London. I want to see
how Canterbury looks in the direction.—When once Unc. H. has left
us I shall wish him with you. London is become a hateful place to him,
and he is always depressed by the idea of it.—I hope he will be in time
for your sick. I am sure he must do that part of his Duty as excellently
as all the rest. He returned yesterday from Steventon, & was with us by
breakfast, bringing Edward with him, only that Edwd staid to breakfast
at Wyards. We had a pleasant family-day, for the Altons dined with
us;—the last visit of the kind probably, which *she* will be able to pay us
for many a month;—Very well, to be able to do it so long, for she *expects*
much about this day three weeks, and is generally very exact.—I hope
your own Henry is in France and that you have heard from him. The
Passage once over, he will feel all Happiness.—I took my 1st ride yesterday and liked it very much. I went up Mounters Lane, and round by
where the new Cottages are to be, and found the exercise and everything
very pleasant, and I had the advantage of agreable companions, as At
Cass: and Edward walked by my side.—At Cass. is such an excellent
Nurse, so assiduous and unwearied!—But you know all that already.—

Very affecly Yours   J. Austen

HENRY AUSTEN

Biographical Notice of the Author †

The following pages are the production of a pen which has already
contributed in no small degree to the entertainment of the public. And
when the public, which has not been insensible to the merits of "Sense
and Sensibility," "Pride and Prejudice," "Mansfield Park," and

† Preface to *Northanger Abbey and Persuasion*, London, 1818. All notes are by the editor of this
Norton Critical Edition.

"Emma," shall be informed that the hand which guided that pen is now mouldering in the grave, perhaps a brief account of Jane Austen will be read with a kindlier sentiment than simple curiosity.

Short and easy will be the task of the mere biographer. A life of usefulness, literature, and religion, was not by any means a life of event. To those who lament their irreparable loss, it is consolatory to think that, as she never deserved disapprobation, so, in the circle of her family and friends, she never met reproof; that her wishes were not only reasonable, but gratified; and that to the little disappointments incidental to human life was never added, even for a moment, an abatement of goodwill from any who knew her.

Jane Austen was born on the 16th of December, 1775, at Steventon, in the county of Hants.[1] Her father was Rector of that parish upwards of forty years. There he resided, in the conscientious and unassisted discharge of his ministerial duties, until he was turned of seventy years. Then he retired with his wife, our authoress, and her sister, to Bath, for the remainder of his life, a period of about four years. Being not only a profound scholar, but possessing a most exquisite taste in every species of literature, it is not wonderful that his daughter Jane should, at a very early age, have become sensible to the charms of style, and enthusiastic in the cultivation of her own language. On the death of her father she removed, with her mother and sister, for a short time, to Southampton, and finally, in 1809, to the pleasant village of Chawton, in the same county. From this place she sent into the world those novels, which by many have been placed on the same shelf as the works of a D'Arblay and an Edgeworth.[2] Some of these novels had been the gradual performances of her previous life. For though in composition she was equally rapid and correct, yet an invincible distrust of her own judgement induced her to withhold her works from the public, till time and many perusals had satisfied her that the charm of recent composition was dissolved. The natural constitution, the regular habits, the quiet and happy occupations of our authoress, seemed to promise a long succession of amusement to the public, and a gradual increase of reputation to herself. But the symptoms of a decay, deep and incurable, began to shew themselves in the commencement of 1816. Her decline was at first deceitfully slow; and until the spring of this present year, those who knew their happiness to be involved in her existence could not endure to despair. But in the month of May, 1817, it was found advisable that she should be removed to Winchester for the benefit of constant medical aid, which none even then dared to hope would be permanently beneficial. She supported, during two months, all the varying pain, irksomeness, and tedium, attendant on decaying nature, with more than

1. Hampshire.
2. Frances Burney (1752–1840), whose married name was D'Arblay, and Maria Edgeworth (1767–1849), both popular novelists.

resignation, with a truly elastic cheerfulness. She retained her faculties, her memory, her fancy, her temper, and her affections, warm, clear, and unimpaired, to the last. Neither her love of God, nor of her fellow creatures flagged for a moment. She made a point of receiving the sacrament before excessive bodily weakness might have rendered her perception unequal to her wishes. She wrote whilst she could hold a pen, and with a pencil when a pen was become too laborious. The day preceding her death she composed some stanzas replete with fancy and vigour. Her last voluntary speech conveyed thanks to her medical attendant; and to the final question asked of her, purporting to know her wants, she replied, "I want nothing but death."

She expired shortly after, on Friday the 18th of July, 1817, in the arms of her sister, who, as well as the relator of these events, feels too surely that they shall never look upon her like again.

Jane Austen was buried on the 24th of July, 1817, in the cathedral church of Winchester, which, in the whole catalogue of its mighty dead, does not contain the ashes of a brighter genius or a sincerer Christian.

Of personal attractions she possessed a considerable share. Her stature was that of true elegance. It could not have been increased without exceeding the middle height. Her carriage and deportment were quiet, yet graceful. Her features were separately good. Their assemblage produced an unrivalled expression of that cheerfulness, sensibility, and benevolence, which were her real characteristics. Her complexion was of the finest texture. It might with truth be said, that her eloquent blood spoke through her modest cheek. Her voice was extremely sweet. She delivered herself with fluency and precision. Indeed she was formed for elegant and rational society, excelling in conversation as much as in composition. In the present age it is hazardous to mention accomplishments. Our authoress would, probably, have been inferior to few in such acquirements, had she not been so superior to most in higher things. She had not only an excellent taste for drawing, but, in her earlier days, evinced great power of hand in the management of the pencil.[3] Her own musical attainments she held very cheap. Twenty years ago they would have been thought more of, and twenty years hence many a parent will expect their daughters to be applauded for meaner performances. She was fond of dancing, and excelled in it. It remains now to add a few observations on that which her friends deemed more important, on those endowments which sweetened every hour of their lives.

If there be an opinion current in the world, that perfect placidity of temper is not reconcileable to the most lively imagination, and the keenest relish for wit, such an opinion will be rejected for ever by those who

3. For drawing.

have had the happiness of knowing the authoress of the following works. Though the frailties, foibles, and follies of others could not escape her immediate detection, yet even on their vices did she never trust herself to comment with unkindness. The affectation of candour[4] is not uncommon; but she had no affectation. Faultless herself, as nearly as human nature can be, she always sought, in the faults of others, something to excuse, to forgive or forget. Where extenuation was impossible, she had a sure refuge in silence. She never uttered either a hasty, a silly, or a severe expression. In short, her temper was as polished as her wit. Nor were her manners inferior to her temper. They were of the happiest kind. No one could be often in her company without feeling a strong desire of obtaining her friendship, and cherishing a hope of having obtained it. She was tranquil without reserve or stiffness; and communicative without intrusion or self-sufficiency. She became an authoress entirely from taste and inclination. Neither the hope of fame nor profit mixed with her early motives. Most of her works, as before observed, were composed many years previous to their publication. It was with extreme difficulty that her friends, whose partiality she suspected whilst she honoured their judgement, could prevail on her to publish her first work. Nay, so persuaded was she that its sale would not repay the expense of publication, that she actually made a reserve from her very moderate income to meet the expected loss. She could scarcely believe what she termed her great good fortune when "Sense and Sensibility" produced a clear profit of about £150. Few so gifted were so truly unpretending. She regarded the above sum as a prodigious recompense for that which had cost her nothing. Her readers, perhaps, will wonder that such a work produced so little at a time when some authors have received more guineas than they have written lines. The works of our authoress, however, may live as long as those which have burst on the world with more éclat.[5] But the public has not been unjust; and our authoress was far from thinking it so. Most gratifying to her was the applause which from time to time reached her ears from those who were competent to discriminate. Still, in spite of such applause, so much did she shrink from notoriety, that no accumulation of fame would have induced her, had she lived, to affix her name to any productions of her pen. In the bosom of her own family she talked of them freely, thankful for praise, open to remark, and submissive to criticism. But in public she turned away from any allusion to the character of an authoress. She read aloud with very great taste and effect. Her own works, probably, were never heard to so much advantage as from her own mouth; for she partook largely in all the best gifts of the comic muse. She was a warm and judicious admirer of landscape, both in nature and on canvass. At

4. Generosity.
5. Brilliance, dazzling effect.

a very early age she was enamoured of Gilpin[6] on the Picturesque; and she seldom changed her opinions either on books or men.

Her reading was very extensive in history and belles lettres; and her memory extremely tenacious. Her favourite moral writers were Johnson in prose, and Cowper in verse.[7] It is difficult to say at what age she was not intimately acquainted with the merits and defects of the best essays and novels in the English language. Richardson's[8] power of creating, and preserving the consistency of his characters, as particularly exemplified in "Sir Charles Grandison," gratified the natural discrimi‐ation of her mind, whilst her taste secured her from the errors of his prolix style and tedious narrative. She did not rank any work of Fielding[9] quite so high. Without the slightest affectation she recoiled from every thing gross. Neither nature, wit, nor humour, could make her amends for so very low a scale of morals.

Her power of inventing characters seems to have been intuitive, and almost unlimited. She drew from nature; but, whatever may have been surmised to the contrary, never from individuals.

The style of her familiar correspondence was in all respects the same as that of her novels. Every thing came finished from her pen; for on all subjects she had ideas as clear as her expressions were well chosen. It is not hazarding too much to say that she never dispatched a note or letter unworthy of publication.

One trait only remains to be touched on. It makes all others unimportant. She was thoroughly religious and devout; fearful of giving offence to God, and incapable of feeling it towards any fellow creature. On serious subjects she was well-instructed, both by reading and meditation, and her opinions accorded strictly with those of our Established Church.

London, Dec. 13, 1817.

POSTSCRIPT

Since concluding the above remarks, the writer of them has been put in possession of some extracts from the private correspondence of the authoress. They are few and short; but are submitted to the public without apology, as being more truly descriptive of her temper, taste, feelings, and principles than any thing which the pen of a biographer can produce.

The first extract is a playful defence of herself from a mock charge of

6. William Gilpin (1724–1804) articulated a theory of the picturesque in *Three Essays: On Picturesque Beauty, On Picturesque Travel, and On Sketching Landscape* (1792).
7. Samuel Johnson (1709–1784), essayist and author of the moral tale *Rasselas;* William Cowper (1731–1800), poet, author of *The Task*.
8. Samuel Richardson (1689–1761), didactic novelist, who published *Sir Charles Grandison* in 1753.
9. Henry Fielding (1707–1754), whose best-known novel was *Tom Jones.*

having pilfered the manuscripts of a young relation.

"What should I do, my dearest E. with your manly, vigorous sketches, so full of life and spirit? How could I possibly join them on to a little bit of ivory, two inches wide, on which I work with a brush so fine as to produce little effect after much labour?"

The remaining extracts are from various parts of a letter written a few weeks before her death.

"My attendant is encouraging, and talks of making me quite well. I live chiefly on the sofa, but am allowed to walk from one room to the other. I have been out once in a sedan-chair, and am to repeat it, and be promoted to a wheel-chair as the weather serves. On this subject I will only say further that my dearest sister, my tender, watchful, indefatigable nurse, has not been made ill by her exertions. As to what I owe to her, and to the anxious affection of all my beloved family on this occasion, I can only cry over it, and pray to God to bless them more and more."

She next touches with just and gentle animadversion on a subject of domestic disappointment. Of this the particulars do not concern the public. Yet in justice to her characteristic sweetness and resignation, the concluding observation of our authoress thereon must not be suppressed.

"But I am getting too near complaint. It has been the appointment of God, however secondary causes may have operated."

The following and final extract will prove the facility with which she could correct every impatient thought, and turn from complaint to cheerfulness.

"You will find Captain ——— a very respectable, well-meaning man, without much manner, his wife and sister all good humour and obligingness, and I hope (since the fashion allows it) with rather longer petticoats than last year."

London, Dec. 20, 1817.

[RICHARD WHATELEY]

[A New Style of Novel] †

The times seem to be past when an apology was requisite from reviewers for condescending to notice a novel; when they felt themselves bound in dignity to deprecate the suspicion of paying much regard to such trifles, and pleaded the necessity of occasionally stooping to humour the taste of their fair readers. The delights of fiction, if not

† From [Richard Whateley], Review of *Northanger Abbey and Persuasion, Quarterly Review* 24(1821): 352–75. All notes are by the editor of this Norton Critical Edition.

more keenly or more generally relished, are at least more readily acknowledged by men of sense and taste; and we have lived to hear the merits of the best of this class of writings earnestly discussed by some of the ablest scholars and soundest reasoners of the present day.

We are inclined to attribute this change, not so much to an alteration in the public taste, as in the character of the productions in question. Novels may not, perhaps, display more genius now than formerly, but they contain more solid sense; they may not afford higher gratification, but it is of a nature which men are less disposed to be ashamed of avowing. We remarked, in a former Number, in reviewing a work of the author now before us, that 'a new style of novel has arisen, within the last fifteen or twenty years, differing from the former in the points upon which the interest hinges; neither alarming our credulity nor amusing our imagination by wild variety of incident, or by those pictures of romantic affection and sensibility, which were formerly as certain attributes of fictitious characters as they are of rare occurrence among those who actually live and die. The substitute for these excitements, which had lost much of their poignancy by the repeated and injudicious use of them, was the art of copying from nature as she really exists in the common walks of life, and presenting to the reader, instead of the splendid scenes of an imaginary world, a correct and striking representation of that which is daily taking place around him.'

Now, though the origin of this new school of fiction may probably be traced, as we there suggested, to the exhaustion of the mines from which materials for entertainment had been hitherto extracted, and the necessity of gratifying the natural craving of the reader for variety, by striking into an untrodden path; the consequences resulting from this change have been far greater than the mere supply of this demand. When this Flemish painting, as it were, is introduced—this accurate and unexaggerated delineation of events and characters—it necessarily follows, that a novel, which makes good its pretensions of giving a perfectly correct picture of common life, becomes a far more *instructive* work than one of equal or superior merit of the other class; it guides the judgment, and supplies a kind of artificial experience. It is a remark of the great father of criticism,[1] that poetry (i.e., narrative, and dramatic poetry) is of a more philosophical character than history; inasmuch as the latter details what has actually happened, of which many parts may chance to be exceptions to the general rules of probability, and consequently illustrate no general principles; whereas the former shews us what must naturally, or would probably, happen under given circumstances; and thus displays to us a comprehensive view of human nature, and furnishes general rules of practical wisdom. It is evident, that this will apply only to such fictions as are quite *perfect* in respect of the probability of their story; and

1. Aristotle.

that he, therefore, who resorts to the fabulist rather than the historian, for instruction in human character and conduct, must throw himself entirely on the judgment and skill of his teacher, and give him credit for talents much more rare than the accuracy and veracity which are the chief requisites in history. We fear, therefore, that the exultation which we can conceive some of our gentle readers to feel, at having Aristotle's warrant for (what probably they had never dreamed of) the *philosophical character* of their studies, must, in practice, be somewhat qualified, by those sundry little violations of probability which are to be met with in most novels; and which so far lower their value, as models of real life, that a person who had no other preparation for the world than is afforded by them, would form, probably, a less accurate idea of things as they are, than he would of a lion from studying merely the representations on China tea-pots.

Accordingly, a heavy complaint has long lain against works of fiction, as giving a false picture of what they profess to imitate, and disqualifying their readers for the ordinary scenes and everyday duties of life. And this charge applies, we apprehend, to the generality of what are strictly called novels, with even more justice than to romances. When all the characters and events are very far removed from what we see around us,— when, perhaps, even supernatural agents are introduced, the reader may indulge, indeed, in occasional day-dreams, but will be so little reminded of what he has been reading, by any thing that occurs in actual life, that though he may perhaps feel some disrelish for the tameness of the scene before him, compared with the fairy-land he has been visiting, yet at least his judgment will not be depraved, nor his expectations misled; he will not apprehend a meeting with Algerine[2] banditti on English shores, nor regard the old woman who shews him about an antique country seat, as either an enchantress or the keeper of an imprisoned damsel. But it is otherwise with those fictions which differ from common life in little or nothing but the improbability of the occurrences: the reader is insensibly led to calculate upon some of those lucky incidents and opportune coincidences of which he has been so much accustomed to read, and which, it is undeniable, *may* take place in real life; and to feel a sort of confidence, that however romantic his conduct may be, and in whatever difficulties it may involve him, all will be sure to come right at last, as is invariably the case with the hero of a novel.

On the other hand, so far as these pernicious effects fail to be produced, so far does the example lose its influence, and the exercise of poetical justice is rendered vain. The reward of virtuous conduct being brought about by fortunate accidents, he who abstains (taught, perhaps, by bitter disappointments) from reckoning on such accidents, wants that encouragement to virtue, which alone has been held out to him. 'If I

2. Algerian.

were *a man in a novel,*' we remember to have heard an ingenious friend observe, 'I should certainly act so and so, because I should be sure of being no loser by the most heroic self-devotion, and of ultimately succeeding in the most daring enterprises.'

*   *   *

When, therefore, the generality, even of the most approved novels, were of this character, (to say nothing of the heavier charges brought, of inflaming the passions of young persons by warm descriptions, weakening their abhorrence of profligacy by exhibiting it in combination with the most engaging qualities, and presenting vice in all its allurements, while setting forth the triumphs of 'virtue rewarded') it is not to be wondered that the grave guardians of youth should have generally stigmatized the whole class, as 'serving only to fill young people's heads with romantic love-stories, and rendering them unfit to mind any thing else.' That this censure and caution should in many instances be indiscriminate, can surprize no one, who recollects how rare a quality discrimination is; and how much better it suits indolence, as well as ignorance, to lay down a rule, than to ascertain the exceptions to it: we are acquainted with a careful mother whose daughters, while they never in their lives read a *novel* of any kind, are permitted to peruse, without reserve, any *plays* that happen to fall in their way; and with another, from whom no lessons, however excellent, of wisdom and piety, contained in a *prose-fiction*, can obtain quarter; but who, on the other hand, is no less indiscriminately indulgent to her children in the article of tales in *verse*, of whatever character.

The change, however, which we have already noticed, as having taken place in the character of several modern novels, has operated in a considerable degree to do away this prejudice; and has elevated this species of composition, in some respects at least, into a much higher class. For most of that instruction which used to be presented to the world in the shape of formal dissertations, or shorter and more desultory moral essays, such as those of the Spectator and Rambler,[3] we may now resort to the pages of the acute and judicious, but not less amusing, novelists who have lately appeared. If their views of men and manners are no less just than those of the essayists who preceded them, are they to be rated lower because they present to us these views, not in the language of general description, but in the form of well-constructed fictitious narrative? If the practical lessons they inculcate are no less sound and useful, it is surely no diminution of their merit that they are conveyed by example instead of precept: nor, if their remarks are neither less wise nor less important, are they the less valuable for being represented as thrown out

---

3. *The Spectator,* the work of Joseph Addison and Richard Steele, appeared daily from March 1711 to December 1712; *The Rambler,* by Samuel Johnson, was published from 1750 to 1752. Both periodicals consisted of short essays, often with moral emphasis.

in the course of conversations suggested by the circumstances of the speakers, and perfectly in character. The praise and blame of the moralist are surely not the less effectual for being bestowed, not in general declamation, on classes of men, but on individuals representing those classes, who are so clearly delineated and brought into action before us, that we seem to be acquainted with them, and feel an interest in their fate.

Biography is allowed, on all hands, to be one of the most attractive and profitable kinds of reading: now such novels as we have been speaking of, being a kind of fictitious biography, bear the same relation to the real, that epic and tragic poetry, according to Aristotle, bear to history: they present us (supposing, of course, each perfect in its kind) with the general, instead of the particular,—the probable, instead of the true; and, by leaving out those accidental irregularities, and exceptions to general rules, which constitute the many improbabilities of real narrative, present us with a clear and *abstracted* view of the general rules themselves; and thus concentrate, as it were, into a small compass, the net result of wide experience.

Among the authors of this school there is no one superior, if equal, to the lady whose last production is now before us, and whom we have much regret in finally taking leave of: her death (in the prime of life, considered as a writer) being announced in this the first publication to which her name is prefixed. We regret the failure not only of a source of innocent amusement, but also of that supply of practical good sense and instructive example, which she would probably have continued to furnish better than any of her contemporaries.

* * *

Miss Austen has the merit (in our judgment most essential) of being evidently a Christian writer: a merit which is much enhanced, both on the score of good taste, and of practical utility, by her religion being not at all obtrusive. She might defy the most fastidious critic to call any of her novels, (as Cœlebs[4] was designated, we will not say altogether without reason,) a 'dramatic sermon.' The subject is rather alluded to, and that incidentally, than studiously brought forward and dwelt upon. In fact she is more sparing of it than would be thought desirable by some persons; perhaps even by herself, had she consulted merely her own sentiments; but she probably introduced it as far as she thought would be generally acceptable and profitable: for when the purpose of inculcating a religious principle is made too palpably prominent, many readers, if they do not throw aside the book with disgust, are apt to fortify themselves with that respectful kind of apathy with which they undergo a

---

4. *Cœlebs in Search of a Wife* (1809), a highly didactic novel—with considerably more instruction than fiction—by Hannah More.

regular sermon, and prepare themselves as they do to swallow a dose of medicine, endeavouring to *get it down* in large gulps, without tasting it more than is necessary.

The moral lessons also of this lady's novels, though clearly and impressively conveyed, are not offensively put forward, but spring incidentally from the circumstances of the story; they are not forced upon the reader, but he is left to collect them (though without any difficulty) for himself: her's is that unpretending kind of instruction which is furnished by real life; and certainly no author has ever conformed more closely to real life, as well in the incidents, as in the characters and descriptions. Her fables appear to us to be, in their own way, nearly faultless; they do not consist (like those of some of the writers who have attempted this kind of common-life novel writing) of a string of unconnected events which have little or no bearing on one main plot, and are introduced evidently for the sole purpose of bringing in characters and conversations; but have all that compactness of plan and unity of action which is generally produced by a sacrifice of probability: yet they have little or nothing that is not probable; the story proceeds without the aid of extraordinary accidents; the events which take place are the necessary or natural consequences of what has preceded; and yet (which is a very rare merit indeed) the final catastrophe is scarcely ever clearly foreseen from the beginning, and very often comes, upon the generality of readers at least, quite unexpected. We know not whether Miss Austin ever had access to the precepts of Aristotle; but there are few, if any, writers of fiction who have illustrated them more successfully.

The vivid distinctness of description, the minute fidelity of detail, and air of unstudied ease in the scenes represented, which are no less necessary than probability of incident, to carry the reader's imagination along with the story, and give fiction the perfect appearance of reality, she possesses in a high degree; and the object is accomplished without resorting to those deviations from the ordinary plan of narrative in the third person, which have been patronized by some eminent masters.

* * *

Miss Austin, though she has in a few places introduced letters with great effect, has on the whole conducted her novels on the ordinary plan, describing, without scruple, private conversations and uncommunicated feelings: but she has not been forgetful of the important maxim, so long ago illustrated by Homer, and afterwards enforced by Aristotle, of saying as little as possible in her own person, and giving a dramatic air to the narrative, by introducing frequent conversations; which she conducts with a regard to character hardly exceeded even by Shakspeare himself. Like him, she shows as admirable a discrimination in the characters of fools as of people of sense; a merit which is far from common. To invent, indeed, a conversation full of wisdom or of wit, requires that the writer should himself possess ability; but the converse does not hold good: it is no fool that can describe fools well; and many who have succeeded pretty well in painting superior characters, have failed in giving individuality to those weaker ones, which it is necessary to introduce in order to give a faithful representation of real life: they exhibit to us mere folly in the abstract, forgetting that to the eye of a skilful naturalist the insects on a leaf present as wide differences as exist between the elephant and the lion. Slender, and Shallow, and Aguecheek, as Shakspeare has painted them, though equally fools, resemble one another no more than Richard, and Macbeth, and Julius Cæsar; and Miss Austin's Mrs. Bennet, Mr. Rushworth, and Miss Bates, are no more alike than her Darcy, Knightley, and Edmund Bertram.[5] Some have complained, indeed, of finding her fools too much like nature, and consequently tiresome; there is no disputing about tastes; all we can say is, that such critics must (whatever deference they may outwardly pay to received opinions) find the Merry Wives of Windsor and Twelfth Night very tiresome; and that those who look with pleasure at Wilkie's pictures,[6] or those of the Dutch school, must admit that excellence of imitation may confer attraction on that which would be insipid or disagreeable in the reality.

Her minuteness of detail has also been found fault with; but even where it produces, at the time, a degree of tediousness, we know not whether that can justly be reckoned a blemish, which is absolutely essential to a very high excellence. Now, it is absolutely impossible, without this, to produce that thorough acquaintance with the characters, which is necessary to make the reader heartily interested in them. Let any one cut out from the Iliad or from Shakspeare's plays every thing (we are far from saying that either might not lose some parts with advantage, but let him reject every thing) which is absolutely devoid of importance and of interest *in itself*; and he will find that what is left will have lost more than half its charms. We are convinced that some writers have diminished the effect of their works by being scrupulous to admit nothing into them which had not some absolute, intrinsic, and independent merit. They have acted like those who strip off the leaves of a fruit tree, as being of themselves good for nothing, with the view of securing more nourishment to the fruit, which in fact cannot attain its full maturity and flavour without them.

* * *

5. Mrs. Bennet belongs to *Pride and Prejudice*, Mr. Rushworth to *Mansfield Park*, Miss Bates to *Emma*. The last three characters named come respectively from *Pride and Prejudice*, *Emma*, and *Mansfield Park*.
6. David Wilkie (1785–1841) often painted such conventionally unpleasant realistic situations as "The Rent Day." The Dutch School is known for extremely realistic detail.

But we must proceed to the publication of which the title is prefixed to this article. It contains, it seems, the earliest and the latest productions of the author; the first of them having been purchased, we are told, many years back by a bookseller, who, for some reason unexplained, thought proper to alter his mind and withhold it. We do not much applaud his taste; for though it is decidedly inferior to her other works, having less plot, and what there is, less artificially wrought up, and also less exquisite nicety of moral painting; yet the same kind of excellences which characterise the other novels may be perceived in this, in a degree which would have been highly creditable to most other writers of the same school, and which would have entitled the author to considerable praise, had she written nothing better.

We already begin to fear, that we have indulged too much in extracts, and we must save some room for 'Persuasion' or we could not resist giving a specimen of John Thorpe,[7] with his horse that *cannot* go less than 10 miles an hour, his refusal to drive his sister 'because she has such thick ankles,' and his sober consumption of five pints of port a day; altogether the best portrait of a species, which, though almost extinct, cannot yet be quite classed among the Palæotheria, the Bang-up Oxonian.[8] Miss Thorpe, the jilt of middling life, is, in her way, quite as good, though she has not the advantage of being the representative of a rare or a diminishing species. We fear few of our readers, however they may admire the naiveté, will admit the truth of poor John Morland's postscript, 'I can never expect to know such another woman.'

The latter of these novels, however, 'Persuasion,' which is more strictly to be considered as a posthumous work, possesses that superiority which might be expected from the more mature age at which it was written, and is second, we think, to none of the former ones, if not superior to all. In the humorous delineation of character it does not abound quite so much as some of the others, though it has great merit even on that score; but it has more of that tender and yet elevated kind of interest which is aimed at by the generality of novels, and in pursuit of which they seldom fail of running into romantic extravagance: on the whole, it is one of the most elegant fictions of common life we ever remember to have met with.

Sir Walter Elliot, a silly and conceited baronet, has three daughters, the eldest two, unmarried, and the third, Mary, the wife of a neighbouring gentleman, Mr. Charles Musgrove, heir to a considerable fortune, and living in a genteel cottage in the neighbourhood of the Great house which he is hereafter to inherit. The second daughter, Anne, who is the

---

7. A minor character in *Northanger Abbey*.
8. Palæotheria is an extinct species of mammal. Whateley is saying that the perfect representation of the Oxford man (a role to which John Thorpe aspires) is almost but not quite extinct. Miss Thorpe and John Morland both belong to *Northanger Abbey*.

heroine, and the only one of the family possessed of good sense, (a quality which Miss Austin is as sparing of in her novels, as we fear her great mistress, Nature, has been in real life,) when on a visit to her sister, is, by that sort of instinct which generally points out to all parties the person on whose judgment and temper they may rely, appealed to in all the little family differences which arise, and which are described with infinite spirit and detail.

*   *   *

We ventured, in a former article, to remonstrate against the dethrone-ment of the once powerful God of Love, in his own most especial domain, the novel; and to suggest that, in shunning the ordinary fault of recommending by examples a romantic and uncalculating extrava-gance of passion, Miss Austin had rather fallen into the opposite extreme of exclusively patronizing what are called prudent matches, and too much disparaging sentimental enthusiasm. We urged, that, mischie-vous as is the extreme on this side, it is not the one into which the young folks of the present day are the most likely to run: the prevailing fault is not now, whatever it may have been, to sacrifice all for love.

*   *   *

We may now, without retracting our opinion, bestow unqualified approbation; for the distresses of the present heroine all arise from her prudent refusal to listen to the suggestions of her heart. The catastrophe however is happy, and we are left in doubt whether it would have been better for her or not, to accept the first proposal; and this we conceive is precisely the proper medium; for, though we would not have prudential calculations the sole principle to be regarded in marriage, we are far from advocating their exclusion. To disregard the advice of sober-minded friends on an important point of conduct, is an imprudence we would by no means recommend; indeed, it is a species of selfishness, if, in listening only to the dictates of passion, a man sacrifices to its gratifi-cation the happiness of those most dear to him as well as his own; though it is not now-a-days the most prevalent form of selfishness. But it is no condemnation of a sentiment to say, that it becomes blameable when it interferes with duty, and is uncontrouled by conscience: the desire of riches, power, or distinction,—the taste for ease and com-fort,—are to be condemned when they transgress these bounds; and love, if it keep within them, even though it be somewhat tinged with enthusiasm, and a little at variance with what the worldly call prudence, i.e., regard for pecuniary advantage, may afford a better moral discipline to the mind than most other passions. It will not at least be denied, that it has often proved a powerful stimulus to exertion where others have failed, and has called forth talents unknown before even to the possessor. What, though the pursuit may be fruitless, and the hopes visionary?

The result may be a real and substantial benefit, though of another kind; the vineyard may have been cultivated by digging in it for the treasure which is never to be found. What, though the perfections with which imagination has decorated the beloved object, may, in fact, exist but in a slender degree? still they are believed in and admired as real; if not, the love is such as does not merit the name; and it is proverbially true that men become assimilated to the character (i.e., what they *think* the character) of the being they fervently adore: thus, as in the noblest exhibitions of the stage, though that which is contemplated be but a fiction, it may be realized in the mind of the beholder; and, though grasping at a cloud, he may become worthy of possessing a real goddess. Many a generous sentiment, and many a virtuous resolution, have been called forth and matured by admiration of one, who may herself perhaps have been incapable of either. It matters not what the object is that a man aspires to be worthy of, and proposes as a model for imitation, if he does but *believe* it to be excellent. Moreover, all doubts of success (and they are seldom, if ever, entirely wanting) must either produce or exercise humility; and the endeavour to study another's interests and inclinations, and prefer them to one's own, may promote a habit of general benevolence which may outlast the present occasion. Every thing, in short, which tends to abstract a man in any degree, or in any way, from self,—from self-admiration and self-interest, has, so far at least, a beneficial influence in forming the character.

On the whole, Miss Austin's works may safely be recommended, not only as among the most unexceptionable of their class, but as combining, in an eminent degree, instruction with amusement, though without the direct effort at the former, of which we have complained, as sometimes defeating its object. For those who cannot, or will not, *learn* any thing from productions of this kind, she has provided entertainment which entitles her to thanks; for mere innocent amusement is in itself a good, when it interferes with no greater; especially as it may occupy the place of some other that may *not* be innocent. The Eastern monarch who proclaimed a reward to him who should discover a new pleasure, would have deserved well of mankind had he stipulated that it should be blameless. Those, again, who delight in the study of human nature, may improve in the knowledge of it, and in the profitable application of that knowledge, by the perusal of such fictions as those before us.

Anonymous

[Austen's Characters] †

* * * Without any wish to surprise us into attention, by strangeness of incident, or complication of adventure,—with no great ambition of being amazingly facetious, or remarkably brilliant,—laboriously witty, or profoundly sentimental,—of dealing out wise saws and deep reflections, or keeping us on the broad grin, and killing us with laughter;— the stream of [Austen's] Tale flows on in an easy, natural, but spring tide, which carries us out of ourselves, and bears our feelings, affections, and deepest interest, irresistably along with it. She has not been at the trouble to look out for subjects for her pencil of a peculiar and eccentric cast, nor cared to outstep the modesty of nature, by spicing with a too rich vein of humour, such as fell in her way in the ordinary intercourse of life. The people with whom her works bring us acquainted were, we feel certain, like those among whom she herself shared the good and ill of life,—with whom she thought and talked—danced and sung— laughed and wept—joked and reasoned. They are not the productions of an ingenious fancy, but beings instinct with life;—they breathe and move, and think and speak, and act, before our mind's eye, with a distinctness, that rivals the pictures we see in memory of scenes we ourselves have beheld, and upon the recollections of which we love to dwell. They mingle in our remembrances with those, whom we ourselves have known and loved, but whom accident, or coldness, or death, have separated from us before the end of our pilgrimage.

Into those of her characters in particular, who engage our best affections, and with whom we sympathise most deeply, she seems to have transfused the very essence of life. These are, doubtless, the finest of her compositions, and with reason; for she had only, on any supposed interesting occurrence of life, to set her own kind and amiable feelings in motion, and the tide sprang up from the heart to the pen, and flowed in a rich stream of nature and truth over the page. Into one particular character, indeed, she has breathed her whole soul and being; and in this we please ourselves with thinking, we see and know herself.

And what is this character?—A mind beautifully framed, graceful, imaginative, and feminine, but penetrating, sagacious, and profound.— A soul harmonious, gentle, and most sweetly attuned,—susceptible of all that is beautiful in nature, pure in morals, sublime in religion;—a soul—on which, if, by any accidental contact with the vulgar, or the

† From anonymous review of *Life and Adventures of Peter Wilkins, Retrospective Review* 7 (1823): 131–35.

vicious, the slightest shade of impurity was ever thrown, it vanished instantaneously, like man's breath from the polished mirror; and, retreating, left it in undiminished lustre.—A heart large and expansive, the seat of deep, kind, honest, and benevolent feelings.—A bosom capacious of universal love, but through which there flowed a deeper stream of domestic and holy affections,—as a river through the lake's broad expanse, whose basin it supplies with its overflowing waters, and through which its course is marked only by a stronger current.—A temper even, cheerful, gladdening, and serene as the mild evening of summer's loveliest day, in which the very insect that lives but an hour, doth desport and enjoy existence.—Feelings generous and candid,—quick, but not irritable,—sensitive to the slightest degree of coolness in friend or lover, but not easily damped;—or, if overwhelmed by any heart-rending affliction, rallying, collecting, settling into repose again, like some still and deep waters disturbed by the fall of an impending rock.—Modest in hope, sober in joy, gay in innocence,—sweet soother of others' affliction,—most resigned and patient bearer of her own. With a sunny eye to reflect the glad smiles of happy friends,—dim and cloudy at the sight of others' grief; but not revealing the deep seated woes of the remote chambers of her own breast, by aught but that wild, pensive, regardful, profound expression, which tells nothing to a stranger or acquaintance, but, if a parent or friend, might break your heart but to look upon.— The beloved confidante of the young and infantine—at once playmate and preceptress;—the patient nurser of their little fretful ailments;—the more patient bearer of their rude and noisy mirth, in her own moments of illness or dejection;—exchanging smiles, that would arrest an angel on his winged way, for obstreperous laughs;—and sweet low accents, for shrill treble screams. The friend of the humble, lowly, and indigent; respecting in them, as much as in those of highest degree and lordliest bearing, the image of their common Maker. Easy, pleasant, amusing, playful, and kind in the intercourse of equals—an attentive hearer, considerate, patient, cheerfully sedate, and affectionate in that of elders. In scenes of distress or difficulty, self-dependent, collected, deliberate, and provident,—the one to whom all instinctively turned for counsel, sympathy, and consolation. Strong in innocence as a tower, with a face of serenity, and a collectedness of demeanour, from which danger and misery—the very tawny lion in his rage—might flee discomfited,—a fragile, delicate, feeble, and most feminine woman!

Whether, in this enumeration of female excellencies, one of those deeply attached friends, of whom she was sure to have had many, might recognize some, or most of the admirable qualities of JANE AUSTEN, we cannot say;—but sure we are, if our memory have not failed us, or our fancy deceived us, or our hearts betrayed us, such, or nearly such, are those of which she has herself compounded one of the most beautiful female characters ever drawn;—we mean, the heroine of *Persuasion*.

But we have digressed farther than we intended.—Indeed, so fast and thick do recollections of what is beautiful and good in the works of this admirable woman, throng into our mind, that we are borne away involuntarily and irresistibly. They stole into the world without noise,—they circulated in quiet,—they were far from being much extolled,—and very seldom noticed in the journals of the day,—they came into our hands, as nothing different from ordinary novels,—and they have enshrined themselves in the heart, and live for ever in the thoughts,— along with the recollections of all that is best and purest in our own experience of life. Their author we, ourselves, had not the happiness of knowing,—a scanty and insufficient memoir,[1] prefixed to her posthumous work, not written in the best taste, is all the history of her life, that we or the world have before us; but, perhaps, that history is not wanted,—her own works furnish that history. Those imaginary people, to whom she gave their most beautiful ideal existence, survive to speak for her, now that she herself is gone.

The mention of her works happened to fall in our way as the noblest illustration we could give of that improvement in this department of literature, which we are fond to believe in; but we frankly confess, we would, at any time, have travelled far out of it to pay our humble tribute of respect to the memory of Jane Austen. Nor is it so foreign to our regular speculations, as the reader may be apt to imagine. Our conversation, as one of our own number has well observed, is among the tombs and *there* dwells all that once enshrined in a form of beauty a soul of exceeding and surpassing brightness.—O lost too soon to us!—but our loss has been thy immortal gain.

JULIA KAVANAGH

[The Language of Feeling] †

* * *

Beyond any other of Miss Austen's tales, *Persuasion* shows us the phase of her literary character which she chose to keep most in the shade: the tender and the sad. In this work, as in *Sense and Sensibility*, and in *Mansfield Park*, but with more power than in either, she showed what can be the feelings of a woman compelled to see the love she most longs for, leaving her day by day. The judicious Elinor[1] is, indeed,

---

1. The memoir printed above, pp. 191–96 [*Editor*].
† From Julia Kavanagh, *English Women of Letters*, 1862, 251–74. All notes are by the editor of this Norton Critical Edition.
1. A central character in *Sense and Sensibility*.

conscious that she is beloved; but her lover is not free, and she long thinks him lost. Fanny[2] is her lover's *confidante*, and must be miserable when he is blest, or happy when he is wretched. The position of Anne Elliot has something more desolate still. The opposition of her relatives, and the advice of friends, induce her to break with a young naval officer, Captain Frederick Wentworth, to whom she is engaged, and the only man whom she can love. They part, he in anger, she in sorrow; he to rise in his profession, become a rich man, and outlive his grief; she to pine at home, and lose youth and beauty in unavailing regret. Years have passed when they meet again. Captain Wentworth is still young, still handsome and agreeable. He wishes to marry, and is looking for a wife. Anne Elliot, pale, faded, and sad, knows it, and sees it—she sees the looks, the smiles of fresher and younger beauties seeking him, and apparently not seeking him in vain.

Here we see the first genuine picture of that silent torture of an unloved woman, condemned to suffer thus because she is a woman and must not speak, and which, many years later, was wakened into such passionate eloquence by the author of *Jane Eyre*. Subdued though the picture is in Miss Austen's pages, it is not the less keen, not the less painful. The tale ends happily. Captain Wentworth's coldness yields to old love, Anne's beauty returns, they are married, yet the sorrowful tone of the tale is not effaced by that happy close. The shadow of a long disappointment, of secret grief, and ill-repressed jealousy will ever hang over Anne Elliot.

This melancholy cast, the result, perhaps, of some secret personal disappointment, distinguishes *Persuasion* from Miss Austen's other tales. They were never cheerful, for even the gentlest of satire precludes cheerfulness; but this is sad.

Of the popularity of Miss Austen's six novels, of the estimation in which they are held, we need not speak. It is honourable to the public that she should be so thoroughly appreciated, not merely by men like Sir Walter Scott and Lord Macaulay,[3] but by all who take up her books for mere amusement. Wonderful, indeed, is the power that out of materials so slender, out of characters so imperfectly marked, could fashion a story. This is her great, her prevailing merit, and yet, it cannot be denied, it is one that injures her with many readers. It seems so natural that she should have told things and painted people as they are, so natural and so easy, that we are apt to forget the performance in the sense of its reality. The literary taste of the majority is always tinged with coarseness; it loves exaggeration, and slights the modesty of truth.

2. Heroine of *Mansfield Park*.
3. Sir Walter Scott (1771–1832), the best-known novelist of his period, wrote appreciatively about all of Austen's work in his review of *Emma* in *The Quarterly Review* (March 1816; number dated October 1815). Thomas Babington Macaulay (1800–1859), best-known as a historian, praised Austen in an essay on Frances Burney in the *Edinburgh Review* (1843).

Another of Miss Austen's excellencies is also a disadvantage. She does not paint or analyze her characters; they speak for themselves. Her people have never those set sayings or phrases which we may refer to the author, and of which we may think, how clever! They talk as people talk in the world, and quietly betray their inner being in their folly, falsehood, or assumption. For instance, Sir Walter Elliot is handsome; we are merely told so; but we never forget it, for he does not. He considers men born to be handsome, and, deploring the fatal effect of a seafaring life on manly beauty, he candidly regrets that 'naval gentlemen are not knocked on the head at once,' so disgusted has he been with Admiral Baldwin's mahogany complexion and dilapidated appearance. And this worship of personal appearance is perfectly unaffected and sincere. Sir Walter Elliot's good looks have acted on him internally; his own daughter Anne rises in his opinion as her complexion grows clearer, and his first inquiry concerning his married daughter, Mary, is, 'How is she looking? The last time he, Sir Walter, saw her, she had a red nose, and he hopes that may not happen every day.' He is assured that the red nose must have been accidental, upon which the affectionate father exclaims kindly: ' "If I thought it would not tempt her to go out in sharp winds, and grow coarse, I would send her a new hat and pelisse." '

But it was natural that powers so great should fail somewhere, and there were some things which Miss Austen could not do. She could not speak the language of any strong feeling, even though that feeling were ridiculous and unjust. A rumour of Mr. Darcy's marriage with Elizabeth Bennet having reached his aunt, Lady Catherine de Bourgh, she hurries down to Longbourn to tax and upbraid Miss Bennet with her audacity, and to exact from her a promise that she will not marry Mr. Darcy.[4] Elizabeth refuses, and there is a scene, but not a good one. Lady Catherine's interference is insolent and foolish, but it is the result of a strong feeling, and, to her, it is an important, a mighty matter, and this we do not feel as we read. Her assertions of her own importance, her surprise at Elizabeth's independence, are in keeping, but we want something more, and that something never appears. The delicate mind that could evolve, so shrewdly, foolishness from its deepest recesses, was powerless when strong feelings had to be summoned. They heard her, but did not obey the call.

This want of certain important faculties is the only defect, or rather causes the only defect, of Miss Austen's works: that everything is told in the same tone. An elopement, a death, seduction, are related as placidly as a dinner or ball, but with much less spirit. As she is, however, we must take her, and what her extraordinary powers wanted in extent, they made up in depth. In her own range, and admitting her cold views of life to be true, she is faultless, or almost faultless. By choosing to be all but perfect,

---

4. Characters and situation from *Pride and Prejudice*.

she sometimes became monotonous, but rarely. The value of light and shade, as a means of success, she discarded. Strong contrasts, bold flights, she shunned. To be true, to show life in its everyday aspect, was her ambition. To hope to make so much out of so little showed no common confidence in her own powers, and more than common daring. Of the thousands who take up a pen to write a story meant to amuse, how many are there who can, or who dare, be true, like Jane Austen?

GOLDWIN SMITH

From *Life of Jane Austen* †

"Persuasion" was the last work of Miss Austen. When it was written the hand of death was upon her, and when the last touch was put to it she was very near her end. We can therefore hardly help applying in some measure to herself what she says of Lady Elliot, that "she had found enough in her duties, her friends, and her children to attach her to life and make it no matter of indifference to her when she was called on to quit them." That she would feel the value of life, and yet quit it with resignation, is what we should expect of a character like Jane Austen. There is also a passage on the melancholy charms of autumn which reminds us the writer's leaf was falling into the sere, though it is followed and relieved by an allusion to the farmer ploughing in hope of the spring. Perhaps there is a shade of pensiveness over the whole novel, and in parts an increased tenderness of sentiment such as comes with the evening hour. "Persuasion" has had passionate admirers in two persons not unqualified to judge—Miss Martineau and Miss Mitford.[1] Though as a whole not so well constructed as others of Jane Austen's novels, it may be said to contain the finest touches of her art. Its principal character, the tender, sensitive, and suffering Anne Elliot, is also perhaps the most interesting of Jane Austen's women, setting aside the totally different charm of the blooming and joyous Emma. The title denotes the gentle influences which persuade an injured and resentful lover after the lapse of years to return to his early love.

* * *

Admiral Croft is an "old tough," as admirals seem to have been called in those days, drawn evidently from the life by one who knew the navy well. When interrogated about the state of a friend, who it was suspected had been wounded in his affections, he reassures the inquirer by telling

---

† From *Life of Jane Austen* by Goldwin Smith (London: W. Scott, 1890), pp. 167–68, 179–80.
1. Harriet Martineau (1802–1876), writer of fiction, travel books, political treatises, and an autobiography; Mary Russell Mitford (1787–1855), novelist and dramatist [*Editor*].

him that the supposed sufferer had not used a single oath. His wife, as seems to have been the fashion at that time, has been a great deal at sea with him; she is a female "old tough"; and the picture of their strong though refined affection, drawn evidently with hearty relish by Jane Austen, is an "old maid's" tribute to the better state.

It has been already said that there are some weaknesses in the construction of the novel. Sir Walter Elliot and Elizabeth, though they occupy a good deal of space, contribute nothing or hardly anything to the action. They are a little too like the mere character pictures with which we are sometimes presented in place of characters brought into play and developed by the action of a well-constructed plot. Louisa Musgrove on one side, and Mr. William Elliot on the other, serve to add to the complexity and interest of the movement by which Captain Wentworth is to be reunited to Anne. But the destruction of William Elliot's character is needless, and strikes us as inartistic, while there is something unnatural in his whole relation to the Elliot family, and something strained in the account of his motives. The purpose for which he is introduced and afterwards killed off is too obvious. The transfer of Louisa Musgrove from Captain Wentworth to Captain Benwick, again, is abrupt, and forced as well as sudden; nor does Captain Wentworth come quite clear out of the affair. The description of Mrs. Clay's artfulness, and of her sinister relation to the foolish baronet, leads us to expect something lively in that quarter; but nothing comes, and Mrs. Clay leaves the scene at last a "pale and ineffectual" figure, without our being able to see with what object she was brought upon it. Nor does Lady Russell, though she seems intended for an important part, do much more than solemnly seal by her ultimate approbation the match which she had made a grand mistake in breaking off.

GERALDINE EDITH MITTON

From *Jane Austen and Her Times* †

Last Days

The evening of Jane's life had set in, but yet it had not occurred even to those who loved her best that they must inevitably lose her. She was in her forty-first year; recognition from the public had just begun to be accorded to her; in the novels she had lately written no sign of decay could be detected. It is true that in both *Emma* and *Persuasion* there is a particular maturity of rendering, and a kindlier tone that marks per-

---

† From *Jane Austen and Her Times* by Geraldine Edith Mitton (New York: Putnam's, 1905), pp. 313–15. All notes are by the editor of this Norton Critical Edition.

haps a difference, but not degeneracy. If the word seriousness can ever be used of such clear-cut, brilliant work as hers, we might say that a certain sweet seriousness pervaded these two, which are more alike in tone than any of the other novels. *Persuasion* has been called the "most beautiful of all the novels"; it has many excellencies, not the least among which is the character of the heroine, whose girlish weakness develops into a loyal steadfastness. She has also that endearingness that perhaps certain others of the heroines lack. In fact, of all the principal female characters that of Anne Elliot has most of that nameless and indefinable charm, which comes from a combination of qualities such as firmness, gentleness, unselfishness, sympathy and sweetness, a charm which is more lovable than any number of stereotyped graces. Though Anne was at one time weak, we feel that she outgrows it, that it was the weakness of immaturity, not of character, and that her loyalty fully redeems it.

Jane herself says of Anne Elliot, "You may perhaps like the heroine as she is almost too good for me," yet the too-good note seems less obtrusive with Anne than with Fanny Price,[1] whose exceeding surface meekness does sometimes produce a little exasperation. Anne and Fanny have the most in common among the heroines of the novels, yet what a difference is there! Fanny has many virtues, but her intense nervous sensitiveness makes one feel her self-consciousness, and underlying all her shrinking there was a quality of obstinacy that is felt without being insisted upon. It is just the subtle difference that Jane knew so well how to make, the feeling perhaps is that Fanny is not quite a gentlewoman, that she would be difficult to get on with, however meek and self-effacing on the surface, while Anne could never be anything but a delightful companion.

Incidentally some parts of *Persuasion* have already been referred to, Louisa Musgrove's fall on the Cobb, the scenes that take place in Bath, the touching words of Anne when she feels that she has hopelessly lost her lover, which strike a deeper note of feeling than any other in the whole range of the novels. It remains therefore but to say that there is no secondary character to equal those of Miss Bates or Mr. Collins,[2] that the secondary characters are in all cases less sharply defined than those usually depicted by Jane, but that Captain Wentworth is equal to his good fortune, and that as a pair of lovers he and Anne stand unrivalled.

Persuasion was finished in July 1816, but Jane was not satisfied with it, perhaps her own failing health and the sense of tiredness that went with it, had made her lose that grip of the action that she had hitherto held so well; she felt the story did not end satisfactorily, that it wanted bringing together and clinching so to speak; Mr. Austen-Leigh[3] says: "This weighed upon her mind, the more so probably on account of her

---

1. Central character of *Mansfield Park*.
2. In *Emma* and *Pride and Prejudice*.
3. James Edward Austen-Leigh, Austen's nephew, published his *Memoir* of his aunt in 1870.

weak state of health, so that one night she retired to rest in very low spirits. But such depression was little in accordance with her nature, and was soon shaken off. The next morning she woke to more cheerful views and brighter inspirations; the sense of power revived and imagination resumed its course. She cancelled the condemned chapter and wrote two others, entirely different, in its stead."

These were the tenth and eleventh chapters, and contained the scene in which Anne so touchingly expresses her ideas on the theme of woman's love. There is no question that the story as it now stands is improved by the change, and that her instinct was true. Mr. Austen-Leigh gives the cancelled chapter in his *Memoir*, and it certainly is "tame and flat" compared with the others, and had she not made the substitution it might justly have been said that *Persuasion*, however charming, did show signs of failing power.

This book was not published until after her death, when it appeared in one volume with *Northanger Abbey*, the first to which her name was prefixed, this came out in 1818 with a Memoir by her brother Henry. Up to the time of her death she had received nearly seven hundred pounds for the published books, which, considering her anonymity, and entire lack of publicity and influence, must have appeared to her, and indeed was, wonderful, though in comparison with the true value of the work very little indeed.

* * *

MODERN CRITICAL
VIEWS

A. WALTON LITZ

New Landscapes †

As we seek to define the special qualities of Jane Austen's late work our attention is inevitably drawn to the new importance she gives to natural landscapes. In the earlier fiction we visualize the characters against a man-made landscape; when the setting is not a drawing-room or ball-room it tends to be the civilized nature of eighteenth-century gardens and paintings. Trees and grass and hills are there, but they are drawn from the repertory of the picturesque, and belong in their small way to what Kenneth Clark has called the "landscape of fantasy."[1] Nature is contemplated with Gilpin[2] and the "improvers" in mind; the landscape is described and criticized as if it were a work of art. Although the young Jane Austen delighted in ridiculing the "sublime" nature of Gothic fiction, with its rhetorical imitations of Salvator Rosa,[3] we know from her brother Henry that she had been "enamoured of Gilpin on the Picturesque" at an early age. It is not surprising, then, that Elizabeth Bennet's interest in the Lake Country is that of the amateur artist, or that she views Pemberley Woods with an eye to picturesque stage-effects. But with *Mansfield Park* a new feeling for external nature begins to emerge, and in *Emma* we find an expressive use of landscape that contrasts sharply with the descriptions of the early fiction. The course of Emma Woodhouse's life is subtly related to the cycle of the seasons: Mr. Elton's distressing proposal takes place against the background of a dark and snowy December evening, while Knightley's confession of love occurs on a delightful day in July. The chapter in which Jane Austen brings Emma and Mr. Knightley together opens with a descriptive passage that foreshadows the human changes:

> The weather continued much the same [a cold stormy rain] all the following morning; and the same loneliness, and the same melancholy, seemed to reign at Hartfield—but in the afternoon it cleared; the wind changed into a softer quarter; the clouds were carried off; the sun appeared; it was summer again. With all the eagerness which such a transition gives, Emma resolved to be out of doors as soon as possible. Never had the exquisite sight, smell, sensation of nature, tranquil, warm, and brilliant after a storm, been more attractive to her.

† From A. Walton Litz, *Jane Austen: A Study of Her Artistic Development* (New York: Oxford UP, 1965) 150–60. Reprinted by permission of the author. All notes are by the editor of this Norton Critical Edition. The author's notes have been deleted.
1. Bibliographical information about this and other works cited in the essays included in this section will be found in the bibliography (pp. 315–16).
2. See note 6, p. 194.
3. Neapolitan painter (1615–1673) whose somber, often sinister landscapes were much admired in the eighteenth century.

This symbolic use of the natural setting involves a "sensation of nature" foreign to the early works, and we find the sensation intensified in *Persuasion*, where Anne Elliot's melancholy and "early loss of bloom" are continuously presented through the imagery of autumn. In the following description of a November walk Anne's feeling for the landscape harmonizes with the emotions prompted by the dialogue.

> Her *pleasure* in the walk must arise from the exercise and the day, from the view of the last smiles of the year upon the tawny leaves and withered hedges, and from repeating to herself some few of the thousand poetical descriptions extant of autumn, that season of peculiar and inexhaustible influence on the mind of taste and tenderness . . . After one of the many praises of the day, which were continually bursting forth, Captain Wentworth added,
>
> "What glorious weather for the Admiral and my sister! They meant to take a long drive this morning; perhaps we may hail them from some of these hills. They talked of coming into this side of the country. I wonder whereabouts they will upset to-day. Oh! it does happen very often, I assure you—but my sister makes nothing of it—she would as lieve be tossed out as not."
>
> "Ah! You make the most of it, I know," cried Louisa, "but if it were really so, I should do just the same in her place. If I loved a man, as she loves the Admiral, I would be always with him, nothing should ever separate us, and I would rather be overturned by him, than driven safely by anybody else."
>
> It was spoken with enthusiasm.
>
> "Had you?" cried he, catching the same tone; "I honour you!" And there was silence between them for a little while.
>
> Anne could not immediately fall into a quotation again. The sweet scenes of autumn were for a while put by—unless some tender sonnet, fraught with the apt analogy of the declining year, with declining happiness, and the images of youth and hope, and spring, all gone together, blessed her memory. She roused herself to say, as they struck by order into another path, "Is not this one of the ways to Winthrop?" But nobody heard, or, at least, nobody answered her.
>
> Winthrop, however, or its environs—for young men are, sometimes, to be met with, strolling about near home, was their destination; and after another half mile of gradual ascent through large enclosures, where the ploughs at work, and the fresh-made path spoke the farmer, counteracting the sweets of poetical despondence, and meaning to have spring again, they gained the summit of the most considerable hill, which parted Uppercross and Winthrop, and soon commanded a full view of the latter, at the foot of the hill on the other side.

The effects of this passage are new to Jane Austen's art. Anne's consciousness is the focus of the scene, and our interest is in her reactions, but these reactions are expressed more through descriptive details than through exposition. The tone of the landscape controls the passage: Anne's regret is imaged in the autumn scene, while the reminder of spring—in immediate context a sad reminder—may also be read as a hint of future happiness. This "poetic" reliance on natural landscape is even more striking in *Sanditon*, the fragmentary work that closes Jane Austen's career. As E. M. Forster has observed, the town of Sanditon is "not like Lyme or Highbury or Northanger or the other places that provide scenes or titles to past novels. It exists in itself and for itself. Character-drawing, incident, and wit are on the decline, but topography comes to the front, and is screwed much deeper than usual into the story."

The sources of this new quality in Jane Austen's fiction must have been complex, but one point seems obvious. More than has been generally realized or acknowledged, she was influenced by the Romantic poetry of the early nineteenth century. *Persuasion* and *Sanditon* contain a number of references to contemporary poets, to Byron, Wordsworth, and especially Scott. And although Jane Austen's explicit use of these authors may be for the purposes of satire, her late prose reflects their influence. Nature has ceased to be a mere backdrop; landscape is a structure of feeling which can express, and also modify, the minds of those who view it. In their quiet and restrained fashion, Jane Austen's last works are part of the new movement in English literature. She has learned that the natural setting can convey, more surely than any abstract vocabulary, the movements of an individual imagination.

This method for expressing individual moods was needed in *Persuasion*, for in her work on this novel Jane Austen set herself a new problem of communication. To put it quite simply, the sense of community has disappeared, and the heroine finds herself terribly alone. Anne Elliot has no trustworthy confidante, no Jane Bennet, or Mrs. Weston, or Mr. Knightley.[4] The sympathetic brothers, sisters, and fathers of the earlier novels have disappeared; Lady Russell cannot comprehend Anne Elliot, and the heroine is locked in the world of her own consciousness. Anne's need is as much communication as it is love, and in spite of the happy ending the deepest impression we carry away from *Persuasion* is one of human isolation. D. H. Lawrence's well-known attack on Jane Austen is directly relevant here:

> The sense of isolation, followed by the sense of menace and of fear, is bound to arise as the feeling of oneness and community with our fellow-men declines, and the feeling of individualism and personality, which is existence in isolation, increases. . . . Class-hate and class-consciousness are only a sign that the old togetherness, the old blood-warmth has collapsed, and every man is really aware of himself in apartness. . . . In the old England, the curious

4. Characters from *Pride and Prejudice* (Jane Bennet) and *Emma*.

blood-connections held the classes together. The squires might be arrogant, violent, bullying and unjust, yet in some ways they were at one with the people, part of the same blood-stream. We feel it in Defoe or Fielding. And then, in the mean Jane Austen, it is gone. Already this old maid typifies "personality" instead of character, the sharp knowing in apartness instead of knowing in togetherness . . .

After we have discounted Lawrence's masculine antagonism toward Jane Austen, and his characteristic identification of art with life, we are left with a penetrating statement of the essential themes in *Persuasion*. In a sense, *Persuasion* begins where the other novels end: Anne knows her own heart, and is not deluded about herself. Yet she is isolated, haunted by a "sense of menace and fear"; she knows only in "apartness." Her despair is that of the modern "personality," forced to live within itself. We may attribute this quality in *Persuasion* to the frustrations of Jane Austen's middle-age (for the first time there is no fictional counterpart to Cassandra), but such biographical speculations are of limited usefulness. It is better to view *Persuasion* as a final variation on one of Jane Austen's most persistent themes, the perils of the free spirit in its search for social identity. Here this theme is given its darkest treatment. Anne Elliot is denied the retreat into obsolete manners symbolized by Mansfield Park, just as she is cut off from the fatherly advice of a Mr. Knightley. The social world of *Persuasion* seems cruelly unhelpful, and one must conclude that Jane Austen is expressing in the novel her alarm at contemporary changes in English manners. In spite of the final marriage and the brave flourishes of the last chapter, *Persuasion* looks forward to a society where the burdens of personality must be borne without a compensating "feeling of oneness and community." The familiar world of the nineteenth-century novel is at hand.

The technical difficulties Jane Austen faced in her work on *Persuasion* were formidable, the direct result of her chosen subject. The drama of self-deception and self-recognition which holds our interest in the earlier novels is almost totally absent from *Persuasion*, and without it the field for irony is greatly reduced. The personality of Anne Elliot must carry all our interest without the benefit of dramatic irony, and to accomplish this Jane Austen has made Anne's point-of-view that of the reader. Everything depends on our sympathy with Anne, and our interest in her fate. The contrast between this narrative method and that of *Emma* is highly significant. Since Emma Woodhouse does not know her own mind, we soon learn that we cannot identify our vision with hers; and although most of the action of *Emma* is seen through the heroine's eyes Jane Austen has supplied us with glimpses into other minds, and with reliable commentary from herself and Knightley. But, as Wayne Booth has pointed out, the only significant break in "angle of vision" between the first and last chapters of *Persuasion* occurs in the scene where Anne meets Captain Wentworth for the first time in many years. The sympathetic reader is likely to assume that he is still in love with Anne. As Booth says,

> All the conventions of art favor such a belief: the emphasis is clearly on Anne and her unhappiness; the lover has returned; we have only to wait, perhaps with some tedium, for the inevitable outcome. Anne learns (chap. vii) that he has spoken of her as so altered "he should not have known her again." "These were words which could not but dwell with her. Yet she soon began to rejoice that she had heard them. They were of sobering tendency; they allayed agitation; they composed, and consequently must make her happier." And suddenly we enter Wentworth's mind for one time only: "Frederick Wentworth had used such words, or something like them, but without an idea that they would be carried round to her. He had thought her wretchedly altered, and, in the first moment of appeal, had spoken as he felt. He had not forgiven Anne Elliot. She had used him ill"—and so he goes on, for five more paragraphs. The necessary point, the fact that Frederick believes himself to be indifferent, has been made, and it could not have been made without some kind of shift from Anne's consciousness.

This isolated excursion into the mind of another character does not disturb us, since in the opening chapter the author has presented the situation and characters to us in her own voice; but I doubt if it has convinced many readers. We know that Wentworth's love will be easily reawakened, and our real interest lies in Anne's struggle to overcome the barriers of social isolation and communicate with the man she once knew so well. It is for this reason that Jane Austen presents almost all the action from her point-of-view.

Of the surviving Austen manuscripts, the two "canceled" chapters of *Persuasion* reveal the most about her artistic methods. On 18 July 1816 she wrote "Finis" at the end of the second volume, which then contained eleven chapters; but the handling of the reconciliation scene still did not satisfy her, and during the next two weeks or so she recast the tenth chapter into the present tenth and eleventh chapters, recopying the last chapter (now the twelfth) with verbal corrections. In his separate edition of the two original chapters R. W. Chapman has recorded manuscript corrections and variants from the posthumous first edition, and a study of these corrections and additions reveals the same care for phrasing and rhythm we discovered in the revisions of *The Watsons*. Presumably more verbal changes would have been made in the final preparation for the press, if Jane Austen had lived. But these small changes are less illuminating than the structural changes which occurred when the original Chapter X was transformed into the present Chapters X and XI.[5] By comparing the two versions we can gain a new sense of Jane Austen's skill in construction, and a feeling for the artistic ideals that governed her work on *Persuasion*.

In the ninth chapter of the second volume Anne pays her visit to Mrs. Smith at Westgate-buildings, in the course of which she learns of Mr. Elliot's true character. This revelation is the subject of Anne's thoughts at the beginning of the original Chapter X. She is walking down Gay Street, considering the implications of her new knowledge, when she encounters Admiral Croft. His home is only a few steps away, and Anne is persuaded—much against her wishes—to enter and speak to Mrs. Croft. It is only when she has reached the threshold of the drawing room that Anne is casually informed, "there is nobody but Frederick here." As soon as she is confronted with Captain Wentworth, Admiral Croft draws him outside the door and begins a conversation in which Anne hears "her own name and *Kellynch*" mentioned repeatedly. Captain Wentworth re-enters the room, and, after a moment of embarrassment, begins to speak on the Admiral's behalf.

> "The Adml, Madam, was this morning confidently informed that you were—upon my word I am quite at a loss, ashamed—(breathing and speaking quick)—the awkwardness of *giving* Information of this sort to one of the Parties—You can be at no loss to understand me—It was very confidently said that Mr Elliot—that everything was settled in the family for an Union between Mr Elliot—and yourself. It was added that you were to live at Kellynch—that Kellynch was to be given up. This, the Admiral knew could not be correct—But it occurred to him that it might be the *wish* of the Parties—And my commission from him Madam, is to say, that if the Family wish is such, his Lease of Kellynch shall be cancel'd . . ."

Falteringly, Anne informs Wentworth that the Admiral has been misinformed; and, encouraged by her denial and countenance, the Captain confesses his love.

> Her Countenance did not discourage.—It was a silent, but a very powerful Dialogue;—on his side, Supplication, on her's acceptance.—Still, a little nearer—and a hand taken and pressed—and "Anne, my own dear Anne!"—bursting forth in the fullness of exquisite feeling—and all Suspense and Indecision were over.

The rest of the canceled chapter is given over to Wentworth's account of his own feelings and behavior during their separation.

It is easy to see why Jane Austen was dissatisfied with this handling of

5. In the present edition, chapters are numbered consecutively, without regard for the divisions of the original two volumes. Chapters X and XI of the second volume thus become Chapters XXII and XXIII in the single-volume version.

the reconciliation. The climax comes so close on the heels of Anne's visit to Mrs. Smith that we are taken by surprise; the two critical scenes are so close together that they detract from each other. Furthermore, Anne's difficulties with her family have almost been forgotten. In rewriting the chapter Jane Austen retained a good portion of Wentworth's account of his own feelings; this needed little revision. But she completely altered the circumstances of the reconciliation, and separated it from the visit to Westgate-buildings by a new chapter devoted to Anne's family.

In the final version of the novel Chapter X opens with Anne returning home after her visit to Mrs. Smith. She is exposed to the humiliating behavior of Elizabeth and Mrs. Clay; Mr. Elliot enters, and is treated coldly by Anne. We then shift to the next day; Anne is preparing to visit Lady Russell and tell her of Mr. Elliot's true nature, when the Musgroves suddenly arrive. The visit to Lady Russell is postponed, and Anne joins her friends of the past autumn at the White Hart. Captain Wentworth arrives, and Anne must shortly suffer another meeting between the Captain and her family. Mr. Elliot, supposedly out of town, is glimpsed in the company of Mrs. Clay. The next day (Chapter XI) Anne returns to the White Hart and finds that Captain Wentworth has already arrived. He soon calls for writing materials and begins a letter. Encouraged by the events of the previous day and the tenor of her conversation with Captain Harville, which he overhears, Wentworth composes a hasty love letter and contrives to place it in Anne's hands. The reconciliation has been accomplished, and when they meet a short time later Wentworth launches into an explanation of his past feelings and actions.

Even this crude summary of the changes made in revision can show the complexity of Jane Austen's aims and the sureness of her execution. The new tenth chapter reasserts Anne's isolation, and—through the momentary revelation of the affair between Mr. Elliot and Mrs. Clay—confirms the impressions of the previous chapter. By decelerating the pace of events Jane Austen has given full weight to Mr. Elliot's duplicity, and prepared us for the understanding between Anne and Captain Wentworth. In this connection the indirect appeal by letter seems far superior to the direct confrontation of the earlier version; it emphasizes that difficulty of communication which has been the novel's major theme. Significantly, the final version sustains the internal point-of-view, allowing us to follow the turns of Anne's mind, while the shorter draft had threatened to break this psychological consistency and collapse into straight summary. It is fortunate that this fine example of Jane Austen's structural revisions has survived, since it gives us a clear sense of the rigorous self-criticism and technical control which went into the making of her mature novels.

*　*　*

MARILYN BUTLER

[On *Persuasion*] †

In Captain Frederick Wentworth *Persuasion* has a classic case-study of a modern-minded man from the conservative point of view. Wentworth is personally attractive and an idealist, but he has the fault of trusting too implicitly in his own prior conceptions. When, eight years before the novel opens, he first fell in love with Anne Elliott, he impulsively demanded that she should marry him, contrary to the wishes of her family, and (since he had no money for them to live on) contrary at that stage to common prudence. He put his faith in himself, and in his powers to realize his own destiny; and because, two years later, he did make a fortune, he has always blamed Anne for not showing the same degree of confidence in him, or the courage to defy her connections, know her own mind, and trust her own will. 'She had shewn a feebleness of character in doing so, which his own decided, confident temper could not endure.' When he returns to the neighbourhood, and Anne has to listen to snatches of his conversation with Louisa on the walk to Winthrop, she hears him reiterate his faith in the self. Louisa states that she would rather be overturned by the man she loves than driven safely by anyone else, and Wentworth exclaims 'with enthusiasm,' 'I honour you!' Later, when Anne overhears their conversation within the hedge, she hears him praise 'resolution,' 'decision,' 'firmness,' 'spirit,' and finally, in truly Godwinian phraseology, 'powers of mind.' His personal philosophy approaches revolutionary optimism and individualism and he is impatient of, or barely recognizes, those claims of a mentor which for him can be dismissed in the single word, 'persuasion.'

With Captain Wentworth thus established as its well-intentioned but ideologically mistaken hero, the novel takes a course familiar to the reader of Jane Austen's other novels. At Lyme his eyes are opened. On the Cobb he perceives that what he took for firmness of character in Louisa is really an extreme self-will which disregards rational restraints. After the accident, Anne's behaviour reveals to him another kind of strength, which includes self-forgetfulness, self-control, and the ability to act. He reflects over the lessons of the incident, and afterwards is able to admit to Anne that his judgement of her was prejudiced by his bitterness at the broken engagement. He learns to accept that Anne's submission to Lady Russell was neither a symptom of weakness, nor cold-hearted prudence, but a further sign of principle and fortitude. In the image characteristic of Jane Austen's faulty heroines—that of blind-

† From Marilyn Butler, *Jane Austen and the War of Ideas* (Oxford: Clarendon, 1975), 275–84. Reprinted by permission of Oxford University Press. All notes are by the editor of this Norton Critical Edition. The author's notes have been deleted.

ness upon which light suddenly breaks—he says of his own errors, 'I shut my eyes, and would not understand you, or do you justice.'

The problem about this explanation of the action of *Persuasion* is that although Captain Wentworth is the protagonist of the novel he is not the central character. What *happens* in *Persuasion*, Wentworth's choice of Anne for a wife, and the discovery of true values which is implicit in that choice, remains in line with the conservative philosophy of all of Jane Austen's other novels. But the novel's actual effect is, notwithstanding, distinct, because many of its techniques lead the attention away from the moral implications of action, and the kind of truth expressed by over-all form.

On the whole, though it is not clear how far this effect is intended, the action and most of the characters in *Persuasion* seem meaningful primarily in terms of the impression they make upon Anne. The slow, static, at times rather laborious opening is indirectly all about her: its function is to establish her setting, first in an atmosphere of bankrupt family pride and cold formality at Kellynch Hall, and afterwards among the comfortable, unexacting Musgroves at Uppercross. Morally the Musgroves are not nearly as censurable as the Elliotts. If we feel that there is a great deal wrong with them, it is largely because they are stupid and undiscriminating about Anne.

Just as the first half of the first volume is written in a way to bring out the sorrows of Anne's situation, so Captain Wentworth's entrance is delayed for the same purpose. When at last they meet, the scene is given through the blurred, rushed imprint it makes on Anne's senses:

> Mary, very much gratified by this attention, was delighted to receive him; while a thousand feelings rushed on Anne, of which this was the most consoling, that it would soon be over. And it was soon over. In two minutes after Charles's preparation, the others appeared; they were in the drawing-room. Her eye half met Captain Wentworth's; a bow, a curtsey passed; she heard his voice—he talked to Mary, said all that was right; said something to the Miss Musgroves, enough to mark an easy footing: the room seemed full—full of persons and voices—but a few minutes ended it. Charles showed himself at the window, all was ready, their visitor bowed and was gone; the Miss Musgroves were gone too, suddenly resolving to walk to the end of the village with the sportsmen; the room was cleared, and Anne might finish her breakfast as she could.
>
> 'It is over! it is over!' she repeated to herself again, and again, in nervous gratitude. 'The worst is over!'
>
> Mary talked, but she could not attend. She had seen him. They had met. They had been once more in the same room!

In *Emma* syntax is used to suggest heightened emotion, but there is nothing approaching the exclusively subjective viewpoint of *Persuasion*.

In the earlier novel dialogue is important, and even Emma's free indirect speech can incorporate the tones of another character's conversation. Here Anne is before us, and no one else. Her selective view of external 'reality,' her overwhelming emotional sense of a climax that is also anti-climax, is suggested by the novelist's distortion of the two 'normal' outward dimensions: time is recklessly speeded up, space grotesquely contracted. The implication, as so consistently in the presentation of Anne, is that the senses have a decisive advantage over reason and fact. 'Alas! with all her reasonings, she found, that to retentive feelings eight years may be little more than nothing.'

Especially after the cold, distanced beginning to the novel, with its unsympathetic handling of Elliotts and Musgroves, the intimacy with which Jane Austen approaches Anne's consciousness appears to be something extraordinary. So, too, is the effect of high-wrought nervous tension, compared with the mental worlds of other characters, whose attention is dissipated among the trivia of their external relationships. Unlike the lesser figures, Wentworth is certainly capable of feeling, but immediately after his meeting with Anne we are deliberately shown that his frame of mind is calm and nearly dispassionate. Every technique of contrast is used to throw her abnormally intense experience into high relief.

There is nothing in subjective writing in any earlier English novel to compare in subtlety of insight or depth of feeling with the sequence of nervous scenes between the hero and the heroine in *Persuasion*. The rival realist Maria Edgeworth correctly singles out three episodes for special praise:

> Don't you see Captain Wentworth, or rather don't you in her place feel him taking the boisterous child off her back as she kneels by the sick boy on the sofa? And is not the first meeting after their long separation admirably well done? And the overheard conversation about the nut?

Overheard conversations are part of the technique of *Emma*, but there the inference is that the evidence supplied by the dialogue approaches objectivity; it is the interpretation placed upon the conversation by its observer which is liable to be biased and faulty. When Anne overhears Captain Wentworth's remarks to Louisa about the nut, the two elements, the heroine's consciousness and the hero's conversation, have precisely the reverse connotations. Captain Wentworth's praise of the beauty of the nut, his symbol for hidden richness, perfection, and strength, suggests an intelligent, attractive, witty man, of high moral aspirations; but at the same time a man who is in the grip of a strongly subjective frame of mind, a personal bias which perverts his judgement. Anne, the hidden listener, has, as we already know, and he will rediscover, all the richness and secret strength he is attributing to Louisa.

Once again the inference is that Anne's inner life has an unassailable quality and truth. Nothing like this image of the nut—richest at the kernel, made private by its strong, defensive exterior—is even suggested in an earlier Austen novel.

It is of course precisely this 'inward interest' of *Persuasion*, its access to Anne's feelings, that has given it a relatively high standing in the twentieth century. A very large factor in securing the admiration of posterity must be the subjectivism of later thinking. We find the book peculiarly 'true,' that is to our current attitudes, while *Emma* is true only to itself and to Jane Austen's so-called 'Augustan' objectivity. The sad scenes of autumn in the novel, the desolation of winter rain, are as they are because they are felt by Anne. The world of her consciousness is so all-absorbing that it is not clear whether the outer world (the farmer's outer world, for example) has objective existence or not.

And yet, even while she seems to invite the reader's emotional identification with Anne, Jane Austen orders other parts of her novel in terms that imply her continued acceptance of the old ethical certainties. Both at the beginning of the first volume, where she contrasts the values of Kellynch and Uppercross, and at the end, with the big set-piece scene at Lyme, she reverts to a form of presentation which is near-objective and presented to the reader dramatically rather than refracted through Anne's consciousness. At Lyme we continue to be aware of Anne's emotion. But the meaning of the accident on the Cobb—that Anne is strong while Louisa is only childishly wilful—is directed at the moral understanding of Captain Wentworth and of the reader. The change of focus, or the dual focus, is awkward, and it points to the weakness of *Persuasion*.

That weakness, a failure to integrate the novel's two planes of reality, becomes more acute when in the second volume the scene moves to Bath. In so far as Jane Austen is writing a novel of subjective experience, she continues to do it beautifully. Anne's nervous impatience, her acute state of suspense, is beautifully countered within her own consciousness by her mature knowledge that she and Captain Wentworth must eventually make their feelings known. But enveloping this nineteenth-century novel of the inner life is an eighteenth-century novel in search of a centre. The cold prudential world of Sir Walter and Elizabeth properly belongs within a two-dimensional tradition of social comedy, such as Fielding's. Within such terms they would convince: put in the same novel as Anne, they seem out of focus, and for various reasons. One is that the pain they give Anne, and the spiritual isolation they impose on her, are out of scale in comedy. Another is that beside Anne's consciousness their very being seems sketchy. In no other Austen novel since *Sense and Sensibility* is the social group surrounding the heroine so thin as the Elliotts' circle at Bath.

Far more glaringly wrong—and perhaps more relevant to the question of Jane Austen's mastery of her material—is Mr. William Walter Elliott, the alternative claimant for Anne's hand. His entry into the novel at Lyme, which serves no function, is unusually clumsy stage-management. In his scenes with Anne at Bath he seems curiously inexpressive and featureless. Jane Austen's unease in dealing with him is reflected in the inferior writing he inspires. He provokes from Anne herself some moralistic reflections which include a piece of prudery as disconcerting as anything uttered by Fanny Price. Mrs. Smith's history of his past, that outworn cliché of the eighteenth-century novel, is a device which Jane Austen otherwise allows herself only in *Sense and Sensibility*. The manœuvre by which Mr. Elliott is disposed of, his *affaire* with Mrs. Clay, seems decidedly undermotivated and inconsistent with the worldly wisdom which has hitherto been his leading characteristic. Worse than any of these things, perhaps, is that Mr. Elliott has little or no place in Anne's consciousness. Apparently she does not respond to him as Elizabeth does to Wickham and Emma to Frank. He never represents any kind of real temptation to her. Belonging as he does to the usual Austen format, a novel of moral choices in which each choice is given external bodily reality, in this novel he inevitably loses most of his substance. Failure to define the tempter-figure is surely the most significant of the failures of *Persuasion*. For elsewhere in Jane Austen it is the villain who has always in some form or other embodied self-sufficiency, a whole intellectual system of individualism or self-interest that the more social and outward-turning ethic of the novel was designed to counter. Here, where Anne's inner world is implicitly vindicated, there is very little that is significant for William Walter Elliott to represent.

Persuasion's uneasy compromise between old techniques and new is best exemplified by its two alternative endings. In the original version of the last two chapters, a strong comic plot of a more or less traditional kind binds the events consequentially together. The characters around Anne act in the belief that she is about to marry Mr. Elliott. Anne herself is under the immediate influence of Mrs. Smith's revelations about him, which themselves came about because Mrs. Smith had heard rumours of an engagement. On her way home from talking to Mrs. Smith in Westgate-buildings, Anne encounters Admiral Croft. He too has heard that she is engaged to Mr. Elliott, and assumes that the family may want Kellynch Hall back so that the couple can live there. He takes her into his lodgings and asks his brother-in-law, Wentworth, to find out from Anne if her father would like Kellynch Hall vacated. Wentworth has to account for the question by referring to the supposed engagement; Anne replies by denying it; and the *éclaircissement*[1] is made. In a sense, of course, Mr. Elliott's role is not great, even in this version, since Anne never intended to marry him. But the fact that she

1. Clarification.

has just come from hearing a story which proves him unfit to marry seems to give a moral colouring, in the characteristic Austen fashion, to her acceptance of Wentworth.

The earlier version differs from the dénouement as we know it primarily because it is an essentially objective account of external events, which follow one another in a seemingly rational sequence. Unveiling the truth about Mr. Elliott appears to clarify the attitudes of hero and heroine towards each other—just as the discovery of Frank Churchill's secret brings about the explanatory conversation of Knightley and Emma. The original end of *Persuasion* was to have used the well-tried machinery of Jane Austen's other dénouements.

The new version is a marvellous technical adjustment, in the unique manner of *Persuasion*: it is infinitely better in its access to the feelings. The second volume has been a nervous sequence of half-articulate meetings between Anne and Wentworth—as they shelter from the rain, pass on opposite sides of the street, are separated by circumstances and by Mr. Elliott at the concert. Such occasions are tracked in Anne's consciousness, woven in with intensity among the cold externals of the Elliotts' social life. The first new element of the revised ending is another of these scenes, a meeting which fails to bring about any clarification because Wentworth and Anne are prevented by the crowd from communicating directly with each other. The entirely new-written chapter ten brings the Musgroves to Bath to buy wedding-clothes for Henrietta and Louisa. Shelving her intention to reveal the truth about Mr. Elliott to Lady Russell, Anne goes instead to visit the party from Uppercross at the White Hart hotel. There she also meets Captain Wentworth, and attempts to set his fears at rest about Mr. Elliott, but in the hurried circumstances the task of explaining herself is still left incomplete. The new chapter eleven again reverts to the topic of Mr. Elliott—only, once more, to shelve it:

> One day only had passed since Anne's conversation with Mrs. Smith; but a keener interest had succeeded, and she was now so little touched by Mr. Elliott's conduct, except by its effects in one quarter, that it became a matter of course the next morning, still to defer her explanatory visit in Rivers Street.

She goes instead to spend the day pleasurably with the Musgroves at the White Hart, where she finds Mrs. Croft, Captain Harville, and Captain Wentworth. There follows Anne's beautifully conceived and moving conversation with Harville about the duration of love, which Wentworth overhears: his turn to hear Anne, and to hear her eloquent and unconfined by the hurry and constraint of all their attempted conversations together. She is gentle with Harville; judicious in revealing her own story; rational and general on the subject at issue; but at the end, when her deepest feelings are touched, she speaks straight from her own experience. ' "All the privilege I claim for my own sex (it is not a very enviable one, you need not covet it) is that of loving longest, when existence or when hope is gone." '

All Anne's characteristics find expression in this conversation: her fortitude, gentleness, modesty, integrity. The ideal Wentworth outlined in the conversation she overheard, when he spoke of the hazel-nut, comes vividly to life. Wentworth hears, and writes his letter of proposal, so that she receives it when she is alone; for, in this novel of little dialogue, hardly any of the protagonists' utterances are directed openly to one another. The positive value of replacing the Gay-street proposal scene with the two chapters at the White Hart rests on this change from a direct confrontation between the two (which has never yet occurred successfully throughout the course of the novel) to an indirect one, in which first Anne speaks her thoughts as it were in soliloquy, then Wentworth speaks his through the medium of the pen. The effect is in keeping with the other techniques original to *Persuasion*, for it puts a premium on expression of the self, and avoids direct communication between the self and another.

There can be no question that, of these two endings, the second and final version is infinitely more pleasing—even though it is achieved at the cost of Mr. Elliott's meaningful place in the action. By the same token, Anne, though so out of scale in her social setting, is many people's favourite among Jane Austen's heroines. With an inner life that is rich and feeling, an outer environment that is barren, she looks forward to Maggie Tulliver and Dorothea Brooke.[2] Unfortunately she also looks backward to Elinor and, more immediately, to Fanny.[3] Matching her to her world is not the only problem. Jane Austen has further difficulties within the character—in reconciling Anne's feelings, which are often indistinguishable from those of a victim of her environment, and her exemplary role, which is that of the resolute Christian.

Like Fanny, she is a perceptive bystander, implicitly the conscience and censor of her world. She rebukes the Elliotts because she is above worldly vanity; the Musgrove elders because she is meditative; unlike Louisa, she has the real strength which derives from reflection, principle, and a sense of duty. Anne comes near to being dangerously perfect: 'she is almost too good for me.' Although it is given less explicit Christian colouring than Fanny's, her intense, withdrawn inner life would suggest the 'Saint' even without her hints to Captain Benwick on moral and religious reading, and her sober distaste for Mr. Elliott's Sunday travelling.

The strong contrast between worldly vanity on the one hand and an exemplary train of thought on the other is quite as marked in *Persuasion* as in *Mansfield Park*. Anne's pain at the vanity, selfishness, and inutility

2. Central characters of George Eliot's *Mill on the Floss* (1860) and *Middlemarch* (1871–72).
3. In *Sense and Sensibility* and *Mansfield Park*.

of her father and sister have to be lightly touched upon, because a daughter's denunciations would hardly be in good taste; but the author's severe handling of the baronet comes as near to social criticism as anything she ever wrote. The comparison Jane Austen makes between an idle, useless 'gentleman' proud of his rank, and the eminently useful sailors, has been seen as a notable example of Jane Austen's willingness to be radical. So too has her perception that Lady Russell's wrong advice stemmed from a refined kind of worldliness. On the contrary, the tone of Jane Austen's criticism of her novel's father- and mother-figure— together with its fictional source, in the conscience of a selfless and dutiful daughter—belong to a familiar kind of conservative social comment.

* * *

TONY TANNER

In Between: *Persuasion* †

Persuasion. Not 'Persuasion and . . .'—Resistance, Refusal, Rebellion, for instance. Just *Persuasion.* In previous titles using abstract nouns Jane Austen had deployed pairs. This time the debate, the struggle, the contestation, the contrarieties and ambiguities are all in the one word. As they are all in, or concentrated on, the one girl. Anne Elliot is the loneliest of Jane Austen's heroines. Persuaded by others, she has to repersuade herself.

> Sir Walter Elliot, of Kellynch-hall, in Somersetshire, was a man who, for his own amusement, never took up any book but the Baronetage; there he found occupation for an idle hour, and consolation in a distressed one; there his faculties were roused into admiration and respect, by contemplating the limited remnant of earliest patents; there any unwelcome sensations, arising from domestic affairs, changed naturally into pity and contempt, as he turned over the almost endless creations of the last century—and there, if every other leaf were powerless, he could read his own history with an interest which never failed—this was the page at which the favourite volume was always opened:
>
> 'ELLIOT OF KELLYNCH-HALL'

Jane Austen opens her book with the description of a man looking at a book in which he reads the same words as her book opens with—'Elliot,

---

* From Tony Tanner, *Jane Austen* (Cambridge: Harvard UP, 1986), 208–49. Copyright © 1986 by Tony Tanner. Reprinted by permission of Harvard University Press and Macmillan Press Ltd. All notes are by the editor of this Norton Critical Edition.

of Kellynch-hall.' This is the kind of teasing regression which we have
become accustomed to in contemporary writers but which no one associates with the work of Jane Austen. It alerts us to at least two important
considerations: the dangers involved in seeking validation and self-justi-
fication in book as opposed to life, in record rather than in action, in
name as opposed to function; and the absolutely negative 'vanity' (her
key word for Sir Walter) in looking for and finding one's familial and
social position, one's reality, in an inscription rather than in a pattern of
behaviour, in a sign rather than the range of responsibilities which it
implicitly signifies. We learn how fond Sir Walter is of mirrors and how
hopelessly and hurtfully unaware of the real needs and feelings of his
dependents he is. This opening situation poses someone fixed in an
ultimate solipsism gazing with inexhaustible pleasure into the textual
mirror which simply gives him back his name. The opening of Jane
Austen's text—a title, a name, a domicile, a geographic location—
implies a whole series of unwritten obligations and responsibilities
related to rank, family, society and the very land itself, none of which
Sir Walter, book-bound and self-mesmerised, either keeps or recognises.
He is only interested in himself and what reflects him—mirrors or
daughters. Thus he likes Elizabeth because she is 'very like himself'—
this is parenthood as narcissism—and Mary has 'acquired a little artificial importance' because she has married into a tolerably respectable
family; 'but Anne, with an elegance of mind and sweetness of character,
which must have placed her high with any people of real understanding,
was nobody with either father or sister: her word had no weight; her
convenience was always to give way;—she was only Anne.' Only
Anne—no rank, no effective surname, no house, no location; her words
are weightless, and physically speaking she always has to 'give way'—
that is, accept perpetual displacement. Anne we may call the girl on the
threshold, existing in that limboid space between the house of the father
which has to be left and the house of the husband which has yet to be
found. No longer a child and not yet a wife, Anne is, precisely, in
between, and she lives in in-betweenness. She is a speaker who is
unheard; she is a body who is a 'nobody.' I emphasise this because the
problems of the body who is, socially speaking, a nobody were to engage
many of the great nineteenth-century writers. We might recall here that
in one of the seminal eighteenth-century novels, *La Nouvelle Héloïse*,[1]
Julie's father refuses even to listen to the idea of her marrying Saint-
Preux, because Saint-Preux is what he calls 'un quidam,' which means
an unnamed individual or, in dictionary terms, 'Person (name
unknown).' This is to say that, as far as the father is concerned, Saint-
Preux exists in a state of 'quidamity.' As far as her father is concerned,

1. Published in 1761, by French writer Jean-Jacques Rousseau (1712–1778).

Anne also exists in that state of quidamity—she was nobody, she was only Anne: 'He had never indulged much hope, he had now none, of ever reading her name in any other page of his favourite work.' Until she is, as it were, reborn in terms of writing in the Baronetage, she does not exist—not to be in the book is thus not to *be*. We may laugh at Sir Walter but Jane Austen makes it very clear what kind of perversity is involved in such a radical confusion or inversion of values whereby script and name take absolute precedence over offspring and dependents; or, to put it another way, when you cannot see the body for the book.

Anne Elliot, then, is perpetually displaced, always 'giving way' as opposed to having her *own* way—it is worth emphasising the metaphor. The story of her life consists precisely in having had her own way blocked, refused, negated. One might almost think of the book as being about dissuasion, for she is urged or forced not into doing something which she does not want to do, but into *not* doing something which her whole emotional self tells her is the right thing (that is, marry Captain Wentworth at a time when he had no fortune). Her words carry no weight. The word 'persuasion' echoes throughout the novel of that title just as it is constantly haunting Anne Elliot (it occurs at least fourteen times). It is as if she cannot get away from what she has done in allowing herself to be persuaded not to marry Frederick Wentworth—or dissuaded from marrying him. Yet 'persuasion' implies some sort and source of 'authority'—preferably moral authority; mere power can work by simple imperatives or prohibitions backed up by force. But what is striking about the world of *Persuasion* is the absence of any real centre or principle of authority. Among the possible traditional sources of authority we might include the family, parents, the clergy, social rank and respected names, familiar and revered places, codes of manners and propriety, codes of duty and prudence, the care and concern of friendship, or true love so certain of itself that it becomes self-authorising. But in this novel all such potential sources of authority have gone awry, gone away, gone wrong; they are absent, dispersed or impotent; they have become ossified, stagnant or—worse—totally unreliable and misleading. Everything is in a condition of change in this novel, and as often as not it is change as deterioration or diminution. In such a world it becomes a real question, what can and should remain 'constant'? To retain an uncritical allegiance to certain decaying inert social hierarchies and practices means dehumanising the self for the sake of rigidifying deathly formulae; to abandon oneself to the new might be to opt for a giddy dissolution. Just about all the previous stabilities of Jane Austen's world are called into question in this novel—in which things really are 'changed utterly,' with no terrible beauty being born.[2] It is a novel of

2. See William Butler Yeats, "Easter 1916": "All changed, changed utterly:/A terrible beauty is born."

great poignancy and sadness, as well as one of real bitterness and astrin-
gency, for it is deeply shadowed by the passing of things, and the
remembrance of things past.

It is hardly surprising, then, that time plays a larger part in this novel
than in any other of Jane Austen's works. It is the only one of her novels
which gives a specific date for the opening action—'summer 1814'—as
Emma is the only novel to use a single name as a title. The significance
of that date (the end of the Napoleonic wars—apart from 'the hundred
days' of Napoleon's abortive return, concluded by the battle of Waterloo
in 1815), becomes increasingly obvious: it marks a big change in English
history and society. But in the novel the crucial passage of time is that
which has elapsed since Anne was 'persuaded' to give up Wentworth
and he disappeared into the navy—'more than seven years were gone
since this little history of sorrowful interest had reached its close.' Indeed
Persuasion is in effect a second novel. (Part of its rare autumnal magic—
not unlike that of one of Shakespeare's last plays—is that it satisfies that
dream of a 'second chance' which must appeal to anyone who has experienced the sense of an irreparably ruined life owing to an irrevocable,
mistaken decision.) The 'first novel' is what might be called (warily) a
typical Jane Austen novel and is told in telescopic brevity in a few lines
in chapter 4:

> He [Wentworth] was, at that time, a remarkably fine young man,
> with a great deal of intelligence, spirit and brilliancy; and Anne an
> extremely pretty girl, with gentleness, modest taste and feeling.—
> Half the sum of attraction, on either side, might have been
> enough, for he had nothing to do, and she had hardly any body to
> love; but the encounter of such lavish expectations could not fail.
> They were gradually acquainted, and when acquainted, rapidly
> and deeply in love. It would be difficult to say which had seen the
> highest perfection in the other, or which had been the happiest;
> she, in receiving his declarations and proposals, or he in having
> them accepted.

End of story. To get there could have taken the younger Jane Austen
some hundreds of pages. But times and things have changed. That was
a happy novel of yesteryear, here no more than a distant trace, a radiant
but receding, summarisable memory in this second novel. 'More than
seven years were gone since this little history of sorrowful interest had
reached its close.' The first novel ended when the totally vain, egotistical
anti-father (he is even described as womanly in his vanity) Sir Walter
Elliot 'gave it all the negative of great astonishment, great coldness, great
silence.' His 'negative' blocked the marriage and the novel alike. It is a
'negative' which is against generational and narrative continuity and
renewal and it has far-reaching social implications.

Here it is enough to point out that it provides the starting-point for a new kind of novel for Jane Austen; a novel which arises precisely out of the thwarting and 'negating' of her first (earlier type of) novel. Hence the stress on time past. What has happened in between then and now? And what can happen next? It must be something quite different from the action and resolution of any previous Jane Austen novel, because something—history, society or whatever it is that is embodied in the sterile, life-denying figure of Sir Walter—has given that kind of novel 'all the negative.' What Jane Austen does say is this: 'She [Anne] had been forced into prudence in her youth, she learned romance as she grew older—the natural sequence of an unnatural beginning.' Most of Jane Austen's heroines have to learn some kind of prudence (not Fanny Price, who has suffered for her undeviating dedication to prudentiality). Anne, born into repression and non-recognition, has to learn romance—a deliberate oxymoron surely, for romance is associated with spontaneous feelings. But in Anne's case these had been blocked; her father gave them all the negative. To find her own positive she has, as it were, to diseducate herself from the authorities who, whether by silence or disapproval or forceful opposition, dominated that early part of her life when she was—in relation to Captain Wentworth—becoming somebody. Anne has to start on a long and arduous second life, which is based on loss, denial, deprivation. This is the 'unnatural beginning' to her life, and to Jane Austen's novel, which differs quite radically from her previous works in that there, as I said, her heroines tend to graduate from romance to prudence. And because of what she has lost and regretted losing (again an unusual condition for the Jane Austen heroine, who has usually not yet had any significant romance when the book opens) Anne undergoes a new kind of ordeal and tribulation, since any reference to Captain Wentworth offers 'a new sort of trial to Anne's nerves' so that she has to 'teach herself to be insensible on such points.' Among other things, Anne Elliot has to combine sense and *in*sensibility—again, a marked change from Jane Austen's earlier work.

The novel starts, then, with Sir Walter contemplating 'the limited remnants of the earliest patents' in a volume which records 'the history and rise of the ancient and respectable family.' 'Limited remnants' are indeed all that now remain, and *this* volume will complete the work by recording the 'fall' and self-destruction of this 'respectable family'—if not the traditional family in general. Around the unnaturally well-preserved appearance of Sir Walter he can only see the 'wreck of good looks of everybody else.' Did he but realise it, the 'wreckage' goes a good deal deeper than that. What is irremediably wrecked and what might yet remain to generate new life from among the 'remnants' becomes a key question of the book. Anne has to live with the regret for what she has lost, while her one friend and mother-substitute, Lady Russell, while feeling sorry for Anne, 'never wishes the past undone.' As a result 'they knew not each other's opinion, either its constancy or its change.' When

Sir Walter decides to move with his daughters out of the family home, Kellynch Hall, Anne is aware of 'the general air of oblivion among them.' It is an air which partially pervades the book. When Anne does finally meet Wentworth again, her concern is very much with the possible effects of time:

> How absurd to be resuming the agitation which such an interval had banished into distance and indistinctness! What might not eight years do? Events of every description—changes, alienations, removals,—all, all must be compromised in it; and oblivion of the past—how natural, how certain too!

In the event Anne finds that 'to retentive feelings eight years may be little more than nothing.' Time can obviously mean one thing to a couple in love—and something quite different to the society around them. Anne is a lonely figure of emotional constancy living in a society of 'changes, alienations, removals.' She hears that Wentworth finds her 'altered beyond his knowledge,' but his enlightened knowledge will find her essentially unaltered. There is of course much emphasis on the past and the pastness of the past: '*That* was in the year six'; 'There had been a time'; 'those rooms had witnessed former meetings'; and so on. The pluperfect tense is poignantly present. Even painful memories are precious; indeed even precious because painful.

> Scenes had passed at Uppercross, which made it precious. It stood the record of many sensations of pain, once severe but now softened; and of some instances of relenting feeling, some breathings of friendship and reconciliation, which could never be looked for again, and which could never cease to be dear. She left it all behind her; all but the recollection that such things had been.

The dominant mood before the end is autumnal, nostalgic, a sense of the most significant period of experience being in the past, recollectable but irretrievable and unrepeatable. 'One does not love a place the less for having suffered in it.' There are moments when Wentworth speaks to Anne 'which seemed almost restoring the past.' 'Restoration' on this personal level does prove to be joyfully—miraculously—possible. But on the social and familial level no such restoration is possible. This is made clear when the heir to Kellynch, Mr Elliot, enters the novel and is not only keen to marry Anne but *seems* a correct and suitable figure to assist at such restoration after the gross and ruinous derelictions of Sir Walter. Lady Russell, characteristically, would like to forward this marriage and see Anne 'occupying your dear mother's place, succeeding to all her rights . . . presiding and blessing in the same spot'. To Anne herself the idea of 'being restored to Kellynch, calling it her home again, her home forever, was a charm which she could not immediately resist.' But love is stronger than even the most precious property. Anne really has 'left it all behind her.' Whatever else it might be, this is not a 'restoration' age.

The question of 'what lasts' obviously figures most largely in this novel in connection with human feelings—even leading to a recurring debate as to whether man or woman is capable of the greater constancy, of loving longer. Captain Benwick is slightly reproached by Wentworth for having put aside his devotion to the dead Fanny Harville (whom he apparently worshipped) to marry Louisa Musgrove. 'A man does not recover from such a devotion of the heart to such a woman!—He ought not—he does not.' Wentworth obviously has his own motives for such an assertion: he is both indirectly signalling his own unbroken devotion to Anne, and questioning hers. And indeed such pointed exchanges proliferate towards the end of the book: 'You did not like to use cards; but time makes many changes.' Wentworth's statement is of course also a question. To which Anne replies, 'I am not yet so much changed'— 'and stopped, fearing she hardly knew what misconstruction.' In the crucial 'recognition' scene—in the revised chapter 23—the central debate is between Captain Harville and Anne while Wentworth apparently writes a letter. Harville argues that men love longer, that women have a legendary reputation for inconstancy. Anne maintains that 'We certainly do not forget you, so soon as you forget us,' and 'All the privilege I claim for my own sex . . . is that of loving longest, when existence or hope is gone.' This is all said for the benefit of the apparently preoccupied but all-attentive Wentworth. I shall return to the indirect mode of communication in this crucial scene. Here the point to note is that, as Lady Russell says, 'Time will explain'—certainly in this novel, in which time is so central, and 'explanations' (making intelligible, laying things out clearly) are both crucial and difficult to come by. And the novel itself is an inquiry into—an ex-planation of—the effects of time. As I have said, this is the 'second' novel, made necessary by the rude 'negation' of the first one, which remains as an aborted embryo in chapter 4.

I shall return to the relationship between Anne and Wentworth. First we should consider the general state of society as it is represented in this book. The normal sources of stability and order in Jane Austen's world would include social position, property, place, family, manners and propriety, as generating a web of duties and responsibilities which together should serve to maintain the moral fabric and coherence of society. In this novel all these institutions and codes and related values have undergone a radical transformation or devaluation. There *are* values, but many of them are new; and they are relocated or resited. Instead of a heedful regard for position and property and family, we have a new obsession with 'rank,' 'connexions,' money and private relationships. Lady Russell esteems Sir Walter not as a man or father (he is a wretched example of both) but as a baronet: 'she had prejudices on the side of ancestry; she had a value for rank and consequence.' There are discussions of 'rank, people of rank, jealousy of rank.' Mary, the most insufferable snob (she is not comic—she is unbearable), looks not at Mr Elliot but at 'the horses . . . the arms . . . the livery'; she regards only the insignia of rank, empty signifiers of another empty series of signifiers. For 'rank' in this book does not betoken a responsible authoritative position in society: it signifies only itself. It is rigidifying self-reifying system—signifying nothing. It is symptomatic of a 'state of stagnation' existing in the class which should be exemplary and active if it is to serve as, and deserve to be, a ruling class. Mr. Elliot at one time of his life despises 'the honour of the family' and declared that 'if baronetcies were saleable, anybody should have his for fifty pounds, arms and motto, name and livery included.' 'Rank' is degraded into a mere commodity. On the other hand, when it seems that it would be more profitable for him to become the serious heir to baronetcy, he speaks seriously in favour of 'the value of rank and connexion.' This is a mark not of his conversion but of his ruthlessly selfish opportunism and hypocrisy. The discourse and ideology of 'rank' happen to be available to disguise or 'embellish' his crudely egotistical aspirations. The new realm where rank *does* have a genuine significance and is related to a hierarchy of real functions and obligations is the navy—but I shall come back to the navy. The emphasis on the 'value' of 'connexions,' which Lady Russell upholds in an apparently rational way, as the unspeakably foolish Mary does in the crudest possible way ('It is very unpleasant having such connexions,' she declares of the respectable Hayters), is a relatively new one in Jane Austen. It emphasises a merely titular or 'nominal' and fortuitous relationship rather than any true bonding or sense of reciprocal human relatedness. An extreme example of the meaninglessness and folly of this stress on 'rank' and 'connexions' is offered by Sir Walter's and Elizabeth's frantic anxiety and eagerness to cultivate the acquaintance of their titled cousins, Lady Dalrymple and her daughter. As people they are not even 'agreeable'; 'they were nothing.' Mr Elliot asserts that 'rank is rank.' The book confirms this as a meaningless tautology and counterasserts that rank is 'nothing.'

More than one person is said to be 'nothing' or 'nobody.' Anne 'was nobody' because unmarried; Mr Wentworth (Frederick's brother) 'was nobody . . . quite unconnected,' because he was a curate and not 'a man of property'; Charles Hayter is 'nothing but a country curate'; Captain Wentworth, when he reappears as rich 'and as high in his profession as merit and activity could place him' was 'no longer nobody.' These are mainly the verdicts of Sir Walter, a 'foolish spendthrift baronet' who has neither money nor profession nor merit nor activity. He is also no longer married and has rented his property. If anybody is now 'nobody,' it is he. It is indirectly Jane Austen's verdict—through Anne's silent assessment—that the Dalrymples 'were nothing.' But who then is somebody and something—and by what social criteria? It would seem that there are no longer any agreed-on standards, no authoritative modes of assessment, to discriminate the somebodies from the nobodies, to tell a something from a nothing. This in itself is a symptom of a crisis of values—a chaos if not a total absence and loss of 'common' (i.e. communal) standards of modes of identification and evaluation. There seems to be no correlation or connection between social title and social role, between rank and merit.

The honorific term 'gentleman'—always somewhat vague—now means different things to different people (Sir Walter is 'misled' when his agent Mr Shepherd refers to Mr Wentworth as a 'gentleman'), or it is meaningless (as applied to Captain Wallis) or worse it conceals heartless and ruthless anti-social egotism (Mr Elliott passes as "completely a gentleman'). The true 'gentlemen' are now to be found in the navy, but they are neither recognised nor addressed as such. A whole social system of categorisation and terminology is slipping into meaningless or perverse misapplication, dangerously so when the label 'gentleman' is confidently affixed to a man who is the complete opposite (or inversion) of everything a true gentleman should be. Society's very taxonomy seems to have collapsed, being at best misleading and at worst totally corrupt. Names themselves seem to have lost any social significance—at least from the perverse and anachronistic point of view of Sir Walter, who laments thus: 'One wonders how the names of many of our nobility became so common.' One explanation may involve the dilution of aristocratic families with the wealthier members of other classes; another could simply point to the behaviour of Sir Walter himself, who effectively does just about everything he could to bring his family name into disrepute. It is he who, on hearing that Anne is going to visit her crippled and impoverished friend Mrs Smith, says disdainfully, 'Mrs Smith, such a name!' 'Smith' is indeed the archetypal anonymous English name, a name which is in effect no 'name' at all. But, here again, this novel forces us to question all kinds of social assumptions. What really *is* in a name? In the case of Sir Walter Elliot, an impoverished and fatuous vanity; in the case of Mrs. Smith, a wealth of misfortune and misery; in the case of Lady Dalrymple, 'nothing.' Like 'rank' and 'connexions,' names also no longer serve to facilitate any kind of social orientation. They now manifest themselves as truly arbitrary signifiers—designations unrelated to any coherent social design or structure.

Let us now consider property and places, houses and homes and families. We can note immediately that the action of the novel is dispersed among an unusually large number of different places (unusual for Jane Austen). Fanny Price visits her 'home' in Portsmouth; Emma goes to Box Hill. But Anne is variously 'removed' or 'transplanted' from Kellynch Hall to Uppercross cottage; to the Great House (of the Musgroves) to Bath; with a glimpse of Winthrop and a crucial visit to Lyme. This topographical diffusion and 'transplanting' is itself both a symptom and a part of a more far-reaching social fragmentation and mobility. One important scene takes place in an hotel in Bath. 'A morning of thorough confusion was to be expected. A large party in an hotel ensured a quick-changing, unsettled scene.' An hotel is the appropriate edifice for a transient, increasingly uprooted or unrooted society, and that 'quick-changing, unsettled scene' is—in little—the scene of the whole book. The 'thorough confusion' experienced in the hotel pervades society at large. This topographical dispersal and social scattering also have their effect on the style and vocabulary of the novel. Of the incident on the Cobb we are told parenthetically that '(it was all done in rapid moments).' In a way that is true of the book as a whole, which is more episodic, more fragmentary, and more marked by quick and sudden changes and abrupt transitions and jerks of the plot than any of the previous novels. Related to that is a perceptibly new note of emotional volatility and irruptiveness, even excess. After the incident on the Cobb there is, not a cool discussion, but an 'interchange of perplexity and terror'—a significant dissolution of coherent speech in feeling. The word 'burst' appears a number of times in relation to sudden mental and emotional eruptions—'extraordinary burst of mind,' 'bursts of feeling'; phrases such as 'a thousand feelings rushed on Anne,' 'overpowering happiness' contribute to the increased presence of sudden unanticipated and unpredictable inward intensities. And such 'bursts,' 'rushes of feeling,' emotional 'overpowerings' are not always the signs of a potentially dangerous and disorderly (or 'improper') lack of control, as they often are in Jane Austen's earlier work. On the contrary, they can now be the desirable manifestations of a capacity for authentic and spontaneous feeling. This means that there is a much more ruffled 'choppy' surface to the narrative. 'Tranquillity' is often 'interrupted'; 'restraint' gives way to 'disturbance.' 'Every moment rather brought fresh agitation.' This refers to Anne near the end, but in a way it is true of the novel as a whole.

There are further lessons to be learned from Anne's constant 'transplantation.' The following is crucial:

> Anne had not wanted this visit to Uppercross, to learn that a removal from one set of people to another, though at a distance of only three miles, will often include a total change of conversation, opinion, and idea . . . she acknowledged it to be very fitting, that every little social commonwealth should dictate its own matters of discourse; and hoped, ere long, to become a not unworthy member of the one she was now transplanted to . . . she believed she must now submit to feel that another lesson, in the art of knowing our own nothingness beyond our own circle, was becoming necessary for her.

This awareness that within the one common language—English—there can be innumerable discourses according to group, place, and so on, is a very crucial one. It is not the same thing as a dialect but what Roland Barthes calls a 'sociolect'—'the language of a linguistic community, that is of a group of persons who all interpret in the same way all linguistic statements.' It is of course simply a general truth, and one well known to Jane Austen, that people speaking the same language can very often not 'hear' each other because they are operating within different discourses or sociolects. It is characteristic of many of Jane Austen's heroines that they are aware when people are operating within different discourses—an awareness which is an aspect of their sense and linguistic 'conscience' and very often a consequence of their detachment and isolation. And Anne learns another lesson; just as one language is in fact made up of many discourses, so society is made up of many 'circles' and in many of these circles one may be a 'nothing' just as in some discourses one is inaudible. Anne's 'word' initially 'had no weight' precisely because she was regarded as a 'no-body' within the first circle of her family—'negatived' from the beginning. Her speech can only take on its full value when she is truly regarded as a 'some-body'—a person in her own right, not according to rank or status, and taken permanently into a new circle—the navy. In between she is, well, in between. But notice two things. Anne does not fight this state of affairs or lament the plurality of discourses. On the contrary, she is willing to try and adapt herself (within the limits of her unchanging sense of propriety). Yet her speech—like her love—is 'constant' in a society apparently given over to change. Having to negotiate a plurality of partial discourses, Anne comes to embody what we might call the conscience of language. She, and she alone, always speaks truly, and truly speaks. Indeed, Jane Austen may well be intending to depict Anne as in some ways old-fashioned—or, rather, out of fashion (which is by nature ephemeral and fickle). Not all change is regarded as unmitigatedly bad in this book— indeed, given the 'stagnation' and moral paralysis (if not something worse) which seems to prevail among the upper ruling clases, then some change may be not only unavoidable but positively necessary and welcome. But Anne's 'lessons' do point to the fact (glimpsed at the end of *Emma*) that society is breaking up into smaller and smaller 'circles' and units. This implies—indeed involves—the loss of any sense of a true, authoritative 'centre,' and the possible disappearance of any 'common' language (and with that, a shared sense of 'common' values). Add to this the fact that even within the small separate 'sociolects' there are people who tend towards speaking an 'idiolect' (i.e., a language which is really private to themselves and not properly heard or understood by anyone else). This could portend a society which is no longer truly a society in any meaningful sense but rather an aggregate of contiguous but non-communicating groups or just families (or even just individuals), with no *real* connections, no overall coherence, no single structure binding them together. Separate 'commonwealths' with neither 'wealth' not any-

thing much else held in 'common': 'Dictate-orships' perhaps (Jane Austen's words carry a weight of possible irony) of one kind or another. To
a large extent this is our 'society' today. It is not 'society' as Jane Austen
had thought it should or could be. But she saw that the change was
coming and was inevitable. To a large extent she could see why. It is all
there in this unique novel.

In this prevailing atmosphere of change it is not surprising that 'property' no longer plays the assured and essential role it did in earlier novels.
Mary, for instance, 'had merely connected herself with an old country
family and respectability and large fortune.' That 'merely' is Sir Walter's
thought, Jane Austen's irony. The advantage for people 'living on their
own property,' according to the insinuating Mrs Clay, is that they 'are
not obliged to follow any . . . profession' but can just 'follow their own
pursuits.' Just what Sir Walter likes to hear, of course, but not at all what
Jane Austen believed, since for her the owning of 'property' necessarily
involved the recognition of obigations and duties to the community. If
it is merely an arena for self-indulgence and hedonism, it is less than
useless as a part of the maintained and maintaining order of society. It
is still desirable to have property of course; but as a symbol of certain
social values it is undervalued as Mary undervalues Charles Hayter's
'good, freehold property' because it confers no rank (adding, in her
incomparably selfish way, 'it would be shocking to have Henrietta marry
Charles Hayter; a very bad thing for *her*, and a still worse for *me*'), or as
Sir Walter feels 'no degradation in his changes,' seeing 'nothing to regret
in the duties and dignity of the resident land-holder' and finding 'much
to be vain of in the littleness of a town.' His is the quintessential abdication and dereliction of the ruling-class landowner. When he rents Kellynch Hall he causes a 'break-up of the family,' and leaves behind
'deserted grounds' and 'so altered a village.' (There is quite possibly here
a barely ironic allusion to Goldsmith's *The Deserted Village*.[3]) He is an
agent of 'desolation,' helping both to precipitate and to accelerate the
destruction of the old order of society. (Anne will be the first Jane Austen
heroine who will not found her marriage on the once-necessary basis of
'property.') Society in the form of Sir Walter Elliot has become all
empty self-regarding form and display: he has no sense of responsibility
to his position, to the land, and it is significant that he rents his house
to go and participate in the meaningless frivolities in Bath.

This matter of renting his house is worth pausing over for a moment.
The notion 'quit Kellynch-hall' is initially horrendous to Sir Walter.
But he would, as he says, 'sooner quit Kellynch-hall' than undertake
any economies or constraints on his unrestricted pursuit of pleasure. His
relation to his house is not a responsible one: he does not see his house

---

3. A poem (1770) about rural depopulation by Oliver Goldsmith (1728–1774).

as part of a larger context, an interrelated rural society, an ecology, if you will; it is more like a pleasure-dome or a three-dimensional mirror which flatters his vanity. So he agrees to quit if he cannot have those pleasures. But note that 'Sir Walter could not have borne the degradation of being known to design letting his house—Mr Shepherd had once mentioned the word "advertise"—but never dared approach it again.' I shall come back to 'advertising' in the last chapter, but here again we note that Sir Walter wants the profits of 'renting' while still pretending to belong to an aristocracy which did not contaminate itself with contact with any kind of 'trade' or commerce. This is the self-deception of a figure no longer sensible of the significance of his social rank. When he does consider renting it he thinks of it in terms of 'a prize' for the fortunate tenants—'a prize'; he has no appreciation of the real value of his inherited house. And I shall just note the areas to which he does not really want the new tenant to have access: 'The park would be open to him of course . . . , but what restrictions I might impose on the use of the pleasure-grounds, is another thing. I am not fond of the idea of my shrubberies being always approachable.' Funny of course—but again there is no sense of the importance and significance of the house of his fathers, the house in which he so signally fails in *his* paternal duties. To abandon it in exchange for money, for mere pleasure, rather than 'economise' is a very notable dereliction of his duties. This is an alteration which is most definitely not 'perhaps an improvement' but indisputably a degradation.

Even before Sir Walter decided to 'quit Kellynch-hall' we are told of 'the prosperity and the nothingness' of the life there, with nothing to fill 'the vacancies'—'no habits of utility abroad, no talents or accomplishments for home.' Lady Elliot, the true upholder of domesticity, is dead. Anne would carry on her work—but of course is not allowed to. Rather than practise the slightest economy or curtail any of his indulgences, Sir Walter prefers to rent his landed house, which is indeed nothing of a home and merely parasitic on the community it should help to maintain and preserve. (We might note in passing that we are told that, if Sir Walter follows Anne's sensible suggestions, Lady Russell estimates that 'in seven years he will be clear.' Of course he cannot deprive himself of any of his private gratifications for any length of time at all. It is Anne, who can wait and economise scrupulously on her emotional expenditure, who after 'seven years'—when Wentworth returns—will finally 'be clear.' 'Clear,' one might say, of the whole rotten pack of her family; as well as 'clear' of the obstacles, negatives and dissuasions which had blocked the growth and consummation of her true love seven years previously.) Seeing the Crofts in Kellynch Hall after they have rented it, Anne feels that 'they were gone who deserved not to stay, and that Kellynch-hall had passed into better hands than its owners.' Unlike the 'improvements' suggested in *Mansfield Park*, the 'few alterations' the Crofts make to Kellynch Hall are 'all very much for the better.' It is almost as if Jane Austen was passing a verdict on the defection of a whole class in whom she had once invested so much hope. Initially Anne is sad at the thought of 'a beloved home made over to others'—but that home was no longer home. Her loyalties shift and are displaced or realigned elsewhere. For instance: 'how much more interesting to her was the home and the friendship of the Harvilles and Captain Benwick, than her own father's house in Camden Place.' The Harvilles and Benwick are naval officers of course, and, just as there is a shift of significant, active 'rank' from society to the navy, so it is the navy who—apparently paradoxically—reconstitute a meaningful domesticity, re-create the idea of home, ultimately redefine the notion of society itself. It is Mrs Croft who asserts that 'Woman may be as comfortable on board, as in the best house in England,' and clearly her ship was more of a 'home' than Kellynch Hall. But even the house of the Harvilles and Captain Benwick—rather like a ship on shore—in all its apparent oddity and somewhat cramped idiosyncrasy offers to Anne 'the picture of repose and domestic happiness.' Note that the rooms are extremely small and the very limited space is crowded. This was one of the major deficiencies of Fanny's home in Portsmouth which contributed to its 'impropriety.' Nothing of that now. The small space is turned into 'the best possible account' and instead of the chaos of excessive proximity and discord there is the snugness of hospitable ease and intimacy. The 'hospitality' of the navy is emphasised—and usual 'forms' of etiquette are at the same time devalued. There was such a 'bewitching charm in a degree of hospitality so uncommon, so unlike the usual style of give-and-take invitations and dinners of formality and display.' A whole system of socially prescribed 'formal' reciprocities is here effectively displaced by an informal spontaneity. It is not prompted by custom but by 'the heart'—the rooms are so small as none but those who 'invite from the heart' would think of asking people to share their living-space. The shift of emphasis from socially prescribed 'invitations' to those which come from 'the heart' is part of a larger change from a socially based to an emotionally justified code of behaviour. It has quite radical implications. As already intimated, I shall have more to say about the navy, but I want to return to land matters.

There is an example of a relatively happy home unrelated to the navy: the home of the Musgroves, the Great House. But it is 'happy' in a new way. For a start, it is characterised by an 'air of confusion' owing to the accumulating objects belonging to the lively children. The originals of the ancestral portraits would have been 'astonished' at the general 'overthrow of all order and neatness.' So surmises Anne. But, again, though these were characteristics of Fanny's Portsmouth home, the Great

House is in no way another version of that horrific non-home. The tone of the description is worth noting with some care:

> The Musgroves, like their house, were in a state of alteration, perhaps of improvement. The father and mother were in the old English style and the young people in the new. Mr and Mrs Musgrove were a very good sort of people; friendly and hospitable, not much educated, and not at all elegant. Their children had more modern minds and manners . . . and were now, like thousands of other young ladies, living to be fashionable, happy, and merry. Their dress had every advantage, their faces were rather pretty, their spirits extremely good, their manners unembarrassed and pleasant; they were of consequence at home, and favourites abroad.

Alteration, *perhaps of improvement:* the qualification is not barbed. There is no biting irony, no malice in the text. Jane Austen is genuinely open and uncommitted. The gay hedonism of the children is not seen as dangerous or disruptive. The older generation lack education and elegance. Once that would have been a serious defect in Jane Austen's eyes. Now it doesn't matter. Because other values, such as friendship and hospitality, are coming to seem more important. 'There is so little real friendship in the world!' laments poor Mrs Smith later in the book, and it is now becoming for Jane Austen a cardinal virtue. The children's 'modern minds and manners' are not mocked. They may be somewhat giddy, perhaps a little shallow or frivolous. They are lively and good-spirited (*they* are not 'stagnant') and their 'manners' are at least 'unembarrassed and pleasant'—quite unlike the ludicrous snobbery, chilly hauteur, unpleasant seeming-politeness, and mean-spirited psuedo-etiquette of the upper classes. Jane Austen cannot whole-heartedly identify with these 'modern minds and manners,' just as Anne 'would not have given up her own more elegant and cultivated mind for all their enjoyments.' But both Anne and her author can recognise their genuine happiness and applaud their 'good-humoured mutual affection.' Society—England itself—is altering, perhaps improving. Jane Austen does not take sides; she neither mocks the old style nor reprobates the new. Her stance is Anne's. But she is clearly undertaking a radical reassessment and revision of her system of values. She can be gently ironic about the domestic arrangements of the Great House, as when, later, she describes a tolerably confused and noisy scene there with everyone doing something different and contributing to a general disharmony, and comments, 'It was a fine family-piece.' But it is not Portsmouth. A new tolerance and relativism has entered Jane Austen's tone. What for Anne is a rather nerve-racking 'domestic hurricane' is for Mrs Musgrove 'a little quiet cheerfulness at home.' Jane Austen is amused but not censorious: 'Everybody has their tastes in noises as well as in other matters; and sounds are quite innoxious, or most distressing, by their sort rather than their quantity.' (Lady Russell would hear the street noises of Bath as signalling her 'winter pleasures' and would, says Jane Austen, have probably regarded them as part of 'a little quiet cheerfulness' after the deprivations of the country.) I do not believe that Jane Austen could have written that sentence at the time of *Mansfield Park*.

Having mentioned 'manners' I want to point to another major reversal or change in Jane Austen's habitual mode of assessment. We have seen how important manners were to her—as to Burke[4]—and how crucial she made it seem to distinguish (if possible) between Lockean good manners and Chesterfield's type of good manners[5] (alternatively, between English and 'French' manners). Again, this careful distinction—indeed the whole signifying role of manners—has become useless if not treacherously misleading. On Mr Elliot's first appearance he 'proves' by his 'propriety' that 'he was a man of exceedingly good manners.' By contrast, Admiral Croft's 'manners were not quite of the tone to suit Lady Russell.' Mr Elliot indeed serves single-handedly to undermine utterly any code of values attached to manners. 'His manners were so exactly what they ought to be, so polished, so easy, so particularly agreeable' that—as manners—Anne herself finds them as good as Wentworth's! His conversation leaves 'no doubt of his being a sensible man.' And it is not merely the cultivated appearance of manners. Lady Russell finds 'the solid . . . so fully supporting the superficial' that she perceives him as an embodiment of all the virtues. 'Everything united in him.' He even seems to have 'a value for all the felicities of domestic life.' True, Anne begins to have her suspicions and reservations, and Lady Russell is capable of erroneous judgements. But *nothing* in Mr Elliot's manners could have prepared anyone for the revelation of the 'true' man.

> Mr Elliot is a man without heart or conscience; a designing, wary, cold-blooded being, who thinks only of himself; who, for his own interest or ease, would be guilty of any cruelty, or any treachery, that could be perpetrated without risk of his general character. He has no feeling for others. Those whom he has been the chief cause of leading into ruin, he can neglect and desert without the smallest compunction. He is totally beyond the reach of any sentiment of justice or compassion. Oh! he is black at heart, hollow and black!

Mrs Smith's description of the true Mr Elliot is never challenged or controverted. It is the most unqualified summary of unmitigated evil in all Jane Austen's work. Yet his manners are so perfect that even Anne

4. Edmund Burke (1729–1797), statesman and political writer, who celebrated conservative values.
5. An allusion to John Locke (1632–1704), philosopher, author of the important treatise *On Education* (1693), and Philip Dormer Stanhope, fourth Earl of Chesterfield (1694–1773), whose letters to his illegitimate son constitute elaborate prescriptions for polished behavior.

can scarcely differentiate them from her true, beloved, Wentworth's. Anne's own manners are 'as consciously right as they were invariably gentle,' but as usual, in her constancy and genuine 'invariability,' she is an exception. With the vivid example of the absolute non-correlation between 'manners' and character presented by Mr Elliot we have to accept that 'good manners' in the socially accepted and prescribed sense are simply no longer of any use in estimating or infering the inner qualities of anyone. Perhaps a new code of manners altogether is necessary—manners which, however 'incorrect' or even crude according to established social notions of decorum and propriety, do nevertheless reveal the true qualities of the inner man, or woman. Anne, and Jane Austen, find them in the rougher but sincere manners of the navy.

As I have tried to indicate, the usual sources, strongholds and tokens of social values have, in *Persuasion*, dried up, collapsed, or been eroded or travestied into meaninglessness. Even the family—which did seem to offer the possibility of a last stronghold in *Emma*—is at best a good-humoured confusion barely containing generational differences and at worst a hollow mockery or a claustrophobic prison of cohabiting egotists or a dreary vacancy. It may indeed have already 'broken up'—specifically in Anne's case, but that might be taken as a paradigm for a more general dissolution of the institution of the family. Mrs Smith seems to recognise this when she gives her opinion that 'even the smooth surface of family-union seems worth preserving, though there may be nothing durable beneath.' It would be idle to speculate whether or not this was Jane Austen's own opinion. It does indicate a felt apprehension that the 'family' was in danger of becoming an empty form, a mere name—or collective noun—when it should be the cornerstone and microcosm of society. The fate and future of 'the family' is an ongoing debate and problem in our own times. Jane Austen could already see that it was at a crisis point. We have very little to add to her diagnosis. What Jane Austen does offer as a potential source of new values, new bondings is the navy. About which now a few comments.

The specific dating of this novel—1814 and after—and its obvious significance has been mentioned. Britain has won the wars against Napoleon and primarily through her navy. Many specific references to the war—including Trafalgar—are made in the book, and indeed the whole novel is not properly comprehensible without appreciating the importance of this background. As Warren Roberts rightly states, '*Persuasion* could only have been written by someone whose life was deeply affected by the Revolutionary and Napoleonic wars' (see *Jane Austen and the French Revolution* for detailed evidence of the relationship between the novel and the wars). The 'peace' brings Captain Wentworth back to England; more generally, 'This peace will be turning all our rich Navy Officers ashore.' That many of them *were* rich—through capturing

enemy ships and the like—is important, since, for example, it enables
the Crofts to rent Kellynch Hall and makes Wentworth completely independent of any snobbish social disapproval (such as had separated him
from Anne). Indeed, it makes him a 'somebody,' since money was
becoming a more powerful means of gaining social acceptance and
esteem than land or even rank. But what is more important is that they
bring back with them a wholly different scheme of values, and a potentially new model of an alternative society or community, alive and func-
tioning where the traditional land society seemed to be moribund and
largely 'stagnant'; a new community which, among other things,
accepted wives as equals. Thus Anne delights in seeing the Crofts walk
about Bath, meeting and warmly greeting their friends, and observing
'their eagerness of conversation when occasionally forming into a little
knot of the navy, Mrs Croft looking as intelligent and keen as any of
the officers around her.' That admiration and respect for 'a little knot
of the navy' brings Jane Austen curiously close to Conrad and his sense
of the hypocrisies of society on land and the values of fidelity within the
ranks in the navy. (As it happens he also uses the word 'knot': 'the dark
knot of seamen drifted in sunshine'—*The Nigger of the 'Narcissus.*';[6])
This, if you like, is Jane Austen's ultimate displacement or shift of values
in the novel: to redefine and relocate her vision of a 'possible' society in
relation to that most potentially precarious of occupations engaged with
the most unstable element—an unlanded and unrooted community of
people committed to the sea. Hardly a stable and fixed community,
since that 'knot' could be disassembled and reassembled, depleted and
augmented, indeed 'tied' or 'untied,' at any time and in any place. In
truth, the extreme of a dispersed community, a floating, drifting, changing, population which would have seemed the antithesis of the kind of
society Jane Austen was writing to secure or maintain. But by 1815
much had changed. For one thing it was the navy which—to Jane Austen's eyes—had saved England, while the ruling aristocratic class had
done almost nothing. Seen in this light, the fact that at Uppercross
'there was a very general ignorance of all naval matters' is deplorable,
while Sir Walter Elliot's unbelievably patronising and condescending
attitude to naval officers is beneath contempt. Without the navy there
quite possibly would no longer have been any society left in England.
(Jane Austen must have been aware of the invasion panics.) Her transfer
of allegiance and emotional investment from the English ruling classes
(about whom she had clearly been growing more and more pessimistic)
to the navy (which not only appealed to her patriotism but also embodied new and welcome alternative values) is doubly understandable at this
point in English history. Among other things, *Persuasion* is notable for
some uncharacteristically lyrical passages about the sea, which also help

6. Novel published in 1897 by Joseph Conrad (1857–1924).

to give the novel its markedly different atmosphere. (Emma, we may recall, had never seen the sea, and one of her father's more significant fatuities is, 'I have been long perfectly convinced . . . that the sea is very rarely of use to any body.' By this time the sea was 'of use'—of inestimable use—simply to the whole of England!) In the first description of the coast and sea at Lyme, so enchanting and beautiful in contrast to the 'melancholy looking rooms' and undistinguished buildings of the town, there is a curious sentence referring to the group 'lingering' on the sea-shore 'as all must linger and gaze on a first return to the sea, who ever deserve to look on it at all.' *Deserve* to look on the sea? Is this Jane Austen—or Melville? Here is a shift indeed. Not the awed and humble approach to Pemberley[7] or Mansfield Park; but the privilege, for those who deserve it, of gazing at—the sea. Jane Austen seems to be turning her back on more than just the local inanities of a Sir Walter Elliot.

Of course the navy is on shore throughout the novel, and it is the effect they have there and the part they play in Jane Austen's redefinition and relocation of values that we must consider. At one point the enthusiastic Louisa

> burst forth into raptures of admiration and delight on the character of the navy—their friendliness, their brotherliness, their openness, their uprightness; protesting that she was convinced of sailors having more warmth than any other set of men in England; that they only knew how to live, and they only deserved to be respected and loved.

Allowing a little for her youthful hyperbole, this is in many ways—and with moderation—the verdict of the book. Anne finds Captain Harville 'a perfect gentleman, unaffected, warm and obliging'—it would seem that, by another shift, only sailors can be true 'gentlemen': Mrs Harville is 'a degree less polished' but has the 'same good feelings.' Above all, this naval group (or knot) are sincere, hospitable, open, warm and genuinely friendly. What they might lack in 'polish' they more than made up for in 'heart.' In any case, Jane Austen never set great store by *mere* 'polish' and by now she clearly distrusts it. The older values seem to have lost much of their force and degenerated into snobbish reflexes. Where the older civilities are somewhat peremptorily adhered to, it is often in 'an improper style.' Anne of course holds on to what was best in the older practices and codes. She believes in 'duties,' in 'prudence' in 'propriety.' If she is somewhat shy and reserved, she appreciates the decent lack of these potentially inhibiting traits in others. Quiet herself, she responds to 'heartiness.' She suspects Mr Elliot precisely because he seems too controlled and good-mannered:

> Mr Elliot was rational, discreet, polished—but he was not open. There was never any burst of feeling, and warmth of indignation or

7. The splendid estate owned by Darcy in *Pride and Prejudice*.

delight, at the evil or good of others. This, to Anne was a decided imperfection. Her early impressions were incurable. She prized the frank, the open-hearted, the eager character beyond all others. Warmth and enthusiasm did captivate her still. She felt she could so much more depend upon the sincerity of those who sometimes looked or said a careless or hasty thing, than of those whose presence of mind never varied, whose tongue never slipped.

The passage speaks for itself; we remember that Emma's most significant transgression occurs precisely because her tongue slips and she says 'a careless and hasty thing' to Miss Bates, and to get some idea of the kind of change in Jane Austen's values it represents just think how a Darcy or Knightley would appear if tested by these criteria. These are primarily the manners of feeling, which may dispense with manners: spontaneity is always likely to annihilate etiquette. If we want to see a 'Romantic' side to Jane Austen, it would be in such passages. In a sense Jane Austen was fortunate to have the navy to turn to. Otherwise it is something of a question whether she would not have had to have gone further afield— perhaps into socially 'dangerous' areas—to find suitable embodiments of these preferred values and characteristics.

Anne is also always 'useful,' and willingly so, in anybody's home. (When Mary leaves her sick child in the care of Anne so that she can go to a dinner party, her excuse is 'I am of no use at home—am I?' It is the literal truth. In fact she is 'no use' anywhere. In this, she is not alone in the book.) When Anne speaks up for the navy—'The navy, I think, who have done so much for us, have at least an equal claim with any other set of men, for all the comforts and all the privileges which any home can give. Sailors work hard enough for their comforts, we must all allow'—Sir Walter speaks disparagingly of them as a class and merely allows that 'the profession has its utility.' But 'utility' is becoming a very positive word in this book. When someone is sick, Anne is glad to know herself 'to be of the first utility.' Whether or not there is some influence of Bentham[8] here it is impossible to say. But it is clear that for Jane Austen 'utility' was becoming a word of approval. We must allow, for instance, that Sir Walter and his ilk have no 'utility' whatsoever. 'Utility' is something which Anne has in common with the navy. All the more appropriate that she should find her true home here at last. Of course, there is already an example of a 'useful' woman happily integrated into the 'little knot of the navy'—Mrs Croft. From the start we gather that she is no 'lady' of idleness leaving the 'real' world to men. She is in fact better at business than her husband. 'A very well-spoken, genteel, shrewd lady, she seemed to be . . . [she] asked more questions about the

8. Jeremy Bentham (1748–1832) founded the Utilitarian movement in philosophy, which made usefulness the test of value.

house, the terms, and taxes than the admiral himself, and seemed more conversant with business.' Thus Mr Shepherd. When Anne meets Mrs Croft we are given the description of effectively a new kind of woman in Jane Austen's world. Quite outside any structure of dominance and deference, she seems to belong to no class at all. She is both inseparable from her husband—does all that may become a man—sharing all his travels; and also strongly independent—and still very much a woman. If she seems 'rougher' than many Jane Austen heroines, she is also in many not unadmirable ways tougher. Anne is not (yet!) like Mrs Croft. But she admires her.

> Mrs Croft, though neither tall nor fat, had a squareness, upright-ness and vigour of form, which gave importance to her person. She had bright dark eyes, good teeth, and altogether an agreeable face; though her reddened and weather-beaten complexion, the conse-quence of her having been almost as much at sea as her husband, made her seem to have lived some years longer in the world than her eight and thirty. Her manners were open, easy, and decided, like one who had no distrust of herself, and no doubts of what to do; without any approach to coarseness, however, or any want of good humour.

Anne is 'pleased' with her, and so are we. So, obviously, was Jane Aus-ten—and in that depiction of Mrs Croft she is offering a new model of a new kind of woman, scarcely imaginable in any of her previous novels. (One odd note: she is childless. But then Jane Austen never does actually *show* us a good mother. I think we must infer from this what we choose.)

A key area of the debate concerning old and new values concerns resolution and wilfulness. A central problem here hinges on Anne's early 'yielding' to the negative persuasion of Lady Russell, which effec-tively involved her supressing the love she felt for Wentworth and pre-venting a marriage both of them desired. Was she wrong? Did she show insufficient resolution and belief in her own instinct and desires? We shall leave a final adjudication until later, but her behaviour in fact poses a problem which reverberates through the book. For instance, in talking to Louisa (who boasts that she is not so 'easily persuaded' and derides 'nonsensical complaisance') Wentworth praises her for her 'char-acter of decision and firmness' and speaks with understandable bitterness against the opposite: 'It is the worst evil of too yielding and indecisive a character, that no influence over it can be depended on. . . . Everybody may sway it; let those who would be happy be firm.' And to emphasise his point he picks up a hazel nut—one of the rare emblematic aids to discourse in Jane Austen!—praising its exemplary enduring strength and hardness, and asserting, rather foolishly, that its 'happiness' is a function of its unpunctured 'firmness.' A 'nutty' happiness indeed, but not perhaps a very helpful model for a young—and virgin—woman! Is this fair to Anne? Was she too easily 'swayed'—too indecisive and lacking in firmness? It is at least something of a question. But Louisa's 'decision and firmness' reveal themselves most graphically on the Cobb. We have been told that Louisa has the habit of 'doing as she liked' and believed in 'the merit in maintaining her own way' (against 'parental wishes or advice') and is quick to advance 'heedless schemes.' On the Cobb she also wants her own way: this times it involves jumping from the steps into the arms of Wentworth. Enjoying the sensation, she expresses a wish and an intention to do it again. Wentworth 'reasoned' against it, but 'in vain': she smiled and said, 'I am determined I will.' And 'maintaining her own way' she jumps—too precipitously ('heedlessly'?)—and as everyone knows she falls and suffers a dangerous concussion. There lies the 'nut' of 'decision and firmness'! She indeed would not 'yield' to any 'persuasion,' however 'rational'—and she will not be 'swayed.' But how 'meritorious' or 'admirable' is that now? Is such a character trait of determined wilfulness a virtue or a rashness? Is it a real strength or an egotistical rashness (she not only causes damage to herself but great anguish and a lot of trouble to other people)? Is that jumping girl a finer character than the sedate and self-effacing—and apparently 'persuadable'—Anne? We might remember that another of the Musgrove children sustains a 'bad fall': young Charles falls and dislocates his collarbone in chapter 7. On that occasion 'Anne had every thing to do at once,' since Mary retires into useless hysterics, and all the duties and responsibilities devolve on Anne. As, of course, they do after Louisa's accident on the Cobb. There even Wentworth reveals an uncharacteristic sense of helplessness: 'Is there no one to help me?' These are unusual words from a Jane Austen hero. He is not omni-competent and once again all eyes turn to Anne for advice and direction. She effectively has to help and advise them all. These modern youngsters are attractive and lively, and perhaps engagingly adventurous and independent in their wilful heedlessness of external constraints—or advice. The Musgrove girls are 'wild for dancing,' 'wild to see Lyme'—'wild' is one of their favourite words and, as a word, harmless enough as a youthful hyperbole (as for a more recent young generation everything was 'fabulous,' 'fantastic,' and so on). But are they perhaps in fact *too* wild? After all, Elizabeth Elliot is also accustomed to 'go her own way' and there is nothing at all attractive about her ice-cold selfishness. After the Cobb incident Anne might well wonder whether

> it ever occurred to him [Wentworth] now, to question the justness of his own previous opinion as to the universal felicity and advantage of firmness of character; and whether it might not strike him that, like all other qualities of the mind, it should have its proportions and limits. She thought it could scarcely escape him to feel,

that a persuadable temper might sometimes be as much in favour
of happiness, as a very resolute character.

Of course she is right. Louisa, in 'jumping' at will, shows herself to have
a very 'yielding' character, but she yields to her own whims and caprices.
At least Anne thought that she was 'rationally' persuaded to yield to Lady
Russell. It comes back to the problem of authority in a period of change
when all traditional sources of authority are in doubt, if not disqualified
or defunct. Whose persuasion or advice should one—anyone—listen
to? When Wentworth cries for help he is articulating a larger need. In
the event, in this novel it is the apparently yielding but actually steadfast
Anne who becomes the authority to whom others turn. Wentworth's
'nut' lies sufficiently crushed to make us (and him) realise that she would
be in no way an appropriate wife for him. He says he wants 'A strong
mind, with sweetness of manner' in any wife he chooses. There is of
course only one candidate. Anne is not a 'nut'—that visual image for
the ideal wife was curiously infelicitous. For nuts are either totally hard
or totally smashed (I suppose they can also go rotten). Anne's strength
of character is peculiarly human. Which means that it must combine
flexibility and firmness, the concessionary and the adamant, the rights
of self with the obligations of selflessness, in a complex, ever-demanding
way. Wentworth is right in seeking for an alliance of strength and sweetness (the lion and the honeycomb). He is only wrong temporarily and
perhaps understandably—in not seeing that that ideal admixture is only
to be found in one woman (in this novel). Anne. Only Anne.

How Anne will discover Wentworth's true state of feelings, how she
will be able to convey her still 'unyielding' love for him, raises a problem
familiar in Jane Austen's work: namely, that of private communication
in a predominantly public world in which various taboos on certain
forms of direct address between the sexes are still operative. It is again a
problem of hermeneutics. 'Now, how were his sentiments to be read?'
After his return they are 'repeatedly in the same circle,' but that offers as
many chances for misreadings (on both sides) as it does opportunities for
reliable interpretation. People talk too little or too much. (As when
Anne finds herself the unwilling repository of the 'secrets of the complaints of each house.' Regarded as nothing herself, a permanently available pair of hands or ears, she is 'treated with too much confidence by
all parties.' On the other hand, the one man she wants to hear most
from says least. She cannot control these asymmetries and excesses or
shortfallings of communication.) Mary, inevitably, provides a constant
example of lack of all communicative tact—as when she asks Anne to
tell their father they have seen Mr Elliot. To Anne 'it was just the circumstance which she considered as not merely unnecessary to be communicated, but as what ought to be supressed.' For Jane Austen the
imperatives of verbal repression were as important as the obligations of

communication: social harmony depends on getting the balance right. Needless to say, in the world of *Persuasion* most people have lost that tact. Anne often has to 'smother' her own feelings and preoccupations, realising that they are of little or no interest to her interlocutors. She knows what it is to have to 'converse' without 'communicating.' She also knows what it is like to talk without being heard. 'They could not listen to her description of him. They were describing him themselves.' But of course her main concern is somehow to communicate with Wentworth and this in fact provides the climax of the book. At the concert near the end she is sure of his feelings and desperate to communicate hers. But she cannot contrive the necessary propinquity. As other Jane Austen women do, she has recourse to the eye—trying to catch Wentworth's when she is prevented from speaking to him: 'she was so surrounded and shut in: but she would rather have caught his eye.' But she is trapped by the unwelcome attentions of Mr Elliot and the general 'nothing-saying amongst the party.' How to find or create a place or position which would make 'something-saying' possible is again a recurrent problem for Jane Austen's heroines. Interestingly, she manages to choose a seat on the bench with a 'vacant space' next to her. Wentworth nearly takes it, but Mr Elliot breaks in. Here is a small parabolic tableau of the problem for a woman. She can create a space for the man but cannot invite him to take it. Man has to initiate, and if there is any hesitation the wrong (and more assertive) male may take advantage of that space. Mr Elliot does this—and a jealous Wentworth takes his departure. Anne still has her problem: 'How was the truth to reach him? How, in all the peculiar disadvantages of their respective situations, would he ever learn her real sentiments?'

So crucial is this problem that Jane Austen revised her first—excessively simple—resolution of it into two longer chapters which dramatise in detail the strategies of indirection to which the lovers have recourse. This revision (chapters 22 and 23) is of great subtlety and importance and is worth some particular examination and comment. In the first version Admiral Croft crudely contrives to leave them alone in his house and very quickly everything is cleared up. There is 'a hand taken and pressed; and "Anne, my own dear Anne!" bursting forth in the fulness of exquisite feeling,—and all suspense and indecision were over. They were re-united.' This is summary to a degree and a very lame solution to a problem which has been growing in importance until it becomes *the* main problem in the book. The revised and substituted chapters do not merely prolong the suspense and defer narrative gratification through gratuitous complication of plot: they comprise an infinitely richer and more searching examination of the whole problem of communication between man and woman.

The revised chapters add much. We learn more of the 'odious insin-

cerity' of Mr Elliot and his dubious connection with that other plotting
'hypocrite,' Mrs Clay, whose name is suggestive enough of a weak vessel
and whose 'freckles' not only indicate a flawed and 'spotted' moral inte-
rior but may indeed suggest the remnants or traces of syphilis. (In a very
interesting letter to *The Times Literary Supplement* on 7 October 1983,
Nora Crook points out that 'Gowland's Lotion,' which Sir Walter recommends to Anne 'on the strength of its supposed benefits to Mrs Clay's
freckles,' contained 'corrosive sublimate of mercury,' which 'had a particular connection with the old-fashioned treatment of syphilis.' Mrs
Crook produces evidence from contemporary journals such as *Reece's
Gazette of Health* and, while admirably tentative in drawing any conclusions, rightly points out that 'so few are references to actual trade-
names in Austen that one feels that this one must have had some sort of
function other than "realism." ' I agree completely and feel surer than
she does—though on no more evidence—that a hint of syphilis must be
intended. After all, Mrs Clay ends up in London as Mr Elliot's mistress
and thus with a status little better than that of a prostitute. The fact that
she was a welcome intimate of Sir Walter's and Elizabeth's, in preference to Anne, not only confirms the worst we feel about their utterly
corrupted judgement: it also suggests the presence of the most ruinous
sexual disease among the upper classes. She is a fitting 'partner' for the
totally corrupt Mr Elliot—who is also the heir of Kellynch Hall. A fine
end to be inscribed in that volume chronicling the 'history and rise of
the ancient and respectable family'!) We learn that Louisa is 'recovered'
but 'altered' (perhaps improved?). There is no 'running or jumping
about, no laughing or dancing.' Her newly acquired 'stillness' is not the
result of achieved moral poise and undistractability—the stillness which
Jane Austen admired—but the timorous cowering of a nervous wreck.

But centrally there is the extended problem of how Anne can communicate with Wentworth. It is he now who is acting under an 'unfortunate
persuasion': namely, that she loves Mr Elliot. In the crowded hotel
scene 'he did not seem to want to be near enough for conversation' and
the 'circumstances' only expose them to 'inadvertencies and misconstructions of the most mischievous kind.' Eyes and glances—surrepti-
tious, anxious, inquiring—are again active. More venturesomely (or
desperately) Anne speaks words to others which are meant obliquely for
Wentworth—as when she loudly proclaims her complete lack of interest
in a party being organised for the theatre which would include Mr
Elliot. She trembles as she speaks, 'conscious that her words were listened to, and daring not even to try to observe their effect.' When they
do have to exchange social conversation, Anne has recourse to another
strategy. Referring to trivia—whether she still enjoys card games—Anne
uses the occasion to transmit a second meta-message by emphasising
that 'I am not yet so much changed,' hoping that the generalising

response will not be lost on Wentworth—though she still fears 'she hardly knew what misconstructions.' It is indeed a tricky and dangerous game when a lifetime's happiness depends on the outcome. We may wonder at the need for all these tormenting ploys of indirection. Why cannot Anne be open and direct—qualities she admires in other people? The contrast is indeed made in the next chapter when Mrs Musgrove is talking. Her talk is marked by 'open-hearted communication,' but it is all concerned with personal 'minutiae' and Anne feels that 'she did not belong to the conversation.' The obstacle—effectively a double-bind— seems to be that you cannot speak 'openly' and 'directly' about such important matters as your feelings of love, *to* the person you love, until you have achieved a certain intimacy (tantamount to engagement) which *then* permits such open talk. But how do you ever manage to get intimate enough to be intimate, as it were? I don't think this is just a matter of tiresome, overdelicate etiquette or the repressive interdictions of propriety. It certainly has something to do with true modesty. More generally I think it dramatises the delicacy and difficulty of identifying and establishing the right sexual partner. That social conditions and codes made this particularly difficult in Jane Austen's period we can hardly doubt. But one feels that there is some deeper correlation between the delicacy of the approach and the value and quality of the ensuing union. We have gained much by our less inhibited and less formalised ways of achieving sexual and marital *rapprochements*. Argu- ably our loss has been no less great.

Be that as it may, we now approach the actual moment of full com- munication. How it is achieved—the context, the method—could hardly be more interesting. The general talk has become meaningless to Anne—'only a buzz of words in her ear.' She must look for (and send) the right signal in the noise. Then Captain Harville approaches Anne with a 'small miniature painting.' It is a portrait of Captain Benwick which was commissioned for Captain Harville's dead sister, Fanny. Benwick now wants it reset to give to Louisa, whom he is to marry. Harville finds the commission too painful and Wentworth has gallantly agreed to take care of it. He is seated nearby—'writing about it now,' as Harville explains. Harville almost tearfully muses that 'Fanny . . . would not have forgotten him so soon' and there ensues that debate about the relative constancy of men and women in their love. Anne argues that women do not forget so soon. 'We cannot help ourselves. We live at home, quiet, confined, and our feelings prey upon us. You are forced upon exertion . . . continual occupation and change soon weaken impressions.' Then follows a famous exchange in which Har- ville has recourse to the evidence and authority of literature—writing:

> But let me observe that all histories are against you, all stories, prose and verse. If I had such a memory as Benwick, I could bring

you fifty quotations in a moment on my side the argument, and I do not think I ever opened a book in my life which had not something to say upon women's inconstancy. . . . But perhaps you will say, these are all written by men.

Anne replies,

> 'Perhaps I shall.—Yes, if you please, no reference to examples in books. Men have had every advantage of us in telling their own story. Education has been theirs in so much higher a degree; the pen has been in their hands. I will not allow books to prove any thing.'
> 'But how shall we prove any thing?'
> 'We never shall.'

Painting, writing, speech. The portrait is a fixed representation or 'quotation' of the man which he can dispatch to different women. The man changes in his affections; the portrait remains 'constant.' In this it is precisely a misrepresentation—an ideal image of the man which leaves all his emotional changeableness out. However accurate as to physiognomy, it is untrue to life. It is a detached token which can be sent through intermediaries—Harville, Wentworth—to now this woman, now that. And potentially any other. It is in all respects the opposite of an unmediated confrontation of, and communication between, a living man and a living woman. In this the portrait comes dangerously close to being like a piece of money, a coin of fixed, arbitrary 'value' which can circulate through different hands and purchase any object to be obtained at the price on the coin. There need be no relationship between the purchaser and the object. Indeed, the whole mode of transaction is marked by separation and im-personality. The model for this kind of 'relationship' is ultimately the open market. This is not to impugn the feelings of reciprocity which may have gone into the 'relationship' of Benwick, but only to point out that it is *excessively* mediated. Benwick is a man who lives in and by books. He woos and wins Louisa by quotations and a portrait (as he did Fanny and, we feel, would have tried to do with Anne). They are signs which are precisely *not* his own, not himself. They are substitutions for an essential absence—emotional if not ontological. Anne has no access to totally unmediated communication, but she must avoid the kind of mediation briefly but tellingly here alluded to. And so must Wentworth. Benwick's books and Harville's allusion to his 'quotations' might remind us that at the start of *this* book Anne was effectively written *out* of meaningful life because she was not written *in* to Sir Walter's 'book of books.' She has suffered from male 'writing' since indeed 'the pen has been in their hands'—starting with the originating male authority, the father. Her argument has of course a general and very important validity, relevant to the condition of all women in her—and our—society. But one crucial little incident gives it a vividly local and specific point.

As she is arguing with Harville—and of course her words have a double target and dual purpose, as she hopes that the nearby Wentworth, seated and writing, will hear them and detect the personal message contained in the general statements—a 'slight noise' draws their attention to Wentworth. 'It was nothing more than that his pen had fallen down.' Nothing more—in many ways it is the most quietly dramatic and loaded incident on the book. The pen may, generally speaking, be in 'their hands'; but at this crucial moment the pen—a specific one—had dropped from *his*—specific—hand. However unintentionally, however momentarily, he is disproving the generalisation which Anne is enunciating. He is, perhaps by a 'slip,' excepting himself from—revealing himself as an exception to—the rule. We tend to read a lot of significance into 'slips' now, but, at no matter what level of conscious or unconscious intention, Wentworth's 'slip' in dropping the pen at that moment is perhaps the most important signal—or unvoiced communication—in his entire relationship with Anne. I am not concerned with possible phallic interpretations of 'the pen': literalness is quite powerful enough here. No single definitive reading of the incident is either possible or desirable. But we can say at least this: Wentworth at this critical moment has, however inadvertently, dropped (let go of, lost his grip on) that instrument which is at once a tool and a symbol of men's dominance over women; the means by which they rule women's destinies, literally *write* (through inscription, prescription, proscription) their lives. It is as if he is open to a more equal (unscripted) relationship in which the old patterns of dominance and deference are abandoned, deleted—dropped. Benwick quotes from already written books; Sir Walter wrote in his book according to an ancient and now non-functional scriptural tradition (his 'book of books' is only a bible for himself—a mere mirror instead of the authorising and authoritative sacred text). Wentworth was writing a commission for another person—he drops the pen and, after that crucial lacuna or interruption, when he picks it up again it is to 'speak' to Anne. Under the 'public' letter he writes for Harville and Benwick he now writes a 'private' letter—like a sub-text—to Anne, which he hides under scattered paper. He goes out—formally—with Harville, and returning under false pretences (left gloves), furtively delivers the hidden—but 'true'—letter to Anne. Significantly the writing is 'hardly legible': we may guess that the impersonal 'public' letter was in a perfect hand. The hidden letter was indeed not really written, but rather 'spoken.' As he writes in it, 'I must speak to you by such means as are within my reach.' It is the desperate calligraphy of the heart—written under pressure and social constraints. No wonder it is 'hardly legible.' For this speechwriting is not done according to prescribed formulae or convention: it is an 'exceptional'

writing which seeks to find a way through all the restraining and silenc-
ing rules and codes to communicate directly to the chosen woman. It
attempts the apparently impossible—mediated im-mediacy. Like love.
There is no need here to reproduce the contents of that letter-under-the-
letter. With its delivery and reading the 'union' is assured. But two final
points about it. Anne realises that, 'while supposed to be writing only to
Captain Benwick, he had been also addressing her.' No doubt some of
this final drama (or game) can be traced to the specific difficulties of
intersexual communication in Jane Austen's society. But the episode
points up and dramatises a larger truth. All 'writing' or communication
is potentially double (at least exoteric and esoteric, to go no further: there
may always be another message in—under—the ostensible message); we
can 'address' more than one person at the same time, and likewise be
'addressed' by messages not apparently meant for us. Indeed, one might
say that the addresser and the addressee of the letter—all 'letters'—are
potentially indeterminate and plural. There is ultimately no single,
definitively correct 'address.' The problems and difficulties which Anne
and Wentworth have to negotiate are not a function of early nineteenth-
century English society. They are inherent in language and communication itself. How important is this rather singular little parlour 'game'?
Well—'On the contents of that letter depended all which this world
could do for her!' Life, and all that it might offer, can indeed depend on
'the letter.' It is a final joke that informs us that, as Wentworth is now
rich enough to be 'accepted' as a husband for Anne by her father, it
'enabled Sir Walter at last to prepare his pen with a very good grace for
the insertion of the marriage in the volume of honour.' It is of course a
dead volume by now and the paternal pen is as irrelevant as it is power-
less. Anne and Wentworth will 'write' their own marriage elsewhere, in
a new book, in their own hands. Of course they will never 'prove' anything by the book, any book. When it comes to matters of love we can
never *prove* anything—by writing, or speaking, or painting. And we
never shall. When Othello asks Iago for 'ocular proof' of Desdemona's
infidelity, he is lost. Her honour is 'an essence that's not seen.' You may
fake 'proof' of infidelity (nothing easier for an Iago) and misread signs
(and books) as evidence of inconstancy. But you cannot *prove* love—any
more than you can 'see' honour or constancy. You must finally trust
beyond the available evidence. The proof of the loving can only be in
the living.

Before leaving the matter of language and communication in this
novel, I want to draw attention to a rather surprising notion which Jane
Austen inserts into Anne's thoughts while she is listening to another
social conversation which combines the vacuous and the hyperbolic.
'Allowances, large allowances, she knew, must be made for the ideas of
those who spoke. She heard it all under embellishment. All that sounded
extravagant or irrational in the progress of the reconciliation might have

no origin but in the language of the relators' (emphasis added). Of course social conversation can lie and fabricate—nothing unusual in such an observation. But Anne's thought is potentially more radical. Allow that language 'embellishes'; but what if *all* that people talk about has 'no origin but in the language of the relators'? Put it another way: language may be the origin of all that people relate. It is perhaps not such a new idea for us, but, coming out of the context in which Jane Austen was writing, the hint (it is perhaps no more) that language itself might be the origin of what we talk about—i.e., that language is the origin of what we think of as reality—is here startling. Language thus becomes capable of creating its own referents *and* referends—an awesomely autonomous, generative, and 'originating' power. If in fact we live primarily in the world we speak, then we should be careful indeed about the words we use. Jane Austen herself exemplifies that indispensable vigilance and scrupulousness.

What follows the final achieving of clarification and communication between Anne and Wentworth is characteristically summary. They stroll along a 'retired gravel-walk' and there can indulge their 'private rapture' in 'public view.' As usual Jane Austen does not pursue them into their private passional discourse. Whether we ascribe this to ignorance, repression or delicacy hardly matters. Jane Austen has shown us all that is essential to her novel; now she maintains a tactful distance.

> There they exchanged again those feelings and those promises which had once before seemed to secure every thing, but which had been followed by so many, many years of division and estrangement. There they returned again into the past more exquisitely happy, perhaps, in their re-union, than when it had been first projected. . . .

And so on. There they are oblivious of the passing groups—'sauntering politicians, bustling house-keepers, flirting girls, nursery-maids and children.' The 'world' is temporarily lost, and well lost. They have made 'a separate peace.' But we should add a few words about Anne and her marriage. In some respects she is like Fanny Price, with her 'still' virtues, her essential loneliness, her general desire 'not to be in the way of any body'; her pleasure is only to be 'unobserved,' her plight to be generally overlooked. She is glad just to do her duty and to be 'useful,' however unappreciated. In her apparent weakness she is the real source of strength. But there is a crucial difference, related to the larger difference between the two worlds of the novels. At one point in the confusion of Uppercross, we are told of an insuperable problem: 'How was Anne to set all these matters to rights?' Fanny Price does effectively 'set to rights' all the wrongs, neglects, and partial deteriorations of Mansfield Park—which becomes something of a microcosm of society as it should be and might be. Anne's healing efforts are necessarily more local and limited in the scattered and diffused world of *Persuasion*. She would have put her father's house 'to rights' but is not allowed to. She can nurse a sick child here, tend a wounded girl there, sympathise with a grieving bereft lover, provide concrete help when Wentworth cries out for it (a hint of a possible new equality there). But society is too far gone in disarray to be 'put to rights' by an exemplary heroine. Fanny Price's marriage to Edmund symbolises and seals the restoration and renewal of a whole social order and structure. Anne's marriage to Wentworth signifies nothing larger than their own refound and reconstituted happiness in love. Their 're-union' is not a sign of any larger re-established harmony. To borrow that enigmatic and resonant phrase of Jay Gatsby's,[9] it is 'just personal.'

Their marriage is not grounded in property—as all the previous concluding marriages in Jane Austen are. Mary—of course—gloats that Anne 'had no Uppercross-hall before her, no landed estate, no headship of a family.' And indeed it is one of Anne's regrets that she has 'no relations to bestow' on Wentworth, 'no family to receive and estimate him properly.' In fact it is he who offers a family—the new 'family' of the navy. She brings to him only her 'undistracted heart,' in Henry James's memorable phrase. The marriage itself does not portend an endless stability: there will always be 'the dread of a future war.' She has to 'pay' for her marital happiness in a way unknown to any previous Jane Austen heroine. Thus the conclusion: 'She gloried in being a sailor's wife, but she must pay the tax of quick alarm for belonging to that profession which is, if possible, more distinguished in its domestic virtues than in its national importance.' (Contrast the conclusion of *Mansfield Park* and Fanny's return to the 'paternal abode' of Mansfield, which formerly 'Fanny had been unable to approach but with some painful sensation of restraint and alarm' but which 'soon grew as dear to her heart, and as thoroughly perfect in her eyes as every thing else within the view and patronage of Mansfield Park, had long been.' Her 'alarm' was definite but is in the past, replaced by an extended future of assured happiness and 'perfection.' Anne's 'alarm' is indefinite and in the future—an integral part of her happy marriage, out of an old society and into a new one, far away from the abandoned 'paternal abode,' with nothing assured except her joy in her reciprocated love.) The final words of *Persuasion* effectively point to that radical redefinition and relocation of values which marks the whole novel. Established society and domesticity are now, as we say, 'all at sea'—metaphorically (they are in a state of chronic confusion, chaotic flux) but also literally. For the new social and domestic virtues are now to be found, indeed, 'at sea'—for those 'who ever deserve to look on it at all.'

(To base a marriage almost exclusively on feelings, no matter how

---

9. Protagonist of *The Great Gatsby* (1925) by F. Scott Fitzgerald (1896–1940).

tested and proved those feelings may be, inevitably entails a *new* kind of 'risk.' It is more than apt that this new kind of model for a more personal society, in which actions come 'from the heart,' is situated both metaphorically and actually on the sea—traditionally regarded as 'the unstable element.' Even though Anne and Wentworth are models of emotional stability and constancy, the emotions are by nature inherently potentially unstable, and, without the reinforcement of some forms—formalities—and conventions, any society based on feelings must be precarious and in danger of ensuring its own impermanence. In founding a possible new society on the sea, even metaphorically, Jane Austen was engaging deliberately in what is almost a contradiction of terms. It is some measure of her disenchantment with 'landed' society that she felt prepared, or compelled, to take that risk.)

Was Anne right to give in to the 'persuasion' of Lady Russell? There is rich ambiguity or hesitation here, and phrases such as 'the fair interference of friendship' in their poised ambivalence indicate that Jane Austen knew all about the multiple motivations which are at work in the impulse to exert some apparently beneficent control over a person in a weaker position. There is, perhaps, no point at which you can clearly distinguish persuasion from constraint or constraint from coercion. It is something of a blur, a confusion if you will—and it is out of just that confusion that Anne the nobody has somehow to come to clarification and remake her life. In discussing the point with Wentworth at the end of the book, when they are privately conversing while 'apparently occupied in admiring a fine display of green-house plants' (a somewhat more auspicious adjunct to a discussion of love than 'nuts'!), Anne defends her decision without wholly exculpating Lady Russell:

> I must believe that I was right, much as I suffered from it, that I was perfectly right in being guided by the friend whom you will love better than you do now. To me, she was in the place of a parent. Do not mistake me, however. I am not saying that she did not err in her advice. It was, perhaps, one of those cases in which advice is good or bad only as the event decided; and for myself, I certainly never should, in any circumstance of tolerable similarity, give such advice.

Lady Russell is by no means one of Jane Austen's malign characters. On the contrary she is a 'benevolent, charitable, good woman, and capable of strong attachments.' She is genuinely fond of Anne and truly appreciates all her qualities and virtues. Anne loves her to the end. She is indeed regarded by all who know her as a person of 'the greatest influence with every body,' and that 'influence' is often wisely employed and invariably with disinterested concern for what is right or best. If she has a fault, it is not a kind of masked will-to-power masquerading as good advice. But

'she had prejudices on the side of ancestry . . . a value for rank and consequence, which blinded her a little to the faults of those who possessed
them.' In a word, she favours the old order of society and cannot always
see its derelictions and delinquencies. She is not—as she insists—a
'match-maker,' though we can see her as a 'match-marrer' when it comes
to not appreciating the reality and value of Anne's and Wentworth's love
for each other. But her real importance and significance is that, for
Anne, 'she was in the place of a parent'—a surrogate mother. This brings
me back to the central problem of the lack of any reliable properly constituted authority in the book. Effectively Lady Russell fills—and is allowed
to fill—an authority vacuum. As far as my memory and my notes go, I
think I am right in saying that that key word is only once applied to any
character in the book, and that is Lady Russell. When Wentworth is
explaining to Anne that he could only think of her as 'one who had
yielded,' who had been 'influenced by any one rather than by me,' he
is referring to his apprehensions about the persuasive power which Lady
Russell might still be exerting over Anne: 'I had no reason to believe her
of less *authority* now' (emphasis added). As Anne explains, she thought
she was yielding to 'duty,' and, while she now admits she was wrong, she
makes the point that she was yielding to 'persuasion exerted on the side
of safety, not of risk.' Perhaps she was too cautious, but she learnt her
lesson and she is justified, in the event, when Wentworth comes to see
where 'risk' can lead to—as in Louisa's foolish jump. (Emma, in her
capricious wilfulness, often abuses her powers of 'persuasion': for example, in relation to Harriet's 'rejection' of the perfectly suitable Robert
Martin—as Knightley angrily accuses her, 'You persuaded her to refuse
him'; and in relation to herself, as when she excuses herself for her 'deficiency' in not visiting the Bateses by 'the persuasion of its being very
disagreeable—a waste of time—tiresome women'—a perverse act of self-
persuasion which, at 'heart,' she herself knows to be a culpable rationali-
sation for a more selfishly and snobbishly motivated disinclination and
neglect.)

Wentworth had to learn his own lesson, 'to distinguish between the
steadiness of principle and the obstinacy of self-will, between the darings
of heedlessness and the resolution of a collected mind.' The old order
was wrong; but Louisa's reaction is not the right one—self-destructive
rather than reconstructive. Lady Russell's 'authority' was capable of
error, but with no other reliable authority available in this society-with-
out-a-centre (as in Anne's family-without-parental-guidance), it seemed
to Anne—as to others—the only reliable substitute. But it *was* a substitute. Lady Russell is *not* Anne's mother and she is not a true central
authority in society. And it is the lesson that *she* has to learn that is as
important as any in the book. It is a lesson which centres on her radically
incorrect appraisals of the respective worth of Mr Elliot and Wentworth:

She must learn to *feel* that she had been mistaken with regard to both; that she had been unfairly influenced by appearances in each; that because Captain Wentworth's *manners* had not suited her own ideas, she had been too quick in suspecting them to indicate a character of dangerous impetuosity; and that because Mr Elliot's manners had precisely pleased her in their *propriety* and *correctness*, their general *politeness* and suavity, she had been too quick in receiving them as the certain result of the most correct opinions and well regulated mind. There was nothing less for Lady Russell to do, than to admit that she had been pretty completely wrong and to take up a new set of opinions and of hopes. [Emphasis added]

There is no more important passage in the novel. We remember that Anne had been 'prudent' (an old and basic Jane Austen value) but had had to learn 'romance.' Similarly Lady Russell will have to learn to re-educate her 'feelings' when judging people and not rely on the once-reliable signs of 'propriety' and 'correctness,' 'manners' and 'politeness.' In a changing society a more emotional, 'romantic' personal code is emerging as both desirable and necessary—with a proper appreciation of the difference between 'spontaneity' and 'impetuousness,' between the mere rashness of 'risk' and the securely grounded independence of individual feelings, whether or not these seem to be approved and ratified by the old standards and codes of society. The lesson that Lady Russell has to learn is not in itself revolutionary or subversive, but it does represent a radical assessment—and turning away from—many of the old values. I have said that Anne was initially 'in between,' an uncertain status both socially and ontologically. The novel shows that English society is similarly 'in between': in between an old social order in a state of decline and desuetude, and some new 'modern' society of as yet uncertain values, hierarchies and principles. It may precipitately 'jump' to its own destruction and wreckage (like Louisa). It may, though it is a slim hope, reconstitute itself and its values as Anne—and 'only Anne'— has learnt to do with Wentworth. Meanwhile the message within the message of the book, the not-so-hidden 'letter' under the text of the story, reads like this: 'There was nothing less for English society to do, than to admit that it had been pretty completely wrong, and to take up a new set of opinions and hopes.'

ROBERT HOPKINS

Moral Luck and Judgment in Jane Austen's *Persuasion* †

> *Prospero.* they prepared
> A rotten carcass of a butt, not rigged,
> Nor tackle, sail, nor mast; the very rats
> Instinctively have quit it. There they hoist us,
> To cry to th' sea that roared to us.
> . . . .
> *Miranda.* How came we ashore?
> *Prospero.* By providence divine.
> —*The Tempest*

> ". . . and here was another instance of luck. We had not been six hours in the Sound, when a gale came on, which lasted four days and nights, and which would have done for poor old Asp, in half the time; . . . Four-and-twenty hours later, and I should only have been a gallant Captain Wentworth, in a small paragraph at one corner of the newspapers; and being lost in only a sloop, nobody would have thought about me." —*Persuasion*

I shall begin with a hypothetical case involving a moral judgment: Anne, a nineteen-year-old woman with "elegance of mind and sweetness of character," is living in England in 1806. Her mother had died five years earlier. Anne's father is a self-centered baronet with no male heir who is living well beyond his means, and her unmarried oldest sister is equally vain. She also has a younger sister. An aristocratic widow lives nearby who was a close friend of the deceased mother and who is a trusted moral advisor of Anne. A handsome, dynamic naval captain on shore leave meets Anne, and they fall "rapidly and deeply in love." Although having "been lucky in his profession," the captain has no fortune and faces a dangerous future in naval combat. He proposes to Anne. The father does not overtly oppose the marriage but thinks it a "degrading alliance." Anne's moral advisor discourages her and finds the marriage proposal "unfortunate." What is Anne to do? (One stipulation: there can be no long engagement.)

The moral judgment occurs, of course, in Jane Austen's last great novel *Persuasion* (1816, publ. 1817). Anne Elliot turns down Captain Frederick Wentworth on the advice of Lady Russell who "persuaded" her to believe the engagement "a wrong thing—indiscreet, improper, hardly capable of success, and not deserving it." Why else does Anne turn down the proposal? Not for a "merely selfish caution" but in a

† Robert Hopkins, "Moral Luck and Judgment in Jane Austen's *Persuasion*," *Nineteenth-Century Literature* 42(1987): 143–58. Reprinted with the permission of the author. All notes are by the editor of this Norton Critical Edition. The author's notes have been deleted.

"belief of being prudent, and self-denying principally for [Captain Wentworth's] advantage" as well. Dismayed, hurt, and angered, the Captain returns to the sea to assume his first command of a sloop, the Asp, to succeed wonderfully in capturing prizes of war, and eight years later to return to Anne's neighborhood with a fortune of over twenty thousand pounds. *Persuasion* gives Anne Elliot a second chance at happiness with Wentworth after he overcomes his pride and diffidence to propose to her again at the end of the narrative in Jane Austen's most memorable love scene. This time Anne accepts but, reflecting on her earlier moral judgment, she believes that because Lady Russell was "in the place of a parent" she was right to take her advice. "Perhaps," Anne rationalizes to Wentworth, this was "*one of those cases in which advice is good or bad only as the event decides*" (italics mine).

This is an extraordinary statement! How can a subsequent event be the determinant of whether a moral decision is right or wrong? Suppose, for example, that Captain Wentworth had married Anne, returned to sea, been severely wounded in battle and then returned to Anne, like Rochester in *Jane Eyre*, blinded, and, in addition, destitute? Would this scenario have proved Lady Russell morally right? Or suppose Anne had married and had a daughter, and Wentworth had died at sea but had not yet earned his fortune? This scenario will immediately remind Austenites of Jane Fairfax's origins in *Emma*: "The marriage of Lieut. Fairfax, of the——regiment of infantry, and Miss Jane Bates, had had its day of fame and pleasure, hope and interest; but nothing now remained of it, save the melancholy remembrance of him dying in action abroad—of his widow sinking under consumption and grief soon afterwards—and this girl."

Is Anne Elliot merely assuming a providential universe in which whatever happens is right? Is she intuitively recognizing what twentieth-century moral philosophy calls "consequentialism"? And is Jane Austen projecting into her last novel a reconsideration of the moral implications of her earlier prudential plots that, in spite of her hard-boiled, no-nonsense vision, reward her heroines with marriage and with fortune? Leopold Damrosch, Jr., who has studied Puritan and eighteenth-century "providential fiction" metaphysically modelling itself on "God's plan" believes that after Fielding English novelists bid "farewell to providential fiction" (with some exceptions) and that "Jane Austen based her fictions firmly in the contemporary social order" with heroines "learning to accommodate [themselves] to the world as it is." Austen's fiction might be viewed as *prudential* fiction because of its emphasis on individual moral judgments being made in the context of a secular problematic social world. Anne Elliot's rationalization that "the event" may decide the goodness or badness of moral judgment suggests consequentialism—defined by Alan Donagan as actions "judged morally solely according to the nature of their consequences per *se*"—or, more specifically, "act-consequentialism," described by Michael Slote as "a theory that judges the rightness of actions in terms of whether those actions have optimal consequences."

Although consequentialism is an outgrowth in twentieth-century ethics of utilitarianism, the moral problem it reflects, whether we judge an action's rightness or wrongness by its effects or by the purity of the agent's motive (as Kant had insisted), had been wrestled with by Adam Smith in *The Theory of Moral Sentiments* (1759):

> But how well soever we may seem to be persuaded of the truth of this equitable maxim [that a moral action should not be judged by it unintended consequences], when we consider it . . . in abstract, yet when we come to particular cases, the actual consequences which happen to proceed from any action, have a very great effect upon our sentiments concerning its merit or demerit.

It is precisely the "particular cases" and "actual consequences" of a novel like Henry Fielding's *Tom Jones* (1749) that can best spotlight the difficulties of judging moral actions solely by motives. Squire Allworthy is a well-intentioned, morally obtuse magistrate/patriarch whose moral judgments in the first third of the narrative are well-nigh catastrophic. Martin C. Battestin has shown how the narrator's thesis that "Goodness of Heart, and Openness of Temper" are not enough to do "Business in the World," that "Prudence and Circumspection are necessary even to the best of Men," relates to Fielding's focus on Christian practical wisdom, to *Prudentia*, one of the four cardinal virtues. Allworthy, then, means well but lacks prudence when he is emotionally involved. He judges that Jenny Jones is Tom's mother because Jenny tells him so, not realizing that Jenny is covering up for Tom's real mother Miss Bridget Allworthy. Next he judges Partridge to be Tom's father on the basis of Mrs. Partridge's perjury. (Partridge is condemned by the community, his wife dies, he loses his annuity and his school, is forced to leave the area, and is eventually sent to prison.) Black George is judged falsely for wiring hares because of Blifil's lying. Allworthy almost sends Molly Seagram to Bridewell prison for bastardy until Tom intercedes. Eventually Tom himself is exiled from Paradise Hall when Blifil again lies to Allworthy. R. S. Crane grossly understated the case when he wrote of Allworthy that "in spite of his excellent principles, it is hard for us to maintain entire respect" for him, particularly when he could "dispose so precipitously" of Jenny Jones and Partridge. Though the comic tone of the work tends to suspend our moral judgment, we are horrified by the failures of Allworthy's moral judgment, particularly on subsequent readings of the novel when we no longer share his ignorance. We could argue that judged purely on motive Allworthy is intrinsically good but that judged solely on the consequences of his judgments he has much to answer for. The problem of Allworthy is the ethical dilemma raised by consequentialism.

Bernard Williams and Thomas Nagel, two well-known contemporary philosophers, have dealt with the complexities of this dilemma in two essays entitled "Moral Luck." Williams, writing in the Humean tradition of skepticism, coined the provocatively shocking term "moral luck" to show that no matter how far back "in the "direction of motive and intention" we place "the dispositions of morality," they are "as 'conditioned' as anything else." Williams' fictitious case study is that of a would-be painter named Gauguin who deserts his wife and five children in order to dedicate himself to the vocation of artist. Should Gauguin drown while crossing the English Channel, his decision will be judged as immoral. Should he succeed in his vocation and become a world famous painter, his decision will be judged consequentially. Since his paintings will benefit mankind his decision would be a right one. Thomas Nagel cites the case of Chamberlain signing the Munich agreement. Suppose Hitler had died of a heart attack after occupying the Sudetenland, and then Germany had not overrun Europe exterminating millions? Since Chamberlain's motives and intentions were presumably moral, to prevent war, his action at Munich while betraying the Czechs would "not be the great moral disaster that has made his name a household word." Nagel defines moral luck as occurring where "a significant aspect of what someone does depends on factors beyond his control, yet we continue to treat him in that respect as an object of moral judgment." He outlines "four ways in which the natural objects of moral assessment are disturbingly subject to luck":

> One is the phenomenon of constitutive luck—the kind of person you are, where this is not just a question of what you deliberately do, but of your inclinations, capacities, and temperament. Another category is luck in one's circumstances—the kind of problems and situations one faces. . . . [Then there is] luck in how one is determined by antecedent circumstances, and luck in the way one's actions and projects turn out.

"However jewel-like the good will may be in its own right," Nagel continues, "there is a morally significant difference between rescuing someone from a burning building and dropping him from a twelfth-storey window while trying to rescue him." (Were I that someone, needless to say, I or my estate's attorney would take a consequentialist rather than a Kantian point of view stressing intention.) Not himself a consequentialist, Nagel agrees with Williams that there is a genuine "philosophical problem" involved with any attempt to insist on the purity of moral judgments isolated from events: "The view that moral luck is paradoxical is not a *mistake*, ethical or logical, but a perception of one of the ways in which the intuitively acceptable conditions of moral judgment threaten to undermine it all."

In the context of moral luck so formidably presented by Williams and Nagel how are we to interpret Anne Elliot's event-governed moral judgments? And what does Jane Austen mean us to think? In *Pride and Prejudice* Charlotte Lucas had claimed that "Happiness in marriage is entirely a matter of chance," and Elizabeth Bennet had replied, "You make me laugh, Charlotte; but it is not sound. You know it is not sound, and that you would never act in this way yourself." (Charlotte does "act in this way" when she marries Mr. Collins.) All of Austen's heroines in her earlier novels seem clearly to argue for *not* relying on chance or luck in marital matters. Not only do these heroines judge prudently, but they are rewarded with marriage to like-minded men who are comfortably situated. Their judgments are based on what David A. J. Richards (a twentieth-century Kantian philosopher) defines as a "principle of mutual love requiring that people should not show personal affection and love to others on the basis of arbitrary physical characteristics alone, but rather on the basis of traits of personality and character related to acting on moral principles."

Bernard Williams refers to this position as "righteous absurdity." Why do Austen's admiring readers—and I count myself among them—experience a similar reaction to some of the too prudish moral judgments of the two problem novels *Sense and Sensibility* and *Mansfield Park*? Williams objects to Kantian moral philosophy for its tendency to treat "persons in abstraction from character," for abstracting "moral thought" from "particular circumstances and particular characteristics of the parties" involved, and for failing to recognize that "love, even love based on 'arbitrary physical characteristics,' is something which has enough power and even authority to conflict badly with morality." This conflict between truth and morality poised by Williams is what we surely must feel when Austen marries off Marianne Dashwood to Colonel Brandon *before* she falls in love with him.[1] We know that Edward Ferrars is too indecisive for Elinor Dashwood and that it is Elinor who should have married Brandon. We resent a plot ending morally at the expense of truth.

Barbara Hardy has noted how even in *Persuasion* the conventions of the romantic novel save Anne Elliot from the "consequences of her choice." She has also noted the emphasis in *Persuasion* on "human luck or chance" but disapprovingly, as if Austen were using it to resolve the plot at the expense of genuine artistry. As Paul N. Zietlow showed over twenty years ago, however, Austen's emphasis on luck in the novel is intentional and not to be taken lightly. Since Zietlow's 1965 essay, the important new insights in ethical philosophy on "moral luck" and consequentialism now enable us to see that Jane Austen is struggling with a

---

1. The situations alluded to in this and the next sentence belong to *Sense and Sensibility*.

major dilemma of moral judgment by placing that judgment in the context of moral luck where a providential universe is invisible to the moral agent.

How radical this is can be illustrated by a little-known episode involving Samuel Johnson's friend, the editor of the *Adventurer* paper, John Hawkesworth. In 1773 Hawkesworth's edition of the *Voyages* to the South Seas was published, an edition containing the first publication of Captain Cook's first voyage to Tahiti, New Zealand, and Australia. Eagerly awaited by the public, this authorized edition shocked readers not only by its salacious descriptions of Tahitian mores, but by Hawkesworth's "Providential heresy" in his general introduction. When Cook's ship, the Endeavour, risks being sunk on a reef but is saved by the wind subsiding, Hawkesworth refuses to see providence at work but merely a "natural event." For the next five months until his death in November, 1773, Hawkesworth was hounded by reviews and letters in the major periodicals attacking his rejection of particular providence. The episode resurfaces in Boswell's *Life of Johnson*. On their tour of the Hebrides, Boswell and Johnson are caught in rough seas off the Isle of Skye. Johnson is below deck while Boswell is above. Terrified, Boswell claims to have remembered Hawkesworth's objection against a particular providence and the "arguments of those who maintain that it is in vain to hope that the petitions of the individual, or even of congregations, can have any influence with the Deity." Boswell regains his equilibrium, however, when he remembers "Dr. Ogden's excellent doctrine on the efficacy of intercession."

Providence has been traditionally a tacit frame for mariners' discourse as evidenced by *Robinson Crusoe*, Boswell, or by Cowper's "The Castaway" illustrating religious despair. It should have come as a bit of a shock to Jane Austen's readers, then, when Captain Wentworth, just before his first proposal, is described as follows:

> Captain Wentworth had no fortune. He had been lucky in his profession, but spending freely, what had come freely, had realized nothing. But, he was confident that he should soon be rich;—full of life and ardour, he knew that he should soon have a ship, and soon be on a station that would lead to every thing he wanted. He had always been lucky; he knew he should be so still.

This description has an insouciant ring to it, capturing perhaps the attitude of Jane Austen's own two brothers who were naval officers confronted with the random nature of naval warfare and of storms at sea. Even Lady Russell, who earlier had been so cautious, tries to persuade Anne to consider the attentions of Mr. Elliot, but first explains that she is "no match-maker . . . being much too well aware of the uncertainty of all human events and calculations." "Uncertainty" indeed! Had Lady Russell genuinely recognized that many moral actions involve "judg-

ment under uncertainty," that risk and moral luck are especially inherent in match-making, she would not have discouraged Anne from
marrying Wentworth.

Anne suffers throughout *Persuasion* for her earlier moral failure to
take risks for love. Admiral and Mrs. Croft did take such risks. When
the Crofts speculate about Wentworth proposing to one of the Miss
Musgroves, the Admiral exclaims, "If it were war, now, he would have
settled it long ago.—We sailors, Miss Elliot, cannot afford to make long
courtships in time of war. How many days was it, my dear, between the
first time of my seeing you, and our sitting down together in our lodgings
at North Yarmouth?" Mrs. Croft replies, "We had better not talk about
it, my dear, . . . for if Miss Elliot were to hear how soon we came to an
understanding, she would never be persuaded that we could be happy
together. I had known you by character, however, long before." A long
engagement would clearly not have been an alternative action for Anne
Elliot and Wentworth, and the Crofts' discussion is extremely painful
for Anne. Mrs. Croft later repeats her objection to long engagements to
Mrs. Musgrove while Anne and Wentworth overhear: "I would rather
have young people settle on a small income at once, and have to struggle
with a few difficulties together, than be involved in a long engagement."

And what of Wentworth's own sense of providence, divine intercession, or moral luck when at sea? When Admiral Croft and Wentworth
reminisce—Anne and the Musgroves are listening—Wentworth jests
about the admiralty "now and then . . . sending a few hundred men to
sea, in a ship not fit to be employed" because they "have a great many
to provide for; and among the thousands that may just as well go to the
bottom as not, it is impossible for them to distinguish the very set who
may be least missed." The Admiral counters twice with "Lucky fellow,"
reminding Wentworth that there were at least "twenty better men" who
had applied for command of the Asp. "I felt my luck, admiral," replies
Wentworth. The emphasis on moral luck continues with Wentworth
never having "two days of foul weather all the time he was at sea,"
having "the good luck" then to capture a French frigate, and, finally, as
"another instance of luck," bringing his vessel into Plymouth just before
a four-day gale which would have almost certainly sent it to the bottom:
"Four-and-twenty hours later, and I should only have been a gallant
Captain Wentworth, in a small paragraph at one corner of the newspapers." No wonder that Anne shudders to herself.

The supreme irony of all this occurs when Anne learns that Captain
Benwick was engaged to Captain Harville's sister, that *he* had been waiting two years for a promotion and fortune before marrying, only to discover tragically that his fiancée had died the previous summer while he
was at sea. Suppose in another scenario that Anne had insisted on a prudent long engagement, that Wentworth had returned to sea to seek his
fortune, and that Anne had died! At numerous places in the narrative

Anne is reminded of moral luck: to try to avoid in marriage "the uncertainty of all human events and calculations" is to avoid living itself.

Clearly Jane Austen is struggling in *Persuasion* with the problem of moral judgment under uncertainty. I believe that she is also reconsidering the ethical implications of her earlier plots which too readily reward prudential moral judgments with fortunate resolutions. Authorial ambivalence seems to me to be unmistakably articulated in the first three sentences of the final chapter of the novel:

> Who can be in doubt of what followed? When any two young people take it into their heads to marry, they are pretty sure by perseverance to carry their point, be they ever so poor, or ever so imprudent, or ever so little likely to be necessary to each other's ultimate comfort. *This may be bad morality to conclude with, but I believe it to be truth.* [italics mine]

Had Anne and Wentworth married eight years sooner, they would have been poor, imprudent,—and very much in love. All the weight of the narrative—the Crofts, Captain and Mrs. Harville, Captain Benwick and his deceased fiancée—argues in favor of Anne and Wentworth marrying earlier. Given a choice between prudential morality and the truth of love, *Persuasion* argues for love.

Alasdair MacIntyre has called Jane Austen "the last great representative of the classical tradition of the virtues." By doing so he joins other Austenites, notably Wayne Booth, Lionel Trilling, and Martin Price, in recognizing the importance of moral judgment in Austen's works, but he has not had the benefit of Mary Poovey's more recent radical reading of *Persuasion*.

Brilliantly applying feminist theory and Marxist assumptions to *Persuasion*, Poovey finds at the heart of the novel an "epistemological relativism," a "mortal vertigo," from which it follows that "ethical judgment will be based at least initially on appearances and that all moral evaluation will be at least implicitly subjective": "Anne's intuitions are meant to be morally responsible and hence authoritative." Poovey finds that "the centralizing narrative authority taken for granted in the earlier novels has almost completely disappeared from *Persuasion*" so that the "subjectivity of the heroine" dominates "at nearly every level." Poovey clearly recognizes that the truly radical nature of *Persuasion* is in its ethical philosophy.

Where I disagree strongly with Poovey is in her linking this supposed "epistemological relativity" with a supposed "state of total collapse" of a "social and ethical hierarchy superintended by the landed gentry" as symbolized by the "fiscal and moral bankruptcy of Sir Walter Elliot." Such a reading gives Sir Walter far more social significance than Jane Austen intended. Such interpretations—and they are numerous—have been thoroughly demolished by the historian David Spring whose essay

"Interpreters of Jane Austen's Social World" is surely one of the most significant contributions to Austen scholarship in the last twenty years. What Spring shows is that "landed society" was *not* losing power in the Regency period, that the use of the word "bourgeois" to apply to Austen's world is woefully inadequate, and that Sir Walter's renting out his country house while living elsewhere more cheaply "was an ancient expedient for debt-ridden landowners" and not "a portent of the imminent downfall of landed society." Without denying the French Revolution, the Industrial Revolution, or Jane Austen's interest in the meritocracy of the British Navy, Spring reminds us what we knew all along from our reading of Trollope's fiction, our viewing of nineteenth-century English country houses, and our reading of Winston Churchill biographies: English landed society continued to be enormously powerful. (In fact, in a published version of his 1981 Tawney Memorial Lecture, David Spring says that it was not until after 1870 that an "erosion of landed society" gathered force and that only after World War I was the "English aristocracy's sense of purpose" for the first time "seriously shaken.") In response to Frederic Jameson's admirable exhortation in *The Political Unconscious* (1981) always to historicize, and in response to radical political interpretations of *Persuasion* by literary critics, David Spring would seem to be replying, "Fine, but you have not historicized enough." The crisis in *Persuasion*, I believe, is not a socio-economical-political crisis, but a moral one.

In all fairness to Poovey, however, I must grant that she recognizes Jane Austen's essential conservatism that gives "individual feeling moral authority" and places it in a private sphere "qualitatively different from the public spheres" (by Marxist analysis corrupt). Poovey also argues that only in this private sphere can "the premises and promises of romantic love," "one of the fundamental myths of bourgeois society," be perpetuated. The problem with this thesis is that, as Hannah Arendt, Michael Walzer, and numerous other political theorists have observed, the private sphere has been shown again and again to be the last bastion of moral value and personal integrity against the totalitarian (authoritarian) pressures of regimes of both the left and the right. A commitment to the private sphere or to romantic love, particularly when it is earned as it is in *Persuasion*, can be moral. Precisely because *Persuasion* places a heavy burden on individual choice, on personal judgment by an agent when confronted with the complexities of consequentialism and the context of moral luck, it has become my favorite Jane Austen novel. In this work I also find Austen's position to be essentially liberal and acutely prescient by showing the enormous burden that the modern Western world places on individual moral choice.

In *Persuasion* Jane Austen has transcended the limitations of a potentially too-calculating, closed system of communitarian morality present in her earlier novels, where male suitors are either too obviously

immoral or too priggishly moral. (Mr. Elliot is never a real threat to
Anne as a suitor in *Persuasion*.) Captain Wentworth, in contrast to such
clerical suitors in Austen's other novels as Henry Tilney or Edmund
Bertram,[2] presents a thoroughly admirable *secular* character. His marriage to Anne seems based less on moral calculus and more on the mysterious biology of desire, love, and psychological compatibility.
Courtship becomes the arena in which choices may not be obviously
right or wrong, good or bad, until proved out consequentially in a context of moral luck. This is *not* to say that *any* choice is equally plausible
because of a context of "epistemological relativism," but rather that each
individual cannot fall back on an external checklist or on an authoritarian moral adviser to evade personal choice. The burden of choice
henceforth is on the self and on character.

Finding this burden of choice endemic to a "classic liberal theory"
rooted in an "ontology of individual freedom," Charles Fried argues that
such theory has "trouble" accounting for "love and friendship" while
offering a "stringent code of moral constraint and of obligation":

> The theory of classical liberalism locates man's nobility and the
> source of his moral worth in his capacity of judgment (his rational-
> ity) and his capacity to conform his conduct to the deliverances of
> that judgment (his freedom). This power of judgment and choice
> distinguishes all men, and entitles all men to our equal respect.

This definition seems to me to apply perfectly to Anne Elliot in *Persuasion*. (No "righteous absurdity" here!) "If I was wrong in yielding to persuasion once, remember that it was to persuasion exerted on the side of
safety, not of risk," explains Anne to Wentworth. By the end of the
novel she is willing to opt for risk.

Although Austen's last known surviving letter referring to her imminent death as "the appointment of God, however secondary causes may
have operated" affirms her Christian courage and belief in a particular
providence, it reveals also her awareness of an alternative view suggested
by "secondary causes." Is it possible that while writing *Persuasion*, her
health already deteriorating from the fatal effects of Addison's Disease,
Jane Austen is reconsidering her earlier plot resolutions and projecting
a deep sense of anxiety about a universe governed providentially (what
ought to be) versus a universe governed by moral luck (what is)? Such a
very human anxiety throws more of an existential choice back onto the
individual. Like it or not, Jane Austen's men and women—especially
women—must make moral judgments on their own and be prepared—
as Anne Elliot is admirably willing to do even when she is wrong the
first time—to live with the consequences of those judgments. Above all,
not to judge, or to let others judge for you, is to fail in the conduct
of life.

2. From *Northanger Abbey* and *Mansfield Park*.

ANN W. ASTELL

Anne Elliot's Education: The Learning of Romance in *Persuasion* †

Most readers will agree with Richard Simpson (Review), C. S. Lewis, ("A Note"), Karl Kroeber *(Styles)*, D. D. Devlin *(Jane Austen)* and others that the Austen literary corpus reveals an overriding concern with the educational process in character formation—a process which, in the case of most of Austen's heroines, leads through love from self-deception to self-knowledge. Critics, however, have always had difficulty in approaching Austen's *Persuasion* from a pedagogical perspective. As Sylvia Sieferman recently observed, they usually argue that Anne Elliot's education has been completed before the novel begins; that she maintains a clear-sighted, morally elevated, central but static position throughout, while Captain Wentworth's gradual learning of love and truth defines the forward movement of the plot. In him the reader sees the educational process; in her, only the product.

This interpretation of the novel is, it seems to me, unsatisfactory for a variety of reasons. First of all, it identifies the educational process exclusively with what C. S. Lewis calls the "pattern of undeception" without making provision for a broader understanding of learning. Secondly, it assumes that the process of education ceases, in Austen's understanding, after a person has achieved a fundamental self-knowledge. Third, it fails to take into account the explicit and repeated references in *Persuasion* itself to Anne's on-going self-education. Fourth, it provides an aesthetic model of interpretation that is frankly at variance with our reading experience of the novel. It is Anne's mental processes, her perceptions, actions, and modulations of feeling—not Wentworth's—that absorb our attention. As John Wiltshire observes, "The process of [Wentworth's] unblinding is so lightly charted that it is plain that Jane Austen is not deeply interested in it." *Persuasion* cannot, I think, be said to be about Wentworth's education when it is so obviously Anne's story.

The narrator defines the object of Anne's instruction in the fourth chapter: "She had been forced into prudence in her youth, she learned romance as she grew older—the natural sequence of an unnatural beginning." Critics, it seems to me, have been too quick to assign Anne's learning of romance exclusively to the past—in particular, to her eight years of separation from Wentworth—when her romantic experience so clearly belongs to the present action of the novel which unfolds

† Ann W. Astell, "Anne Elliot's Education: The Learning of Romance in *Persuasion*," *Renascence* 40 (1987): 2–14. Reprinted by permission of the publisher. The author's notes have been deleted.

in time as the "natural sequence" of prior events. Anne's knowledge of romance does not stop short with a clear cognition of what might or could or should have been; it becomes an experiential knowledge, mediated through the emotions, which tests her moral maturity, her psychic stamina, to the utmost. Anne's feelings for Wentworth are not new; but the ethical context in which she must deal with them is. The intense interiority of the novel, which draws us into the world of Anne's thinking, feeling, and willing, invites us to participate in a learning of romance that is colored by the passions without being blinded by them, that is both intellectually and emotionally true, and that is increasingly independent of surrounding circumstance. In the end Anne's happiness depends less on Wentworth's loving her than on her loving him, freely, unconditionally, and eternally. Indeed, there is something silently Augustinian in Austen's transformation of a youthful romance, which is simply defined by strong, mutual attraction, into a mature romance which derives its spiritual splendor from selfless intentionality, and the ordering power of a directed will.

If the object of Anne's education is romance, then it must also be said that the pedagogical process involved in her instruction is a Romantic one. The Romantic features of the novel—its celebration of nature, its revolutionary impulse, its affirmation of emotion, its focus on the individual, its ranging homelessness, its poignant emphasis on remembrance—have often been noted (see Wiesenfarth, Spence), but the relationship between Romantic theories of composition and Anne's own method of self-education has not been sufficiently explored. *Persuasion* presents a series of incidents, each of which trigger a strong emotional response in Anne, who first withdraws to recollect herself, testing her perception of the present against her memory of the past, and then exerts herself to virtuous action, drawing on the strength of those same emotions. As Wiltshire has said, "Her goal, and the goal of the novel, is a harmonizing of her agitation that shall involve no giving in, no compromise, no suppression of one part of the personality by another." The gradual process of Anne's psychic integration in *Persuasion* parallels the process William Wordsworth describes in the Preface to *Lyrical Ballads*:

> our continued influxes of feeling are modified and directed by our thoughts, which are indeed the representatives of all our past feelings; and, as by contemplating the relation of these general representatives to each other we discover what is really important to men, so, by the repetition and continuance of this act, our feelings will be connected with important subjects.

The Romantic view of the educational process, then, as outlined by Wordsworth and imitated by Austen, involves the conversion of essentially passive and spontaneous *reactions* to the world of sensory experience—that is, our "continued influxes of feeling"—into freely-willed and energetic *responses*—that is, the purposeful connection of our feelings with important subjects—through the habitual exercise of the intellect in the close examination, modification, and direction of our emotions. The feelings, then, are an essential factor in the educational process—not only because, properly understood, they enable one to discover what is essential to human nature, "what is really important to men," what is timeless and universal in the individual life-experience; but also because the emotions impel one to act. As Wordsworth notes in his 1815 "Essay Supplementary to the Preface," "To be moved . . . by a passion is to be excited, often to external, but always to internal, effort; whether for the continuance and strengthening of the passion, or for its suppression."

If Wordsworth's discussion of the effect of the passions on poet and reader alike looks forward to Thomas de Quincey's "Literature of power," it also looks backward to Lockean treatments in the eighteenth century. As Devlin has shown, John Locke clearly understood the end of education to be the acquiring of virtues, an attainment dependent both on the clear, rational discernment of right and wrong, and on the ability to act in accord with that recognition. Locke realized that, because the passions can impair our reasoning powers and deprive us of inner freedom, the art of controlling the emotions is central to the educational enterprise. In *On the Conduct of the Understanding* Locke writes:

> When the fancy is bound by passion, I know no way to set the mind free and at liberty to prosecute what thoughts the man would make choice of, but to allay the present passion, or counterbalance it with another; which is an art to be got by study and acquaintance with the passions.

In *Some Thoughts on Education* (1693) Locke urges the early practice of the *agere contra* [1] as a way of achieving "the principle of all virtue and excellency" which "lies in a power of denying ourselves the satisfaction of our own desires where reason does not authorize them." In the same treatise Locke affirms that "the great principle of all virtue and worth" consists in the mind's ability to "endure hardships" and "purely follow what reason directs as best, though the appetite lean the other way." This is clearly a life-long educational objective that can only be learned by being practiced.

If Locke's discussion of vigorous and virtuous resolve as a counterforce to emotional impulse seems far-removed from Austen's *Persuasion*, one only needs to recall how Anne Elliot's "strong sense of duty" defines her peculiar heroism, and determines her actions from beginning to end. When the nineteen-year-old Anne submits to Lady Russell, a woman

---

1. Literally, "to act against." Locke is recommending acting against the grain, against one's immediate desires [*Editor*].

who has taken "the place of a parent" for her, she follows her conscience and yields "to duty," renouncing her desire to marry Wentworth. She considers herself to be "consulting his good, even more than her own," and this conviction empowers her to give him up at a time when she feels exceedingly drawn to him. When Wentworth returns after years of separation, Anne's long-dormant feelings of attraction for him are aroused with all their former intensity; at the same time, however, her breaking of their engagement has changed their relationship in such a way that those feelings have virtually no outlet, no direct and immediate means of outward expression. Anne and Wentworth are "repeatedly in the same circle" but they can allow themselves "no intercourse but what the commonest civility" requires. "Once so much to each other" they are "nothing" now, existing in "perpetual estrangement." Before Anne lived apart from Wentworth without him; his return forces her to endure an existential separation from him in his physical presence.

The same "strong sense of duty" which moved Anne to break their engagement initially now challenges her to allow Wentworth to exercise the freedom she has given him. She understands that he wishes "to avoid seeing her"; that he is "actually looking around, ready to fall in love" with anyone else but her. She silently witnesses him "accepting the attentions" of both the Musgrove girls, and sees his intimacy with Louisa advance to such a point that others consider him "an engaged man." The accident at Lyme calls upon Anne in a dramatic way to fulfill "the office of a friend" toward the young woman who is her chief rival for Wentworth's affection, and we are told that "she would have attended on Louisa with a zeal above the common claims of regard, for his sake," directing the strength of her love for Wentworth into the charitable service of another. Event after event stirs painful emotions with which Anne must deal within an objective frame of conduct dictated by social norms and her own fine conscience.

Anne's heroic struggle to master her own emotions, to deal with what Wordsworth calls "continued influxes of feeling," defines her program of self-education. Her success is measured in two ways: first of all, by her unfailing usefulness to others in the performance of duty; secondly, by her free decision to bind her affection finally and irrevocably to Wentworth, whether or not he returns her love, whether or not she receives any other proposal of marriage. If Anne's resolute sublimation of emotion in socially consequent action recalls Locke, her affirmation of a single, radical affection as the well-spring of that virtuous behavior recalls Wordsworth who maintains that poetry, imitating life, finds its first origin in "the spontaneous overflow of powerful emotions." Indeed, Austen's summary phrase—"the resolution of a collected mind"—unites the polar focuses of Locke and Wordsworth in a description of the personal integrity Anne strives to attain through a rigorous and uncompromising self-education.

Austen emphasizes Anne's need to educate herself by pointing out the inadequacy of the would-be mentor figures who surround her. Lady Elliot, long dead, is only a shadowy presence in the novel. Sir Walter, foolish, vain, and indifferent to Anne, is morally incapable of offering his daughter guidance. Lady Russell is good, well-mannered, well-intended, and genuinely attached to Anne. She has, however, "prejudices on the side of ancestry" and a "value for rank and consequence" which tend to blind her to the faults of the gentry. She is always quick to find reasons to approve her own liking, even if, as in advocating the Elliots' move to Bath, she has to "oppose her dear Anne's known wishes." When Lady Russell exerted her influence over Anne, urging her to break off her engagement with young Wentworth, she did so because, in her opinion, he "had nothing but himself to recommend him, and no hopes of attaining affluence." Unlike Anne, Lady Russell finds "nothing suspicious or inconsistent, nothing to require more motives than appeared" in William Elliot's renewed cordiality; indeed, she delights in the prospect of Anne's assuming her mother's position in Kellynch Hall as the heir's wife. Anne's disapproval of her "overanxious caution which seems to insult exertion and distrust Providence" suggests that Lady Russell's errors in judgment—both in opposing Wentworth's suit and in favoring Elliot's—stem from a way of thinking that is too naturalistic and worldly, too little founded on the faith in God which, according to Locke, must be the very basis of education. The reference to trust in Providence, in a literary context saturated with the imagery of flowering and bloom, recalls the Sermon on the Mount and the scriptural discourse on the lilies of the field, thus providing an implicit counter-text to Lady Russell's pattern of counsel.

Anne's mother, "an excellent woman, sensible and amiable," had turned in her final illness to Lady Russell, hoping that her friend would support and maintain "the good principles and instruction which she had been anxiously giving her daughters." Anne was only fourteen when her mother died, but her sensitive, docile nature must have been particularly receptive to her mother's early influence, for Lady Russell fancies "the mother to revive again" in her. The assimilation between mother and daughter—which might have gained fictive expression in their warm intimacy, shared principles, and parallel judgments—becomes a fusion in Austen's novel. We do not see Anne's mother; we only see Anne—the daughter who bears her name, and whose "elegance of mind and sweetness of character" reflects her mother's own "superior character."

As D. D. Devlin has pointed out, Austen's handling of the mentor figure clearly demonstrates the relation of her individual talent to the tradition of the eighteenth century novel. According to Devlin, however, Anne Elliot functions directly as a mentor for Captain Wentworth, and indirectly as the reader's mentor, while she herself has nothing to learn. What Devlin and other critics have failed to recognize is that Anne only instructs others in the process of instructing herself. The world of appearances, which exerts so great an influence in *Persuasion* on Anne's tender sensibility, is continually tested by her in her search for truth, a search which leads her from the present into the past to discover what is real and unchanging, the only fit foundation for futurity. If Anne Elliot has suffered, and continues to suffer, without becoming embittered, it is because she has found a way to supply the need for a mentor within her own consciousness. Throughout the novel Anne is depicted as a composite figure who is simultaneously mother and child, teacher and learner, and who carries on the dialogic, didactic discourse within her own mind.

When Anne is called upon to advise others, she only teaches lessons she is learning herself. At Uppercross, for instance, she finds herself "being treated with too much confidence by all parties." After listening to all the complaints, she can only "soften every grievance, and excuse each to the other," giving "hints of the forebearance necessary between such near neighbors." Anne herself exercises "perseverance in patience, and forced cheerfulness" in Mary's company. Her "pleasure" at the happiness of the Musgroves over their daughters' musical performance overrides her own feelings of "mortification" at the keyboard. Her conduct consistently exemplifies the forebearance she urges others to practice.

That, however, is an achievement that involves considerable self-sacrifice on Anne's part. When she arrives at Uppercross she tells herself "that another lesson, in the art of knowing our own nothingness beyond our own circle, was become necessary for her." When she is surprised by the Musgroves' lack of interest in the Elliots' affairs, she resolves "to avoid such self-delusion in future" and put aside any notions of her own importance. Indeed, she takes it as her aim to detach herself from Kellynch Hall, and "clothe her imagination, her memory, and all her ideas in as much of Uppercross as possible." If Anne masters this lesson, it is because she submits to the discipline of her own sense for what is fitting.

At Lyme Anne converses with Captain Benwick, a man afflicted by his fiancée's recent death. Once again the narrative emphasizes that Anne identifies with the one she instructs. She tells herself that his heart is not "more sorrowing" than hers; she compares his loss and "blighted" prospects with her own. After preaching "patience and resignation" to him, she admits to herself the fear that she has been "eloquent on a point in which her own conduct would ill bear examination." She only tells Benwick what she must tell herself over and over again as she struggles to maintain an inner equilibrium.

Anne's conversation with Benwick reveals that she herself attaches a great importance to books as a means of self-education. She has certainly read the "works of our best moralists," the letters, and the memoirs she recommends to Benwick as a way of fortifying her own mind "by the highest precepts, and the strongest examples of moral and religious endurances." On the other hand, she is clearly familiar with the poetry Benwick discusses and recites, including "all the tenderest songs . . . and all the impassioned descriptions of hopeless agony." Anne's sophisticated understanding of the psychology of reading affirms the value of the lyrical expression of sentiment as a way to grow in self-knowledge and understanding for others. At the same time, however, she clearly understands the dangers it entails. She urges Benwick to include in his daily study "a larger allowance of prose," and cautions him against reading too much poetry, observing that the "strong feelings" which make a person capable of really appreciating poetry also expose him to poetry's dangers, and require him in prudence "to taste it but sparingly."

Anne's counsel reveals much about her own reaction to poetry, her own need to practice temperance. The reader recalls that Anne "occupied her mind" with snatches of poetry during the walk to Winthrop—an occupation which increased her susceptibility to the influence of autumn at a time when Wentworth's attentions to Louisa Musgrove were renewing her own painful sense of loss. Indeed, she endeavored at that time to avoid overhearing them by reciting to herself tender autumnal sonnets "fraught with . . . the images of youth, and hope, and spring, all gone together."

The advice Anne gives to Benwick indicates that she regulates her own emotional response to poetry, first of all, by limiting her reading of it, and secondly, by submitting the strong emotions aroused by poetry to the order of reason reflected in expository writing on moral and religious themes. Anne, in short, is the mature reader of poetry that Wordsworth celebrates in his 1815 "Essay Supplementary to the Preface" of *Lyrical Ballads*. Wordsworth begins by affirming that

> The appropriate business of poetry, . . . her appropriate employment, her privilege and her *duty*, is to treat of things not as they *are*, but as they *appear*; not as they exist in themselves, but as they *seem* to exist to the *senses*, and to the *passions*.

He goes on to admit that the poetic "world of delusion" necessarily entails dangers for the young and inexperienced, whose feelings are flammable and "little disciplined by the understanding." After differentiating various classes of readers by age and interest, Wordsworth describes the one group whose judgment can be trusted in the criticism of poetry: "those and those only who, never having suffered their youthful love of poetry to remit much of its force, have applied . . . the best power of their understanding" to a study of poetry's laws within a broader literary context. Such readers possess "a mind at once poetical and philosophical," and "a natural sensibility that has been tutored into correctness without losing anything of its quickness." Like Anne Elliot they have the "strong feelings" that respond to poetry's passionate appeal; at the same time, they possess the mental discipline to examine those same emotions, and the cause of their arousal, within a larger frame of reference. Like her, they are both young and old; they are able to guide others because they first instruct themselves.

Anne's way of dealing with the passions stirred by poetry parallels her method of mastering the emotions aroused by life. Indeed, her practice conforms to the stages outlined in Wordsworth's theoretical discussion of lyrical composition. Again and again she withdraws and struggles to recollect in tranquillity the powerful feelings which agitate her. She thinks about what she feels—and finds enough calm in that contemplation to mobilize the inner strength needed to act, to re-engage the world, to give herself in the performance of her duties. The "sublimation of grief" merges with the fulfillment of her love and makes it possible for Wentworth, in turn, to find himself in love with her.

Austen consistently describes Anne's struggle with her emotions as an educational process that is triggered by the events she experiences. Those events belong to a narrative order that is often so colored by Anne's emotional perception of things that the ordinary distinction between first and third person narrators no longer applies. The impressionistic, fragmentary account of the Musgroves' discussion of Wentworth, for instance, is clearly an instance of free indirect discourse:

> To hear them talking so much of Captain Wentworth, repeating his name so often, puzzling over past years, and at last ascertaining that it *might*, that it probably *would*, turn out to be the very same Captain Wentworth whom they recollected meeting, once or twice, after their coming back from Clifton;—a very fine young man; but they could not say whether it was seven or eight years ago,—was a new sort of trial to Anne's nerves.

The "so much" and "so often," and the selection of details reflects Anne's inner experience of the talk that evening. She is clearly agitated, and she responds to her own emotional turmoil with the resolution to "teach herself to be insensible." As an inhabitant of Uppercross, Anne feels she cannot allow her personal distress to mar the "comfort" of the Musgroves, who are grateful to Wentworth, and eager to meet him.

Anne's own first meeting with Wentworth after years of separation is narrated in a fragmented style that suggests the rush of "a thousand feelings." When he leaves she begins "to reason with herself, and tries to be feeling less"—only to discover "that to retentive feelings eight years may be little more than nothing." She asks herself about Wentworth's sentiments, and then hates herself "for the folly which asked the question." After seeing him she acknowledges to herself that she has definitely seen "the same Frederick Wentworth"—whether or not he sees the same, or an altered, Anne. The dialogue she carries on within herself affirms that her present feelings match her remembered ones, and she knows that she still loves him.

The first kindness Wentworth shows to Anne—in carrying off little Walter, who had bound himself to her back and neck—produces "such a confusion of varying, but very painful agitation" in Anne that she is forced to leave the room. She is "ashamed of herself," honestly admits her own weakness, and grants herself the "long application of solitude and reflection" which is necessary for her recovery.

During the walk to Winthrop Anne inadvertently overhears a conversation between Wentworth and Louisa that reveals his opinion of her character. Once again she experiences "extreme agitation." As long as her emotions hold her "fixed," she cannot move; she takes the time she needs to recover. Later that same day, when her fatigue becomes apparent to Wentworth and he assists her into the Crofts' carriage, Anne is so distracted by this unexpected kindness that she does not even hear what the Crofts are saying. Through the use of free indirect discourse Austen lets us overhear Anne as she contemplates the act and its significance, and reflects on her own emotions "compounded of pleasure and pain."

Anne's affections increase, rather than limit, her powers of perception, even as her memories give her insight into present happenings. "From her knowledge of [Wentworth's] mind" Anne feels assured that he cannot speak about "former times" without recalling their engagement. She dares to judge from her "observations" based on "memory and experience" that Wentworth is not really in love with either of the Musgrove daughters, nor they with him. Because she loves (and therefore knows) Wentworth, she can interpret the "momentary expression" on his face, and know the meaning of his "contemptuous glance." Because she connects the "little circumstance" of the carriage ride with "all that had gone before," she is suddenly able to understand that Wentworth still feels for her without being able to forgive her. Her own suffering consistently increases her empathy for others, her insight into their character.

Nor do Anne's painful emotions keep her from virtuous action; they rather strengthen her to exert herself. Like her mother, whose unhappiness in marriage led her to devote herself to "her duties, her friends, and her children," Anne directs the energy of her passions into useful deeds. Sad about leaving Kellynch Hall, and dreading the move to Bath, Anne goes to Uppercross to help Mary, feeling "glad to have anything marked out as a duty." Distressed at Wentworth's return, she devotes herself to little Charles, knowing herself "to be of first utility to the child." When dancing is proposed at the Musgroves' party, Anne offers her services at the keyboard. Her eyes fill with tears as she plays, but she is "extremely glad to be employed." She accepts the invitation to go on the walk "as she might be useful" in lessening Mary's interference in the plans of the

Musgrove girls. At Lyme she keeps Benwick company, and thus performs "a good deed." Her greatest service there, of course, is the leadership she provides when Louisa injures herself severely in her jump from the stiles. There is, as Wentworth says, "no one so proper, so capable as Anne." During the last days of Anne's stay at Uppercross she has "the satisfaction of knowing herself extremely useful there" as a companion, counsellor, and practical assistant to the Musgroves.

Anne's ability to compose her emotions, and channel their forceful flow into service, has two results. First of all, it provides a series of lessons which teach Anne her own value. She who had felt herself "rejected as no good at all" comes to know herself as someone "extremely useful." The gratitude of Benwick and the Musgroves, and Wentworth's words of praise at Lyme, awaken in her "a second spring of youth and beauty." Secondly, Anne's resourcefulness and kindness teach others her true worth. Wentworth sees her nursing little Charles and caring for Louisa, and learns to appreciate her anew. Benwick praises her "elegance, sweetness, beauty." William Elliot is delighted by her visits to her old schoolfellow, and considers her "a model of female excellence."

While Anne disciplines her feelings and directs their energy into virtuous action, she never denies them. She remains true to herself, and that truth becomes a standard by which she assesses the character of others. She instinctively distrusts William Elliot, in particular, because he is "not open," because he never has a "burst of feeling" which leads him to reveal his true sentiments. He is, she thinks, "too generally agreeable," too polished in his manner, too skilled in the art of pleasing everyone. His pliability suggests a lack of principle. Anne realizes from passing remarks that he has been, and perhaps still is, "careless on all serious matters," including religious obligations. She notes that Elliot's "value for rank and connexion"—which leads him, like her father, to pay court to the Dalrymples—is greater than hers. Finally, when she compares Elliot with Wentworth, she discovers that she continues to prize "the frank, the open-hearted, the eager character beyond all others." Her early impressions inform her present ones, even as her own principles test those of others.

Anne's "continued influxes of feeling" at Bath serve to teach her about her own unchanging sentiments. Agitated by the news of Louisa Musgrove's engagement to Captain Benwick, she withdraws to her room in an attempt "to comprehend it." She discovers that she is "ashamed to investigate" her feelings because they are "too much like joy, senseless joy." Her chance meeting with Wentworth at Molland's produces "agitation, pain, pleasure, a something between delight and misery." She confesses to herself that she is not yet "wise and reasonable" for she cannot "be quite herself" without knowing his sentiments toward her. She must continue to educate herself. The conversation with Wentworth at the concert, which reveals so much to her, leaves her "in need of a little interval for recollection." She recalls his every word, his tone, his look, and her observations lead her to believe that he "must love her."

In the final movement of *Persuasion* Anne becomes reconciled to herself. Through the repeated contemplation of her own emotions she learns that she has always loved Wentworth, and becomes convinced that she always will:

> be the conclusion of the present suspense good or bad, her affection would be his forever. Their union, she believed, could not divide her more from other men, than their final separation.

The inner peace which attends this "yes" to her own unconditional love for Wentworth marks an atmospheric change in Anne's soul which symbolically affects the world around her: "It was almost enough to spread purification and perfume all the way." At this point in the narrative, before Wentworth declares his love, Anne discovers the meaning of her life—past, present, and future—in her unchanging love for him—a love that has strengthened her and empowered her endurance. As she tells Captain Harville, a woman's privilege consists in "loving longest, when existence or when hope is gone." If the ending of *Persuasion* is aesthetically satisfying, even haunting (and it is), that is because it is a story of love *without* end, a love that has been tested and become increasingly independent of outward circumstance—be it physical separation, the passage of time, the interference of others, or the outbreak of a Napoleonic War.

Even the marriage of Anne and Wentworth is secondary to the achievement of Anne's inner freedom to love, "the harmonizing of her agitation." Their mature, mutual "recollection in tranquillity" of their youthful love for one another mirrors Anne's independent achievement, and leaves them both "more equal to act, more justified in acting." Indeed, their marriage becomes an outward sign, a symbol, of the integrity Anne has achieved within herself. Anne, like Mrs. Smith, possesses an "elasticity of mind" which disposes her "to be comforted," to turn "from evil to good," to find "employment which [carries] her out of herself." Austen's novel shows that this spiritual capacity, which is simultaneously a gift "from Nature alone" and "the choicest gift of Heaven," is also a talent to be developed, a task to be undertaken willfully and freely. Because Anne dares to let herself be educated by life with all its tempests and trials, and does not shrink from the challenge posed by her own passionate reactions to persons and events, she succeeds in learning a romance that is all the more wonderful because it represents an ordered synthesis, an integration of elements initially chaotic and potentially destructive. *Persuasion* moves us to believe that such transcendent lessons can be learned—at least by minds which possess an elasticity comparable to Anne's own.

CLAUDIA L. JOHNSON

Persuasion: The "Unfeudal Tone of the Present Day" †

Persuasion has always signified more than what it singly comprises: its two slender volumes have been made to bear the imprint of Austen's entire career. Whereas *Pride and Prejudice* and *Emma* can be and most often are discussed without reference to Austen's other works, *Persuasion* is above all else the last novel, the apparent conclusion that determines the shape of everything that has come before. The critical tradition has designated *Persuasion* the "autumnal" novel, and this adjective brings with it a parcel of value-laden and often quite pedestrian assumptions about both the course of Austen's career and the course of literary history in general. Wistful and romantically unfulfilled in the twilight of her life, so the argument goes, the author grows tenderer on romantic subjects she had disparaged in the confidence and severity of her youth; with her own opening out onto a new world of emotion, eighteenth-century "objectivity" yields to nineteenth-century "subjectivity"; the assured, not to say simple-minded, gives way to the ambiguous and complex. The underlying assumption that Anne's autumn and Austen's are complementary—in other words, that *Persuasion*, like the other novels, indeed like all novels by women, is the author's own love story, composed with little or no aesthetic distance—is of course teeming with fallacies, not the least glaring of which in this particular case are those which result from the imposition of specious teleology. *Persuasion* will not look so unequivocally like Austen's last and most mature word about love and the changing world before death stopped her lips if we recollect that *Sanditon*, which recapitulates the raucous energy and renews the literary debates characteristic of Austen's earliest work, followed so closely on its heels. Austen, unlike her latter-day readers, did not have the benefit of knowing that her impending death would be imparting a gently resigned, autumnal melancholy to all her observations. Many prominent, yet seldom-discussed, elements of *Persuasion* call the youthful *Sense and Sensibility* to mind—the apparently unfeeling allusion to Mrs. Musgrove's "fat sighings," the conventionalized villainy of William Elliot and the conspicuously artificial means of disclosing it, the overtness of its sarcasms at the expense of silly and uninformed people. To judge them in terms of the autumnal paradigm, with which they are at odds, these features can only be dismissed as unfortunate lapses in morbid foresight.

This of course is not to say that *Persuasion* gives us nothing new, but

* From Claudia L. Johnson, *Jane Austen: Women, Politics, and the Novel* (Chicago: U of Chicago P, 1988), 144–66, 181–82. Reprinted by permission of The University of Chicago Press. All notes are by the editor of this Norton Critical Edition. The author's notes have been deleted.

only that it should be considered without using the benefit of hindsight to beg so many important questions. Most readers note, for example, that *Persuasion* ridicules the ruling class. This fact appears distinctive, however, only when we assume that it is a departure from the practice of the earlier novels. But surely nothing said in *Persuasion* about the Musgroves or Elliots surpasses the satire to which the Middletons, Palmers, and John Dashwoods are treated in *Sense and Sensibility*. What is different about *Persuasion* is not that it shows how the improvident landowners, proving themselves unworthy of their station, have left England poised on the brink of a new world dominated by the best and the brightest, the Royal Navy. As one historian has observed, foolish and financially embarrassed landowners are nothing new to English social history or to Austen's fiction. Eventually, Sir Walter will reassume Kellynch, and yield it in the time-honored way to his heir William Elliot, a man who, knowing how to serve "his own interest and his own enjoyment," will doubtless not, as Sir Thomas had, lose his hold on "the situation in which Providence has placed him."

But if in *Persuasion* the landed classes have not lost their power, they have lost their prestige and their moral authority for the heroine. Whereas *Pride and Prejudice* could, with elaborately wrought qualifications and finely modulated discriminations, finally vindicate the highly controversial practice of "prejudice," Lady Russell's "prejudices on the side of ancestry" and "value for rank and consequence" are never allowed to be anything more than amiable but groundless articulations of self-interest. Like her idea of what constitutes a "little quiet cheerfulness" or, for that matter, Admiral Croft's idea of proper decor, Lady Russell's "prejudices on the side of ancestry" are not favored with any corroborative footing in "objective" reality. As Admiral Croft puts it, "Ay, so it always is, I believe. One man's ways may be as good as another's, but we all like our own best. And so you must judge for yourself . . ." *Sense and Sensibility* makes it hard to believe that Austen ever shared Lady Russell's prejudices, yet even there she evinces a heartier tolerance for booby squires than what she somewhat wearily musters here. For all his absurdity, Sir John Middleton's bluff generosity commands some respect. But whether darting eagerly after weasels, defending the claims of eldest sons, or extolling the virtues of "good, freehold property," Charles Musgrove has little to recommend himself. His ideas, like his activities, are tediously predictable, and his "old country family of respectability and large fortune" has no charm: Anne never regrets her refusal to attach herself to this inoffensive, but unredeemably mediocre gentleman and the long-established kind of domestic life he represents.

Persuasion, then, distinctively minimizes problems which had before been so momentous to the heroines. By centering her novel on a maturer heroine, of course, Austen is free to explore female independence without being obliged to explore the concomitant impertinence which always seems to accompany the self-assurance of younger heroines. The duty of filial piety, for example—Fanny Price's "great rule to apply to"—is nowhere dignified with the status of being at issue here. Even though her "word" has "no weight" within her family circle, Anne, like Emma, is an autonomous heroine. For this reason, to conceptualize *Persuasion*, as readers so often do, as a debate between individualism and propriety is not only to employ an opposition already curiously loaded in favor of conservative arguments, but it is also to underestimate the degree of Anne's independence from traditional, paternal authority and to misplace the emphasis of the plot. Starting as early as the second chapter, for example, when we learn that she regards paying one's debts as an "indispensable duty," Anne distances herself from an impropriety that is specifically paternal. General Tilney's wrath with Catherine is the catastrophe of *Northanger Abbey*. But the crisis in *Persuasion*—Anne's decision to break off her engagement—has little to do with Sir Walter's paternal displeasure. On the contrary, it has everything to do with the advice, not the authority, of a trusted friend, Lady Russell, to whom Anne does not owe the comparable duty of obedience. Such is Anne's filial disposition at nineteen. At twenty-eight she pays Sir Walter even less mind. While Sir Walter pursues Lady Dalrymple, Anne visits a "nobody"—Mrs. Smith—without as much as informing him, let alone seeking his permission, and once his disapproval is expressed, it is ignored without fuss. For Anne, no hard conflict between duty and inclination is implied by defying or simply ignoring her father. Indeed, it is all too easy: "Anne kept her appointment; the others kept theirs."

Although Anne's indifference to filial propriety can show us the distance Austen has come since *Northanger Abbey*, Austen's earlier novel is nevertheless tied up with *Persuasion*. Published together posthumously in 1817, they seem unlikely companions, but in Austen's mind their partnership was deeper than the accident of their copublication. *Persuasion* itself speaks to problems that to all appearances pressed on Austen while she was reviewing, perhaps even revising, Northanger Abbey for publication. The "hand of time" may have been "lenient" to Catherine Morland's feelings, but Austen considered it harsh to her novel. In the "Advertisement" to *Northanger Abbey* she dwells on the "thirteen years" during which "places, manners, books, and opinions have undergone considerable changes," changes which render parts of her novel "comparatively obsolete." The "thirteen years" marked here, of course, are the same thirteen years that cause such dislocation in *Persuasion*. This novel is constantly calling attention to a temporal gap, to the time unwritten, but everywhere felt, to the missing third volume, as it were. Austen's handling of time in her plots is famously exact, carefully coordinated with reference to almanacs. But for all her exactitude, once Austen forges the temporal schemata of her narratives, she generally proceeds to submerge them, and only the most determined of students would wish to note down references to years and dates and then arrange them sequentially. But *Persuasion* is a calculated tangle of years and dates, and the passage of time itself is foregrounded. Here, as in no other novel, we are constantly being pointed backwards—to the knell-like repetition of "thirteen years" that have left Elizabeth husbandless, to the heavy "eight years" that have changed everything but Anne's feelings for Wentworth, to the tolled "twelve years" that have transformed the smart young Miss Hamilton into the poor and crippled Mrs. Smith; in short, to the inconjurable difference time makes.

The years alluded to in the "Advertisement" to *Northanger Abbey* and throughout *Persuasion* as the occasion of so much change are not just any years which would work changes at any time. With the benefit of hindsight, we look back upon those thirteen years as having sealed the reaction,[1] but as they appear in *Persuasion* they do not present a repressive and politically monolithic aspect. Sir Walter himself seems firmly enough entrenched, to be sure, but he is not all there is. In his related capacities as general, pamphleteer, and stern paterfamilias, General Tilney is the obstacle in *Northanger Abbey* whose authority must be confronted and in some ways, however limited, overcome. But now, some two decades later, defenders of the nation appear under a different guise and are envisioned as alternatives to, rather than representatives of, the establishment. Admiral and Mrs. Croft are not gentry. Far from presiding over a neighborhood, they live most contentedly at sea, unconcerned with the production of heirs or the reproduction of ideologically correct values through the cultivation of local attachments. From some points of view, the differences between Admiral Croft and General Tilney may be minimal. The former, to be sure, nowhere expresses or implies progressive opinion. But to Anne, the difference is great. The years which bring the Admiral into prominence are those which mark off the disparity between the "old English style" of the senior Musgroves, and the "new" English style of their "accomplished" daughters, and which have brought changes with them accounting for what William Elliot calls the "unfeudal tone of the *present* day" (emphasis added). But the causes and the processes of such transformation are not themselves the subject of *Persuasion*. Instead they are the pervasive backdrop Austen establishes throughout *Persuasion* in order to consider the psychological impact that social arrangements have on women and the apparent possibilities which the "unfeudal tone of the present day" may hold out for them.

Of all Austen's novels, *Persuasion* is, in point of mere years, the farthest removed from the pressures of political controversy that animate the fiction of her time. And yet, though it is often viewed as a forward-

---

1. This was a period of political reaction and repression, in response to fears of radicalism raised by the French Revolution.

looking novel, it makes a concerted effort to embrace a prerevolutionary context as well. Many of the most basic terms in the novel have a decidedly Johnsonian[2] ring to them, and this should not surprise us, not only because Johnson is so sympathetic a figure to Austen generally, but also because he is probably foremost among the "best moralists" Anne recommends to the stylishly melancholy Benwick. *Persuasion* continually contrasts the merits of fortitude, which can be "headstrong" or daringly heedless, with the merits of prudence, which can be "over-anxious caution which seems to insult exertion and distrust Providence." The opposition itself, of course, is Johnson's trademark. He frequently juxtaposes "heartless pusillanimity" to "heady confidence" (*Rambler* 25) and opposes the "presumption and arrogance" of expecting sure success to the "weakness and cowardice" of anticipating sure defeat (*Rambler* 43). Although neither Johnson nor Austen definitively resolve this opposition, both writers are self-consciously unconventional in refusing the moral authority of prudential maxims.

Writing when she does, however, Austen cannot treat temerity and timidity as neutral poles in a disinterested debate, nor can she omit scrutinizing their tacit reference to sexual difference. For Lady Russell, they are political attitudes. Lady Russell does not share the mindlessness typical of the squires, ladies, and baronets in this novel. Much to Elizabeth's irritation, in fact, she is always reading "the new poems and states of the nation that come out," and as we might expect, her opinions about Anne's suitors bespeak her absorption in and sympathies for conservative apologetics. She aims her approval of William Elliot at Anne in such a way as to show Wentworth's boldness in what she considers to be the worst possible light:

> He [William Elliot] was steady observant, moderate, candid; never run away with by spirits or by selfishness, which fancied itself strong feeling; and yet with a sensibility to what was amiable and lovely, and a value for all the felicities of domestic life, which characters of fancied enthusiasm, and violent agitation seldom really possess..

Lady Russell's argument is a manifestly sentimental one whose object is to establish the priority of that most basic unit of the social structure, the patriarchal family. She awards the prize for true, as opposed to "fancied," feeling to the man whose sensibility evinces the most responsiveness to women—the "amiable and lovely" being of course their province—and dismisses Wentworthian impetuosity as only fitful in its loyalties and subversive in its effects.

Of course Lady Russell is drastically wrong about Sir Walter's heir. Like all the villainous gentlemen and peers of progressive fiction who manipulate other people's domestic lives in order to secure their own

---

2. A reference to their similarity to the terminology of Samuel Johnson (1709–1784), the great moralist.

power, he is out for himself, and if a semblance of sensibility to the fair sex is needed to acquire prestige, then so be it. Lady Russell is wrong about Wentworth as well, although in this case her error is plausible, since Wentworth is a complex figure whose own sensibility bears the deep marks of ideological contradiction. The action of *Persuasion* begins eight years before the opening of the novel, when Wentworth angrily spurns young Anne Elliot because he believes she showed "feebleness of character" in relinquishing their engagement. Wentworth's anger deserves particular attention, because it is anything but customary to fault women for diffidence. In another kind of novel by another kind of novelist, Anne's initial hesitation would strike Wentworth and us alike as exemplary and he, like the enthusiastic Henry Crawford[3] glorying in his chains, would, rather than take umbrage at her maidenly doubt, manfully seize an occasion to prove his worth. But Wentworth does not appear to believe that the inconvenient modesty of the maiden will be redeemed by the submission of the wife, or to value the "feebleness" so often held to be part of woman's duty as well as her charm. Conservative fiction and conduct literature tirelessly preach to women about the duty of submission. In her avowedly counterrevolutionary *Letters Addressed to a Young Man*, Jane West assures young men of the kingdom that they have every right to expect their wives to give way, whatever the "pestiferous doctrines" of revolutionaries urge to the contrary. The "wise and beautiful subordination which Providence has instituted to avoid domestic contention" dictates precisely the kind of persuadableness in women that Wentworth scorns: "submission is the *prescribed* duty of the female; peace must be preserved, and she must yield."

Maria Edgeworth was, as we shall see, a careful reader of the very passages of *Persuasion* which specifically address how the different social conditioning of men and women creates differences in their psychological makeup. The political agenda of her *Practical Education*, co-authored with her progressive father, is not so unashamedly clear as West's. Here Edgeworth disclaims—though she does not outright dismiss—any progressive concern for the condition of women, illuminating their problems, but disavowing any intention to solve them: "Their happiness is of more consequence than their speculative rights." Accordingly, she recommends that female children should be taught restraint, sweetness, and submission, because these, like it or not, are to be expected from them throughout their lives as adults. Women, she continues, "*must* trust to the experience of others; they cannot always have recourse to what *ought to be*, they must adapt themselves to what is. . . . Timidity, a certain tardiness of decision, and reluctance to act in public situations, are not considered as defects in a woman's character." Edgeworth's statement, of course, is already a stunning piece of intertex-

3. In *Mansfield Park*.

tuality, imbedded as it is with a number of conservative truisms: it is wiser to trust to the accumulated experience of others than to advance and pursue one's own ideals, to submit to what "is" rather than quixotically striving for what "ought to be," and to habituate male, but especially female, children to what Edgeworth a little later terms dutiful "forebearance" rather than self-willed "precipitation."

Wentworth's contempt for what he perceives as Anne's failure to be decided, forward, and strong thus implicates and dissents from an already firmly established and widely available tradition of debate about women's manners. To Wentworth, a woman is guilty of "weakness and timidity" when she evinces a readiness "to oblige others," and when, deferring to the judgment of family or friends, she credits fearful rather than hopeful predictions about her betrothed. A strong man himself, Wentworth knows, or at least thinks he knows, that he wants the same qualities in a woman. He "seriously described the woman he should wish to meet with. 'A strong mind, with sweetness of manner,' made the first and the last of the description." Wentworth's description appears straightforward enough. But as his subsequent remarks attest, he is in fact caught within highly charged tensions about women's manners, and his description of the ideal woman is oxymoronic, because however much he may desire "strength" in women, he considers it essentially inconsistent with the sweetness he also exacts. The narrator's remarks on the "large fat sighings" of Mrs. Musgrove "over the destiny of a son, whom alive nobody had cared for" are relevant here. They will appear less like the gratuitous and tasteless cruelties which the subversive school has so relished when we consider them in light of Wentworth's contradictory assumptions about women. The narrator in fact brings up the grotesqueness of Mrs. Musgrove's grief only to ponder the irrationality of our response to it: "Personal size and mental sorrow have certainly no necessary proportions. A large bulky figure has as good a *right* to be in deep affliction, as the most graceful set of limbs in the world. But, fair or not fair, there are unbecoming conjunctions, which reason will patronize in vain,—which taste cannot tolerate,—which ridicule will seize" (emphasis added).

The tendency of *Persuasion* as a whole is to consider conjunctions which perhaps have even less basis in reason, but which are so much more pervasive that their arbitrariness is not even noticed. This discredited association of physical size with emotional delicacy prefaces a debate between Wentworth and Mrs. Croft about female manners, in which Wentworth takes a position very different from what Lady Russell would expect. If a large, bulky figure has a "right" to affliction, then conversely perhaps a "graceful set of limbs" has a "right" to venturesomeness as well. To Wentworth, however, the very idea seems as ludicrously incongruous, if not indeed as repellent, as fat grief may be to us, and this despite his declared wish to find "a strong mind, with sweetness of manner" in a woman. With the haughtiness typical of him, Captain Wentworth announces his principled opposition to carrying women on board ships precisely on account of their delicacy. His objections, he explains, arise not from mean-spirited misogyny, but rather from high-minded chivalry: "There can be no want of gallantry, admiral, in rating the claims of women to every personal comfort *high*—and this is what I do. I hate to hear of women on board, or to see them on board; and no ship, under my command, shall ever convey a family of ladies any where, if I can help it." Having spent the best years of her life on a man-of-war, Mrs. Croft regards her brother's opinions as "idle refinement!" But Mrs. Croft's claim that "any reasonable woman" can be "perfectly comfortable" on board actually loses points with her brother. To a man fixed in his ideas about female delicacy, women so "reasonable" are simply not ladies. He is willing to transport women on his ships insofar as they are a dear friend's property—"I would bring any thing of Harville's from the world's end, if he wanted it"—but the possibility that women themselves may not consider such journeys a violation of their lovely and amiable natures is obnoxious to him: "I might not like them the better for that, perhaps. Such a number of women and children have no *right* to be comfortable on board" (emphasis Wentworth's).

The objections not only to female sturdiness, but also to a female "*right*" to it, that Wentworth expresses here explain why it was and still is impossible for him to recognize "strength of mind" and "sweetness of manner" in Anne Elliot, until Anne's sturdiness and her forwardness to take control after the the catastrophe at Lyme oblige him to surrender his notions about delicacy. Like female modesty, which is suspected to the same degree as it is commanded, female strength is disapproved to the same degree as it is desired. Although the introduction of the tearful Benwick and the domestic Harville upsets conventional conjunctions of ideas about gender, for Wentworth delicacy and strength are sex-typed oppositions reinforced by class, and where he finds them conjoined in women of his own class—officer's wives—he is by his own admission displeased. Mrs. Croft's extraordinary rebuttal seizes on what she regards as absurd in her brother's ideas about manners and class: "I hate to hear you talking so, like a fine gentleman, and as if women were all fine ladies, instead of rational creatures." As we recall, Mr. Knightley can convincingly oppose the modish primitivism of Mrs. Elton's projected "gipsy party" to the "nature and simplicity of gentlemen and ladies, with their servants and furniture," because *Emma* as a whole is predicated upon the worthiness of the gentry ideal and the gentlemen and ladies who comprise it. But in *Persuasion*, gentlemen and ladies are excluded from the category of "rational creatures." Not that rational creatures of either sex here abandon the amenities of life, like Mrs. Elton's impossibly idealized gypsies. Indeed, the conditions Wentworth imagines to be too grueling for a lady to bear turn out to be quite accommodating after all. It is Wentworth himself who ridicules land-loving civilians for supposing that sailors rough it, "living on board without any thing to eat, or any cook to dress it if there were, or any servant to wait, or any knife or fork to use."

But though Mrs. Croft may not repudiate some of the comforts of gentility, she does repudiate the system of sexually differentiated manners ladies and gentlemen depend upon. Her views on the subject are actually quite remarkable, given the renewed importance ascribed to female manners during the period in question. Conservatives and radicals alike agreed that amiable weakness and loveliness in women guarantee the continuance of patriarchy itself. "The age of chivalry is gone," as Burke famously wailed in a passage of the *Reflections* which Lady Russell seems to remember, and along with the chivalric sensibility, he predicts, will die the conditions which make the old regime possible: the gallant disposition in men to feel fondly disposed to the amiable softness of women restrains the otherwise indecent and uncivilized rapacity of their appetites, and the retiring docility and dutiful chastity of women insures the identity and survival of the blood lines of good families.[4] Of course not all of Burke's allies believed that the civilized world was held together by chivalrous opinion. Jane West, for one, opined that Burke's notions of chivalry bordered on idolatry, and granted women far more than they intrinsically deserved, filling their weak heads with silly ideas about their own importance, when it is they instead who should study to please, and to be sensible helpmates and useful companions rather than lovely and ever-distressed females.

While conservative and progressive discourse sometimes intersects on the phrase "rational creatures," the insistence that men and women's shared status as rational creatures takes precedence over sexual difference in questions relating to their manners and their morals was generally perceived to be the progressive position. Wollstonecraft's critique of the cultivation of speciously differentiating delicacy in women was often treated as though it were a wholesale recommendation of grossly viraginous[5] strength. Thus Robert Bisset, for example, scoffs that Wollstonecraft included among the *"rights of women"* the right to serve as "soldiers, sailors, senators, politicians, scholars, philosophers, and rakes. . . . She trusted the time would soon arrive when the sex would require high renown in boxing matches, sword and pistol." Seen in this light, Mrs. Croft is a tour de force of characterization. Though her comportment has not the slightest hint of mannish impropriety about it—Lady Russell, for one, finds her a pleasing and sensible neighbor—her manners are conspicuous by their lack of features usually construed as femi-

4. Edmund Burke, *Reflections on the Revolution in France* (1790), in a passage bemoaning the fact that "ten thousand swords" failed to leap from their scabbards to "avenge even a look that threatened [the Queen of France] with insult."
5. Characteristic of viragoes: bold, quarrelsome, aggressive women.

nine, such as bashfulness, roundness, sweetness, and daintiness. She "had a squareness, uprightness, and vigour of form, which gave importance to her person" and "a weatherbeaten complexion, the consequence of her having been almost as much at sea as her husband." She omits that self-doubt and reluctance that Edgeworth, for one, exacted from women, particularly in public situations. She looks "as intelligent and keen as any of the officers around her," and her manners are "open, easy, and decided, like one who had no distrust of herself, and no doubts of what to do; without any approach to coarseness, however, or any want of good humour." And finally, without ever really appearing to be the eccentric she is, Mrs. Croft prefers warships to the most comfortable manors in the kingdom, throwing overboard as needless weight the excellencies of the proper lady, and she "shares with him [Admiral Croft] in everything."

Mrs. Croft appears never to consider robustness and self-confidence an oxymoronic violation of her feminine nature, and she could bid farewell to the age of chivalry without worrying much about the future of the civilized world. To her chivalry and the way of life it guarantees are superfluous: Wentworth's solicitude for women's comfort is a "superfine, extraordinary sort of gallantry," which appears even more unnecessary in his case, since he in particular, as his sister implies, has the good fortune not to be a "fine gentleman" to begin with. Sir Walter, for his part, does not regard Wentworth as a "gentleman" at all, and his usage, however unpleasant, is far from idiosyncratic. Wielding a fortune in war prizes of mythically immense proportions, Wentworth is nouveau riche with a vengeance. Sir Walter restricts the term *"gentlemen"* to "some man of property," and thus does not recognize the claim even of Wentworth's clerical brother to the title: "Mr. Wentworth was nobody, I remember; quite unconnected, nothing to do with the Strafford family." He objects besides to the tendency of Wentworth's profession itself to contend with and confound the established networks of social prestige, for the military is "the means of bringing persons of obscure birth into undue distinction, and raising men to honours which their fathers and grandfathers never dreamt of." In all fairness, the contempt is entirely mutual. To a man who prides himself on "the gratification of believing myself to earn every blessing that I enjoyed" the famous "Elliot pride" in membership within their own family—as well as the precedence-, title-, and pedigree-mongering that goes along with it—is offensive. Mary Musgrove's eagerness to assure him that she regards the Hayters as unworthy connections only arouses in him "a contemptuous glance, as he turned away, which Anne perfectly knew the meaning of." Furthermore, the record of filial piety which makes up an important part of Darcy's characterization,[6] for example, has no place in Wentworth's

6. Darcy is the hero of *Pride and Prejudice*.

history, and his impatience with Anne's hesitation at nineteen to defy
paternal displeasure surely suggests how little store he sets by paternal
authority in general. Since Wentworth has no place in, and indeed is
actually hostile to, the patriarchal world of family and neighborhood
which Sir Walter represents, though none too well, his "superfine" gallantry has no rationale and operates at political cross-purposes with his
own designs and energies.

Wentworth's argument with Admiral and Mrs. Croft does not settle
any issues, for no sooner does the subject reach an impasse than Wentworth breaks off and withdraws altogether. To their assurance that he
will change his mind when he marries, he rather angrily returns: " 'I
can only say, "No, I shall not;" and then they say again, "Yes, you will,"
and there is an end of it.' He got up and moved away." Wentworth's
words here both recapitulate his quarrel with Anne Elliot eight years ago
and prefigure the same dilemma he will face in a matter of days when
Louisa wants to jump down from the stiles at the new Cobb: "He [Went-
worth] advised her against it, thought the jar too great; but no, he reasoned and talked in vain; she smiled and said, 'I am determined I will.' "
Recurring to the imagery of hardness and to such related concepts as
complaisance and determination, elasticity and fixation, impressionabil-
ity and obstinacy, *Persuasion* continues to explore the antinomies of
autonomy and authority that figure prominently in Austen's other novels as well. The subject of one of Elizabeth's and Darcy's first debates,
after all, is the worth of ductility and resoluteness: "To yield readily—
easily—to the *persuasion* of a friend," Elizabeth taunts, "is no merit with
you" (emphasis Elizabeth's). But while both novels attempt to delimit
the legitimate boundaries of authoritative interference, the later novel
deals with conflicts which, as with the conceit of fat sighings, "reason
will patronize in vain," and where persuasion accordingly is more problematic.

In *Persuasion* neither giving in on the one hand, nor holding out to
get one's way on the other, are very attractive options. Conservative
apologists, of course, cut the Gordian knot by submitting such conflicts
to the arbitration of persons wisely vested by tradition with the authority
to decide. But if *Persuasion* does not specifically indict this method, it
also stops far short of adopting it, since the "authorities" so vested are
inadequate. In Anne's case, an older woman friend, and no venerable
father, carried the day. Lady Russell stands not in place of a mother,
but rather "in the place of a parent," and the very need to replace a
living but morally dysfunctional father itself points to a problem with the
conservative model. Moreover, although Anne is steadfast in refusing to
apologize for having once been persuaded by a woman who takes the
place of a parent, she soon eschews Lady Russell's prudential reasonings
on the grounds that they "insult exertion and distrust Providence," and
she never allows herself to be persuaded again. When Anne receives a

proposal from Charles Musgrove, she solicits neither her father's opinions nor Lady Russell's, but "left nothing for advice to do." Anne's gentle imperviousness to interference is fortunate, for Lady Russell's approval of Charles Musgrove's suit and her championship of William Elliot's do not testify to her powers of discrimination. Like *Northanger Abbey*, *Persuasion* reflects on its own refusal to ratify received notions: the narrator validates the perseverance of young people in carrying their points even though doing so is, as she says, "bad morality to conclude with." In erased notes of the cancelled chapter covering the same material, Austen dwells at greater length on her departures from conventional wisdom in fashioning a story where the older and unassailably "proper" woman is wrong, not once, but twice: "Bad Morality again. A young Woman proved to have . . . more discrimination of Character than her elder—to have seen in two Instances more clearly what a Man was . . . But on the point of Morality, I confess myself almost in despair . . . and shall leave it . . . to the mercy of Mothers and Chaperons and Middle-aged Ladies in general." Even though Anne finally avers in defense of her own infelicitous, but not culpable, deference to Lady Russell, "if I mistake not, a strong sense of duty is no bad part of a woman's portion," the efficacy of "submission" is, if not utterly undone, then at least called into question by authorially emphasized criticism of the principles which underpin and valorize such duty.

The unyielding firmness and independence Wentworth advocates is likewise tested and found wanting. After persuading Henrietta to visit Charles Hayter despite the interference of Mary Musgrove, Louisa proclaims:

> "And so I made her go. . . . What!—would I be turned back from doing a thing that I had determined to do, and that I knew to be right, by the airs and interference of such a person?—or, of any person I may say. No,—I have no idea of being so easily persuaded. When I have made up my mind, I have made it."

This speech, and Wentworth's enthusiastic response to it, are not the simple assertions of principled self-determination they appear to be. Louisa, after all, did not disinterestedly supplement her sister's faltering powers of mind with the strength of her own. Instead, she took advantage of her sister's persuadability in order to clear the field for Wentworth and herself. Further, Louisa recommends independence even as she congratulates herself for her own interference: "I made her go." Finally, Wentworth disdains the feeble malleability of "too yielding and indecisive a character" when it defies him as Anne's did, but he does not seem to mind or even to notice the same qualities when they malleably conform to his own influence. Louisa has really done no more than give Wentworth what he wants to hear, and unaware that Louisa's strength of mind is really only persuadability to him in disguise, he rewards her with his praise: "Happy for her [Henrietta], to have such a mind as yours at hand."

Clearly, Wentworth's preference for singlemindedness is as indiscriminating and self-serving in its own way as Lady Russell's prejudice in favor of wealth and family is in its. If "complaisance" can be, as Louisa terms it, "nonsensical," inflexibility can be so as well. Wentworth takes little notice of this possibility. "[L]et those who would be happy be firm," he intones, anticipating the moral of his parable about the hazelnut: "To exemplify,—a beautiful glossy nut, which, blessed with original strength, has outlived all the storms of autumn. Not a puncture, not a weak spot anywhere.—This nut . . . while so many of its brethren have fallen and been trodden under foot, is still in possession of all the happiness that a hazel-nut can be supposed capable of." The most salient feature of the glossy hazel-nut, however, is not that it holds impressions well, but that it is not susceptible to them at all. The efficacy of determination is undermined when Louisa, "armed with the idea of merit in maintaining her own way," withholds herself from advice and falls headlong onto the pavement at the Cobb. Even Wentworth eventually surrenders resolution so fixed and intransigent. After the accident, he turns desperately to Anne for help, to be ordered and told what to do. And throughout the novel, his immovable resentment of her loosens under the influence of other peoples' admiration of her. He arrives at Uppercross swearing that Anne has aged beyond recognition, but he changes his tune when he observes William Elliot to be struck by her, and later when connoisseurs of beauty sing Anne's praises in his hearing.

Wentworth's determination is generally considered to mark him as a "new man," temperamentally as well as ideologically opposed to the way of life Sir Walter represents. But like his gallantry towards women, his steadfastness to the point of inflexibility actually aligns him with Sir Walter, and he must mitigate his self-will before reconciliation is possible. When Anne defies him by suspending their engagement, she encounters "all the additional pain of opinions, on his side, totally unconvinced and unbending, and of his feeling himself ill-used by so forced a relinquishment." Wentworth's tenacity in holding "unbending" opinions, his tendency to remain "unconvinced" by and inaccessible to opposition, and most alarmingly of all, his readiness to feel "ill-used" place him in the unflattering fellowship of none other than the Elliots themselves. Like spoiled children, Elizabeth and Sir Walter bitterly blame the world for the necessities their own debts place them under. They feel "ill-used and unfortunate," and steadfast in their foolishness, they refuse to forego expensive "decencies"—"Journeys, London, servants, horses, table"—that alone make life supportable even to "private" ladies and gentlemen. Having inherited "a considerable share of the Elliot self-importance" without commanding any comparable hauteur,

Mary Musgrove manifests their tyrannical self-pity in a particularly degraded form. She always fancies herself "neglected or ill-used," always thinks with bullheaded obstinacy "a great deal of her own complaints," and feels everything as a wound. Wentworth has his own version of the "Elliot self-importance" which prompts him in like fashion to be headstrong and absolute. True, he may not have behaved like "an ill-used man" when Louisa falls for Benwick, but this is not, as the Admiral thinks, because he has "too much spirit" to kick against the goad, but rather because he came to regret their flirtation to begin with. As the Admiral could not have known, eight years ago, when it counted, Wentworth did feel like "an ill-used man," and he does "murmur" and "whine and complain"—not with Mary's sorts of whimpers, but rather with icy vindictiveness nursed over a period of eight years.

In the Elliots' case, of course, self-importance is a birthright, a benefit conferred upon them by their social position. Sir Walter believes he is somebody to the "nobody" of virtually everyone else. But though Sir Walter is convinced that, as a public figure, he carries his importance around with him irrespective of place, people only three miles away at Uppercross are contentedly oblivious to "the affairs which at Kellynch-hall were treated as of such general publicity and pervading interest" by Sir Walter himself. Anne's mortification to discover that Sir Walter and Elizabeth "see nothing to regret" in relinquishing "the duties and dignity of the resident land-holder" bespeaks her lingering sympathy with the life of the manor, but landholders less distinguished than her father are not spared either. As presented in *Persuasion*, at least, landed existence itself fosters an immobility that fixes delusions of self-consequence which cause so much conflict. Anne is an adept in "the art of knowing our own nothingness beyond our own circle," and this is what makes her wise. But the otherwise unobjectionable Musgroves, whose views are bounded by the narrowness of their neighborhood, cannot share such wisdom. Except in *Pride and Prejudice*, where a countrified Mrs. Bennet takes umbrage at Darcy's cosmopolitan pretentions, only in *Persuasion* does Austen portray the provinciality of her characters as a disadvantage. Taken by himself, Charles Hayter, for example, could appear as an earnest and respectable gentleman. But placed alongside Frederick Wentworth and ineffectually pleading with a troublesome child, he fades into nonentity. And just as the Admiral's tendency to confuse Henrietta and Louisa suggests their indistinguishability, so the redundancy of Hayter's Christian name, doubling with that of Charles Musgrove, calls attention to what is undistinctive about eldest sons in general. And in no other novel is a gentry matron exposed to such painful comparisons with a woman with wider horizons. When Mrs. Croft summarizes her travels, adding "We do not call Bermuda or Bahama, you know, the West Indies," poor Mrs. Musgrove finds herself baffled:

"Mrs. Musgrove had not a word to say in dissent; she could not accuse herself of having ever called them any thing in the whole course of her life."

Landed life is not taken to task simply because it promotes mediocrity or ignorance, but rather because its insularity is psychologically damaging, especially for women. Conservatives laud membership within a neighborhood precisely on account of the strong and stabilizing attachments, the changeless pace, and the unceasing familiarity that it carries with it. But for women it also carries with it a particularly narrow and unwholesome confinement, and discussion of this problem in *Persuasion* is specific, prolonged, and dramatically charged. Whatever baronetcy does for Sir Walter, it has not helped a daughter who has reached the age of twenty-nine without marrying. For Elizabeth the *Baronetage* cannot be the never-ending fund of solace unalloyed it is for her father. Every reading mercilessly reiterates an ever-receding birthdate and an unchanging status as spinster. Mr. Bennet's sarcasm—"a girl likes to be crossed in love a little now and then. . . . It is something to think of"— has a disturbing relevance to *Persuasion*, where such crosses are all that women have to think of. Being the mistress of Kellynch-hall—"doing the honours, and laying down the domestic law at home"—is not as engaging, as satisfying, and as adequate to Elizabeth's imagination as running Hartfield and its environs is to Emma's. Elizabeth is haunted by her disappointment in love, and the cares and duties of "her scene of life" are not enough to keep her from revisiting and fixing her pain. Bitterness, mortification, regret, and worry are all she has "to give interest to a long, uneventful residence in one country circle, to fill the vacancies which there were no habits of utility abroad, no talents or accomplishments for home, to occupy." Nor is Elizabeth's condition unique. Anne has more "resources," as they are termed in *Emma*, than her sister Elizabeth, yet she understands that her regret over Wentworth lingers because "no aid had been given in change of place . . . or in any novelty or enlargement of society" that could dislodge and eventually efface her painful impressions.

Whether it is because we typically exclude Austen in general from access to, capability for, or interest in arcana of any sort, or whether it is because we have a habit of regarding *Persuasion* in particular as a tender love story that is not conducive to such considerations, rather scant attention has been accorded to Austen's affiliation with the eighteenth-century tradition of liberal psychology. But readers of Johnson's essays, who recall his fears about the corrosiveness of hopes and disappointments, his recommendation of "change of place" (*Rambler* 5, 47), and his anxieties about the "vacuities of recluse and domestick leisure" (*Rambler* 85), will recognize the provenance of her concerns and the character of her diction, and will appreciate how, by linking women's confinement within their changeless neighborhoods to the strength and longevity of their feelings, she develops this tradition with particular emphasis on women's problems. Anne herself tells Harville that women do "not forget you [men], so soon as you forget us." But far from presenting the constancy of woman's love in the light of a virtue, for example, loyalty, she presents it as a burden—"our fate rather than our merit." Men will love faithfully "so long as [they] have an object," but woman's love can subsist indefinitely as fantasy alone: "All the privilege I claim for my own sex . . . is that of loving longest, when existence or when hope is gone." A dubious privilege indeed, this liability to hopeless fixation. Anne's rather technical explanation for the stubborn durability of women's love combines social criticism with psychological acuity:

> "We live at home, quiet, confined, and our feelings prey upon us. You are forced on exertion. You have always a profession, pursuits, business of some sort or other, to take you back into the world immediately, and continual occupation and change soon weaken impressions."

To Maria Edgeworth, whose access to moral psychology, unlike Austen's, is undisputed, Anne's analysis held special interest. The marginalia in her personal copy of *Persuasion* are very sparse until this episode, which prompts a flurry of scratches, underlinings, and comments. She, for example, reiterates Anne's socio-psychological argument here with "our mind is continually fixt on one object"; to the claims that occupation and change weaken impressions, she writes a heartily concurring "That it does"; and she brushes aside Harville's analogy between the strength of men's "bodily frames" and the constancy of their feelings with an emphatic "No." But whereas Edgeworth in conservative fashion upholds the traditional social arrangements that expose women to the problems she herself laments, on the grounds that defying such arrangements will not promote their happiness, *Persuasion* asks us to consider whether women's happiness may not be better served by cutting loose from those arrangements. Mrs. Croft disapproves of long and uncertain engagements because they expose women to perilous anxieties and fantasies—and her brother, eavesdropping, appears to acknowledge that the application to his own case with Anne has a compelling legitimacy which he had never before considered. Mrs. Croft's example as a wife suggests that life on the high seas, for all its dangers, is to be preferred to the "safety" of helpless immobility she experienced when she lived conventionally, as most wives such as Mrs. Musgrove do: "The only time I ever really suffered in body or mind, the only time I ever fancied myself unwell, or had any ideas of danger, was the winter that I passed by myself at Deal, when the Admiral (*Captain* Croft then) was in the North Seas. I lived in perpetual fright at that time, and had all manner of imaginary complaints from not knowing what to do with myself."

The phenomena of change and relativity in *Persuasion* have long been considered symptoms of the dizzying modernity to come, a modernity usually described as either brave or degenerate, according to the axis of the critic. But to those characters who take notice at all, the deracination and relativity presented in *Persuasion* are not felt to be disturbing or disorienting. Except when she has pangs in tender remembrance of her dear mother, Anne cannot regret the Croft's tenancy at Kellynch-hall. She cannot say of her family seat what she knows social orthodoxy would have her say: "These rooms ought to belong only to us. . . . How unworthily unoccupied! An ancient family to be so driven away!" Rather than feel that their removal to the diminished accommodations at Camden-place constitutes a fall, Sir Walter and Elizabeth themselves find more than enough "extent to be proud of between two walls, perhaps thirty feet asunder." Anne is not bewildered to learn that our somethingness is tenuous and relative, or sad to confront her nothingness beyond her family circle—she, after all, is rather less than something *in* her family circle as well. Only from within a mentality which organizes people hierarchically from somebodies down to nobodies, and often according to whether or not they yield or are yielded to, does that status of nothingness feel so degrading. Anne does not possess such a mentality, and detached from a single neighborhood and a fixed world of traditional institutions that make that mentality possible, she allows the alienation she experiences upon first coming to Uppercross to be a benefit. Anne finds it "very fitting, that every little social commonwealth should dictate its own matters of discourse," and by learning different social discourses she is able to be a citizen of many commonwealths. Accordingly, she considers it "highly incumbent on her to clothe her imagination, her memory, and all her ideas" in Uppercross. Though first undertaken as a duty, this reinvestiture is later experienced as a boon. After leaving, Anne discovers that subjects which she had felt obliged to "smother among the Musgroves" assume only "secondary interest." She is "sensible of some mental change": her sorrow about Kellynch and even her tenacious loyalty to Wentworth loosens, and she now entertains thoughts of Benwick, and even of Walter Elliot.

If processes of inuring can be therapeutic—Anne, for example, "was become hardened to such affronts" as she receives at home—some kinds of malleability can bring relief as well, even if it makes possible a certain erasure. Anne finally refuses to take sides in the debate about hardness and softness, and determination and submission, setting her sights instead on "elasticity of mind, that disposition to be comforted, that power of turning readily from evil to good, and of finding employment." When Wentworth wittily explains how in marrying Anne he is not getting what he deserves, he elaborates on this quality: " 'Like other great men under reverses,' he added with a smile, 'I must endeavour to subdue my mind to my fortune.' " The ironic mode of his statement is oddly fitting, for the "reverse" in question of course is the happiness of reconciliation, possible only after relinquishing the obduracy of his resentment and becoming susceptible to opposition. But the people in *Persuasion* who are preeminent for elasticity of mind are significantly far more remote than Wentworth, who after all by the end of the novel is acceptable even to Sir Walter. By the standards set in Austen's fiction, in fact, they are unusual, and by those set in conservative fiction, far too marginal to be the models they are here. They are mostly without the kinds of affiliations, idealized in such writing, that exact a high cost—confinement, unventuresomeness, fixity, boredom—for the stability they guarantee. Some Sir Walter regards as scarcely human: "A Mrs. Smith. A widow Mrs. Smith. . . . And what is her attraction? That she is old and sickly.—Upon my word, Miss Anne Elliot, you have the most extraordinary taste! Every thing that revolts other people, low company, paltry rooms, foul air, disgusting associations are inviting to you." Yet Mrs. Smith above all others typifies the "elasticity of mind" Anne values, and this is not only despite the reverses that have marginalized her, but also in some ways because she has undergone them.

Insofar as salvos like these would console the unfortunate by contending that it is better to suffer after all, they condone the processes and conditions which cause such suffering to begin with, and so may be considered implicitly conservative. *Persuasion* is sometimes deeply tinged with such quietism. And yet Anne's preference of "low company, paltry rooms, foul air" to the companionship of her father and those he would choose for her is nevertheless a pretty piece of social criticism. Fortune, Providence, luck, chance—these are extremely prominent entities in the novel, and are emblemized here by the sea itself. And the person with "elasticity of mind"—the "choicest gift of Heaven"—takes and resigns what they give with equal cheer, and makes her- or himself malleable to their impressions, much as the Crofts have let the sea air write itself onto their complexions without bothering with applications of Gowland's Lotion. On Mrs. Smith, who lives beyond the margins of "good" society, their marks have been the deepest: "She had been very fond of her husband,—she had buried him. She had been used to affluence,—it was gone. She had no child to connect her with life and happiness again, no relations to assist in the arrangement of perplexed affairs, no health to make all the rest supportable." But though she is the least sheltered from fortune's blows—and as Mrs. Croft says, "We none of us expect to be in smooth water all our days"—she is also the most resilient for having "weathered it," the least inclined to feel "ill-used." Her bodily immobility—roughly similar in kind, if not in degree, to the confinement undergone by proper ladies in their provincial homes—serves only to highlight her resources more brilliantly. In a similar way Harville lives just beyond society, bordering out onto the sea itself, which has not served him a fraction so generously as it has Wentworth. If his case is not so dire as Mrs. Smith's—he is less crippled, less cramped, less destitute, and with a loving family, less disattached—by Sir Walter's standards he still ranks as a "disgusting association." But though even Anne herself suffers a "moment's astonishment" at the meanness of his lodgings, she later regards them as the seat of "great happiness."

While the people Anne casts her lot with are well-traveled citizens of many different commonwealths, to recall Anne's metaphor, they are proprietors of none. Always ready to determine orders of precedence and to feel "ill-used" if opposed or neglected, Mary Musgrove decides after only a little consideration that even though Anne's accession to marriage restores her "to the rights of seniority," her own situation is still superior: "Anne had no Uppercross-hall before her, no landed estate, no headship of a family; and if they could but keep Captain Wentworth from being made a baronet, she would not change situations with Anne." To Anne, however, these lacks are a virtue. Religious intimations are more frequent in *Persuasion* than in any of Austen's other novels and more enmeshed into its outlook. But whereas in other novels the world of wealthy gentry in which Mary takes such pride is either genuinely or at the very least nominally in the service of such intimations, in *Persuasion* it is not. Characters here who are most like the glossy but impermeable and therefore irredeemable hazelnut in Wentworth's parable are not Wentworth himself, who finally yields after all, but members of the privileged class, such as Sir Walter, who is devoted to avoiding crow's-feet, and the "polished" William Elliot, who is suspect precisely because he "endured too well" and gives no evidence of friction or wear.

From the very beginning of the novel, Anne has valued "cheerful confidence in futurity" and scorned to "distrust Providence!" Peopled more with friends than family, and accepting the "dread of war" that sometimes dims the "sunshine" of domestic felicity, the society Anne finally selects—the "best" company—removes itself from the institutions of the country manor to front more directly and hospitably onto Providence. But while the break Anne accomplishes with those institutions is more complete than what we find in any other novel, and while her efforts at accommodation are the most perfunctory, she and the alternative society she joins are also the least prone to overt indictment, and this constitutes a departure from Austen's early fiction especially. Whereas *Sense and Sensibility* and *Northanger Abbey* derive much of their dramatic tension from the defiance of tyrannical parents, *Persuasion* eludes, even frowns upon, overt rebellion. Social forms may be neglected—Anne dislikes "give-and-take invitations, and dinners of formality and display"—but not outright opposed. Accordingly, Anne herself is capable of betraying some shame about her association with Lady Dalrymple and Miss Carteret, but she politely keeps it under wraps: " 'Yes,' sighed Anne, 'we shall, indeed, be known to be related to them!'—then recollecting herself . . . not wishing to be answered." But William Elliot's history of expressed disrespect for rank itself is not acceptable. The narrator makes no bones about averring that "Sir Walter was not very wise," but Anne shudders "with shock and mortification" to learn that his heir applies words as irreverent as "fool" to him. But before we conclude that Austen's willingness to cover for Sir Walter betrays deplorable bad faith, or perhaps less damningly, loyalties too deep and residual to permit penetrating social criticism, we would do well to ponder the typically confounding twist in her characterization of William Elliot. Surely to identify the person who mouths social disrespect with the person who then panders to the very people of "credit and dignity" whom he admits are "nothing in themselves" is to underscore the particularly sterile conventionality of the entire system of "blood and connexion" and the cynicism on which it subsists.

Of none of Austen's works, but of *Persuasion* perhaps least of all, can it be said, as Trilling has, "Nothing in the novels questions the ideal of the archaic 'noble' life which is appropriate to the great beautiful houses with the ever-remembered names—Northanger Abbey, Donwell Abbey, Pemberly, Hartfield, Kellynch Hall, Norland Park, Mansfield Park. In them 'existence is sweet and dear,' at least if one is rightly disposed. . . . With what the great houses represent the heroines of the novels are, or become, completely in accord." Northanger Abbey is far from a haven to Catherine Morland, and this is not because *she* fails to be "rightly disposed"; Norland Park provides no values with which the Dashwood sisters can accord;[7] and Kellynch Hall, not even "ever-remembered" by its own proprietors, is bidden a rather wistful good riddance by a daughter far superior to what it now "represents." Works of fiction written on the conservative model tirelessly exhort us to accept infelicity as the condition of life and urge us instead to seek our modest satisfactions in the consciousness of prescribed attachments well honored, and duties well done. But Austen's novels are pervasively concerned, not with according ourselves to an existence "sweet and dear," but with achieving a more active, expansive, and personally fulfilling happiness, and they persistently suggest that this is well worth the striving. Sometimes, as in *Pride and Prejudice*, Austen contrives to locate such happiness within conservative institutions themselves, but . . . it takes some work before Pemberly will accommodate Elizabeth. And once Pemberly does make a place for her, one suspects that it is the "great beautiful house" itself, rather than Elizabeth, that will be essentially improved for her presence there, because whatever its previous dignity, it never seemed a place of pleasure. The word "happy" rings as frequently across the pages of *Persuasion* as it does those of *Pride and Prejudice*, and it should tell us something that in *Persuasion* it is the nefarious Walter Elliot who wishes to dissuade Anne from pursuing the highest happiness she can conceive of. When he discovers that she pre-

7. In *Sense and Sensibility.*

fers the "best" company to merely "good" company, he warns, "You have a better right to be fastidious than almost any other woman I know; but will it answer? Will it make you happy? Will it not be wiser to accept the society of these good ladies in Laura-place, and enjoy all the advantages of the connexion as far as possible?" Fortunately, Anne's fastidiousness, like Elizabeth's, finally does "answer." But unlike Elizabeth's, it is achieved not at a great beautiful house with an ever-remembered name, but rather in a disposition only discernible in people who do not belong to such houses, people such as the Crofts, who walk "along in happy independence," or like Harville, whose weather-beaten lodgings are a "picture of repose and domestic happiness."

The interests of happiness, piety, and well-being demand removal from Kellynch Hall, its proprieties and priorities. But whether moving beyond Kellynch or any equivalent bespeaks a victory of autonomy from what a great house represents, or a despair of its ever improving enough to be desirable, is hard to say. Not surprisingly, since they belong exclusively to the years which assured the reaction, Austen's last three novels reflect a strong sense of the increasing immovability of established authority. While *Sense and Sensibility* concludes with an opposition and a withdrawal that are angry, permanent, and committed, in *Northanger Abbey* General Tilney finally does yield, if minimally, and in *Pride and Prejudice* Darcy is improved by confrontation, and eventually even Lady Catherine comes around. But even though Sir Thomas's judgment in *Mansfield Park* is thoroughly impeached, his authority is fixed. In *Emma*, when his kind of authority is transformed and feminized, and joined with Knightley's, it assumes a benign aspect. But in *Persuasion*, stately houses and their proprietors are no longer formidable, and their intransigence is matched only by their vapidity. Good characters depart from them without a breach, differ from them without defiance. Thus the overarching structure of *Persuasion* as a whole reproduces and asks us to accept the same sorts of unresolved tensions found in so many of its shorter, characteristically oxymoronic formulations— such as "fat sighings," or "she was deep in the happiness of such misery, or the misery of such happiness." *Persuasion* settles little: it resumes a debate interrupted eight years in the past without reaching an agreement, and without requiring one. Wentworth does not concede that Lady Russell had been right, Anne refuses to concede that yielding was wrong: "cheerful confidence in futurity" precludes such regret, and Providence has been equally served by delay.

The "elasticity of mind" celebrated in *Persuasion* accepts and surpasses both of these, as well as the broader social conflicts the book details. It is tempting to see in this effort to define and endorse extensive difference from established institutions, without effecting an overt or impassible breach from them, as the perfection of the strategies and the positions that have marked Austen's fiction from the start. Austen, no less than Blake,[8] wrote for an audience with what one critic has called "war-manacled minds," and her works, no less than Blake's, attempt—inevitably with only limited success—to shed those manacles which she perforce wore too. Among the least doctrinaire of all her contemporaries, Austen from the outset took on the materials which political controversy endowed with such importance, without inviting or aggravating partisan impulses. During a time when all social criticism, particularly that which aimed at the institution of the family in general and the place of women in particular, came to be associated with the radical cause, Austen defended and enlarged a progressive middle ground that had been eaten away by the polarizing polemics born of the 1790s. If she very early opted definitely not to ratify the anarchism of the radical opposition, despite an allegiance to the liberal tradition which underlay much of it, she also avoided its irritability, its confusion, and its very early defeat. Conservative fiction was Austen's medium because it very quickly became the only fiction there was, other voices being quelled, and Austen persistently subjected its most cherished mythologies to interrogations from which it could not recover. The highly parodic style developed in the juvenilia, when applied to the stuff of conservative fiction, constituted a kind of piracy which commandeered conservative novelistic discourse and forced it to hoist flags of different colors, so to speak, to say things it was not fashioned to say—as when Catherine Morland, for example, assures herself with perfect trust that the good General Tilney "could not propose any thing improper for her"; or when Marianne's "sensibility" and Elinor's "sense" turn out not to be antithetically opposed; or most optimistically, when Darcy himself absorbs the values of his antagonist in order to make her as well as himself happy. In none of the novels can conservative ideology be entirely overcome, but in all, as most forcibly in *Mansfield Park*, its basic imperatives—benevolence, gratitude, family attachment, female modesty, paternal authority—are wrested from their privileged claims and made, like Edmund Bertram, to relinquish their "moral elevation."

CHERYL ANN WEISSMAN

Doubleness and Refrain in Jane Austen's *Persuasion* †

Among the characters in Jane Austen's canon of fiction, the heroine of *Persuasion* is supremely mysterious. Anne Elliot suggests a residual

8. William Blake (1757–1827), revolutionary poet.
† Cheryl Ann Weissman, "Doubleness and Refrain in Jane Austen's *Persuasion*," *Kenyon Review* n.s. 10 (1988): 87–91. Copyright 1992 by Kenyon College. Reprinted by permission. The author's notes have been deleted.

depth of personality that eludes narrator as well as reader in this, Austen's last completed work. Yet even as character emerges with extraordinary subtlety, this novel's structure and language call themselves to our attention by virtue of their contrasting and conspicuous schematism. The wistful tone of *Persuasion* is informed by a bizarre and implacable emphasis on doubleness and refrains in diction, plot, themes, and even syntax.

Symmetric doubling is not intrinsically remarkable in Austen's fiction, of course. The titles *Pride and Prejudice* and *Sense and Sensibility* reflect the harmoniously epigrammatic rhythm of eighteenth-century prose. But in that tradition, as in Austen's earlier novels, structural symmetry suggests the dependable order of a stable, rational world. In *Persuasion*, names and events recur in a disturbingly irrational way, reflecting a transient, uneasy one.

It is a world keenly reminiscent of the stylized and gloomy milieu of fairy tales. Anne Elliot is a Cinderella figure dominated by a vain and unloving parent (Sir Walter) and two selfish sisters. In a mythical past, eight years prior to the novel's time frame, she was persuaded by a well-intentioned godmother (Lady Russell) to reject Frederick Wentworth, a suitor with modest financial expectations, and that submission to persuasion has proved to be the mistake of her life. Now Wentworth returns, having improbably made his fortune after all, and to Anne's profound anguish he courts both of her sisters-in-law; no Prince Charming was ever more misguided! Anne has become faded and impoverished, but she remains deeply in love with him. She regrets her decision, although she refuses to repent it; it was the correct choice under the circumstances, she insists, even though it chanced to be the wrong course of action.

Meanwhile, chance further contrives to present her with a second suitor, William Elliot. As heir to her father's estate, this man would offer her the unique opportunity to succeed her long-deceased mother in name, fortune, and even place of residence. With fairy tale symmetry, Anne could thus be restored to her home and in some measure be compensated for the wrongs done her by a godmother's error in judgment and a natural mother's symbolic abandonment. We, as readers, can see that the legacy also includes her mother's terrible folly of marrying an unworthy man, but for a time Anne's perception of this remains uncertain.

Fortunately but not accidentally, she is *not* persuaded to be inconstant in favor of this specious continuity. The problematic options of sameness and difference do not double her vision; she recognizes the opportunity for authentically changing the bleakness of her life by remaining faithful to Wentworth, her original and only lover. Consistency of character and of attachment prevail over the menacing forces of chance and confer a happy ending upon the revised fairy tale after all.

Inlaying this hauntingly elemental story are stylistic devices that emphasize its kinship with fairy tales; Austen appears to have gone out of her way to focus attention on the artifice of fiction. We find a surprising occurrence of coincidentally shared names, for example. In the plot, the dramatic turning point is foreshadowed by an earlier, strikingly similar contrivance. And both the narrator's and characters' diction are studded with arresting refrains. Presented from its outset as a sequel to an implicitly meaningful, unwritten earlier story, this novel is a puzzling play on the notion of doubleness.

Beginning with names, the first page contains a breezily irreverent reference to "all the Marys and Elizabeths" that ancestral Elliots have married, alerting us to a quirk of repetitiveness that the coming story will vigorously display. In Anne's contemporary world, Charles Musgrove has both a son and a cousin (his brother-in-law-to-be) with the same Christian name, and Mrs. Smith's deceased husband was a Charles as well. This is an oddly extravagant gesture, coming from an otherwise tautly economical crafter of novels. Ironically, Admiral Croft remarks that he wishes "young ladies had not such a number of fine christian names"; how much simpler "if they were all Sophys, or something of the sort."

William Walter Elliot, heir to Sir Walter Elliot, incorporates a remarkable range of identities within his semi-original name. Morally duplicitous, he has been a false friend to Sir Walter and to Charles Smith. Narratively he is accorded an odd versatility as well. He appears first as an unidentified traveler, spontaneously smitten with Anne at Lyme, then later is shown to have had a calculated plan to court her. Yet, despite his characteristic deviousness, his admiration at the inn was genuine, arising in ignorance of her identity. It was simply a coincidence—a narrative doubleness.

A striking doubleness characterizes the plot as well as the cast of characters. Anne's anticipated first meeting with her former lover, Wentworth, is scuttled by a domestic accident in the Musgrove household: little Charles is injured in a fall. And with a thud that is uncannily familiar, the turning point of the novel will occur when the boy's aunt, Louisa Musgrove, falls on the Cobb at Lyme. The symmetry is as significant as the similarity; as the child's fall heralds a courteous and cold reacquaintanceship, Louisa's precipitates Wentworth's recognition of love and his return to Anne.

Freud was intrigued by the congruence of chronological and spatial patterning in the grammar of dreams, observing that *"temporal repetition of an act is regularly shown . . . by the numerical multiplication of an object."* Repetitions inform Louisa's accident with just such dreamlike ciphering. The company at Lyme are taking their second walk along the Cobb, owing to Louisa's determination, and she further, obstinately insists that Wentworth "jump" her down the steps once, and then again.

After she has fallen and her sister Henrietta has fainted from shock, we are told that the passersby are especially delighted with the entertainment of seeing not merely one, "nay, two dead young ladies, for it proved twice as fine as the first report."

Along with such doubling in names and actions, a cadence of poetic refrain characterizes much of the novel's diction. For example, an unusually long and spiraling sentence expresses Anne's piteous solitude in the wake of events following Louisa's accident:

> She was the last, excepting the little boys at the cot, she was the very last, the only remaining one of all that had filled and animated both houses, of all that had given Uppercross its cheerful character.

This nostalgic sentence echoes another description of lingering lastness, the reference to the old nursery-maid who is delightedly rehabilitated by Louisa's fall:

> A chaise was sent for from Crewkherne, and Charles conveyed back a far more useful person in the old nursery-maid of the family, one who having brought up all the children, and seen the very last, the lingering and long-petted master Harry, sent to school after his brothers, was now living in her deserted nursery to mend stockings, and dress all the blains and bruises she could get near her, and who, consequently, was only too happy in being allowed to go and help nurse dear Miss Louisa.

The sentence is a chanting, balladlike story; the image of the nursery is presented with the soothingly monotonous rhythm of a nursery rhyme, another variation on the theme of refrain.

And refrain *is* a theme. Implicit in the novel's premise is a doubleness of time, for *Persuasion* is constructed like a palimpsest, an overlay through which we must decipher an original. The dramatic action that occurred in the novel's implied past is reflected and reflected upon throughout the text. We need only consider the way in which Anne is presented; until the events at Lyme precipitate her "second spring of youth and beauty," she belongs more to the ghostly past than to her dismal present circumstances. She lives amid the resonant tension of simultaneous time periods.

The passage which most pivotally expresses this impossible doubleness of time occurs just before the story's turning point. In the poised, held moment before Louisa jumps down the Cobb steps and sets in motion a tumultuous rearrangement of the characters' romantic pair-bonds, Austen pauses in her story for a haunting reverie on the sea:

> The party from Uppercross passing down by the now deserted and melancholy looking rooms, and still descending, soon found themselves on the sea shore, and lingering only, as all must linger and

gaze on a first return to the sea, who ever deserve to look on it at all, proceeded towards the Cobb. . . .

Anne's first view of the sea is paradoxically not her first view, it is a "first return." And all of the radical patterning in *Persuasion*'s plot structure and diction emphasizes this tremulous union of beginnings and returns.

The motif of first returns opens the apparently closed story of Anne's life. It suggests the possibility for recovery of what was thought to have been irrevocably lost. And as the story of a misunderstanding that is revisited, the novel challenges the reader's convictions regarding his own perceptions. In the earlier Austen novels, the anticipation of the happy ending invests the whole with a promise of pleasing resolution. But the anticipated ending of *Persuasion* must provoke apprehension; we cannot be sure where this return will lead, or if it will have an ultimate destination at all.

Even Anne's dizzyingly narrow escape from a wasted life is not as properly satisfying as we expect fictional escapes to be. A painful residue of doubt clings to the ending, and we wince with ambivalent desires and beliefs when we are told that

> They returned into the past, more exquisitely happy perhaps, in their re-union, than when it had been first projected; more tender, more tried, more fixed in a knowledge of each other's character. . . .

Analogue of a first return, here is a redeemed past. And Anne teasingly denies us our sigh of relief with her paradoxical insistence that Lady Russell had been wrong in her advice, yet she herself had been right to follow it. We want to agree, yet we are left frowning; like Dr. Johnson's Rasselas, we are being asked to drink from the mouth of the Nile even as we drink from its source. Anne's defense of her terrible error feels like a flirtation with disaster even as the novel is about to close, grinding against her miraculous, precarious rescue.

It is the nature of storytelling to etch patterns and simultaneously to violate them. In *Persuasion* this aesthetic conflict is brought into the foreground; the will to conserve the patterns of the past inviolate abrades against the impulse to disrupt and reform them. As the "imaginist" Emma Woodhouse in *Emma* wishes to preserve authority over her world and yet wishes to make matches (which must necessarily undermine her control over those matched), so the narrator of *Persuasion* expresses contradictory impulses toward enshrinement of the past and toward implacable progress.

Narrative ambivalence is apparent from the start. If the promised story of Anne Elliot is introduced as the wistful remnant of a lost past, then the scene with which that story commences farcically counterpoints the yearning to return there. We meet the fatuous Sir Walter gazing tirelessly at the two handsome duodecimo pages of the Baronetage upon which his family's historical existence is summarily acknowledged. He delights in beholding his own name, feeling an endless glow radiated by his ancestors' prestige. He favors the pursuit of no profession at all, any sort of employment being necessarily deleterious to one's original personal substance. Absurd as such a caricature of conservatism is, his compulsion to hold his story still brings into relief the narrator's and heroine's inclinations to cut Anne's losses, to deny the potentially dangerous possibilities of hope and change.

In change there is loss, of course, but there can be more than compensatory gain as well. On a thematic level, both characters and narrator frequently express faith in justice and the value of suffering. On another level, Anne's losses can be equated with the missing elements of the narrative. The story that overflows the banks of fictional knowledge is in a sense lost, but as with Anne's and Wentworth's lost days, absent features of the text are pledges of a greater richness to come.

The more information we are given about a character's inner life, the sparser that information seems. Who was Anne Elliot before the novel began, and how can we account for the eight years that transformed the persuadable girl of nineteen into the firm woman we are shown? And further, how has this narrator elicited from us such unconventional, seemingly inappropriate curiosity?

She has done so at least in part by contrasting a playfully contrived, non-mimetic fictional background with an earnestly realized, provocatively elusive central figure. Figure and ground resonate, creating a tension that invests the text with powerful emotional authenticity, and anticipating the direction taken by such later novelists as Proust and Joyce.

In place of the unobtrusive mimetic foundation that persuasively supports earlier Austen heroines, here is fictional scaffolding illuminated with narrative searchlights. Patterns of doubleness and refrain have taken the place of progressive momentum, creating a cadence exquisitely suited to this heroine's step. For she is no Elizabeth Bennet, coming of age and learning to distinguish between appearances and reality; Anne Elliot begins her narrative journey with maturity and discernment, and in her world such phenomenological distinctions are no longer possible. Here the focus has veered from character to the perception of character, and knowledge of another person's motives and idiosyncratic vision is always insufficient. Grounded by *Persuasion's* schematically patterned narrative surface, personality emerges with a residual richness that extends beyond the borders of the text.

Jane Austen:
A Chronology

1775	Jane Austen born, December 16, at Steventon, Hampshire, the seventh of eight children of the Rev. George Austen. George III is on the throne of England.
1784	Formal education ends at age 9, at school in Reading.
1789–91	Between the ages of 14 and 16, she writes a novel called "Love and Freindship," a "History of England," and stories called "Lesley Castle" and "A Collection of Letters."
1793–96	Writes "Lady Susan" and "Elinor and Marianne," the earliest version of *Sense and Sensibility*.
1797	Writes "First Impressions," the earliest version of *Pride and Prejudice*.
1797–98	Rewrites "Elinor and Marianne" as *Sense and Sensibility* (which remains unpublished until 1811).
1798–99	Writes *Northanger Abbey* (published posthumously in 1818).
1801	Austen family moves to Bath.
1804–05	Now at Southampton, she writes "The Watsons," possibly an early version of *Emma*.
1805	Her father dies and the following year the family moves to Southampton, where after an interval of several years her major works were composed.
1809	Rewrites "First Impressions" as *Pride and Prejudice*, and revises *Sense and Sensibility* for publication.
1811–20	The Regency: George, Prince of Wales, takes over the powers of George III, who lives on until 1820.
1811	*Sense and Sensibility* published at last, anonymously—like all her other works; writes *Mansfield Park*.
1813	*Pride and Prejudice* published.
1814	Writes *Emma* and publishes *Mansfield Park*.
1815	Writes *Persuasion*.
1816	*Emma* published.
1817	Jane Austen dies at the age of 42 in Winchester, of Addison's disease, leaving "Sanditon," an unfinished novel.
1818	*Northanger Abbey* and *Persuasion* published, again anonymously.

Selected Bibliography

The first section of this bibliography lists the editions of Jane Austen essential to serious study of her work. The second section includes the titles of works that bear indirectly on Austen's modes of thought. All are cited in the essays included in this edition. Works of biography and criticism, with emphasis on relatively recent criticism, are listed in the third section, which provides bibliographic data for other critical citations from the essays. Except for the editions in the first section, nothing listed is the source of any excerpt appearing in the present text.

JANE AUSTEN: WORKS AND LETTERS

The Novels of Jane Austen. Ed. R. W. Chapman. 5 vols. 3rd ed., Oxford, 1933. A sixth volume, including minor works by Austen, appeared in 1954.
Jane Austen's juvenilia have appeared in three volumes:
  Volume the First. Ed. R. W. Chapman. Oxford, 1933.
  Volume the Third. Ed. R. W. Chapman . Oxford, 1951.
  Volume the Second. Ed. B. C. Southam. Oxford, 1963.
Jane Austen's Letters to Her Sister Cassandra and Others. Ed. R. W. Chapman. 2nd ed. London, 1952.

RELATED MATERIAL

Donagan, Alan. *The Theory of Morality.* Chicago, 1977.
Fried, Charles. "Liberals and Love." *The New Republic* (December 24, 1984).
MacIntyre, Alasdair. *After Virtue: A Study in Moral Theory.* London, 1981.
Nagel, Thomas. *Mortal Questions.* Cambridge, 1979.
Richards, David A. J. *A Theory of Reasons for Action.* Oxford, 1971.
Slote, Michael. *Common-sense Morality and Consequentialism.* London, 1985.
Spring, David. "Land and Politics in Edwardian England." *Agricultural History* 58 (1984): 17–42.
Williams, Bernard. *Moral Luck: Philosophical Papers, 1973–1980.* Cambridge, 1981.

BIOGRAPHY AND CRITICISM

Austen-Leigh, J. E. *A Memoir of Jane Austen.* London, 1870.
Battestin, Martin C. *The Providence of Wit: Aspects of Form in Augustan Literature and the Arts.* Oxford, 1974.
Booth, Wayne C. *The Rhetoric of Fiction.* Chicago, 1983.
Brown, Julia Prewitt. *Jane Austen's Novels: Social Change and Literary Form.* Cambridge, MA, 1979.
Brown, Lloyd. *Bits of Ivory: Narrative Techniques in Jane Austen's Fiction.* Baton Rouge, 1973.
Crane, R. S. "The Concept of Plot and the Plot of *Tom Jones.*" *Critics and Criticism: Ancient and Modern.* Ed. R. S. Crane. Chicago, 1952.
Damrosch, Leo. *God's Plot and Man's Stories: Studies in the Fictional Imagination from Milton to Fielding.* Chicago, 1985.
Devlin, D. D. *Jane Austen and Education.* London, 1975.
Duckworth, Alistair M. *The Improvement of the Estate: A Study of Jane Austen's Novels.* Baltimore, 1971.
Duffy, Joseph M. "Structure and Idea in *Persuasion.*" *Nineteenth Century Fiction* 8 (1953): 272–79.
Dussinger, John A. *In the Pride of the Moment: Encounters in Jane Austen's World.* Columbus, OH, 1990.

Forster, E. M. *Abinger Harvest.* London, 1936.

Gard, Roger. *Jane Austen's Novels: The Art of Clarity.* New Haven, 1992. Unlike most recent criticism, this book returns to a mode of "appreciation" for Austen's accomplishment.

Garrod, H. W. "Jane Austen, a Depreciation." *Essays by Divers Hands . . . Transactions of the Royal Society of Literature.* N.s. 8 (August 1957): 21–40. One of the first negative appraisals.

Greene, D. J. "Jane Austen and the Peerage." *PMLA* 68 (1953): 1017–31. Useful for understanding Austen's treatment of social class.

Halperin, John, ed. *Jane Austen: Bicentenary Essays.* Cambridge, 1975.

Harding, D. W. "Regulated Hatred: An Aspect of the Work of Jane Austen." *Scrutiny* 8 (1940): 346–62.

Hardy, Barbara. *A Reading of Jane Austen.* New York, 1976.

Honan, Park. *Jane Austen: Her Life.* New York, 1987. The best recent biography.

Kaplan, Deborah. *Jane Austen and the World of Women.* Baltimore, 1992. A fresh treatment of Austen's cultural situation.

Kroeber, Karl. *Styles in Fictional Structure: The Art of Jane Austen, Charlotte Brontë, George Eliot.* Princeton, 1971.

Lawrence, D. H. *Apropos of Lady Chatterley's Lover.* London, 1930.

Lewis, C. S. "A Note on Jane Austen. *Essays in Criticism* 4 (1954): 359–71.

Monaghan, David M. *Jane Austen: Structure and Social Vision.* Totowa, 1980.

Mooneyham, Laura G. *Romance, Language, and Education in Jane Austen's Novels.* London, 1988.

Poovey, Mary. *The Proper Lady and the Woman Writer: Ideology as Style in the Works of Mary Wollstonecraft, Mary Shelley, and Jane Austen.* Chicago, 1984.

Price, Martin. *Forms of Life: Character and Moral Imagination in the Novel.* New Haven, 1983.

Sieferman, Sylvia. "*Persuasion:* The Motive for Metaphor." *Studies in the Novel* 11 (1979): 283–301.

Southam, B. C., ed. *Critical Essays on Jane Austen.* London, 1968.

Spence, Jon. "The Abiding Possibilities of Nature in *Persuasion.*" *SEL* 21 (1981): 625–36.

Spring, David. "Interpreters of Jane Austen's Social World: Literary Critics and Historians." In *Jane Austen: New Perspectives.* Ed. Janet Todd. New York, 1983. Pp. 53–72.

Sulloway, Alison G. *Jane Austen and the Province of Womanhood.* Philadelphia, 1989.

Tave, Stuart M. *Some Words of Jane Austen.* Chicago, 1973.

Trilling, Lionel. *Sincerity and Authenticity.* Cambridge, MA, 1971.

Weinsheimer, Joel. "Chance and the Hierarchy of Marriages in *Pride and Prejudice.*" *ELH* 39 (1972): 404–19.

Wiesenforth, Joseph. "History and Myth in Jane Austen's *Persuasion.*" *The Literary Criterion* 2 (1977): 76–85.

Wilson, Edmund. "A Long Talk about Jane Austen." *Classics and Commercials.* New York, 1950. 196–203.

Wiltshire, John. "A Romantic *Persuasion?*" *The Critical Review* 14 (1971): 3–16.

Wordsworth, William. "Essay Supplementary to the Preface" and "Preface to Lyrical Ballads." In *Wordsworth's Literary Criticism.* Ed. W. J. B. Owen. London, 1974.

Zietlow, Paul N. "Luck and Fortuitous Circumstance in *Persuasion:* Two Interpretations." *ELH* 32 (1965): 179–95.